Mariah Kammerer

04- __

8282-7788-0477-7264

W9-AWC-621

HOUGHTON MIFFLIN

Spelling and Vocabulary

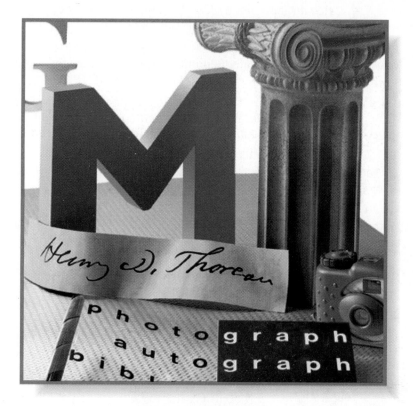

Senior Author
Shane Templeton

Consultant
Rosa Maria Peña

HOUGHTON MIFFLIN

Boston • Atlanta • Dallas • Denver • Geneva, Illinois • Palo Alto • Princeton

Acknowledgments

For each of the selections listed below, grateful acknowledgment is made for permission to excerpt and/or reprint original or copyrighted material as follows:

Select definitions in the Spelling Dictionary are adapted and reprinted by permission from the following Houghton Mifflin Company publications: Copyright © 1998, 1994 *The American Heritage Student Dictionary.* Copyright © 1989 *The Houghton Mifflin Student Dictionary.* Copyright © 1991 *The American Heritage Dictionary, Second College Edition.* Copyright © 1997 *The American Heritage High School Dictionary, Third Edition.*

Selection from *Hook a Fish, Catch a Mountain*, by Jean Craighead George. Copyright © 1975 by Jean Craighead George. Reprinted by permission of Curtis Brown, Ltd.

Selection from "If Pandas Scream . . . an Earthquake Is Coming!" by Phylis Magida. Copyright © 1977 by Phylis Magida, International Wildlife. Reprinted by permission of the National Wildlife Federation.

Selection from "Up from the Deep," by Ray Bradbury. Originally appeared in *The Saturday Evening Post*, June 20, 1951, under the title "The Beast from 20,000 Fathoms." Copyright © 1951 by Curtis Publishing Co., renewed © 1979 by Ray Bradbury. Reprinted by permission of Don Congdon Associates, Inc.

Selection from "The Warehouse," by Walter Dean Myers. Copyright © 1986 by Houghton Mifflin Company. Reprinted by permission of Harriet Wasserman Literary Agency, Inc., as agents for the author.

Selection from "Weathering the World of Snow," by Donald Stokes. Copyright © 1983 by Donald Stokes. Abridged and reprinted by permission of the National Wildlife Federation.

Copyright © 2000 by Houghton Mifflin Company. All rights reserved.

No part of this work may be reproduced or transmitted in any form or by any means, electronic or mechanical, including photocopying and recording, or by any information storage or retrieval system without the prior written permission of Houghton Mifflin Company unless such copying is expressly permitted by federal copyright law. Address inquiries to School Permissions, Houghton Mifflin Company, 222 Berkeley Street, Boston, MA 02116.
Printed in U.S.A.

ISBN: 0-395-97008-3

3456789-DW-05 04 03 02 01 00

Contents

Student's Handbook Contents   9

How to Study a Word   10

Using Spelling Strategies   11

Cycle 1

Unit 1

Silent/Sounded Consonants   12

- Proofreading and Writing
  Proofread: Spelling and Commas in Compound Sentences
- Expanding Vocabulary
  Using a Thesaurus
  Test-Taking Tactics: Analogies
- Real-World Connection
  Language Arts: Journalism

Unit 2

Greek Word Parts I   18

- Proofreading and Writing
  Proofread: Spelling and Fragments or Run-ons
- Expanding Vocabulary
  Context Clues
- Real-World Connection
  Performing Arts: Music

Unit 3

Number Prefixes   24

- Dictionary: Alphabetical Order/Guide Words
- Proofreading and Writing
  Proofread for Spelling
- Expanding Vocabulary
  More Number Prefixes
- Real-World Connection
  Science: Astronomy

Unit 4

Words from Names   30

- Dictionary: Parts of a Dictionary Entry
- Proofreading and Writing
  Proofread for Spelling
- Expanding Vocabulary
  Informal Words
  Test-Taking Tactics: Vocabulary-in-Context
- Real-World Connection
  Science: Plant Life

Unit 5

Homophones   36

- Proofreading and Writing
  Proofread: Spelling and Commas with Appositives
- Expanding Vocabulary
  Synonyms
- Real-World Connection
  Social Studies: World Capitals

Unit 6

Review   42

- Spelling-Meaning Strategy
  The Latin Root *sign*
- Literature and Writing
  Literature
  from "The Warehouse"
  by Walter Dean Myers
  The Writing Process
  Personal
  Narrative

Contents

Cycle 2

Unit 7

Consonant Changes 48

- Proofreading and Writing
  Proofread: Spelling and Subject-Verb Agreement
- Expanding Vocabulary
  The Suffixes -*ate* and -*en*
  Test-Taking Tactics: Analogies
- Real-World Connection
  Careers: Criminal Law

Unit 8

Greek Word Parts II 54

- Dictionary: Spelling Table
- Proofreading and Writing
  Proofread for Spelling
- Expanding Vocabulary
  Compound Words
- Real-World Connection
  Math: Geometry

Unit 9

Noun Suffixes 60

- Proofreading and Writing
  Proofread: Spelling and Comparing with Adjectives
- Expanding Vocabulary
  The Latin Root *frag/fract*
  Test-Taking Tactics: Sentence Completion
- Real-World Connection
  Social Studies: Famous Monuments

Unit 10

Words from Spanish 66

- Proofreading and Writing
  Proofread: Spelling and Comparing with Adverbs
- Expanding Vocabulary
  Context Clues
- Real-World Connection
  Social Studies: Mexico

Unit 11

Words Often Confused 72

- Dictionary: Homographs
- Proofreading and Writing
  Proofread for Spelling
- Expanding Vocabulary
  Antonyms
- Real-World Connection
  Social Studies: Deserts

Unit 12

Review 78

- Spelling-Meaning Strategy
  The Latin Root *gest*
- Literature and Writing
  Literature
  from "Weathering the World of Snow"
  by Donald W. Stokes
  The Writing Process
  Cause and Effect

Contents

Cycle 3

Unit 13

Vowel Changes I   84

- Proofreading and Writing
  Proofread: Spelling and Negatives
- Expanding Vocabulary
  The Greek Word Part *scope*
  Test-Taking Tactics: Analogies
- Real-World Connection
  Careers: Firefighting

Unit 14

Latin Roots I   90

- Dictionary: Parts of Speech
- Proofreading and Writing
  Proofread for Spelling
- Expanding Vocabulary
  Figurative Language
- Real-World Connection
  Science: Volcanoes

Unit 15

The Suffixes *-ary, -ery,* and *-ory*   96

- Proofreading and Writing
  Proofread: Spelling, Usage of Adjectives
  and Adverbs
- Expanding Vocabulary
  Multiple Meanings
  Test-Taking Tactics: Vocabulary-in-
  Context
- Real-World Connection
  Language Arts: Mysteries

Unit 16

Words from French   102

- Proofreading and Writing
  Proofread: Spelling, Proper Nouns and
  Proper Adjectives
- Expanding Vocabulary
  Context Clues
- Real-World
  Connection
  Performing Arts:
  Ballet

Unit 17

Unusual Plurals   108

- Dictionary: Usage Notes
- Proofreading and Writing
  Proofread for Spelling
- Expanding Vocabulary
  The Greek Word Part *cris/crit*
- Real-World Connection
  Science: The Study of Cells

Unit 18

Review   114

- Spelling-Meaning Strategy
  The Latin Root *cis*
- Literature and Writing
  Literature
  from *Hook a Fish, Catch a Mountain*
  by Jean Craighead George
  The Writing Process
  Story

5

Contents

Cycle 4

Unit 19

Vowel Changes II   120

- Proofreading and Writing
  Proofread: Spelling and Commas
- Expanding Vocabulary
  Jargon
  Test-Taking Tactics: Vocabulary-in-Context
- Real-World Connection
  Performing Arts: Songwriting

Unit 20

Latin Roots II   126

- Dictionary: Stress
- Proofreading and Writing
  Proofread for Spelling
- Expanding Vocabulary
  Context Clues
  Test-Taking Tactics: Analogies
- Real-World Connection
  Art: Graphic Arts

Unit 21

Greek and Latin Prefixes   132

- Proofreading and Writing
  Proofread: Spelling, Dates and Addresses
- Expanding Vocabulary
  Exact Words
- Real-World Connection
  Health: First Aid

Unit 22

Words from Other Languages   138

- Dictionary: Pronunciation
- Proofreading and Writing
  Proofread for Spelling
- Expanding Vocabulary
  Slang
- Real-World Connection
  Social Studies: The Arctic

Unit 23

Words Often Misspelled   144

- Proofreading and Writing
  Proofread: Spelling, Capitalizing and Punctuating Letters
- Expanding Vocabulary
  Idioms
- Real-World Connection
  Industrial Arts: Auto Mechanics

Unit 24

Review   150

- Spelling-Meaning Strategy
  The Latin Root solv
- Literature and Writing
  Literature
  from "Up from the Deep"
  by Ray Bradbury
  The Writing Process
  Description

Contents

Cycle 5

Unit 25

Absorbed Prefixes I   156

- Dictionary: Etymology
- Proofreading and Writing
  Proofread for Spelling
- Expanding Vocabulary
  Connotation
- Real-World Connection
  Language Arts: History of Writing

Unit 26

Latin Roots III   162

- Proofreading and Writing
  Proofread: Spelling and Direct
  Quotations
- Expanding Vocabulary
  Context Clues
  Test-Taking Tactics: Analogies
- Real-World Connection
  Language Arts: Dictionary

Unit 27

The Suffixes *-able* and *-ible*   168

- Proofreading and Writing
  Proofread: Spelling and Titles
- Expanding Vocabulary
  Synonyms
- Real-World Connection
  Math: Statistics

Unit 28

Words from Places   174

- Dictionary: Variations in Spelling and
  Pronunciation
- Proofreading and Writing
  Proofread for Spelling
- Expanding Vocabulary
  Regional Differences
- Real-World Connection
  Health: Nutrition

Unit 29

Single or Double Consonants   180

- Proofreading and Writing
  Proofread: Spelling, Subject and Object
  Pronouns
- Expanding Vocabulary
  The Latin root *cred*
  Test-Taking Tactics: Sentence Completion
- Real-World Connection
  Science: Meteorology

Unit 30

Review   186

- Spelling-Meaning Strategy
  The Latin Root *mem*
- Literature and Writing
  Literature
  based on "The History of Soccer"
  by Ross R. Olney
  The Writing Process
  Persuasive Letter

7

Contents

Cycle 6

Unit 31

Absorbed Prefixes II   192

- Proofreading and Writing
  Proofread: Spelling and Pronouns
- Expanding Vocabulary
  Context Clues
- Real-World Connection
  Life Skills: Job Interviews

Unit 32

Suffixes -ant/-ance, -ent/-ence   198

- Dictionary: Prefixes and Suffixes
- Proofreading and Writing
  Proofread for Spelling
- Expanding Vocabulary
  The Latin Root *sist*
  Test-Taking Tactics: Sentence Completion
- Real-World Connection
  Careers: Physical Therapy

Unit 33

Verb Suffixes   204

- Dictionary: Word Forms
- Proofreading and Writing
  Proofread for Spelling
- Expanding Vocabulary
  Synonyms and Antonyms
  Test-Taking Tactics: Analogies
- Real-World Connection
  Language Arts: Research Skills

Unit 34

Words New to English   210

- Proofreading and Writing
  Proofread: Spelling and Agreement with Indefinite Pronouns
- Expanding Vocabulary
  Blends and Clipped Forms
- Real-World Connection
  Performing Arts: Television

Unit 35

Words Often Mispronounced   216

- Proofreading and Writing
  Proofread: Spelling and Pronouns after Prepositions
- Expanding Vocabulary
  British English
- Real-World Connection
  Careers: Pharmacy

Unit 36

Review   222

- Spelling-Meaning Strategy
  The Latin Root *pet*
- Literature and Writing
  Literature
  from "If Pandas Scream . . . an Earthquake Is Coming!"
  by Phylis Magida
  The Writing Process
  Research Report

Student's Handbook

Extra Practice and Review 229

Writer's Resources

Capitalization and Punctuation Guide
Abbreviations 247
Bibliography 248
Titles 249
Quotations 250
Capitalization 250
Punctuation 252

Letter Models
Friendly Letter 255
Business Letter 256

Thesaurus
Using the Thesaurus 257
Thesaurus Index 259
Thesaurus 263

Spelling-Meaning Index
Consonant Changes 271
Vowel Changes 271
Absorbed Prefixes 272
Word Parts 274

Spelling Dictionary
Spelling Table 279
How to Use a Dictionary 281
Spelling Dictionary 282

Content Index 352
Credits 355
Handwriting Models 356

How to Study a Word

1 ▶ Look at the word.

- How is the word spelled?
- Do you see any familiar word parts?

2 ▶ Say the word.

- How are the consonant sounds pronounced?
- How are the vowel sounds pronounced?

3 ▶ Think about the word.

- What does it mean?
- What do you know about the word's origin?
- Would thinking of a related word help you remember the spelling?

> inspire
> inspiration

4 ▶ Write the word.

- Think about the sounds and the letters.
- Form the letters correctly.

column
columnist
design
designar

5 ▶ Check the spelling.

- Did you spell the word the same way it is spelled on your word list?
- Do you need to write the word again?

Using Spelling Strategies

Sometimes you want to write a word that you are not certain how to spell. For example, one student writer wanted to spell the word that named the document at the right. She followed these steps to figure out the spelling.

1 ▶ Say the word softly. Listen to all the sounds. Then think about the letters and patterns that usually spell each sound. Listen for familiar word parts, such as roots, prefixes, suffixes, and endings.

> The word root *script* at the end of the word is clear.

mannuscript
manyuscript

2 ▶ Write the word a few different ways to see which way looks right.

> I didn't find it spelled m-a-n-n-u.

3 ▶ Do you recognize one spelling as the correct one? If you're not sure, look up your first try in a dictionary.

Spelling Strategies

1. Listen for familiar sounds and patterns.
2. Listen for familiar word parts—roots, prefixes, suffixes, and endings.
3. Use the Spelling-Meaning Strategy. Is there a word related in meaning that can help you spell your word?
4. Write the word a few different ways.
5. Use a dictionary.

4 ▶ It's not there? Look up your second try.

> Oh, here it is. It's spelled m-a-n-u-s-c-r-i-p-t.

5 ▶ Write the word correctly to help you remember its spelling.

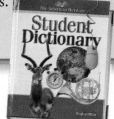

Silent/Sounded Consonants

Read and Say

Basic

READ the sentences. SAY each bold word.

1. column — I read your magazine **column** every month.
2. columnist — Is she a sports **columnist** for that newspaper?
3. design — He will **design** and then build the house.
4. designate — We must **designate** a new group leader.
5. debt — Is this loan your only **debt**?
6. debit — Did the bank **debit** my account?
7. heir — The prince is the **heir** to the throne.
8. inherit — Ted will **inherit** his aunt's property.
9. hasten — She had to **hasten** home to avoid the rain.
10. haste — The thief left in great **haste**.
11. autumn — My favorite season is **autumn**.
12. autumnal — Red and brown are **autumnal** colors.
13. resign — Her choice was to **resign** or be fired.
14. resignation — Meg handed in her **resignation** from the firm.
15. doubt — Many people **doubt** the boy's wild tales.
16. dubious — He is **dubious** about his chances of winning.
17. vehicle — A sled is a **vehicle** that has no wheels.
18. vehicular — The road is closed to **vehicular** traffic.
19. muscle — Is her limp due to a sore leg **muscle**?
20. muscular — Marathon runners are often **muscular**.

Spelling Strategy   To spell a word with a silent consonant, think of a related word in which the consonant is sounded.

Think and Write   Write the pairs of Basic Words. In each pair, underline the letter that is silent in one word and sounded in the other.

Review	23. bomb
21. assign	24. exhaust
22. receipt	25. reign

Challenge	28. condemn
26. solemn	29. condemnation
27. solemnity	

Independent Practice

Vocabulary: Definitions Write the Basic Word that matches each definition.
Use your Spelling Dictionary.

1. one who writes a regular feature for a newspaper or a magazine
2. to indicate or point out
3. the act of leaving or retiring from a job
4. something that is owed
5. having to do with a car or a truck
6. a regular feature in a newspaper or a magazine
7. a drawing giving the details of how something is to be made
8. to move swiftly or hurry
9. one who receives a person's property after that person's death
10. to be uncertain
11. having to do with the fall season
12. to charge an account with an amount that is owed
13. body tissue that controls movement

Vocabulary: Analogies A verbal analogy shows how two pairs
of words are related. The second two words are related to each
other in the same way as the first two. An analogy can be written
as a sentence or with colons.

   String is to guitar as key is to piano.
   string : guitar :: key : piano

Write the Basic Word that completes each analogy.
Use your Spelling Dictionary.

14. month : April :: season : _____
15. happy : joyful :: uncertain : _____
16. coat : clothing :: car : _____
17. weak : flabby :: strong : _____
18. heat : cold :: slowness : _____
19. push : shove :: quit : _____
20. give : donate :: receive : _____

Challenge Words Write the Challenge
Word that completes each sentence. Use your
Spelling Dictionary.

21. "I must report the truth," the journalist said in a _____ tone.
22. The editorial's _____ led to the closing of the unsafe factory.
23. The usually cheery newsroom had an odd air of _____ today.
24. People should _____ newspapers that print gossip and lies.

Review: Spelling Spree

Rhyming Clues Write the Basic or Review Word that rhymes with the underlined word or words in each sentence.

1. <u>Millionaires</u> may be rare, but lucky me, I'm an _____.
2. Harry is a speedy <u>mason</u> because he really likes to _____.
3. Maria's in a <u>wee pickle</u> now that she's dented her _____.
4. When I gave the soup a <u>taste</u>, I burned my tongue in my _____.
5. I want to be the king of <u>Spain</u> and wear a crown as I _____.
6. Have you met a banker <u>yet</u> who forgets to collect on a _____?
7. Wrestling is a way to <u>tussle</u>; athletes must use every _____.
8. Anxiety turns you inside <u>out</u>, as do worry, fear, and _____.
9. The movie plot was fairly <u>calm</u> until the villain made a _____.

Code Breaker The Basic and Review Words below have been written in code. Use the following code key to figure out each word. Write the decoded words correctly.

CODE:	z	y	x	w	v	u	t	s	r	q	p	o	n	m	l	k	j	i	h	g	f	e	d	c	b	a
LETTER:	a	b	c	d	e	f	g	h	i	j	k	l	m	n	o	p	q	r	s	t	u	v	w	x	y	z

Example: evsrxov   *vehicle*

10. xlofnm
11. wvhrtm
12. wvyrg
13. rmsvirg
14. zfgfnmzo
15. ivhrtm

16. vcszfhg
17. wfyrlfh
18. ivxvrkg
19. ivhrtmzgrlm
20. xlofnmrhg
21. wvhrtmzgv

22. zhhrtm
23. zfgfnm
24. evsrxfozi
25. nfhxfozi

How Are You Doing?
Write each spelling word as a partner reads it aloud. Did you misspell any words?

Proofreading and Writing

Proofread: Spelling and Commas in Compound Sentences
Use a comma followed by a conjunction, such as *and*, *or*, or *but*, to separate the parts of a compound sentence.

Have you read the paper, **or** do you want to see my copy?

Find five misspelled Basic or Review Words and two missing commas in this newspaper article. Write the article correctly.

New Stadium Behind Schedule

The new stadium's construction is behind schedule and the building will not be finished by early autum. Project manager Mark Reilly had been dubius for some time about his crew's ability to meet the schedule. "The building's unusual desine caused some delays," Reilly said. "My crew is putting all their skill and mussle into this job. If I exaust them, though, I risk their safety and I won't do that."

Write a Sports Article You are a sports columnist for your school paper. Write a short article about the first sports event to be held in your new school stadium. Try to use five spelling words and at least one compound sentence.

Basic
1. column
2. columnist
3. design
4. designate
5. debt
6. debit
7. heir
8. inherit
9. hasten
10. haste
11. autumn
12. autumnal
13. resign
14. resignation
15. doubt
16. dubious
17. vehicle
18. vehicular
19. muscle
20. muscular

Review

21. assign
22. receipt
23. bomb
24. exhaust
25. reign

Challenge

26. solemn
27. solemnity
28. condemn
29. condemnation

Proofreading Marks
- ¶ Indent
- ∧ Add
- ∧ Add a comma
- ∨ ∨ Add quotation marks
- ⊙ Add a period
- Delete
- ≡ Capital letter
- / Small letter
- ∾ Reverse order

Expanding Vocabulary

**Spelling
Word Link**

hasten

Using a Thesaurus How can you add variety to your writing? Where can you find the most precise words to communicate your ideas? Try using a thesaurus. Look at the sample entry.

main entry
word   part of speech   definition   sample sentence

> **hasten** *v.* to move or act swiftly. *Jim **hastened** to get to school on time.*
>
> **dash** to race or rush with sudden speed. *Lee **dashed** after the runaway dog.*
>
> subentries
>
> **scuttle** to move with quick small steps. *The spider **scuttled** along the floor.*
>
> **antonyms:** dawdle, delay

1–10. Read pages 257–258. Then find the Thesaurus main entry words *strange* and *picture*. Write the five subentries for each word below the main entry.

TEST-TAKING TACTICS

Analogies Many analogy test questions have a multiple-choice format similar to this one:

GIGANTIC : COLOSSAL ::

(A) vague : specific   (B) exacting : careless

(C) tiny : tremendous   (D) doubtful : dubious

(E) habitual : occasional

Knowing some common types of analogy relationships will help you choose the word pair that is related in the same way as the capitalized word pair. Here are four typical types of analogy relationships: an *object* and its *class*, a *cause* and its *effect*, *synonyms*, and *antonyms*.

Answer the following questions to find the answer to the sample analogy.

11. Which of the four types of relationships listed above exists between GIGANTIC and COLOSSAL?

12. Which answer choice contains a pair of words that has the same relationship as GIGANTIC and COLOSSAL? Write its letter.

Real-World Connection

Language Arts: Journalism All the words in the box relate to journalism. Look up these words in your Spelling Dictionary. Then write the words to complete this paragraph.

Spelling Word Link

columnist

journalism
publication
correspondent
source
by-line
masthead
supplement
libel

Reporters work in the field of __(1)__ . A __(2)__ is a reporter who reports on events far away. Daily news stories are usually written in a matter of hours. Special features, such as those that appear in a Sunday __(3)__ or magazine section, may be written over days or even weeks. In a newspaper, the writer's __(4)__ appears above the story. In a magazine, writers and editors are named in the __(5)__ . Though reporting can be exciting, it can also be risky. A reporter may be jailed for refusing to name a secret __(6)__ . Also, if a story is considered damaging to a person's reputation, the __(7)__ in which the story appears can be sued for __(8)__ .

TRY THIS!

Yes or No? Write *yes* if the underlined word is used correctly. Write *no* if it is not.

9. The reporter began a paragraph with a witty <u>by-line</u>.
10. My favorite <u>publication</u> is this weekly news magazine.
11. Tammy gave her story a <u>libel</u> and put it in the file.
12. The editor opened an urgent air-mail <u>correspondent</u>.

Fact File

Pulitzer Prizes have been awarded annually since 1917 for outstanding achievements in American journalism, literature, drama, and music. The prizes were established by newspaper publisher Joseph Pulitzer.

Greek Word Parts I

Read and Say

Basic

READ the sentences. SAY each bold word.

1. symphony — Which composer wrote that **symphony**?
2. microphone — The **microphone** picked up the softest sound.
3. phonograph — Old **phonograph** records can be valuable.
4. xylophone — Does the band have a **xylophone**?
5. choreography — The dancers studied **choreography**.
6. autograph — I have the star player's **autograph**.
7. automobile — Most people call an **automobile** a car.
8. telephone — May I use your **telephone** to call home?
9. homograph — What are the meanings of this **homograph**?
10. bibliography — His report's **bibliography** listed six books.
11. phonetic — Look up the **phonetic** spelling of that sound.
12. geography — We studied major rivers in **geography**.
13. photograph — I used special film to take that **photograph**.
14. graphic — The **graphic** account of the battle was awful.
15. paragraph — A **paragraph** should deal with only one topic.
16. automatic — My camera has an **automatic** flash.
17. telegraph — Many people still send messages by **telegraph**.
18. calligraphy — Each award was written in **calligraphy**.
19. homophone — Study the meaning of each **homophone**.
20. autobiography — My **autobiography** covers my first ten years.

Spelling Strategy   Knowing the Greek word parts *phon* ("sound"), *auto* ("self"), and *graph* ("writing") can help you spell and understand words with these parts.

Think and Write   Write the Basic Words. Underline the Greek word part *phon*, *auto*, or *graph* in each.

Review	
21. instrument	23. musician
22. performance	24. audience
	25. intermission

Challenge	
26. cacophony	28. seismograph
27. autonomy	29. autocrat
	30. topography

Independent Practice

Vocabulary: Using Context Write the Basic Word that completes each sentence. Use your Spelling Dictionary.

1. The singer used a _____ so that everyone could hear her.
2. Dimitri played an old record on the wind-up _____.
3. Karen gave a _____ description of the opera's final scene.
4. The concert invitation was handwritten in beautiful _____.
5. "*Cymbal* is a _____ for *symbol*," said the music teacher.
6. The famous conductor signed his _____ on a fan's ticket.
7. This stereo comes with an _____ shut-off switch.
8. I wanted Jaime to receive the message of congratulations right after his performance, so I sent it by _____.
9. Rosie learned how to pronounce the unfamiliar musical terms by looking up their _____ respellings in the dictionary.
10. Chiu is studying _____ and hopes to perform her own ballet someday.
11. My piano lesson was interrupted by the ringing of the _____.
12. *Scale* is a _____ because it has the same spelling as two other words that have different origins and meanings.

Vocabulary: Classifying Write the Basic Word that fits each word group. Use your Spelling Dictionary.

13. piano, tuba, cello, _____
14. anthem, song, concerto, _____
15. airplane, train, boat, _____
16. history, mathematics, science, _____
17. poetry, fiction, drama, _____
18. word, phrase, sentence, _____
19. filmstrip, slide, video, _____
20. introduction, index, glossary, _____

Challenge Words Write the Challenge Word that answers each question. Use your Spelling Dictionary.

21. What could you call the sound of an orchestra loudly playing the wrong notes?
22. What kind of ruler has absolute power?
23. What is used to measure the force of an earthquake?
24. What do countries want if they are seeking independence?
25. What should every mapmaker be good at?

Review: Spelling Spree

Word Clues Write the Basic Word that fits each clue.

1. This graph is a signature.
2. This graph is usually indented.
3. This graph delivers a message.
4. This graph is a snap.
5. This graph is the study of the earth.
6. This graph has perfect penmanship.
7. This graph spins records.
8. This graph is a series of dance steps.
9. This graph is two words in one.
10. This graph is the story of the writer's life.
11. This graph is a list of books.

Word Horn 12–25. Find the Basic and Review Words hidden in the horn. Write the words in the order in which you find them.

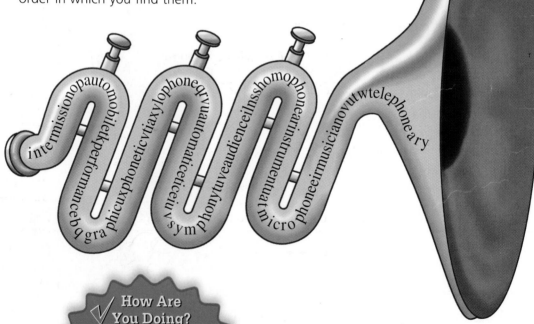

How Are You Doing?
List the spelling words that are difficult for you. Practice them with a partner.

Proofreading and Writing

Proofread: Spelling and Fragments or Run-ons Correct a **sentence fragment** by adding a subject or a predicate. Correct a **run-on sentence** by creating two separate sentences or one compound sentence.

FRAGMENT:	Ran her fingers along the piano keys.
CORRECTION:	**Meg** ran her fingers along the piano keys.
RUN-ON:	The pianist bowed we cheered.
CORRECTION:	The pianist bowed**, and** we cheered.
CORRECTION:	The pianist bowed**. We** cheered.

Find five misspelled Basic or Review Words, one sentence fragment, and one run-on sentence in this excerpt from a concert program. Write the program correctly.

Today's program features a performance of *Work of Nature,*
by Ned Palek he spent weeks on the prairie with a tape
recorder and a mikrophone, recording the sounds of nature.
These sounds form the background to the synphony. From
this natural music. Listeners can picture the geografy of
the land. Mr. Palek will sign autographs at intermision.

Basic

1. symphony
2. microphone
3. phonograph
4. xylophone
5. choreography
6. autograph
7. automobile
8. telephone
9. homograph
10. bibliography
11. phonetic
12. geography
13. photograph
14. graphic
15. paragraph
16. automatic
17. telegraph
18. calligraphy
19. homophone
20. autobiography

Review

21. instrument
22. performance
23. musician
24. audience
25. intermission

Challenge

26. cacophony
27. autonomy
28. seismograph
29. autocrat
30. topography

Proofreading Marks

¶ Indent
∧ Add
⋏ Add a comma
⋎ ⋎ Add quotation marks
⊙ Add a period
⊱ Delete
≡ Capital letter
/ Small letter
∾ Reverse order

Write a Comparison and Contrast Paragraph

Write a paragraph comparing and contrasting two musical performances you have seen or heard. Try to use five spelling words, and check that you have not included any sentence fragments or run-on sentences.

Unit 2 BONUS

Expanding Vocabulary

Spelling Word Link

xylophone

Context Clues You can often use **context clues**, or other words in a sentence, to find the meaning of an unfamiliar word. For example, if you did not know the word *xylophone*, the words *tapped* and *tune* in the sentence below would provide clues to its meaning.

Len **tapped** out a **tune** on the xylophone.

Write the meaning of each underlined word in the sentences below. Then write the context clues that helped you figure out the meaning of that word.

1. Audience members wept over the opera's <u>dolorous</u> ending.
2. The trombonist <u>slaked</u> his thirst with a glass of water.
3. The <u>discordant</u> sounds of the untuned instruments grated on Al's nerves.

MEANING	CONTEXT CLUES
1. ?	?
2. ?	?
3. ?	?

Now write a sentence for each word in parentheses.

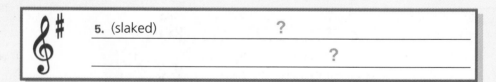

4. (dolorous)　　　?
?

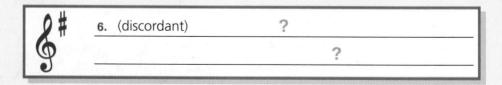

5. (slaked)　　　?
?

6. (discordant)　　　?
?

Real-World Connection

Performing Arts: Music All the words in the box relate to music. Look up these words in your Spelling Dictionary. Then write the words to complete this paragraph.

Last night my family attended a wonderful concert of classical music in Symphony Hall. Applause filled the hall as the __(1)__ appeared and waved her __(2)__ like a magician waving a magic wand. First we heard a __(3)__ of six pieces with a fast __(4)__, performed by a full symphony __(5)__. This was followed by a violin __(6)__. The concert ended with a magnificent __(7)__. Because the building's __(8)__ are so good, the music sounded as clear as a bell.

Spelling Word Link

symphony

orchestra
conductor
baton
tempo
acoustics
suite
concerto
finale

TRY THIS!

Understanding Vocabulary Write *yes* or *no* to answer each question.

9. Could a person get a job as an acoustics player?
10. Can a suite have more than one piece?
11. Can two people form an orchestra?
12. Can a tempo get louder?

Fact File

Wynton Marsalis is a contemporary American musician who plays trumpet and conducts both classical music and jazz. In 1997 he became the first jazz musician to win the Pulitzer Prize, for his composition on the subject of slavery. He has also composed ballet music. He regularly conducts the Lincoln Center Jazz Orchestra.

Number Prefixes

Read and Say

Basic

READ the sentences. SAY each bold word.

1.	universe	Is the **universe** endless?
2.	billion	A **billion** things are hard to imagine.
3.	binoculars	I can see almost a mile with my **binoculars**.
4.	tripod	One leg of the camera **tripod** is bent.
5.	unique	Each snowflake is **unique**.
6.	unison	Please sing this song in **unison**.
7.	triple	Dan can do a **triple** flip.
8.	semicircle	We sat in a **semicircle** around the fire.
9.	triangle	Fold each strip into the shape of a **triangle**.
10.	bicycle	Both tires on his **bicycle** were flat.
11.	unify	How can we **unify** the different groups?
12.	triplets	The **triplets** often wear matching clothes.
13.	semicolon	Use a **semicolon** to connect those clauses.
14.	biceps	Swimmers have strong **biceps** and upper arms.
15.	bimonthly	We have six **bimonthly** art classes a year.
16.	unity	The thirteen colonies pledged their **unity**.
17.	trio	A **trio** of clowns ran around the ring.
18.	university	Mom is a student at the **university**.
19.	biannual	Our **biannual** meetings are in spring and fall.
20.	semifinals	Will our team be playing in the **semifinals**?

Spelling Strategy Remember that *uni-* ("one"), *bi-* ("two; twice"), *tri-* ("three"), and *semi-* ("half") are number prefixes.

Think and Write Write each Basic Word under its prefix.

uni-	bi-	tri-	semi-

Review
21. unite
22. observe
23. gigantic
24. explode
25. confirm

Challenge
26. trigonometry
27. bicentennial
28. bilingual
29. trivet
30. semiprecious

Independent Practice

Vocabulary: Replacing Words Write the Basic Word that means the same thing as the underlined word or words in each sentence. Use your Spelling Dictionary.

1. The flare star suddenly became <u>three times</u> its original size.
2. Gabe used <u>field glasses</u> to observe the craters on the surface of the moon.
3. The astronomer set up her camera on a <u>three-legged stand</u>.
4. The telescope at the observatory is <u>one of a kind</u>.
5. A <u>threesome</u> of scientists studied the photographs of Venus.
6. Professor Vila says that the moon's seas are about four <u>thousand million</u> years old.
7. *The Star-Gazer's Report* is published <u>every two months</u>.
8. The pattern of the stars formed a <u>three-sided geometric figure</u>.
9. The government passed a bill that would <u>combine</u> several scientific research programs.
10. Last night, the moon was a brightly glowing <u>half-circle</u>.
11. Trudy made it to the <u>next to the last round of matches</u> in the science club trivia competition.

Vocabulary: Word Clues Write the Basic Word that fits each clue. Use your Spelling Dictionary.

12. three who celebrate their birthdays on the same day
13. twice a year
14. a part of the arm that is flexed a lot
15. the combination of musical tones of the same pitch
16. a punctuation mark that both separates and joins
17. a school of higher learning
18. all existing things
19. a two-wheeled vehicle
20. what the fifty states have

Challenge Words Write the Challenge Word commonly associated with each word or phrase below. Use your Spelling Dictionary.

21. hot dishes
22. language
23. mathematics
24. anniversary
25. gems

Dictionary

Alphabetical Order/Guide Words Words in a dictionary are listed alphabetically. **Guide words** appear at the top of each page and indicate the first and last entries on the page.

Practice Write each of the following three lists of words in alphabetical order.
1. semicircle, semifinals, semiannual, semicolon, semiarid
2. triplane, triple, tripod, tripedal, triangle
3. biceps, binoculars, billionth, bicycle, billionaire

Look up the following words in your Spelling Dictionary. Write the guide words that appear at the top of the page for each word.

4. unify
5. explode
6. bicycle

7. gigantic
8. colonel
9. semicolon

4. _____ ?
5. _____ ?
6. _____ ?

7. _____ ?
8. _____ ?
9. _____ ?

Review: Spelling Spree

Word Combination Add the prefix of the first word to a letter or group of letters from the end of the second word to write a Basic or Review Word.

Example: trillion + droplets   *triplets*
10. trident + duo
11. bifocal + forceps
12. uniform + reverse
13. biplane + unicycle
14. trial + bipod
15. bisect + semiannual
16. unicorn + person
17. semisoft + encircle
18. tricolor + rectangle
19. univalve + terrify
20. binary + semimonthly
21. union + invite

22. bison + million
23. semiweekly + quarterfinals
24. triplane + droplets
25. unilateral + quality

Proofreading and Writing

Proofread for Spelling Find nine misspelled Basic or Review Words in this article. Write each word correctly.

On May 16, stargazers were able to abserve a uneque sight. A trio of stars blew apart within seconds of one another. The closely grouped stars, which together looked like a semicolin punctuating the night sky, began to expload at 10:38 P.M. The jigantic bursts of light were clearly visible with the help of binoculers. Astronomers at the universaty conferm that a tripple explosion such as this might occur only once in a billion years.

Write the Script of a Conversation While watching the night sky, you and a friend see a meteor shower. Write a script of the conversation you have during the event. Try to use five spelling words, and remember to punctuate your dialogue correctly.

Basic

1. universe
2. billion
3. binoculars
4. tripod
5. unique
6. unison
7. triple
8. semicircle
9. triangle
10. bicycle
11. unify
12. triplets
13. semicolon
14. biceps
15. bimonthly
16. unity
17. trio
18. university
19. biannual
20. semifinals

Review

21. unite
22. observe
23. gigantic
24. explode
25. confirm

Challenge

26. trigonometry
27. bicentennial
28. bilingual
29. trivet
30. semiprecious

Proofreading Marks

- ¶ Indent
- ∧ Add
- ∧ Add a comma
- ∨ ∨ Add quotation marks
- ⊙ Add a period
- Delete
- ≡ Capital letter
- / Small letter
- ∿ Reverse order

Unit 3 BONUS

Expanding Vocabulary

Spelling Word Link

unique
bicycle
triplets
semicircle

More Number Prefixes The spelling words *unique, bicycle, triplets,* and *semicircle* each have a common number prefix. Below are five more.

PREFIX	MEANING	EXAMPLE
quad	four	**Quadriceps** are muscles with four parts.
quint	five	A **quintet** is a group of five people.
hept	seven	**Heptarchy** is rule by seven people.
sept	seven	**Septennial** means "every seven years."
oct	eight	An **octopus** is an eight-armed sea animal.

Write the word that matches each definition.

heptagon   quadrille   quintuplets   septet   octave

1. five children born together
2. a series of eight musical tones
3. a group of seven people
4. a dance performed by four couples
5. a seven-sided flat figure

Now write a sentence for one word from each of these word pairs: *quadriceps/quadrille, quintet/quintuplets, heptarchy/heptagon, septennial/septet, octopus/octave.*

6. _____ ? _____
   _____ ? _____
   _____ ? _____

7. _____ ? _____
   _____ ? _____
   _____ ? _____

8. _____ ? _____
   _____ ? _____
   _____ ? _____

9. _____ ? _____
   _____ ? _____
   _____ ? _____

10. _____ ? _____
    _____ ? _____
    _____ ? _____

Real-World Connection

Science: Astronomy All the words in the box relate to astronomy. Look up these words in your Spelling Dictionary. Then write the words to complete this paragraph.

Spelling Word Link

universe

astronomy
constellation
Milky Way
meteor
light-year
comet
supernova
asteroid

You can learn a lot about __(1)__ simply by observing the sky. For example, the bright, broad band of the __(2)__ is clearly visible from Earth. The group of stars in the __(3)__ called the Big Dipper are also easy to spot. If you gaze long enough, you may see a __(4)__ falling toward Earth. A __(5)__, with its long tail and glowing head, is a rarer sight. Rarest of all is the __(6)__, or exploding star, which you would probably need a telescope to see. Point a telescope between Mars and Jupiter, and you might spot an __(7)__. Although the stars and planets appear crowded together, they are actually so far apart that a unit of measure called a __(8)__, equal to six trillion miles, is used to calculate the distances between them.

TRY THIS!

Riddle Time! Write the Vocabulary Word that answers each riddle.

9. What is a star picture?
10. What is a distance measured by time?
11. What are we part of and able to see at the same time?
12. What has a tail and a head but no legs?

Fact File

Polaris, known as the North Star, shines brightly at the end of the Little Dipper's handle. From its position over the North Pole, Polaris has guided travelers for thousands of years.

Words from Names

Read and Say

| Basic | READ the sentences. SAY each bold word. |

READ the sentences. SAY each bold word.

1. *gardenia* — Each **gardenia** had nearly perfect petals.
2. *zinnia* — A garden of **zinnia** blooms is so colorful!
3. *magnolia* — Our **magnolia** tree blossoms in the spring.
4. *begonia* — Don't forget to water the red **begonia**.
5. *boysenberry* — Do we have any more **boysenberry** jam?
6. *saxophone* — I play the **saxophone** in a band.
7. *leotard* — Each girl wore a **leotard** in dance class.
8. *guy* — Which **guy** is your brother?
9. *graham cracker* — A **graham cracker** and milk is a tasty snack.
10. *volt* — How much power does a **volt** have?
11. *sideburns* — Dad's **sideburns** grew down to his chin.
12. *Braille* — Rosa orders books written in **Braille**.
13. *maverick* — Can a **maverick** ever become a team player?
14. *silhouette* — Turn your head so I can draw your **silhouette**.
15. *cardigan* — This **cardigan** is my warmest sweater.
16. *mackintosh* — Her **mackintosh** and boots kept her dry.
17. *boycott* — Many of us joined the **boycott** of the shop.
18. *derby* — He wore a small brown **derby** on his head.
19. *Ferris wheel* — My favorite fair ride is the **Ferris wheel**.
20. *derrick* — Only a **derrick** could move those huge stones.

Spelling Strategy   Knowing the origin of words that come from names can help you spell and understand the meanings of the words.

Think and Write   Write the Basic Words.

Review		Challenge	
21. diesel	23. panic	26. sequoia	28. fuchsia
22. echoes	24. furious	27. poinsettia	29. mesmerize
	25. volcanoes		30. zeppelin

Independent Practice

Vocabulary: Definitions Write the Basic Word that matches each definition. Use your Spelling Dictionary.

1. a rectangular cracker made of whole-wheat flour
2. a garden plant with showy, variously colored flowers
3. growths of hair down the sides of a man's face
4. a tree or shrub with large white or pink flowers
5. a system of writing and printing for the blind
6. a plant with waxy flowers and often colorfully marked leaves
7. a shrub with glossy evergreen leaves and large, fragrant white flowers
8. a man or fellow
9. a unit of electrical measurement
10. a tight-fitting garment often worn by dancers
11. a stiff felt hat with a round crown and a narrow, curved brim
12. a large crane for lifting and moving heavy objects
13. a wind instrument with a curved metal body

Vocabulary: Using Context Write the Basic Word that completes each sentence. Use your Spelling Dictionary.

14. The tree's _____ was like a dark hand against the sky.
15. Will you join the _____ of Halley's Flower Shop to protest the store's high prices?
16. The red fruit hanging from the _____ bush looked ripe.
17. Mr. Seiji is considered a _____ by other botanists because of his independent views.
18. Emma wore a _____ in case it rained during the nature hike.
19. Each time we reached the top of the _____, we could see the entire fairground and the surrounding gardens.
20. My grandmother knitted me a _____ and added flower-shaped buttons.

Challenge Words Write the Challenge Word that fits each clue. Use your Spelling Dictionary.

21. My upper leaves look like petals.
22. I am a ship of the air.
23. I am a huge tree from California.
24. My drooping flowers are usually red and purple.
25. When I do this, I am hypnotic.

Dictionary

Parts of a Dictionary Entry A dictionary entry gives a great deal of information about a word.

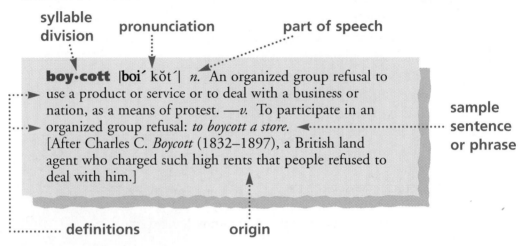

syllable division   pronunciation   part of speech

boy·cott |boi´ kŏt´| *n.* An organized group refusal to use a product or service or to deal with a business or nation, as a means of protest. —*v.* To participate in an organized group refusal: *to boycott a store.* [After Charles C. *Boycott* (1832–1897), a British land agent who charged such high rents that people refused to deal with him.]

sample sentence or phrase

definitions   origin

Practice Study the sample entry above. Then write the answer to each of the following questions.

1. How many definitions are given for *boycott*?
2. What is the origin of *boycott*?
3. Write *boycott* and draw a line between its syllables.
4. What sample phrase illustrates the use of *boycott*?

1. _____?_____   3. _____?_____

2. _____?_____   4. _____?_____

Review: Spelling Spree

Word Origins Write the Basic or Review Word that fits each clue.

Example: a German botanist's flower   *zinnia*

5. a Belgian musician's horn
6. an English earl's hat
7. a U.S. engineer's ride
8. a Scottish chemist's coat
9. a German engineer's engine
10. a U.S. dietician's snack
11. a U.S. general's whiskers
12. an Italian physicist's electrical unit

13. a Texas rancher's calf
14. a Roman god's fiery mountains
15. an English earl's sweater
16. an English executioner's crane
17. a protest of an English officer
18. a French minister's outline
19. a French acrobat's suit
20. a French teacher's writing

Proofreading and Writing

Proofread for Spelling Find nine misspelled Basic or Review Words in this magazine excerpt. Write each word correctly.

It's spring, and you're furius that your garden is the messiest one on the block. Dried stems and stalks provide only echos of last year's glory. Don't panik. With a little work, you can transform your garden into a showpiece. Plant a gracious magnowlia tree or make a border of bright begonnia flowers. Consider the gardenea for its lovely scent or the zinia for a splash of autumn color. To taste the fruits of your labor, plant a boysunberry bush. If you want to be a real maverick, plant daffodil bulbs everywhere. Next spring they'll create a blanket of color that even the giy with the prize roses will envy!

Basic

Basic

1. gardenia
2. zinnia
3. magnolia
4. begonia
5. boysenberry
6. saxophone
7. leotard
8. guy
9. graham cracker
10. volt
11. sideburns
12. Braille
13. maverick
14. silhouette
15. cardigan
16. mackintosh
17. boycott
18. derby
19. Ferris wheel
20. derrick

Review
21. diesel
22. echoes
23. panic
24. furious
25. volcanoes

Challenge
26. sequoia
27. poinsettia
28. fuchsia
29. mesmerize
30. zeppelin

Proofreading Marks
¶ Indent
∧ Add
⋏ Add a comma
⌄⌄ Add quotation marks
⊙ Add a period
⌿ Delete
≡ Capital letter
／ Small letter
∿ Reverse order

Write an Ad What new and exciting products are in stock at the Green Garden Center? Write an ad for the store. Make its plants sound so appealing that people won't be able to resist them. Try to use five spelling words.

Expanding Vocabulary

**Spelling
Word Link**

guy

Informal Words When you say "Look at that guy!" you are using *guy* as an **informal word** for "man." In each pair below, the formal and informal words mean the same thing.

trumpet/horn   detective/private eye

For each sentence below, write the informal word that has the same meaning as the underlined word or words. Use your Spelling Dictionary.

snoop   beat   tacky   gab

1. Everyone wears <u>unstylish</u> clothes to the "Bad Taste Ball."
2. Dirk likes to <u>converse</u> on the telephone with his friends.
3. Nothing can <u>be better than</u> relaxing on the beach.
4. Jessie decided to <u>sneak a look</u> around Zoe's room.

TEST-TAKING TACTICS

Vocabulary-in-Context Some tests require you to answer vocabulary-in-context questions. First, you will read a passage that has line references. Then you will be asked to choose the correct meaning of a word found in a specific line of the passage.

Sample passage excerpt:

Many varieties of cactus grow in the dry regions of the Southwest.
(40) To survive in their arid habitat, most cacti store water in their stems. In turn, the succulent plants attract thirsty desert animals. The plants' sharp spines, however, protect their juices from the animals.

Sample question:

The word "succulent" in line 41 means

(A) hollow   (B) thorny   (C) juicy   (D) greedy   (E) tasty

To answer a question like this one, look for context clues in the sentence in which the tested word appears *as well as* in the surrounding sentences.

Write the answers to these questions about the sample.

5. Which meaning of "succulent" is correct? Write its letter.
6. What context clues helped you select that meaning?

Real-World Connection

Science: Plant Life All the words in the box relate to plant life. Look up these words in your Spelling Dictionary. Then write the words to complete this paragraph from a textbook.

Spelling Word Link

gardenia

botany
pollen
fertilize
spores
germinate
classify
species
parasite

You may think of __(1)__ as the study of green plants. However, this science also includes the study of the various __(2)__ of fungi, such as mushrooms and mold. These plants reproduce in a special way. While flowering plants have grains of __(3)__ that serve to __(4)__ other plants, most fungi reproduce through __(5)__ . Wind and water carry these to environments where they can begin to grow, or __(6)__ , rapidly. Fungi live almost everywhere. Some feed on other living things. Scientists __(7)__ this type of fungus as a __(8)__ .

TRY THIS!

Riddle Time! Write the Vocabulary Word that answers each riddle.

9. What powder determines the shape of things to come?
10. What unwelcome visitor takes and does not give?
11. What field of study can be pursued in a field of grass?
12. What can one plant do to another?

Fact File

What makes the maple trees in New England turn to red, or the aspens in Colorado become gold? As summer draws to a close, leaves stop making chlorophyll, which keeps them green. Red and yellow pigments in the leaves then take over, giving us the vivid autumn colors.

Homophones

Read and Say

Basic

READ the sentences. SAY each bold word.

1. capital	Which city is the state **capital**?
2. capitol	The dome of the **capitol** building is gold.
3. border	We live a few miles from the state **border**.
4. boarder	Their **boarder** rents the whole third floor.
5. core	An apple **core** contains seeds.
6. corps	She served in a special army **corps**.
7. colonel	Mark is a **colonel** in the army.
8. kernel	I ate every **kernel** of corn.
9. hostile	This feels like a **hostile** place.
10. hostel	I spent the night in a youth **hostel**.
11. council	Are you on the student **council**?
12. counsel	His job is to **counsel** troubled students.
13. bail	We had to **bail** out the boat after the storm.
14. bale	Tie the gathered hay into a **bale**.
15. idle	Being **idle** is dull.
16. idol	The rock fans roared when their **idol** appeared.
17. cereal	Does she really put cream on her **cereal**?
18. serial	The last episode of the **serial** was the best one.
19. compliment	Your delicious pie deserves a **compliment**.
20. complement	Certain colors **complement** each other.

Spelling Strategy Remember to think about meaning when using a **homophone**, a word that sounds like another but has a different spelling and meaning.

Think and Write Write the pairs of Basic Words.

Review	23. principal
21. who's	24. principle
22. whose	

Challenge	27. elicit
25. discreet	28. illicit
26. discrete	

Independent Practice

Vocabulary: Question Clues Write the Basic Word that answers each question. Use your Spelling Dictionary.

1. What type of city is Paris, France?
2. What type of behavior might an enemy display?
3. What kind of person stays at a lodging house?
4. What can help a person get out of jail before his or her trial is held?
5. What are you being when you loaf around the house?
6. What do you heat to get a piece of popcorn?
7. What kind of story is presented in installments on television or in magazines or newspapers?
8. What is a rock star to his or her adoring fans?
9. In what kind of building does a state or national legislature meet?
10. What are you giving when you express admiration for something?
11. What can be found in the middle of an apple, a cabbage, or a pineapple?
12. What is a wrapped bundle of hay?
13. What would a new pair of shoes with a matching belt do to an outfit?

Vocabulary: Classifying Write the Basic Word that fits each group. Use your Spelling Dictionary.

14. boundary, rim, outline, _____
15. motel, hotel, inn, _____
16. troop, regiment, division, _____
17. eggs, toast, juice, _____
18. advise, guide, coach, _____
19. major, general, captain, _____
20. committee, cabinet, assembly, _____

Challenge Words Write the Challenge Word that matches each definition. Use your Spelling Dictionary.

21. separate; individual
22. illegal
23. showing good judgment
24. to bring out

Review: Spelling Spree

Homophone Riddles Write the pair of Basic or Review Words that answers each riddle. (Pay attention to the word order!)

Example: What is another name for rabbit fur?   *hare hair*

1–2. What could you call an unemployed movie star?

3–4. What did the nurse ask when she was trying to match a nursery full of babies with their parents?

5–6. What kind of lodging is unfriendly towards its guests?

7–8. What kind of commanding officer is in charge of corn on the cob?

9–10. What could you call a committee made up of lawyers?

11–12. What is the most important rule or standard?

13–14. Who would live in a rooming house on the edge of town?

15–16. What could you call an excellent building in which the legislature meets?

17–18. What could you call a continuing comic strip that appears on the backs of boxes of corn flakes?

19–20. What kind of praise did Mona give when she admired the scarf that completed Ellen's new outfit?

21–22. What could you call a bundle made up of money used to release an arrested person?

23–24. What could you call the central group of soldiers in an army?

✓ **How Are You Doing?**
Write each spelling word in a sentence. Practice any misspelled spelling words with a partner.

Proofreading and Writing

Proofread: Spelling and Commas with Appositives An appositive is a word or group of words that follows a noun and renames or identifies it. Commas usually set off an appositive from the rest of the sentence.

Madame Tussaud's, **a wax museum,** was full of tourists.

Find five misspelled Basic or Review Words and four appositives without commas in this post card. Write the message correctly.

Dear Pete,

Greetings from London the beautiful capitol of England! I'm staying at a youth hostal near Piccadilly Circus. People here are very polite, and they complament me on my nice manners. I was even polite at breakfast when they served me kippers a kind of fish. I would have given anything for a simple bowl of sereal! Colonel Smythe a family friend has shown me around the city. My principle goal is to see my idol the prime minister. Who knows—it could happen!

Bart

Write a Letter If you could make any spot in the country the new capital city, where would you choose? Why? Write a letter to your congressional representative explaining your choice. Try to use five spelling words and at least one appositive.

Basic
1. capital
2. capitol
3. border
4. boarder
5. core
6. corps
7. colonel
8. kernel
9. hostile
10. hostel
11. council
12. counsel
13. bail
14. bale
15. idle
16. idol
17. cereal
18. serial
19. compliment
20. complement

Review
21. who's
22. whose
23. principal
24. principle

Challenge
25. discreet
26. discrete
27. elicit
28. illicit

Proofreading Marks
¶ Indent
∧ Add
⩓ Add a comma
🖙🖙 Add quotation marks
⊙ Add a period
ℐ Delete
≡ Capital letter
/ Small letter
∩ Reverse order

Unit 5 BONUS

Expanding Vocabulary

Spelling Word Link

counsel
hostile

Synonyms A synonym is a word that has the same or nearly the same meaning as another word.

counsel = advise   hostile = unfriendly

Write the word in parentheses that is a synonym for the key word. Use your Thesaurus.

1. boarder (visitor, lodger)
2. idle (inactive, sleepy)
3. compliment (praise, favor)
4. principal (important, primary)
5. border (boundary, region)

The questions below were asked by tourists visiting world capitals. In each question, the underlined word is a synonym of *border*, *principal*, or *idle*. Write a new synonym for each underlined word. Choose the synonym that makes the most sense. Do not use any of the synonyms given in items 1–5.

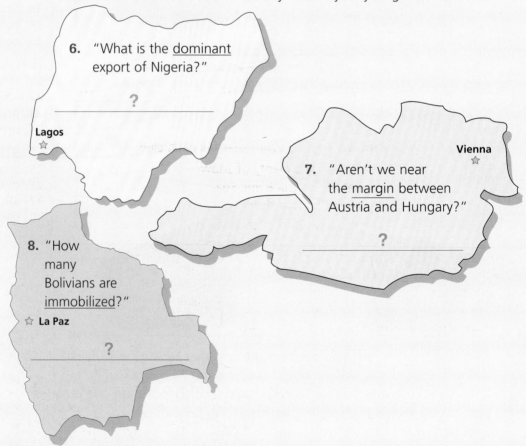

6. "What is the <u>dominant</u> export of Nigeria?"

_____?_____

Lagos ☆

7. "Aren't we near the <u>margin</u> between Austria and Hungary?"

Vienna ☆

_____?_____

8. "How many Bolivians are <u>immobilized</u>?"

☆ La Paz

_____?_____

Vocabulary Enrichment

Real-World Connection

Social Studies: World Capitals All the words in the box relate to world capitals. Look up these words in your Spelling Dictionary. Then write the words to complete the following sentences.

1. The largest city in Russia is _____.
2. The Egyptian capital of _____ has the largest population of any city in Africa.
3. In 1868, Japan's capital moved to its current site, _____.
4. People traveling to Kenya usually fly into _____.
5. The city of _____, Sweden, includes fourteen islands.
6. Pedro de Mendoza founded the city of _____, Argentina.
7. The national government of Canada is based in _____.
8. The capital of China is _____.

Spelling Word Link

capital

Ottawa
Beijing
Buenos Aires
Cairo
Nairobi
Tokyo
Moscow
Stockholm

TRY THIS!

Clue Match Write the Vocabulary Word that fits each clue.

9. This North American city gets plenty of snow.
10. This European capital lies on the Baltic Sea.
11. This Egyptian city lies in the Nile Valley.
12. Russia's government operates from this city.

Fact File

Washington, D.C., the capital of the United States, is one of the few cities in the world that was designed before it was built. Its site was chosen by George Washington, in whose honor the city was named. Washington replaced Philadelphia as the nation's capital in 1800.

6 Review: Units 1–5

pages 12–17

Unit 1 Silent/Sounded Consonants

column	design	haste	resign	muscle
columnist	designate	hasten	resignation	muscular

 Spelling Strategy To spell a word with a silent consonant, think of a related word in which the consonant is sounded.

Write the word that completes each sentence.
1. Carlos put the bread outside to _____ the cooling process.
2. The architect submitted a new _____ for City Hall.
3. Ana's boss was sorry to accept her _____.
4. A hedge helped to _____ the property line.

Write the word that fits each clue.
5. like a body builder
6. a newspaper writer
7. a source of strength
8. what you read in a newspaper
9. one cause of carelessness
10. to quit a job

Unit 2 Greek Word Parts I

pages 18–23

symphony	microphone	autograph	automobile	bibliography
phonetic	photograph	geography	automatic	autobiography

 Spelling Strategy Knowing the Greek word parts *phon* ("sound"), *auto* ("self"), and *graph* ("writing") can help you spell and understand words with these parts.

Write the words that complete the paragraph.
Rory Tyson was the famous conductor of a __(11)__ orchestra. Fans would stop Tyson's __(12)__ in the middle of traffic in order to snap a __(13)__ of him. In his __(14)__, called *The Story of Rory*, he wrote about his life.

Write the word that fits each clue.
15. a list of books
16. without human control
17. the study of the earth
18. a piece of equipment used by singers
19. representing sounds of speech
20. something given by a celebrity

Unit 3   Number Prefixes   pages 24–29

| universe | binoculars | unique | triple | semicircle |
| unity | semicolon | trio | biceps | biannual |

 Spelling Strategy   Remember that *uni-* ("one"), *bi-* ("two; twice"), *tri-* ("three"), and *semi-* ("half") are number prefixes.

Write the word that fits each word group.
21. period, comma, apostrophe, _____
22. sole, unequaled, matchless, _____
23. quartet, duo, quintet, _____
24. telescope, magnifying glass, microscope, _____

Write the word that matches each definition.
25. three times as much   28. twice a year
26. all things   29. a half circle
27. oneness   30. a muscle

Unit 4   Words from Names   pages 30–35

| volt | boysenberry | saxophone | begonia | magnolia |
| Braille | silhouette | maverick | boycott | cardigan |

 Spelling Strategy   Knowing the origin of words that come from names can help you spell and understand the meanings of the words.

Write the word that fits each clue.
31. a kind of outline   34. a measurement of electricity
32. a kind of calf or colt   35. raised dots
33. a musical instrument   36. a plant with colorful leaves

Write the word that completes each sentence.
37. Mia plucked a fragrant _____ blossom from the tree.
38. Harvey was chilly, so he put on his _____.
39. The manufacturers began to lose money as more people joined the _____.
40. Pedro popped a sweet _____ into his mouth.

Unit 5   Homophones

pages 36–41

capital	core	hostile	idle	cereal
capitol	corps	hostel	idol	serial

 Spelling Strategy   Remember to think about meaning when using a **homophone**, a word that sounds like another but has a different spelling and meaning.

Write the word that completes each analogy.

41. individual : soldier :: group : _____

42. tired : weary :: unfriendly : _____

43. lunch : sandwich :: breakfast : _____

44. peach : pit :: earth : _____

Write the word that fits each clue.

45. not busy

46. a leading city

47. a person adored by others

48. a story told in installments

49. lodging for travelers

50. a government building

Challenge Words   Units 1–5

pages 12–41

discreet	autocrat	solemn	bilingual	seismograph
discrete	zeppelin	solemnity	mesmerize	semiprecious

Write the words that complete the paragraph.

Mad King Despota was a powerful __(51)__ . At his coronation, a crown decorated with jewels and __(52)__ stones was placed on his head. Laughing and smiling were strictly forbidden during the __(53)__ ceremony. There was little danger of amusement, however, as the long procession served to __(54)__ any of his subjects who were not already asleep.

Write the word that matches each definition.

55. seriousness

56. a light airship

57. separate or distinct

58. a machine that measures earthquakes

59. able to speak two languages

60. reserved in speech and behavior

Spelling-Meaning Strategy

The Latin Root *sign*

Did you know that *design* and *resignation* are related in meaning? Both words contain *sign*. Although it can stand alone as a word, *sign* is also a Latin root, meaning "mark or seal." Long ago people stamped documents with personal seals. Today, we sign our names, and our signatures serve the same function as those seals. The meaning of a root affects the meaning of each word that contains it. When you design something, you mark a plan. Although today a resignation is something that cancels an agreement, originally it was a mark made to show that a debt or claim had been canceled.

Below are more words that contain *sign*.

signal	as**sign**	en**sign**
signet	**sign**ify	in**sign**ia

> **design**
> **resign**ation
> **sign**ature

Think

- How does the root *sign* affect the meaning of each word? Look up the words in your Spelling Dictionary.
- In Unit 1, you learned that knowing how to spell *resignation* can help you to remember the silent *g* in *resign*. In which of the words above is the letter *g* silent? In which is it sounded?

Apply and Extend

Complete these activities on a separate piece of paper.
1. Write sentences using each word in the list above.
2. Can you think of other words that belong to the same family as *design* and *resignation*? With a partner, make a list of related words. Then look on page 275 of your Spelling-Meaning Index. Add any other related words that you find to your list.

Summing Up

The Latin root *sign* means "mark or seal." Words that come from the same root are often related in spelling and meaning. Knowing some of the words in a family can help you to use and spell the others correctly.

The narrator tells what happened when he, his brother, and his dog were searching for evidence in a deserted warehouse. How does the narrator reveal to you that he is blind?

from

"THE WAREHOUSE"

by Walter Dean Myers

We went up a flight of stairs; I counted eight steps, a turn, and eight more steps to the second landing. I held tightly to Bojangles' harness.

"There's something over there," Jeff said, going to my right. I turned so that Bojangles would know to follow him.

We walked across the floor slowly until we reached another room. It seemed to take forever.

"This is the only place I see that could be an office," Jeff said. "The whole place is nearly empty, but there is a desk in here."

"Is there anything on it?" I asked. . . .

"Nothing here but a few old papers," Jeff whispered.

"Maybe we'd better get out of here," I said.

He tried the drawer a few times before I heard it slide out with a grating noise. He closed it quickly, and I knew it had to be empty.

"I'm sorry," I said, "but it seemed like a good idea."

"It was worth a try to help Dad," he said.

Clang!

I jumped as I heard a door bang heavily shut.

"Jeff, what was that?"

"I don't know," he answered.

We listened, and I heard the sounds of footsteps coming from the first floor. My heart was racing inside my shirt.

Think and Discuss

1. What **details** does the narrator use to show that he is blind?
2. Where does the author rely on **dialogue** alone to tell you what happens?

The Writing Process
Personal Narrative

What embarrassing, funny, thrilling, or scary things have happened to you? Write a personal narrative about one of those experiences. Keep the guidelines in mind, and follow the Writing Process.

1 ▶ Prewriting
- List some interesting experiences you have had.
- Choose as your topic an experience that you can remember in detail and would enjoy writing about.
- List the main events that will make up your narrative.

2 ▶ Draft
- Start to write. Do not worry about mistakes.
- Write three beginnings and then choose the most interesting one.

3 ▶ Revise
- Add details and dialogue to bring your story's action to life. Try to make the dialogue sound like actual conversation.
- Have a writing conference.

4 ▶ Proofread
- Did you spell each word correctly?
- Did you use commas correctly in compound sentences and in appositives?
- Did you correct any sentence fragments or run-on sentences?

5 ▶ Publish
- Copy your narrative neatly and add an interesting title.
- With your classmates, create a book of stories. Display the book in the school library.

Guidelines for Writing a Personal Narrative

✓ Tell the story from your point of view.
✓ Write a good beginning to capture your readers' interest.
✓ Use dialogue and vivid details to make the story real for your readers.

Composition Words

autumn
autograph
microphone
semifinals
idol
unique
Ferris wheel
capital

Consonant Changes

Read and Say

READ the sentences. SAY each bold word.

1. *investigate* — The police will **investigate** the accident.
2. *investigation* — Careful **investigation** will reveal the answer.
3. *detect* — Can you **detect** the scent of burning wood?
4. *detection* — Wolves walk softly to escape **detection**.
5. *violate* — You will be punished if you **violate** the rules.
6. *violation* — Speeding is a traffic **violation**.
7. *exhibit* — I will **exhibit** my sheep at the county fair.
8. *exhibition* — The school has an **exhibition** of student art.
9. *operate* — Were you trained to **operate** this machine?
10. *operation* — I need an **operation** to fix my injured knee.
11. *duplicate* — Use a copy machine to **duplicate** the form.
12. *duplication* — I ordered a **duplication** of the photo for you.
13. *evaluate* — The coach will **evaluate** your hockey skills.
14. *evaluation* — Your **evaluation** helped me improve my report.
15. *participate* — Let everyone **participate** in the discussion.
16. *participation* — I need your **participation** in my drama group.
17. *punctuate* — It is easy to **punctuate** a compound sentence.
18. *punctuation* — Commas and periods are **punctuation** marks.
19. *congratulate* — Let's **congratulate** these excellent actors.
20. *congratulations* — I will send my **congratulations** to the winner.

Spelling Strategy To remember the spelling of the |sh| sound in words such as *detection* and *operation*, think of a word that is related in spelling and meaning.

Think and Write   Write the pairs of Basic Words.

Review
21. connect
22. connection
23. cooperate
24. cooperation

Challenge
25. prosecute
26. prosecution
27. implicate
28. implication

Independent Practice

Vocabulary: Using Context Write the Basic Word that completes each sentence. Use your Spelling Dictionary.

1. Police completed their _____ of the crime by interviewing several witnesses.
2. Did you _____ anything odd about the suspect's actions?
3. Reggie paid a heavy fine for the traffic _____.
4. Special training is required to _____ lie-detector equipment.
5. Did the lawyer _____ the evidence so that the jury could see the stolen goods?
6. Mr. Finch took the document to _____ it on the photocopier.
7. People rushed to _____ the lawyers after they won the case.
8. It is important to _____ legal transcripts correctly, for a single comma can change the meaning of a sentence.
9. A jury makes a decision based on its _____ of the evidence.
10. A detective will _____ to determine the truth of the witness's statements.
11. Professor Wu will _____ in a debate over the anti-crime bill.
12. Jury duty offers an opportunity for _____ in the legal process.
13. The lawyer's closing argument was an _____ of her persuasive skills.

Vocabulary: Analogies Write the Basic Word that completes each analogy. Use your Spelling Dictionary.

Example: teacher : instruct :: detective : _____   *investigate*

14. assistance : thanks :: success : _____
15. actor : performance :: surgeon : _____
16. two : number :: period : _____
17. shield : concealment :: radar : _____
18. show : display :: judge : _____
19. start : stop :: obey : _____
20. telephone : communication :: photocopier : _____

Challenge Words Write the Challenge Word that matches each definition. Use your Spelling Dictionary.

21. involvement or connection with a crime or wrongdoing
22. the act of conducting legal action against someone
23. to involve or connect with a crime
24. to conduct legal action against

Review: Spelling Spree

Code Breaker The Basic and Review Words below have been written in code. Use the code key to write the words correctly.

CODE:	l	m	n	o	p	q	r	s	t	u	v	w	x	y	z	a	b	c	d	e	f	g	h	i	j	k
LETTER:	a	b	c	d	e	f	g	h	i	j	k	l	m	n	o	p	q	r	s	t	u	v	w	x	y	z

1. pistmte
2. opepne
3. zapclep
4. ofawtnletzy
5. nzzapclep
6. afynefletzy

7. pistmtetzy
8. gtzwletzy
9. tygpdetrletzy
10. alcetntaletzy
11. nzyypnetzy
12. opepnetzy

Puzzle Play Write the Basic or Review Word that fits each clue. Circle the letter that would appear in the box.

Example: to discover or notice _ _ _ _ ☐ _   dete©t
13. a form of praise ☐ _ _ _ _ _ _ _ _ _ _ _ _ _
14. to join together _ ☐ _ _ _ _ _ _
15. the act of working together _ _ _ _ _ _ _ _ _ _ ☐
16. to examine carefully _ _ _ _ ☐ _ _ _ _
17. judgment _ _ _ _ _ _ _ ☐ _
18. to disregard or disobey _ ☐ _ _ _ _ _
19. to estimate the worth of _ _ _ _ _ _ ☐ _
20. to copy _ ☐ _ _ _ _ _ _
21. to acknowledge success _ _ _ _ _ _ ☐ _ _ _ _
22. to take part _ _ _ _ _ _ ☐ _ _ _
23. a surgical procedure _ _ _ _ _ _ _ ☐ _
24. to mark the end of a sentence _ _ ☐ _ _ _ _ _

✓ **How Are You Doing?**
Write the spelling words in alphabetical order. Practice any misspelled words with a partner.

Now write the circled letters in sequence. They will spell a mystery word that names a legal document.

Mystery Word:

_ _ _ _ _ _ _ ? _ _ _ _ _

Proofreading and Writing

Proofread: Spelling and Subject-Verb Agreement The subject and the verb of a sentence must **agree** in number. Use a singular verb with a singular subject and a plural verb with a plural subject. Subjects joined by *and* take a plural verb. With subjects joined by *or* or *nor*, use a verb that agrees with the closer subject.

The **judge** presides at a trial.
Lawyers argue in court.
The **judge** and the **jury** discuss the case.
The **lawyer** or her **assistants** research legal issues.

Find five misspelled Basic or Review Words and two verbs that do not agree with their subjects in this newspaper article. Write the article correctly.

THIEVES CAUGHT IN THE ART

Following a long investigasion, police have arrested Michael Morse in conection with a series of art thefts. Morse's partner, Betty Brown, has also been arrested and accused of forgery. Brown's international operation involves the duplacation of artwork stolen by Morse. Dealers or Brown sell the fakes at an exibition in Paris. Both Morse and Brown has been charged with vialation of the Original Art Act.

Basic

1. investigate
2. investigation
3. detect
4. detection
5. violate
6. violation
7. exhibit
8. exhibition
9. operate
10. operation
11. duplicate
12. duplication
13. evaluate
14. evaluation
15. participate
16. participation
17. punctuate
18. punctuation
19. congratulate
20. congratulations

Review
21. connect
22. connection
23. cooperate
24. cooperation

Challenge
25. prosecute
26. prosecution
27. implicate
28. implication

Write a Personal Narrative You are a witness to a crime. Write a personal narrative telling the police what you saw. Record as many details as possible. Try to use five spelling words, and check that the subject and verb of each sentence agree in number.

Proofreading Marks
¶ Indent
∧ Add
⌃ Add a comma
✌ ✌ Add quotation marks
⊙ Add a period
⌐ Delete
≡ Capital letter
/ Small letter
∩ Reverse order

Unit 7 BONUS

Expanding Vocabulary

Spelling Word Link

operate
violate

The Suffixes -ate and -en If you did not know the meanings of the words *operate* and *violate*, how could you tell that they are verbs? The suffix *-ate* means "to become or cause to be." The suffix *-en* has the same meaning. Both *-ate* and *-en* form verbs when they are added to word roots or base words.

active + ate = activate   awake + en = awaken

Add *-ate* or *-en* to each base word below to form a verb. Use your Spelling Dictionary.

1. haste   **2.** threat   **3.** origin   **4.** length   **5.** design

TEST-TAKING TACTICS

Analogies On many analogy tests, the main word pair, or **stem**, is capitalized. To help determine how the stem words are related, first compose a sentence that states the relationship you *think* exists between them. Look at these examples:

Analogy Stem	Sentence	Relationship
HAMMER : TOOL	A hammer is a kind of tool.	item/category
BUTTON : FASTEN	A button is used to fasten.	item/function
PAIN : INJURY	Pain is an effect of an injury.	effect/cause

After stating the stem words' relationship in a sentence, try replacing them with the words in each answer choice.

Study this analogy question, and then write the answers to the questions that follow.

BILLBOARD : ADVERTISE ::   (A) crystal : shatter (B) dictionary : refer
(C) scale: weigh (D) toothpaste : smile (E) newspaper : recycle

6. What sentence could you write to state the stem words' relationship?
7. What type of relationship exists between the stem words?
8. Which answer pair has the same type of relationship as the stem pair? Write its letter.

Real-World Connection

Careers: Criminal Law All the words in the box relate to criminal law. Look up these words in your Spelling Dictionary. Then write the words to complete this paragraph.

Case # 21086

Criminal trials follow a standard procedure. If a person charged with a crime enters a __(1)__ of "not guilty," a trial by jury is arranged. Attorneys then select a jury. They question each possible __(2)__ and may reject anyone who seems prejudiced about the case. A fair jury is important, for they must decide whether the __(3)__ is guilty or innocent. Next, witnesses are notified by __(4)__ that they will have to __(5)__ under oath in court. Because a witness's __(6)__ may lead to either the conviction or the __(7)__ of the accused, a witness who lies may be charged with __(8)__ , which is itself a criminal offense.

Spelling Word Link

exhibit

defendant
plea
testify
juror
subpoena
perjury
testimony
acquittal

TRY THIS!

Yes or No? Write *yes* if the underlined word or phrase is used correctly. Write *no* if it is not.

9. After his <u>acquittal</u>, the prisoner was released.
10. For refusing to testify, he was charged with <u>perjury</u>.
11. The <u>defendant</u> turned to her lawyer for advice.
12. The officer handed me a <u>subpoena</u> to appear in court.

Fact File

A district attorney is a public official responsible for prosecuting a person charged with a crime. District attorneys exist at the local, state, and federal levels. They are elected in some states and appointed in others.

Greek Word Parts II

Read and Say

Basic

READ the sentences. SAY each bold word.

1. geometry — We study shapes and angles in **geometry**.
2. perimeter — Outline the **perimeter** of the court with chalk.
3. diameter — The **diameter** of a circle divides it in half.
4. diagram — Mike drew a **diagram** to describe his room.
5. centimeter — Some rulers can measure a **centimeter**.
6. kilogram — Is a **kilogram** more than two pounds?
7. cyclone — Many trees were blown down by the **cyclone**.
8. thermos — My soup stays warm in this **thermos**.
9. physician — A **physician** cares for people who are ill.
10. encyclopedia — You can look up the dates in an **encyclopedia**.
11. thermometer — I read the **thermometer** to see how cold it was.
12. physics — Matter is a major topic in **physics** class.
13. telegram — The news came by **telegram** instead of by mail.
14. grammatical — Which sentence has a **grammatical** error?
15. barometer — A **barometer** helps to predict the weather.
16. thermostat — She put in a **thermostat** to regulate the heat.
17. physique — Exercise has given him a lean **physique**.
18. motorcycle — Always wear a helmet when riding a **motorcycle**.
19. thermal — My **thermal** hat keeps me warm in winter.
20. cyclical — The seasons repeat in a **cyclical** pattern.

Spelling Strategy   Knowing the Greek word parts *cycl* ("circle"), *phys* ("nature"), *gram* ("something written"), *therm* ("heat"), and *meter/metry* ("measure") can help you spell and understand words with these parts.

Think and Write   Write the Basic Words. Underline the Greek word part *cycl, phys, gram, therm, meter,* or *metry* in each.

Review
21. physical
22. grammar
23. difficult
24. portion
25. example

Challenge
26. parallelogram
27. isometric
28. physiology
29. anagram
30. metronome

54

Independent Practice

Vocabulary: Definitions Write the Basic Word that matches each definition. Use your Spelling Dictionary.

1. the mathematical study of points, lines, surfaces, and angles, and of figures composed of these
2. a straight line that starts on one side of a circle, passes through the center, and ends on the other side
3. producing or caused by heat
4. occurring in a repeated series
5. a device that controls the temperature of an enclosed space
6. following the rules for using words in sentences
7. an instrument that measures and indicates temperature
8. the distance around the sides of a flat figure or shape
9. an instrument that measures the pressure of the atmosphere and indicates changes in the weather
10. a violent rotating windstorm
11. a two-wheeled vehicle, larger than a bicycle and propelled by an engine

Vocabulary: Classifying Write the Basic Word that fits each group. Use your Spelling Dictionary.

12. inch, kilometer, mile, _____
13. chart, graph, illustration, _____
14. ounce, pound, ton, _____
15. dictionary, atlas, thesaurus, _____
16. biology, chemistry, botany, _____
17. letter, postcard, telephone call, _____
18. pitcher, bottle, jug, _____
19. lawyer, teacher, banker, _____
20. body, figure, shape, _____

Challenge Words Write the Challenge Word that fits each clue. Use your Spelling Dictionary.

21. This is an exercise that uses tension.
22. This sounds like a clock but tells no time.
23. This is a word made from the letters of another word.
24. This is a four-sided flat figure.
25. This must be studied by people who want to become doctors.

Dictionary

Spelling Table Suppose you looked up the word |fĭz´ ĭks| under the letter *f* and could not find it. Where in the dictionary would you look next? Check the **spelling table**. It lists the various ways a sound can be spelled.

SOUND	SPELLINGS	SAMPLE WORDS
|f|	f, ff, gh, ph	**f**unny, o**ff**, enou**gh**, **ph**ysical

Practice Write each of the words whose phonetic spellings appear below. Use your Spelling Table and Spelling Dictionary to check your spellings.

1. |ô´ də bəl|
2. |kī´ ăk´|
3. |sûr´ kĭt|
4. |kŏn´ shəs|

5. |krī tîr´ ē ən|
6. |jə nĕt´ ĭk|
7. |ə pō´ nənt|
8. |chĕl´ ō|

1. ?
2. ?
3. ?

4. ?
5. ?
6. ?

7. ?
8. ?

Review: Spelling Spree

Word Perimeter 9–25. Find the Basic and Review Words that are hidden in the perimeter of the park. Write the words correctly in the order in which you find them.

Proofreading and Writing

Proofread for Spelling Find six misspelled Basic or Review Words in this paragraph. Write each word correctly.

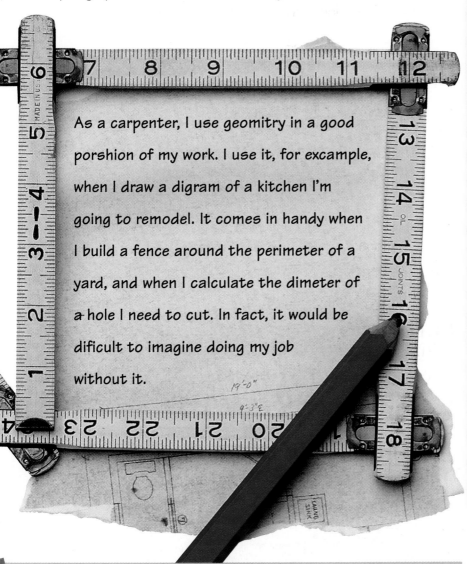

As a carpenter, I use geomitry in a good porshion of my work. I use it, for excample, when I draw a digram of a kitchen I'm going to remodel. It comes in handy when I build a fence around the perimeter of a yard, and when I calculate the dimeter of a hole I need to cut. In fact, it would be dificult to imagine doing my job without it.

Basic

1. geometry
2. perimeter
3. diameter
4. diagram
5. centimeter
6. kilogram
7. cyclone
8. thermos
9. physician
10. encyclopedia
11. thermometer
12. physics
13. telegram
14. grammatical
15. barometer
16. thermostat
17. physique
18. motorcycle
19. thermal
20. cyclical

Review

21. physical
22. grammar
23. difficult
24. portion
25. example

Challenge

26. parallelogram
27. isometric
28. physiology
29. anagram
30. metronome

Proofreading Marks

¶	Indent
∧	Add
⩟	Add a comma
⌄⌄	Add quotation marks
⊙	Add a period
⌐	Delete
≡	Capital letter
/	Small letter
∿	Reverse order

Write a Description Write a description of a common object in terms of the geometric shapes it contains. They may be flat shapes, such as squares and triangles, or three-dimensional shapes, such as cylinders and cubes. Try to use five spelling words.

Expanding Vocabulary

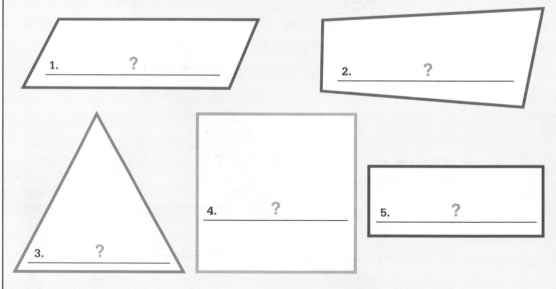

Spelling Word Link

motorcycle

Compound Words A **compound word** is a combination of two or more smaller words. Some compound words are written as one word, some as separate words, and some as hyphenated words.

motor	+	cycle	=	motorcycle
vice	+	president	=	vice-president
seat	+	belt	=	seat belt

Combine two of the words below to write a compound word to match each definition. Use your Spelling Dictionary.

fire	by	year	skate	control
line	proof	remote	light	board

1. a line at the top of a news article, giving the writer's name
2. a measure of distance in space
3. made of material that does not burn
4. a small platform mounted on wheels and propelled by foot
5. a device used to operate a machine from a distance

1. _____ ?

2. _____ ?

3. _____ ?

4. _____ ?

5. _____ ?

Now write a sentence for three of the words you made above.

6. _____ ?

7. _____ ?

8. _____ ?

Real-World Connection

Math: Geometry All the words in the box relate to geometry. Look up these words in your Spelling Dictionary. Then write the words to complete this paragraph.

Last week I showed my little brother how to relate geometry to things around us. I pointed out that a stop sign is a __(1)__ with eight sides, that an intersection often forms __(2)__ lines, and that a sidewalk is a line __(3)__. His sandwich was shaped like a __(4)__, and his orange was a __(5)__. We measured around a bike wheel to find its __(6)__. Then we measured one spoke, which went from the hub to a point on the rim, to find the circle's __(7)__. Finally, a rainbow appeared and gave us an example of an __(8)__!

Spelling Word Link

geometry

rectangle
arc
sphere
polygon
segment
radius
circumference
perpendicular

TRY THIS!

True or False? Write *T* if a sentence is true and *F* if it is false.

9. A segment is the point where perpendicular lines meet.
10. A sphere is a two-dimensional figure.
11. Circumference is the distance around a circle.
12. An arc is part of a circle.

Fact File

A geodesic dome is a self-supporting structure made entirely of linked triangles or other polygons. Designed by Buckminster Fuller, these types of domes are inexpensive and can be quickly assembled anywhere. Because of their shape, they are also incredibly strong and resistant to pressure.

Noun Suffixes

Read and Say

Basic	READ the sentences. SAY each bold word.
1. architecture	Study **architecture** to learn building styles.
2. achievement	It is a rare **achievement** to win first prize.
3. fragment	I cut my foot on a **fragment** of broken glass.
4. sculpture	The artist carved his **sculpture** out of wood.
5. ornament	Mom loves the hair **ornament** I gave her.
6. texture	This cloth has a smooth and silky **texture**.
7. failure	One **failure** will not prevent future success.
8. equipment	Fishing **equipment** includes rods and reels.
9. freedom	We all have the right to **freedom** of speech.
10. judgment	Use good **judgment** when choosing a partner.
11. procedure	I can explain the **procedure** for baking a pie.
12. argument	Their **argument** was over who would go first.
13. literature	Is poetry your favorite form of **literature**?
14. boredom	You can avoid **boredom** by staying busy.
15. legislature	Making laws is the work of the **legislature**.
16. fracture	Did he **fracture** his leg in football practice?
17. gesture	A nod is a **gesture** made with the head.
18. tournament	The top six teams will play in the **tournament**.
19. kingdom	The king ruled his **kingdom** wisely.
20. disappointment	Her **disappointment** at losing was clear.

 Spelling Strategy   The suffixes *-ure, -ment,* and *-dom* form nouns when added to base words or word roots. Remember the spelling patterns for these suffixes.

Think and Write   Write each Basic Word under its suffix.

-ure	-ment	-dom

Review	
21. development	24. replacement
22. document	25. temperature
23. pressure	

Challenge	
26. fissure	29. disclosure
27. caricature	30. horticulture
28. acknowledgment	

Independent Practice

Vocabulary: Using Context Write the Basic Word that completes each sentence. Use your Spelling Dictionary.

1. Delicate carvings of leaves and flowers _____ the pillars.
2. Many fantastic structures were built without cranes, power tools, or other modern _____.
3. The museum's collection of _____ features many beautiful marble statues.
4. In Bev's _____, the White House is grander than the Capitol.
5. The _____ drafted a bill to preserve historic buildings.
6. The _____ for restoring the cathedral included cleaning the walls and replacing any missing stones.
7. Most subjects of the _____ had never seen the royal palace.
8. Students of _____ learn how to design and erect buildings.
9. The building of the huge pyramids was a major _____ of the Egyptians.
10. The handcut stone gave the building a rough _____.
11. A large _____ of the wall lay crumbling in the courtyard.

Vocabulary: Definitions Write the Basic Word that matches each definition. Use your Spelling Dictionary.

12. a contest consisting of a series of games
13. a body of writing
14. liberty
15. a motion of the body
16. the feeling of being let down
17. a dispute
18. a condition resulting from lack of interest
19. to break
20. an unsuccessful attempt

Challenge Words Write the Challenge Word that fits each clue. Use your Spelling Dictionary.

21. a picture or description that exaggerates
22. a statement that lets the cat out of the bag
23. a narrow crack
24. something serious gardeners engage in
25. response or recognition

Review: Spelling Spree

Word Combination In each item, add the beginning letters of the first word to the last letters of the second to form a Basic or Review Word.

Example: mustard + monocle   *muscle*

1. ornery + predicament
2. literally + future
3. doctor + monument
4. genuine + pasture
5. frame + lecture
6. textile + pure
7. frail + segment
8. tourniquet + parliament
9. temperament + nature

Word Forms Add a noun suffix to each base word to form a Basic or Review Word. Write the words.

10. proceed
11. develop
12. disappoint
13. architect

14. argue
15. bore
16. press
17. sculpt
18. replace
19. fail
20. king
21. achieve
22. judge
23. equip
24. free
25. legislate

✓ **How Are You Doing?**
List the spelling words that are difficult for you. Practice them with a partner.

Proofreading and Writing

Proofread: Spelling and Comparing with Adjectives Use the comparative form of an adjective to compare two things. Use the superlative form to compare three or more things.

POSITIVE	COMPARATIVE	SUPERLATIVE
hard	harder	hardest
useful	more useful	most useful

Find five misspelled Basic or Review Words and one incorrect adjective of comparison in this excerpt from a travel guide. Write the excerpt correctly.

While in Cambodia, also known as Kampuchea, be sure to visit the temple of Angkor Wat. In the judgmint of many, it is the greatest achievement in the history of Cambodian architectur. It is certainly the more famous of all Cambodian monuments. Built in the twelfth century, Angkor Wat shows the high level of cultural divelopment of the kingdum of Khmer, as Cambodia was once known. Five huge towers linked by galleries are covered with fine sculpcher and ornament.

Write a Description What interesting building do you see every day? Write a paragraph describing the building as though it were a famous monument. What might the building represent? What makes it special? Try to use five spelling words and at least one comparative or superlative adjective form.

Basic

1. architecture
2. achievement
3. fragment
4. sculpture
5. ornament
6. texture
7. failure
8. equipment
9. freedom
10. judgment
11. procedure
12. argument
13. literature
14. boredom
15. legislature
16. fracture
17. gesture
18. tournament
19. kingdom
20. disappointment

Review

21. development
22. document
23. pressure
24. replacement
25. temperature

Challenge

26. fissure
27. caricature
28. acknowledgment
29. disclosure
30. horticulture

Proofreading Marks

- ¶ Indent
- ∧ Add
- ∧ Add a comma
- “ ” Add quotation marks
- ⊙ Add a period
- Delete
- ≡ Capital letter
- / Small letter
- ∿ Reverse order

Unit 9 BONUS

Expanding Vocabulary

Spelling Word Link

fragment
fracture

The Latin Root *frag/fract* *Fragment* and *fracture* both contain *frag* or *fract*, forms of the same root, meaning "to break." Other English words also contain this root. Their meanings all have something to do with breaking or parts.

fraction   fragile   infraction   refract

Write a word from the list above to complete each sentence. Use your Spelling Dictionary.

1. Lisa was punished for her _____ of the rules.
2. When Joe got home, only a _____ of the pizza was left.
3. The porcelain vase is _____, so handle it carefully.
4. A prism is used to _____ light rays.

TEST-TAKING TACTICS

Sentence Completion Sentence completion questions often appear on tests of verbal skills. These questions typically contain a sentence that has one or two blanks where words have been omitted, followed by four or five answer choices. Your task is to choose the answer that, when inserted in place of the blank(s) in the sentence, best fits the sentence's meaning. Look at this sample question and its answer choices.

Rather than trying to restore the decaying monument, it may be less expensive to _____ it and erect a replacement.

(A) move   (B) raze   (C) repair   (D) remodel   (E) rebuild

To tackle this question, first read the sentence. Then, *before* you look at the answer choices, try to think of a word that makes sense in the blank. Next, look at the answer choices. If one is the word you thought of or a synonym of it, that is the best answer.

Write *A, B, C, D,* or *E* to answer the following question.

5. Which answer choice best fits the sample sentence's meaning?

Real-World Connection

Social Studies: Famous Monuments All the words in the box relate to famous monuments. Look up these words in your Spelling Dictionary. Then write the words to complete these sentences.

Spelling Word Link

architecture

Eiffel Tower
Pantheon
Sphinx
Taj Mahal
Colosseum
Parthenon
Angkor Wat
Stonehenge

1. The _____ lies in the desert in Giza, Egypt.
2. Salisbury Plain, in England, is the site of the great prehistoric monument called _____.
3. Photographs of Paris often feature the _____.
4. The _____ is a Greek temple now in ruins.
5. Cambodians built _____ as a place of worship.
6. Ancient Romans went to the _____ for entertainment.
7. An Indian ruler built the _____ as a tomb for his wife.
8. The _____ is an ancient temple in the heart of Rome.

TRY THIS!

True or False? Write *T* if a sentence is true and *F* if it is false.

9. You can see Paris from the top of the Sphinx.
10. Public contests were held in the Colosseum.
11. Stonehenge was built in the eighteenth century.
12. The Taj Mahal is the tallest building in New York City.

Fact File

The Parthenon sits atop the Acropolis, the highest hill in Athens, Greece. The ancient Greeks built the temple in the fifth century B.C. to honor the patron of the city—Athena, goddess of wisdom.

Words from Spanish

Read and Say

Basic

READ the sentences. **SAY** each bold word.

1. *plaza* — I ran across the broad **plaza** to the hotel.
2. *fiesta* — Will there be music and games at the **fiesta**?
3. *tortilla* — Please fill my **tortilla** with chicken.
4. *siesta* — A short **siesta** is nice after a busy morning.
5. *burro* — A donkey and a **burro** carried our gear.
6. *poncho* — He threw a **poncho** across his shoulders.
7. *sombrero* — A **sombrero** has a broad brim to shade the body.
8. *hammock* — I slept in the **hammock** hanging on the porch.
9. *chocolate* — I love peach ice cream and **chocolate**.
10. *tomato* — A ripe red **tomato** is great in salads.
11. *enchilada* — May I have extra sauce on my cheese **enchilada**?
12. *burrito* — A **burrito** can be filled with meat and beans.
13. *alligator* — The **alligator** is one very scary reptile!
14. *bonanza* — The mine produced a **bonanza** of gold.
15. *patio* — We ate lunch outside on the shady **patio**.
16. *cargo* — The huge ship hauled a **cargo** of trucks.
17. *chili* — I love spicy **chili** topped with onions.
18. *cocoa* — Would a cup of **cocoa** help to warm you up?
19. *vanilla* — Add **vanilla** to the batter for extra flavor.
20. *iguana* — An **iguana** looks like a small dinosaur.

💡 **Spelling Strategy**   Knowing how to pronounce a word from Spanish will often help you spell it.

Think and Write   Write the Basic Words.

Review
21. potatoes
22. ancient
23. custom
24. rural
25. celebrate

Challenge
26. guacamole
27. hacienda
28. guerrilla
29. platinum
30. embargo

Independent Practice

Vocabulary: Word Clues Write the Basic Word that fits each clue. Use your Spelling Dictionary.

1. This is as flat as a pancake.
2. This is filled with meat, beans, or cheese and is eaten with the hands.
3. This is a hot taste with a cold name.
4. This is red and can be eaten raw or cooked.
5. This hangs and can put you to sleep.
6. This is a warm drink good for a cold day.
7. This is a flavor that comes from long, beanlike seed pods.
8. This has a filling inside and a sauce outside.
9. This can be sweet or semisweet, brown or white.
10. This has a big smile, revealing sharp, dangerous teeth.

Vocabulary: Definitions Write the Basic Word that matches each definition. Use your Spelling Dictionary.

11. a spiny tropical American lizard
12. a large, broad-brimmed straw or felt hat worn in Mexico
13. a public square
14. a paved space next to a house or an apartment
15. freight carried by ship, airplane, etc.
16. a source of great wealth
17. a blanketlike cloak
18. a small donkey
19. a rest or nap
20. a festival

Challenge Words

Write the Challenge Word that completes each sentence. Use your Spelling Dictionary.

21. I bought a _____ ring at a jewelry shop in Mexico City.
22. My uncle owns a _____ outside Mexico City, where he raises sheep and cattle.
23. We sat in the Mexican restaurant, eating _____ and chips as we waited for the main dish to arrive.
24. A major trade _____ on coffee or oranges could hurt Mexico's economy.
25. The small _____ band lived and trained at a secret campsite in the hills.

Review: Spelling Spree

Word Riddles Write a Basic or Review Word to solve each riddle.

1. I travel by sea or air and am carried by ship or airplane.
2. I am larger than a cap, made of straw or felt, and offer shade.
3. I am taken with eyes closed, often after a midday meal.
4. In a city, crowds of pigeons and people gather in me.
5. I offer a great opportunity for dancing and singing with friends.
6. We grow in a dark, dirty place and may show up on your plate in many different forms.
7. I am a kind of place that is far removed from the hustle and bustle of the city.
8. I am older than old.

Invisible Vowels Decide which vowels should be added to complete each Basic or Review Word. Write the words correctly.

9. b _ n _ n z _
10. v _ n _ l l _
11. t _ r t _ l l _
12. c _ l _ b r _ t _
13. c _ s t _ m
14. c _ c _ _
15. b _ r r _ t _
16. t _ m _ t _
17. h _ m m _ c k

18. p _ t _ _
19. _ l l _ g _ t _ r
20. p _ n c h _
21. _ g _ _ n _
22. c h _ l _
23. _ n c h _ l _ d _
24. c h _ c _ l _ t _
25. b _ r r _

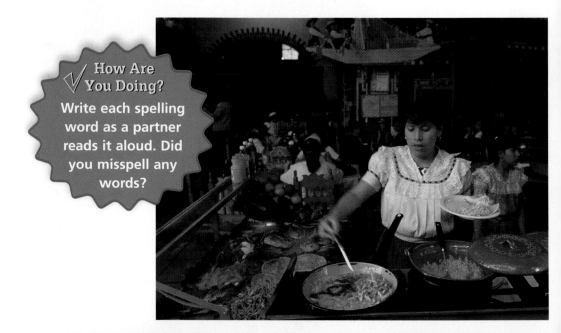

✓ How Are You Doing?
Write each spelling word as a partner reads it aloud. Did you misspell any words?

Proofreading and Writing

Proofread: Spelling and Comparing with Adverbs Use the comparative form of an adverb to compare two actions. Use the superlative form to compare three or more actions.

POSITIVE	COMPARATIVE	SUPERLATIVE
early	earlier	earliest
frequently	more frequently	most frequently

Find six misspelled Basic or Review Words and one incorrect adverb of comparison in this excerpt from a menu. Write the menu correctly.

Vegetarian burito — Lettuce, beans, cheese, and tomatoe chunks are wrapped in a flour tortilla.

Our enchalada special — Of all our dishes, customers demand this item more often.

Spicy chilly — Chef Martinez uses hot peppers more generously than any other chef.

Dessert fiesta — No one can resist this creamy vanila custard sprinkled with dark coco.

Basic

1. plaza
2. fiesta
3. tortilla
4. siesta
5. burro
6. poncho
7. sombrero
8. hammock
9. chocolate
10. tomato
11. enchilada
12. burrito
13. alligator
14. bonanza
15. patio
16. cargo
17. chili
18. cocoa
19. vanilla
20. iguana

Review

21. potatoes
22. ancient
23. custom
24. rural
25. celebrate

Challenge

26. guacamole
27. hacienda
28. guerrilla
29. platinum
30. embargo

Write a Movie Review You have just seen an informative video about Mexico. What were some of the film's highlights? Write a review of the movie, sharing its most interesting parts with your readers. Try to use five spelling words and at least one comparative or superlative adverb form.

Proofreading Marks

¶	Indent
∧	Add
⩘	Add a comma
ᵛᵛ ᵛᵛ	Add quotation marks
⊙	Add a period
⸚	Delete
≡	Capital letter
/	Small letter
∿	Reverse order

Expanding Vocabulary

Context Clues You have learned that an appositive is a group of words that follows a noun and identifies or renames it. When you read, appositives can be context clues to unfamiliar words. Imagine that you did not know the word *iguana*.

The iguana, **a lizard native to Mexico**, is very large.

Write the meaning of each underlined word.

1. Mexican <u>fauna</u>, or animal life, attracts tourists.
2. They take pictures of the <u>saguaro</u>, a tall cactus.
3. Mountain campers hope to see a <u>puma</u>, a kind of cougar.
4. The <u>peccary</u>, a piglike animal, often roams campsites.
5. People come to see the <u>quetzal</u>, a brightly colored bird.

Spelling Word Link

iguana

fauna
saguaro
puma
peccary
quetzal

1.	?
2.	?
3.	?
4.	?
5.	?

Now look up the words *tamale, desperado, piñata, jai alai,* and *bolero* in your Student Dictionary. Decide which word belongs in each sentence below, using the appositive in the sentence as a context clue. Write the word that belongs in each sentence.

6. The children took turns swinging at the _____, a container filled with candy and toys.
7. Try ordering a _____, a Mexican food roll made with corn meal.
8. The dancer's _____, a short jacket, was highly decorated.
9. The _____, a bold outlaw, led the posse into a trap.
10. The ball used in _____, a game similar to handball, travels at very high speeds.

Real-World Connection

Social Studies: Mexico All the words in the box relate to Mexico. Look up these words in your Spelling Dictionary. Then write the words to complete this paragraph.

> On a large __(1)__ that divides the Gulf of Mexico from the Caribbean Sea lies the Mexican state of __(2)__. Here, in the jungle, a giant stone __(3)__ rises seventy-five feet above the undergrowth. It is only one of many crumbling __(4)__ scattered across the region. Here and there, archaeologists have found remains, such as a painted __(5)__ of a religious __(6)__ or fragments of creamy-white __(7)__ ornaments that once decorated buildings. From these, archaeologists can develop an understanding of the extraordinary culture, called the __(8)__ civilization, that flourished here from the third to the tenth century.

Spelling Word Link

hacienda

Mayan
Yucatán
peninsula
pyramid
stucco
ceremony
mural
ruins

TRY THIS!

Yes or No? Write *yes* if the underlined word is used correctly. Write *no* if it is not.

9. The <u>peninsula</u> is cut off from the mainland by water.
10. The outer layer of the wall is made of <u>stucco.</u>
11. Clive gazed up at the slanted sides of the <u>pyramid</u>.
12. I drew a <u>mural</u> of an iguana on the cover of my report.

Fact File

Today, the Yucatán Peninsula is inhabited by descendants of the Mayans and draws tourists by the thousands. Among the area's popular attractions are the capital city of Mérida and the beach resorts of Cancún and Cozumel.

Words Often Confused

Read and Say

Basic		READ the sentences. SAY each bold word.

1. desert — Few plants can grow in this sandy **desert**.
2. dessert — We had fruit for **dessert** after the big meal.
3. access — Can we gain **access** through the park gate?
4. excess — The wet dog shook off the **excess** water.
5. continual — Her dog's **continual** barking kept me awake.
6. continuous — The **continuous** hum of the fan is relaxing.
7. hardy — These **hardy** plants can weather a cold winter.
8. hearty — A **hearty** meal will give us new energy.
9. reality — Can anyone believe a dream is **reality**?
10. realty — The newspaper has a list of **realty** for sale.
11. bizarre — I was startled by his **bizarre** costume.
12. bazaar — One booth at the **bazaar** sells candy apples.
13. formally — Guests behave **formally** at a state dinner.
14. formerly — We **formerly** grew corn in that empty field.
15. hurdle — The horse easily jumped the high **hurdle**.
16. hurtle — We turned to see the express train **hurtle** by.
17. prescribe — What pills did the doctor **prescribe**?
18. proscribe — Schools have rules that **proscribe** cheating.
19. conscious — I was **conscious** of someone staring at me.
20. conscience — Does your **conscience** bother you when you lie?

Spelling Strategy   To avoid confusing words with similar spellings and pronunciations, think of the meanings of the word.

Think and Write   Write the pairs of Basic Words.

Review			Challenge	
21. accept	**23.** advise		**25.** climatic	**27.** ellipse
22. except	**24.** advice		**26.** climactic	**28.** eclipse

Independent Practice

Vocabulary: Synonyms in Context Write the Basic Word that is a synonym for the underlined word. Use your Spelling Dictionary.

1. a <u>deliberate</u> effort
2. to separate fantasy from <u>actuality</u>
3. <u>previously</u> at this address
4. a <u>nourishing</u> breakfast
5. to be <u>officially</u> introduced
6. the <u>uninterrupted</u> supply of blood to the body
7. a <u>strange</u> coincidence
8. <u>strong</u> pioneers
9. to gain <u>entrance</u> to the building
10. the <u>repeated</u> hammering of machinery
11. to <u>prohibit</u> use of the dangerous chemical
12. to <u>speed</u> down the ski slope
13. a <u>surplus</u> of vegetables

Vocabulary: Definitions Write the Basic Word that matches each definition. Use your Spelling Dictionary.

14. to order or recommend the use of something
15. an obstacle or problem that must be overcome
16. the final course of a meal
17. land and the property on it
18. an inner sense that helps a person distinguish between right and wrong
19. a marketplace or fair
20. a dry region, often covered with sand, having little or no vegetation

Challenge Words Write the Challenge Word that fits each clue. Use your Spelling Dictionary.

21. This type of condition is determined by rain, snow, heat, cold, and wind.
22. This event could make a bright, sunny day temporarily dim.
23. The most suspenseful part of a mystery or thriller could be described as this.
24. A tabletop or a platter can have this shape.

Dictionary

Homographs Homographs are words that have the same spelling but different meanings. In the dictionary, homographs are listed as separate entry words, rather than separate definitions, because they have different origins. Some homographs have different pronunciations, as well.

> **des·ert¹** |dĕz´ ərt| *n.* A dry, barren region often covered with sand.
> **des·ert²** |dĭ zûrt´| *v.* To forsake or leave; to abandon.
> **des·ert³** |dĭ zûrt´| *n.* Often **deserts**. Something that is deserved, especially punishment: *He received his just deserts.*

Practice Write *1*, *2*, or *3* to show which of the above homographs is used in each sentence.

1. The criminal got his just *deserts* for the crime he committed.
2. Years of drought had turned the grasslands into *desert*.
3. Though she was afraid, Eve did not *desert* her friend.
4. At night, small animals roam the *desert* in search of food.

1.	?	3.	?
2.	?	4.	?

Review: Spelling Spree

Letter Math Add and subtract letters from the words below to make Basic or Review Words. Write the new words.

Example: ac + forces − for + s =   *access*

5. bi + czar − c + re =
6. sharp − s − p + dy =
7. d + press − pr + ert =
8. h + squirt − sq − i + le =
9. fo + thermal − the + ly =
10. red − d + alter − er + y =
11. he + start − st + y =
12. continent − ent + ual =
13. h + fur − f + dale − a =

14. rex − r + creep − re + t =
15. con + scientist − tist + ce =
16. pre + scroll − oll + ibe =
17. con + ti + strenuous − stre =
18. blaze − l − e + afar − f =
19. reap − p + little − tle + y =
20. ac + reception − re − ion =
21. con + s + precious − pre =
22. prom − m + scribble − bl =

Proofreading and Writing

Basic

Proofread for Spelling Find six misspelled Basic or Review Words in this paragraph. Write each word correctly.

Few plants can live in a dessert. Those that do are very hardy. To get through periods of little rain, some grow long roots to gain acsess to water underground. Others store exess water, using it up a bit at a time. Many of the world's driest areas are expanding. Poor farming methods, too much grazing of livestock, and the cutting of trees dry up the land. To stop this trend and reclaim formally fertile lands, scientists advize planting trees. Other advise includes improving farming methods and limiting livestock in these areas.

Basic
1. desert
2. dessert
3. access
4. excess
5. continual
6. continuous
7. hardy
8. hearty
9. reality
10. realty
11. bizarre
12. bazaar
13. formally
14. formerly
15. hurdle
16. hurtle
17. prescribe
18. proscribe
19. conscious
20. conscience

Review
21. accept
22. except
23. advise
24. advice

Challenge
25. climatic
26. climactic
27. ellipse
28. eclipse

Proofreading Marks
¶ Indent
∧ Add
⅄ Add a comma
⌄⌄ ⌄⌄ Add quotation marks
⊙ Add a period
ᵔ Delete
☰ Capital letter
/ Small letter
∿ Reverse order

Write an Essay   Would you like to live in a desert? Why or why not? Write a short essay presenting your personal views about what desert life would be like. Try to use five spelling words.

Expanding Vocabulary

Spelling Word Link

bizarre

Antonyms What is the relationship between the underlined words in the sentence below?

While a camel would be a <u>bizarre</u> sight on a city street, it is an <u>ordinary</u> one in some desert regions.

Bizarre and *ordinary* are **antonyms**, or words with opposite meanings.

Write an antonym from the list below for each numbered word that follows. Use your Spelling Dictionary.

excess	formally	reality	conscious
continuous	accept	hardy	except

1. weak   **4.** interrupted   **7.** shortage
2. including   **5.** fantasy   **8.** unconscious
3. casually   **6.** reject

1. _____?_____   5. _____?_____
2. _____?_____   6. _____?_____
3. _____?_____   7. _____?_____
4. _____?_____   8. _____?_____

Now choose two pairs of antonyms from items 1–8. Write two sentences, using a different antonym pair in each sentence.

Example: After we <u>capture</u> and treat the injured lizard, we will <u>release</u> it back into the wild.

9. _____?_____
_____?_____

10. _____?_____
_____?_____

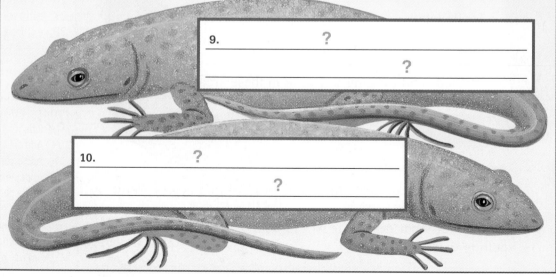

Vocabulary Enrichment

Real-World Connection

Social Studies: Deserts All the words in the box relate to deserts. Look up these words in your Spelling Dictionary. Then write the words to complete this paragraph.

Born in the __(1)__ climate of the Sahara, the __(2)__ was used to the dry air and the parched, __(3)__ landscape. He herded his animals toward a massive __(4)__ formation, whose steep walls might offer some shade. A steady wind whipped the sand around him, slowly continuing the __(5)__ that had carved out the land form. Peering into the distance, he spied a __(6)__, its hump slung with bundles. It must be a __(7)__, he thought, since such illusions were common in the desert. Many pack animals soon became visible, however, and he realized that a merchant's __(8)__ was moving toward him.

Spelling Word Link

desert

arid
barren
erosion
sandstone
caravan
nomad
dromedary
mirage

TRY THIS!

Yes or No? Write *yes* or *no* to answer each question.

9. Could the shape of a mountain be changed by erosion?
10. Could a person climb a mirage?
11. Could a nomad be a farmer?
12. Could a forest be barren?

Fact File

The Sahara is the world's largest desert, covering an area of northern Africa almost as large as the United States. In much of the Sahara, the average rainfall is less than one inch per year. The Sahara supports less plant and animal life than any other desert.

12 Review: Units 7–11

Unit 7   Consonant Changes   pages 48–53

investigate	detect	operate	participate	punctuate
investigation	detection	operation	participation	punctuation

💡 **Spelling Strategy**   To remember the spelling of the |sh| sound in words such as *detection* and *operation*, think of a word that is related in spelling and meaning.

Write the word that completes each sentence.
1. The old mill has not been in _____ for a century.
2. Always try to _____ your sentences correctly.
3. The detective began the _____ by following the suspect.
4. Because of his clever disguise, the colonel escaped _____.

Write the word that matches each definition.
5. active involvement   7. to join in   9. to discover
6. to look into   8. marks used in writing   10. to work or function

Unit 8   Greek Word Parts II   pages 54–59

diagram	perimeter	thermos	physician	encyclopedia
telegram	barometer	physique	thermostat	motorcycle

💡 **Spelling Strategy**   Knowing the Greek word parts *cycl* ("circle"), *phys* ("nature"), *gram* ("something written"), *therm* ("heat"), and *meter/metry* ("measure") can help you spell and understand words with these parts.

Write the word that completes each analogy.
11. steering wheel : car :: handlebars : _____
12. fiction : novel :: reference : _____
13. write : instructions :: draw : _____
14. part : section :: border : _____

Write the word that fits each clue.
15. something sent   18. a device used to forecast weather
16. the form of the body   19. a hospital employee
17. a temperature regulator   20. a container for hot drinks

Unit 9 Noun Suffixes

pages 60–65

equipment	failure	judgment	achievement	architecture
procedure	gesture	boredom	literature	disappointment

 Spelling Strategy The suffixes *-ure*, *-ment*, and *-dom* form nouns when added to base words or roots. Remember the spelling patterns for these suffixes.

Write the word that completes each analogy.

21. victory : defeat :: success : _____   23. color : painting :: words : _____
22. score : music :: blueprint : _____   24. hope : wish :: letdown : _____

Write the word that fits each clue.

25. accomplishment   28. method
26. a hand motion   29. something used in decision making
27. opposite of excitement   30. tools and machinery

Unit 10 Words from Spanish

pages 66–71

sombrero	hammock	plaza	fiesta	tortilla
alligator	bonanza	patio	cargo	cocoa

 Spelling Strategy Knowing how to pronounce a word from Spanish will often help you spell it.

Write the words that complete the paragraph.

   The mayor lay in the __(31)__ that hung across the small __(32)__ just outside his front door. He gazed across the wide open space of the town __(33)__, which was gaily decorated for the annual __(34)__. Waiting for the festivities to begin, he became tired, so he pulled his __(35)__ down over his eyes and was soon asleep.

Write the word that fits each clue.

36. bread made of cornmeal   39. a large reptile
37. a mine rich with ore   40. something transported
38. a hot drink

Unit 11 Words Often Confused   pages 72–77

| desert | access | hardy | hurdle | conscious |
| dessert | excess | hearty | hurtle | conscience |

💡 **Spelling Strategy**   To avoid confusing words with similar spellings and pronunciations, think of the meanings of the words.

Write the word that matches each definition.

41. aware

42. to move speedily

43. passage

44. sincere and enthusiastic

45. an extra amount

46. able to withstand unfavorable conditions

Write the word that completes each sentence.

47. The dry, sandy landscape looked like a _____.

48. The crowd roared as the runner cleared the final _____.

49. After the main course, the guests ate a fruit _____.

50. In making the difficult decision, Ana followed her own _____.

Challenge Words   Units 7–11   pages 48–77

| prosecute | physiology | disclosure | guerrilla | climatic |
| prosecution | metronome | horticulture | embargo | climactic |

Write the words that complete the paragraph.

The __(51)__ final moments of Wiley Snatcher's trial were exciting, especially when Wiley made his sudden confession. His __(52)__ of all the details of the operation provided the evidence needed to arrest at least forty known criminals, all of whom face __(53)__ in the near future. In order to __(54)__ the whole mob at once, however, a special courtroom is being constructed.

Write the word that is associated with each occupation.

55. medicine

56. foreign trade

57. music

58. weather forecasting

59. military

60. gardening

Spelling-Meaning Strategy

The Latin Root *gest*

Did you know that the words *gesture* and *suggest* are related in meaning? Both words contain the root *gest*, meaning "to bear, carry, or bring." The meaning of the root affects the meaning of each word that contains it. Originally, the word *gesture* was used to mean "general bearing or behavior." Today it is used to describe one tiny behavior or movement of the body. *Suggest* means "to bring up an idea."

Below are more words that contain the root *gest*.

di**gest**	con**gest**	sug**gest**ion
di**gest**ion	con**gest**ion	in**gest**

gesture

sug**gest**

Think

- How does the root *gest* contribute to the meaning of each word? Look up the words in your Spelling Dictionary.
- In Unit 7, you learned that when you add *-ion* to a word ending in *t*, the *t* often remains, though its sound can change. How is the *t* pronounced in each word above?

Apply and Extend

Complete these activities on a separate piece of paper.

1. Write six sentences. Use one word from the box above in each sentence.
2. What other words can you think of that belong to the same family as *gesture* and *suggest*? Work with a partner to make a list of related words. Then look up the Latin root *gest* in your Spelling-Meaning Index. Add to your list any other related words that you find on that page.

Summing Up

The Latin root *gest* means "to bear, carry, or bring." Words that contain the same root are often related in spelling and meaning. Knowing some of the words in a family can help you to use and spell the others correctly.

Snowy climates are home to many animals. What effect does snow have on their lives— and their ability to survive?

from

"Weathering the World of Snow"
by Donald W. Stokes

As the snow piles up higher in a woodland over the course of a winter, it creates more problems—and advantages—for animals. For the cottontail rabbit, deep snow provides food. Since it feeds on the winter buds of young trees, the deeper icy blanket helps the animal to reach more buds. What's more, sometimes the weight of snow causes deciduous trees, such as birches and aspens, to bend to the ground. This means their tender tops are easy to reach for the rabbit. . . .

A red fox, on the other hand, meets more difficulties as the snow cover increases. This predator can walk easily in six inches of snow; but when the snow is deeper, the fox must bound through it, using more energy in the process. A fox hunts in winter by zigzagging back and forth over the surface of the snow, listening for faint squeals and scratchings underneath. When a signal is picked up, the fox leaps into the air and lands stiff-legged with its forepaws held together. In this way the fox breaks the snow crust and then quickly grabs its prey in its jaws. However, in heavy wet snow, the fox has trouble hunting. . . .

For deer, deep snow can be particularly hazardous. Because deer are heavy animals with small hoofs and delicate legs, they sink into heavy drifts and become easy targets for predators. When the snow begins to pile high in their area, deer walk single file; each deer steps in the prints made by the animal in front. The deer trails that are formed are often used over and over throughout the winter.

Think and Discuss

1. What effect does the snow have on the rabbit, the fox, and the deer?
2. What is the topic sentence of the second paragraph?

The Writing Process
Cause and Effect

Is there a cause and effect relationship that you find especially fascinating, or that you think others might want to learn more about? Write a cause and effect paragraph about that topic. Use the guidelines, and follow the Writing Process.

1 ▶ Prewriting
- If you don't have a topic in mind, finish these questions. Why does . . . ? What happens when . . . ? What causes . . . ?
- After selecting a topic, list the cause(s) and effect(s) you will explain in your paragraph.

2 ▶ Draft
- Write down your ideas. Don't worry about errors now.
- Keep your purpose and audience in mind. State your main idea in a topic sentence. Include details that help to explain the cause and effect relationship.

3 ▶ Revise
- Add details that support the cause and effect relationship without straying from the main idea. Delete details that don't belong. Reorganize details if necessary.
- Have a writing conference.

4 ▶ Proofread
- Did you spell each word correctly?
- Do all verbs agree with their subjects?
- Have you used comparative and superlative forms of adjectives and adverbs correctly?

5 ▶ Publish
- Copy your paragraph neatly and add an appropriate title.
- Make a poster to illustrate your paragraph.

Guidelines for Writing a Cause and Effect Paragraph

✓ State the main idea clearly in a topic sentence.
✓ Include details that help to explain the cause and effect relationship.
✓ Arrange details in an order that makes sense.

Composition Words

operate
duplicate
cyclone
equipment
procedure
cargo
desert
continual

Vowel Changes I

Read and Say

Basic

READ the sentences. **SAY** each bold word.

1. flame — A bright **flame** burned in the campfire.
2. flammable — Keep **flammable** fabrics away from heat.
3. ignite — Use a match to **ignite** the wood.
4. ignition — A car needs fuel for the **ignition** to work.
5. precise — Gold was discovered at this **precise** spot.
6. precision — A jewel must be cut with careful **precision**.
7. meter — Is a **meter** longer than a yard?
8. metric — The **metric** system is one way of measuring.
9. microscope — This **microscope** magnifies the smallest items.
10. microscopic — This bug is so tiny it is almost **microscopic**.
11. grave — I knew it was serious by his **grave** look.
12. gravity — The **gravity** of the problem had us worried.
13. grateful — I am **grateful** for your help with my report.
14. gratitude — He showed his **gratitude** by giving me a gift.
15. revise — She will **revise** her essay to make it shorter.
16. revision — This **revision** will improve your story.
17. athlete — Our best **athlete** plays football and baseball.
18. athletic — Exercise often if you want an **athletic** body.
19. humane — Our town **humane** society cares for stray cats.
20. humanity — All **humanity** will benefit from the new drug.

Spelling Strategy   Remember that words can be related in spelling and meaning even though they have different vowel sounds.

Think and Write   Write the pairs of Basic Words. In each pair, underline the letter that has the long vowel sound in one word and the short vowel sound in the other.

Review	23. fume
21. fireproof	24. rescue
22. explosion	25. prevention

Challenge	28. impede
26. suffice	29. impediment
27. sufficient	

Independent Practice

Vocabulary: Using Context Write the Basic Word that completes each sentence. Use your Spelling Dictionary.

1. The long, dry summer made the forest timber highly _____.
2. By August the situation had become extremely _____.
3. A stray spark was enough to make a tree burst into _____.
4. One blaze began in the _____ spot in which a huge forest fire had occurred twenty years before.
5. The _____ of the situation increased as the fires spread.
6. Some advanced at the rate of one _____ every two seconds.
7. Sixty kilometers of state roads, the _____ equivalent of about thirty-seven miles, have been closed to traffic.
8. Fighting the fires tested the strength of even the most _____ and energetic volunteers.
9. The exhausted firefighters would have been so _____ for rain.
10. The firefighters were showered with praise and _____.

Vocabulary: Analogies Write the Basic Word that completes each analogy. Use your Spelling Dictionary.

Example: artist : creative :: gymnast : _____   *athletic*

11. one : person :: all : _____
12. preserve : maintain :: alter : _____
13. kitchen : can opener :: laboratory : _____
14. record player : switch :: car motor : _____
15. fix : correction :: change : _____
16. distant : far :: exactness : _____
17. soak : drench :: kindle : _____
18. class : student :: team : _____
19. big : gigantic :: small : _____
20. mean : cruel :: kind : _____

Challenge Words Write the Challenge Word that matches each definition. Use your Spelling Dictionary.

21. something that gets in the way
22. to meet present needs
23. as much as is needed; enough
24. to slow down or block

Review: Spelling Spree

Rhyme Time Read each clue. Then write a Basic or Review Word to complete each rhyme.

Example: serious gesture of farewell

_____ wave   *grave*

1. spark a spat
   _____ a fight
2. change a measurement
   _____ a size
3. keep up the kindness
   remain _____
4. save a sneaker
   _____ a tennis shoe

5. mild blaze
   tame _____
6. tiny subject
   _____ topic
7. exact guidance
   _____ advice
8. all-around competitor
   complete _____

Word Hose 9–25. Find the Basic and Review Words that are hidden in the fire hose. Write the words correctly in the order in which you find them.

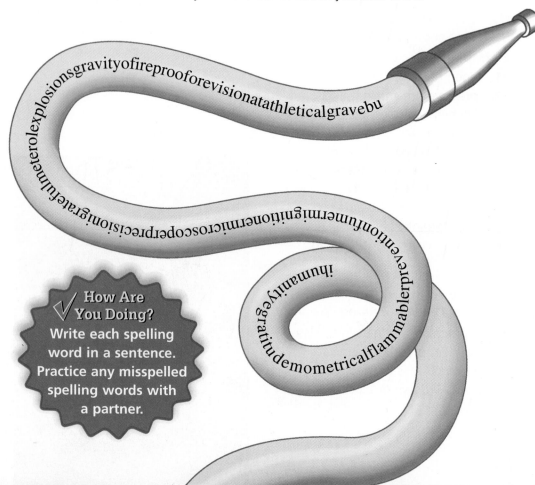

How Are You Doing?
Write each spelling word in a sentence. Practice any misspelled spelling words with a partner.

Proofreading and Writing

Proofread: Spelling and Negatives Negatives are words that mean "no" or "not." A **double negative** is the incorrect use of two negative words to express one idea. Avoid double negatives. To express a negative idea, use only one negative word.

INCORRECT: **Don't never** pull a false alarm.
CORRECT: **Never** pull a false alarm.
CORRECT: **Don't ever** pull a false alarm.

Find five misspelled Basic or Review Words and two double negatives in this list of safety rules. Write the rules correctly.

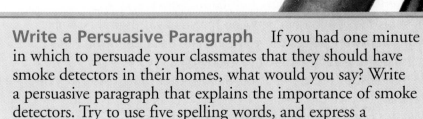

Fire Pravention Rules

1. Keep flamable materials away from heat sources.

2. Use firepruf fabrics in furniture and curtains.

3. Don't leave no irons or hair dryers plugged in.

4. Don't use lighter fluid or gasoline to ignit a fire in the fireplace.

5. Don't never leave an open flame unattended.

6. Report any unusual fume to the

   building manager.

The management is gratful for your consideration.

Basic

1. flame
2. flammable
3. ignite
4. ignition
5. precise
6. precision
7. meter
8. metric
9. microscope
10. microscopic
11. grave
12. gravity
13. grateful
14. gratitude
15. revise
16. revision
17. athlete
18. athletic
19. humane
20. humanity

Review

21. fireproof
22. explosion
23. fume
24. rescue
25. prevention

Challenge

26. suffice
27. sufficient
28. impede
29. impediment

Write a Persuasive Paragraph   If you had one minute in which to persuade your classmates that they should have smoke detectors in their homes, what would you say? Write a persuasive paragraph that explains the importance of smoke detectors. Try to use five spelling words, and express a negative idea at least once.

Proofreading Marks

¶ Indent
∧ Add
⩟ Add a comma
⌄⌄ ⌄⌄ Add quotation marks
⊙ Add a period
⌒ Delete
≡ Capital letter
/ Small letter
∿ Reverse order

Vocabulary Enrichment

Unit 13 BONUS

Expanding Vocabulary

Spelling Word Link

The Greek Word Part *scope* The word *microscope* contains the Greek word part *scope*, meaning "to see." Many other words also contain this word part. Their meanings all have something to do with seeing, detecting, or discovering.

Write the word from the list above that completes each sentence. Use your Spelling Dictionary.

1. With the help of the _____, we could see Saturn's rings.
2. Tina saw a world of fragmented colors through the _____.
3. A _____ helps a doctor detect heart problems.
4. The submarine captain peered into the _____.

1. ?   3. ?

2. ?   4. ?

TEST-TAKING TACTICS

Analogies When answering an analogy question, be careful not to choose an answer pair whose relationship is the *reverse* of the stem pair's relationship. For example, if the relationship between the stem words is *tool* and *user*, you can eliminate as incorrect an answer pair whose relationship is *user* and *tool*.

Study this sample analogy question.

FIREFIGHTER : LADDER ::   (A) police : officer
(B) mechanic : wrench   (C) orchard : picker
(D) tractor : farmer   (E) computer : programmer

Now write the answers to these questions.

5. What is the relationship between the stem words in the sample?
6. Which answer choices can you eliminate because they reverse the stem pair's relationship? Write their letters.
7. Which answer choices can you eliminate for other reasons? Write their letters.
8. What is the letter of the correct answer choice?

88

Real-World Connection

Careers: Firefighting All the words in the box relate to firefighting. Look up these words in your Spelling Dictionary. Then write the words to complete this paragraph.

> Firefighting may seem like a simple job—just go where the __(1)__ sends you, hook up to the nearest __(2)__, aim the __(3)__ of the hose, and spray. In fact, dealing with a burning building involves much more than that. First, firefighters must __(4)__ any people from the building. Even if people manage to avoid the flames, they can suffer serious lung damage from smoke __(5)__. Next, firefighters must decide how to __(6)__ the blaze. To release smoke, heat, and dangerous gases, firefighters __(7)__ the building by opening windows and even cutting holes in roofs and walls. Finally, they check for the cause of the fire. If it appears to be suspicious, the firefighters search for evidence of __(8)__.

Spelling Word Link

flame

extinguish
hydrant
ventilate
evacuate
nozzle
arson
inhalation
dispatcher

TRY THIS!

Yes or No? Write *yes* or *no* to indicate what firefighters do on the job.

9. evacuate a house
10. extinguish flames
11. remove a hydrant
12. commit arson

Fact File

Although some small towns have paid fire departments, most depend chiefly on volunteer firefighters. At the sound of a fire alarm, the volunteers drop whatever they are doing and rush to fight the fire.

ROCKVILLE
E-32
VOLUNTEERS
"Riding With Pride"

Latin Roots I

Read and Say

Basic

READ the sentences. SAY each bold word.

1. eruption — The force of the **eruption** shook the ground.
2. spectacular — The pilots put on a **spectacular** show.
3. abrupt — I jumped at the **abrupt** knock at the door.
4. spectator — A **spectator** in the stands caught the ball.
5. spectacle — What a **spectacle** the circus parade was!
6. description — Vivid details bring a **description** to life.
7. specimen — We will examine the **specimen** in science class.
8. interruption — The rain caused an **interruption** of the game.
9. subscribe — She wants to **subscribe** to that magazine.
10. disrupt — Loud noises **disrupt** my sleep.
11. inspector — The **inspector** checked the roof for holes.
12. rupture — Can water pipes **rupture** in cold weather?
13. respect — I **respect** him for his work with the homeless.
14. manuscript — The author sent her **manuscript** to a publisher.
15. speculate — It is fun to **speculate** on our future careers.
16. aspect — Each **aspect** of the plan had to be considered.
17. transcribe — I must **transcribe** my notes from the lecture.
18. inscription — Can you read the **inscription** on the monument?
19. suspect — I **suspect** they are late because of traffic.
20. bankrupt — He was **bankrupt** after the stock market crash.

Spelling Strategy   Knowing the Latin roots *spect/spec* ("to look at"), *scrib/scrip/script* ("to write"), and *rupt* ("to break; burst") can help you spell and understand words with these roots.

Think and Write   Write each Basic Word under its root.

spect/spec	*scrib/scrip/script*	*rupt*

Review	23. inactive
21. describe	24. fiery
22. prospect	25. dramatic

Challenge	28. nondescript
26. spectrum	29. retrospect
27. conspicuous	30. introspection

Independent Practice

Vocabulary: Definitions Write the Basic Word that matches each definition. Use your Spelling Dictionary.

1. an element or part
2. unable to pay one's debts; financially ruined
3. the process of telling about something
4. the act of breaking in upon or stopping an action or process
5. to think something without having proof
6. to agree to receive and pay for a number of issues of a publication, such as a magazine
7. someone who watches an event
8. a message that is written, printed, carved, or engraved
9. the handwritten or typed version of an article or a book
10. a feeling of honor or esteem for someone
11. someone who examines something carefully in search of flaws
12. a public display or performance; something that is curious or marvelous

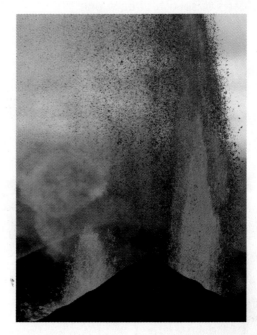

Vocabulary: Synonyms Write the Basic Word that has the same meaning as each word below. Use your Spelling Dictionary.

13. upset
14. break
15. marvelous
16. consider
17. copy
18. sample
19. outburst
20. sudden

Challenge Words Write the Challenge Word that fits each clue. Use your Spelling Dictionary.

21. This helps people get to know themselves.
22. This can be found in a rainbow.
23. This way of looking at things is possible only after all is said and done.
24. This kind of person or thing draws attention.
25. This kind of person or thing draws very little attention.

Dictionary

Parts of Speech One of the many facts a dictionary entry gives about a word is its **part of speech**.

> **a·brupt** |ə **brŭpt´|** *adj.* **1.** Unexpected; sudden.

The abbreviation *adj.* means that *abrupt* is an adjective. On page 282 is a key to the abbreviations used in your Spelling Dictionary.

More than one part of speech may be listed in an entry. In that case, the numbering of the definitions begins over again each time a new part of speech is introduced.

Practice Look up the following words in your Spelling Dictionary. Write the parts of speech of each one.

1. alibi
2. gauge
3. primary
4. doubt
5. draft
6. appropriate

1.	?	4.	?
2.	?	5.	?
3.	?	6.	?

Review: Spelling Spree

Invisible Letters Decide which letters should be added to complete each Basic or Review Word. Write the words correctly.

7. _ a _ k _ u _ t
8. d _ s _ r _ p _ i _ n
9. _ n _ c _ i _ e
10. d _ s _ u _ t
11. _ n _ p _ c _ o _
12. p _ o _ p _ c _
13. _ p _ c _ a _ o _
14. i _ t _ r _ u _ t _ o _
15. _ u _ t _ r _
16. s _ e _ i _ e _

17. _ n _ c _ i _ t _ o _
18. _ b _ u _ t
19. s _ b _ c _ i _ e
20. _ e _ p _ c _
21. t _ a _ s _ r _ b _
22. _ s _ e _ t
23. d _ s _ r _ b _
24. _ a _ u _ c _ i _ t
25. s _ s _ e _ t

Proofreading and Writing

Proofread for Spelling Find six misspelled Basic or Review Words in this paragraph. Write each word correctly.

One day in November 1963, fishermen off the coast of Iceland witnessed a specticle that brought their fishing to an abrupt halt. The ocean was churning from the erupsion of an underwater volcano. For several days, spectaculer explosions created a drumatic fireworks display. Soon, a ridge of ashes poked above the water line. Then hot liquid rock poured out, hardening and cooling around the ash mountain. The result was an island called Surtsey. Scientists spekulate that Iceland was formed in the same firey way.

Basic

1. eruption
2. spectacular
3. abrupt
4. spectator
5. spectacle
6. description
7. specimen
8. interruption
9. subscribe
10. disrupt
11. inspector
12. rupture
13. respect
14. manuscript
15. speculate
16. aspect
17. transcribe
18. inscription
19. suspect
20. bankrupt

Review

21. describe
22. prospect
23. inactive
24. fiery
25. dramatic

Challenge

26. spectrum
27. conspicuous
28. nondescript
29. retrospect
30. introspection

Proofreading Marks
¶ Indent
∧ Add
⩚ Add a comma
ᐺ ᐺ Add quotation marks
⊙ Add a period
ℊ Delete
≡ Capital letter
/ Small letter
∿ Reverse order

Write Interview Questions If you could interview some of the people at the scene of a volcanic eruption, what questions would you ask them? Write a list of interview questions. Try to use five spelling words.

Expanding Vocabulary

Spelling Word Link

eruption

Figurative Language When you use language literally, you create images by describing how things actually look, feel, or sound. When you use **figurative language**, you create images by making comparisons.

LITERAL: The volcano's eruption was seen for miles.

FIGURATIVE: Tom screamed in an eruption of anger.

In the first example, *eruption* refers to a real explosion. In the second one, Tom does not actually explode, but the use of *eruption* compares his anger to an explosion.

Write *literal* or *figurative* to tell how the underlined word is used in each sentence.

1. The first snow would ignite excitement in everyone.
2. A lightning strike can easily ignite a dry forest.
3. Joe went through his room like a cyclone, cleaning it up in ten minutes flat.
4. Yesterday's cyclone destroyed many houses.
5. The scattered pins collected neatly on the magnet.
6. Today I seem to be a magnet for small disasters.

Now write two sentences for one of these words: *ignite, cyclone,* or *magnet.* In one sentence, use the word literally and circle the word. In the other sentence, use the word figuratively and underline the word.

7. _____ ? _____
   _____ ? _____
   _____ ? _____
8. _____ ? _____
   _____ ? _____
   _____ ? _____

Real-World Connection

Science: Volcanoes All the words in the box relate to volcanoes. Look up these words in your Spelling Dictionary. Then write the words to complete this paragraph.

Spelling Word Link

eruption

lava
magma
vapor
mantle
dormant
pumice
Hawaii
extinct

About five hundred of the world's volcanoes are active, or erupting. Many others, referred to as __(1)__, have not erupted in recorded history. In between are those that have not erupted in a long time but could erupt again. These are called __(2)__. Kilauea, in the state of __(3)__, is an active volcano. When it erupts, red-hot liquid rock called __(4)__ is forced up from the earth's __(5)__. Fiery __(6)__ pours from a crater at the top of the volcano and flows down the sides of the mountain. Volcanoes can also spew ash, dust, and __(7)__, or gas. Another volcanic product is __(8)__, a rock that is made so light by trapped air bubbles that it can float.

TRY THIS!

True or False? Write *T* if the statement is true and *F* if it is false.

9. As it cools, lava hardens.
10. The outermost layer of the earth is the mantle.
11. A dormant volcano is one that has erupted recently.
12. Pumice turns to liquid when it leaves a volcano.

Fact File

In Roman mythology, Vulcan, the god of fire and metal-working, had his workshop beneath Mt. Etna, a volcano off the Italian mainland. The Romans called the mountain *vulcano*, which meant "burning mountain."

The Suffixes *-ary*, *-ery*, and *-ory*

Read and Say

Basic

READ the sentences. **SAY** each bold word.

1. mystery — He writes the scariest **mystery** stories!
2. literary — Was her book featured in the **literary** reviews?
3. treachery — The battle was lost because of his **treachery**.
4. theory — Can you prove your **theory** about the comet?
5. bravery — Her **bravery** resulted in lives being saved.
6. primary — My **primary** goal is to graduate with honors.
7. legendary — His skill with a basketball is **legendary**.
8. forgery — Is the signature a **forgery** or the real thing?
9. cemetery — My relatives are buried in this **cemetery**.
10. elementary — We learned the **elementary** dance steps first.
11. observatory — Scientists study the skies at an **observatory**.
12. secretary — A **secretary** should be a good typist.
13. nursery — The baby can have my room as a **nursery**.
14. satisfactory — Did I do a **satisfactory** job cutting the grass?
15. imaginary — The unicorn is an **imaginary** animal.
16. vocabulary — The **vocabulary** in this law book is difficult.
17. ordinary — Nothing unusual happens on an **ordinary** day.
18. machinery — The **machinery** runs better after it is oiled.
19. boundary — A fence marks the **boundary** of our land.
20. temporary — I have a **temporary** job during vacation.

Spelling Strategy   When you hear the final |ə rē| sounds in a word, think of the spelling patterns *ary*, *ery*, and *ory*. When you hear the final |ĕr′ē| sounds, think of the patterns *ary* and *ery*.

Think and Write   Write each Basic Word under its suffix.

-ary	*-ery*	*-ory*

Review
21. weapon
22. disguise
23. horror
24. threat
25. innocent

Challenge
26. preliminary
27. contemporary
28. derogatory
29. itinerary
30. discriminatory

Independent Practice

Vocabulary: Using Context Write the Basic Word that completes each sentence. Use your Spelling Dictionary.

1. A good _____ novel keeps the reader guessing until the end.
2. Investigators found clues among the toys in the _____.
3. The detective questioned everyone who was using a telescope in the _____ on the night the astronomer vanished.
4. The chief inspector found an important piece of evidence lodged in the _____ that operated the drawbridge.
5. When not typing and filing, a detective's _____ may be helping to gather evidence.
6. I waited in the _____, crouched behind a crumbling tombstone.
7. Of the three people with motives, which is the _____ suspect?
8. *Motive* is an important word in any mystery writer's _____.
9. When Miss Jane Marple has a hunch about a crime, she usually keeps her _____ to herself.
10. Detective Frome solved so many cases that his work is _____.
11. The signature on the contract was a _____.
12. That _____ magazine often publishes mystery stories.

Vocabulary: Synonyms Write the Basic Word that has the same meaning as each word below. Use your Spelling Dictionary.

13. passing
14. unreal
15. usual
16. betrayal
17. fundamental
18. edge
19. adequate
20. courage

Challenge Words Write the Challenge Word that matches each definition. Use your Spelling Dictionary.

21. current; modern
22. showing preference or prejudice; biased
23. scornful; harshly critical
24. leading up to or preparing for the main event
25. a schedule of places to be visited on a journey

Review: Spelling Spree

Code Breaker The Basic and Review Words below have been written in code. Use the following code key to figure out each word. Write the decoded words correctly.

CODE:	l	b	g	n	a	o	r	z	s	v	m	h	y	q	w	c	f	k	d	u	e	x	i	t	p	j
LETTER:	a	b	c	d	e	f	g	h	i	j	k	l	m	n	o	p	q	r	s	t	u	v	w	x	y	z

Example: cksylkp *primary*

1. uzawkp
2. nsdresda
3. sqqwgaqu
4. uzkalu
5. ahayaqulkp
6. owkrakp
7. zwkkwk
8. ialcwq

Modular Words Write a Basic Word by adding a word ending from the magnifying glass to each group of letters.

9. ordin ___
10. legend ___
11. liter ___
12. tempor ___
13. nurs ___
14. satisfact ___
15. prim ___
16. cemet ___
17. secret ___
18. imagin ___
19. observat ___
20. machin ___
21. brav ___
22. myst ___
23. treach ___
24. vocabul ___
25. bound ___

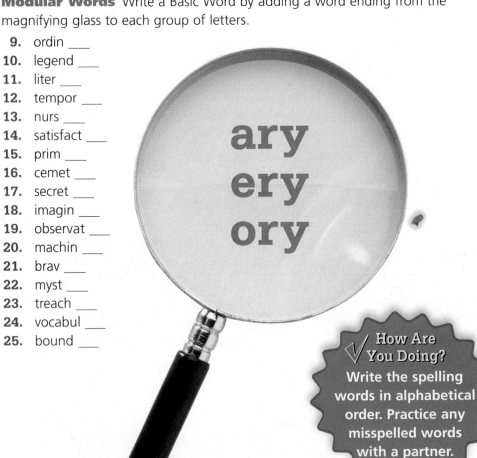

ary
ery
ory

√ **How Are You Doing?**
Write the spelling words in alphabetical order. Practice any misspelled words with a partner.

Proofreading and Writing

Proofread: Spelling, Usage of Adjectives and Adverbs

Some adjectives and adverbs are easy to confuse. Use **adjectives**, such as *good*, *bad*, and *real*, to modify nouns and pronouns. Use **adverbs**, such as *well*, *badly*, and *really*, to modify verbs, adjectives, and other adverbs.

> Finding the **real** criminal was **really** difficult.

Find five misspelled Basic or Review Words and two incorrect adjectives or adverbs in this excerpt from a book report. Write the excerpt correctly.

The Mystry of the Brass Jar

by R.L. Frazier

Liz Bane leads an ordinery life as a secretary until she finds a brass jar. Liz receives a terrible thret and realizes that someone wants the jar bad. Her simple life becomes real complicated as she stumbles into a maze of horrer and trechery.

Basic
1. mystery
2. literary
3. treachery
4. theory
5. bravery
6. primary
7. legendary
8. forgery
9. cemetery
10. elementary
11. observatory
12. secretary
13. nursery
14. satisfactory
15. imaginary
16. vocabulary
17. ordinary
18. machinery
19. boundary
20. temporary

Review
21. weapon
22. disguise
23. horror
24. threat
25. innocent

Challenge
26. preliminary
27. contemporary
28. derogatory
29. itinerary
30. discriminatory

Write a Character or Setting Description Write a paragraph describing a character or a setting that you might find in a mystery story. Include as many vivid details as possible. Try to use five spelling words. Also, try to use one of these adjective or adverb modifiers correctly: *good*, *bad*, *real*, *well*, *badly*, or *really*.

Proofreading Marks
¶ Indent
∧ Add
⅄ Add a comma
⌄⌄ ⌄⌄ Add quotation marks
⊙ Add a period
↲ Delete
≡ Capital letter
／ Small letter
∩ Reverse order

Expanding Vocabulary

Multiple Meanings English words can have multiple meanings.

Spelling Word Link

secretary

> **sec·re·tar·y** |sĕk′rĭ tĕr′ē| *n., pl.* **sec·re·tar·ies.**
> **1.** A person employed to do clerical work, such as typing and filing. **2.** An officer of an organization in charge of the minutes of meetings, correspondence, etc. **3.** The head of a government department. **4.** A desk with a small bookcase on top.

Write a definition number to show which meaning of *secretary* is used in each sentence below.

1. Mrs. Myers asked her secretary to hold all phone calls.
2. Mr. Ahman met with the secretary of education.
3. Leah sat at the secretary to write her thank-you notes.
4. The secretary of the committee read the minutes of the last meeting.

TEST-TAKING TACTICS

Vocabulary-in-Context One tactic for answering a vocabulary-in-context question is to replace the tested word with a word or phrase of your own that makes sense in the sentence. Then compare your word or phrase with each answer choice. Try this technique with the sample below, and then write the answers to the questions that follow.

Sample passage excerpt and question:

> Cal Clew, attending his first Mystery Writers' Convention,
> (30) was awed by the presence of so many famous writers. Although dying to ask for tips on how a fledgling writer could get published, he trembled at the thought of approaching any of his idols.

The word "fledgling" in line 31 means (A) successful (B) promising (C) established (D) inexperienced (E) trained

5. What word or phrase did you use to replace "fledgling" in context?
6. Which meaning of "fledgling" is correct? Write its letter.

Vocabulary Enrichment

Real-World Connection

Language Arts: Mysteries All the words in the box relate to mysteries. Look up these words in your Spelling Dictionary. Then write the words to complete this paragraph.

Spelling Word Link

mystery

sleuth
victim
identity
suspicious
alias
deduction
alibi
intrigue

CONFIDENTIAL

In *Under the Alabaster Mask*, Isabella de Janze is the __(1)__ of a ring of jewel thieves. She hires the famous __(2)__ Mack Blooker to find her stolen jewels. While gathering clues, however, Blooker becomes __(3)__ of Isabella herself. He suspects that she is a fraud and that the name "Isabella de Janze" is an __(4)__, but he does not have a clue to her true __(5)__. Although she has an airtight __(6)__ for the night of the robbery, she could still have planned the crime. The suspense and __(7)__ deepen as Blooker gets closer to the truth. In the end, a brilliant __(8)__ leads him to unravel the mystery.

TRY THIS!

Yes or No? Write *yes* or *no* to answer each question.

9. Is a victim guilty of committing a crime?
10. Does a sleuth look for clues?
11. Does a suspect need an alibi?
12. Can a detective capture an alias?

Fact File

The first mystery and detective stories were written in the 1840s by Edgar Allan Poe. One of America's greatest short-story writers, Poe is also known for his poems, the most famous of which is "The Raven."

Words from French

Read and Say

Basic	READ the sentences. SAY each bold word.
1. ballet	A **ballet** tells a story in dance.
2. technique	Will you teach me your painting **technique**?
3. fatigue	The long hike left us weak with **fatigue**.
4. debut	The young actor was nervous about his **debut**.
5. petite	I am too tall to be called **petite**.
6. amateur	An **amateur** runner does not compete for money.
7. bouquet	She carried a **bouquet** of red and white roses.
8. massage	A **massage** will relax those tight muscles.
9. antique	His **antique** chair is a hundred years old.
10. vague	The directions were so **vague** that we got lost.
11. portrait	Please sit still while I paint your **portrait**.
12. boulevard	The bus crawled along the jammed **boulevard**.
13. reservoir	Heavy rains fill the town **reservoir** in spring.
14. debris	The storm blew **debris** all over the yard.
15. boutique	The dress **boutique** is having a sale.
16. plateau	Is the view from the **plateau** worth the climb?
17. coupon	I have a **coupon** for a free roll of film.
18. depot	His train leaves the **depot** at noon.
19. plaque	Our name is on a **plaque** over the door.
20. crochet	My aunt will **crochet** a scarf for you.

Spelling Strategy   Remember that words from French often contain silent letters, spell the |ē| sound with *i*, and spell the |k| sound with *que*.

Think and Write   Write the Basic Words.

Review		Challenge	
21. routine	23. tragic	26. ensemble	28. coup
22. scene	24. brilliant	27. naive	29. porcelain
	25. detour		30. surveillance

Independent Practice

Vocabulary: Definitions Write the Basic Word that matches each definition.
Use your Spelling Dictionary.

1. not clearly expressed
2. a person who does something without professional skill or who pursues an interest for enjoyment rather than for money
3. a kind of rub given to someone to relax the body or to improve circulation
4. an ornamented or engraved plate, slab, or disk, used for decoration or to carry an inscription on a monument
5. a systematic method or procedure used to accomplish a complicated task
6. the scattered remains or fragments of something destroyed or discarded
7. a bunch of flowers gathered together
8. a feeling of exhaustion or tiredness
9. something very old that is valued for its age
10. the first public appearance of someone or something
11. a printed ticket or advertisement that entitles the bearer to benefits, such as cash or a gift
12. a lake used as a storage place for water
13. a painting, photograph, or other likeness of a person

Vocabulary: Classifying Write the Basic
Word that fits each group. Use your Spelling
Dictionary.

14. modern dance, jazz, tap, _____
15. shop, market, store, _____
16. small, tiny, slender, _____
17. knit, weave, embroider, _____
18. dock, terminal, station, _____
19. mountain, hill, ridge, _____
20. street, avenue, road, _____

Challenge Words Write the Challenge Word that
completes each analogy. Use your Spelling Dictionary.

21. detective : investigation :: spy : _____
22. dough : bread :: clay : _____
23. sport : team :: music : _____
24. sophisticated : worldly :: innocent : _____
25. failure : blunder :: success : _____

Review: Spelling Spree

Coded Clues Write the Basic or Review Word that fits each clue. Circle the letter that would appear in the box.

Example: a muscle pleaser _ _ _ _ _ □ _ *massa(g)e*

1. a body of water _ _ _ _ _ _ _ □ _
2. a train stop _ _ _ □ _
3. a special shop _ _ _ _ _ _ _ □
4. old and valuable _ □ _ _ _ _ _
5. a part of a play _ □ _ _ _
6. work with wool _ _ _ _ □ _ _
7. fuzzy _ □ _ _ _
8. a wide street □ _ _ _ _ _ _ _ _
9. a series of dance steps □ _ _ _ _ _ _ _
10. full of light _ _ _ □ _ _ _ _ _
11. a result of working hard _ _ _ _ □ _ _

Now decode the Mystery Words. The numbers below the blanks are item numbers. Write the circled letters from those items to find the name of a famous choreographer.

Mystery Words:

__ __ __?__ __ __   __ __ __ __ __?__ __ __ __ __
11 3 2 9 11 3   8 7 10 7 4 5 6 1 4 3

Letter Exchange Replace the underlined letters with the same number of letters to write a Basic or Review Word.

12. corsage
13. couple
14. amazing
15. trader
16. unique
17. polite
18. devour
19. banquet
20. debate

21. technical
22. basket
23. platter
24. portable
25. shout

How Are You Doing?
Write each spelling word as a partner reads it aloud. Did you misspell any words?

Proofreading and Writing

Proofread: Spelling, Proper Nouns and Proper Adjectives

A **proper noun** names a specific person, place, or thing. A **proper adjective** comes from a proper noun. Capitalize both. If a proper noun or adjective consists of more than one word, capitalize all the important words.

The (J)offrey (B)allet is a well-known (A)merican dance company.

Find five misspelled Basic or Review Words and two capitalization errors in this excerpt from a newspaper review. Write the review correctly.

Friday's performance by the Danilov festival Ballet featured the brillyant debut of Maria Karoly. Dancing the wedding seen from *Romeo and Juliet*, the russian ballerina conveyed the innocence of Shakespeare's trajic heroine. Karoly's tecknique does need refinement; some movements are vage and uncertain. Still, this new star twinkles with a promising light.

Write a Scene Description What might make an interesting setting for a ballet scene? Write a description of the setting, including details of the props and scenery. Try to use five spelling words and at least one proper noun or adjective.

Basic

1. ballet
2. technique
3. fatigue
4. debut
5. petite
6. amateur
7. bouquet
8. massage
9. antique
10. vague
11. portrait
12. boulevard
13. reservoir
14. debris
15. boutique
16. plateau
17. coupon
18. depot
19. plaque
20. crochet

Review

21. routine
22. scene
23. tragic
24. brilliant
25. detour

Challenge

26. ensemble
27. naive
28. coup
29. porcelain
30. surveillance

Proofreading Marks

¶	Indent
∧	Add
⩕	Add a comma
ꭃꭃ	Add quotation marks
⊙	Add a period
⌔	Delete
≡	Capital letter
/	Small letter
∿	Reverse order

Expanding Vocabulary

Spelling Word Link

fatigue

Context Clues When you come across an unfamiliar word in your reading, look in the sentence for a synonym of the word. Synonyms are excellent context clues. Suppose you did not know the spelling word *fatigue*. The synonym in the sentence below provides a context clue.

Mai complained of tiredness, but her **fatigue** did not show.

Write the word that is a synonym for the underlined word in each sentence.

1. Makeup made the pallid ballerina look less pale.
2. The dancer's sad expression matched the melancholy music.
3. Jules Dubeau is a skilled dancer, but he is even more adept as a choreographer.
4. Though the company expected applause after the performance, the enthusiasm of the ovation surprised them.

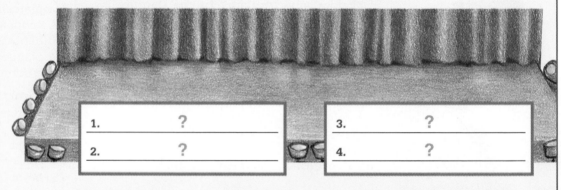

| 1. | ? | 3. | ? |
| 2. | ? | 4. | ? |

Now write your own context clue sentences, using synonyms for *pallid, melancholy, adept,* and *ovation*. You may use the synonyms from items 1–4 or choose others that you know.

5. ?
   ?

6. ?
   ?

7. ?
   ?

8. ?
   ?

Real-World Connection

Performing Arts: Ballet All the words in the box relate to ballet. Look up these words in your Spelling Dictionary. Then write the words to complete this paragraph.

Sitting in the dance studio, Janet thought about what a test of __(1)__ her years as a student of __(2)__ dance at the American Ballet School had been. Janet had always longed to be a __(3)__ . Was it all worth it—the many hours at the __(4)__ , the aching muscles? Dipping the tip of one slipper in __(5)__ , she pictured herself performing in the new dance choreographed by the artistic director, which would have its __(6)__ the following week. She would be dancing a __(7)__ with the incredible Fernando Garcia. In a burst of joy, Janet rose from the bench and twirled in a graceful __(8)__ .

Spelling Word Link

ballet

classical
barre
rosin
endurance
ballerina
pirouette
pas de deux
première

TRY THIS!

True or False? Write *T* if the statement is true and *F* if it is false.

9. A pas de deux is a solo performance.
10. Dancers use a barre to keep their balance.
11. A dancer uses rosin to stay warm during practice.
12. In a pirouette, a dancer turns around.

Fact File

In 1955, Arthur Mitchell began performing with the New York City Ballet. He was the first African American to dance with a major classical ballet company. In 1968, he founded the Dance Theatre of Harlem, which has won praise around the world.

Unusual Plurals

Read and Say

Basic	READ the sentences. SAY each bold word.
1. nucleus	The captain is the **nucleus** of a team.
2. nuclei	Two **nuclei** form when a cell splits in two.
3. bacterium	One tiny **bacterium** can make you ill.
4. bacteria	The **bacteria** in yeast make dough rise.
5. analysis	I completed my **analysis** of the graph.
6. analyses	The experts gave **analyses** of the elections.
7. diagnosis	A blood test will help with the **diagnosis**.
8. diagnoses	Do the **diagnoses** of the doctors agree?
9. criterion	Is correct spelling the only **criterion**?
10. criteria	List your **criteria** for awarding the prize.
11. datum	Each **datum** in the report was checked twice.
12. data	Did you collect **data** from all these sources?
13. thesis	You must support your **thesis** with facts.
14. theses	We debated the opposing **theses** in class.
15. fungus	A blue **fungus** often grows on old bread.
16. fungi	Molds are among the **fungi** we are studying.
17. oasis	The camels hurried to the **oasis** to drink.
18. oases	Palm trees can grow in the dunes at **oases**.
19. cactus	Wet the sand before planting the **cactus**.
20. cacti	Spines protect **cacti** from thirsty animals.

Spelling Strategy

SINGULAR: bacteri**um**, criteri**on**, nucle**us**, analys**is**

PLURAL: bacteri**a**, criteri**a**, nucle**i**, analys**es**

Think and Write
Write each pair of Basic Words under the heading that tells how its singular ending is changed to form the plural.

-um or *-on* Changed to *-a*   *-us* Changed to *-i*   *-is* Changed to *-es*

Review		Challenge	
21. halves	23. heroes	26. phenomenon	28. curriculum
22. shelves	24. studios	27. phenomena	29. curricula
	25. chiefs		

Independent Practice

Vocabulary: Definitions Write the Basic Word that matches each definition.
Use your Spelling Dicitionary.

1. a small one-celled organism
2. plants that have leafless stems and grow in hot, dry places
3. plants that have no green coloring and obtain their food from other plants and from animals
4. a study of a subject, its parts, and the way the parts fit together
5. a fact or piece of information
6. green, fertile places in a desert
7. a rule or standard on which a judgment can be based
8. conclusions reached after medical examinations
9. central parts of cells
10. an idea stated or put forth for consideration

Vocabulary: Word Clues Write the Basic Word that fits each clue. Use your Spelling Dictionary.

11. After hours on the back of a camel, you might rest at this place.
12. If you were this, you might feed off living or dead plants or animals without turning green.
13. If you made detailed studies of several subjects, you would have these.
14. You might base a choice on several of these.
15. When studying a cell through a microscope, you can see this.
16. If you collect a lot of facts, you will have much of this.
17. To write several essays, you would need several of these.
18. A doctor gives you this when explaining why you are sick.
19. Leaning on this would be a painful experience.
20. Some of these can make you sick.

Challenge Words Write the Challenge Word that completes each sentence.
Use your Spelling Dictionary.

21. Cell multiplication is a _____ that causes physical growth.
22. The new _____ at Weston Middle School includes biology.
23. Some school systems offer different _____ that students can choose from.
24. Cell division and cell malfunction are two _____ that biologists study.

Dictionary

Usage Notes When should you use *accept* rather than *except*? Is *datum* or *data* the correct plural form? A **usage note** appears at the end of a dictionary entry for a commonly troublesome word and explains how the word should be used.

> *Usage:* **datum, data**. *Datum* is Latin for "a given fact," and *data* is its plural. Since *data* is often understood as "information" rather than "facts," it is commonly viewed as a collective noun and treated as singular. In formal writing, however, *data* is usually used as a plural: *Numerical data are obtained by counting and measuring.*

Practice Write *yes* or *no* to answer these questions about word usage. Use your Spelling Dictionary.

1. Is *libel* different from *slander*?
2. Is *continual* another word for *continuous*?
3. Could you *assure* an automobile?
4. Do *flammable* and *inflammable* mean the same thing?

Review: Spelling Spree

Word Combination In each item, add the beginning letters of the first word to the last letters of the second to form a Basic or Review Word.

Example: shelter + waves   *shelves*

5. halo + lives
6. date + premium
7. critical + cafeteria
8. theater + poses
9. dialogue + prognoses
10. dare + fiesta
11. study + trios
12. thermal + emphasis
13. analogy + paralysis
14. cackle + spaghetti
15. oak + basis
16. china + chefs
17. cacophony + status
18. herd + volcanoes
19. nucleon + radii
20. funnel + asparagus

Proofreading and Writing

Proofread for Spelling Find nine misspelled Basic or Review Words in this paragraph. Write each word correctly.

Bacterea are found everywhere, from desert oazes to kitchen shelfs. There are many kinds, and they affect our lives in many ways. One type helps us digest food; another works with fungii to destroy wastes; many others cause diseases. A diagnosus of such a disease depends on several criteria. One important criterian used to identify a cell as a bacteriam is the absence of a nucleas. Analysis of size and shape help to distinguish among the different types of these organisms. These kinds of data enable doctors to form accurate diagnoses.

Basic

1. nucleus
2. nuclei
3. bacterium
4. bacteria
5. analysis
6. analyses
7. diagnosis
8. diagnoses
9. criterion
10. criteria
11. datum
12. data
13. thesis
14. theses
15. fungus
16. fungi
17. oasis
18. oases
19. cactus
20. cacti

Review
21. halves
22. shelves
23. heroes
24. studios
25. chiefs

Challenge
26. phenomenon
27. phenomena
28. curriculum
29. curricula

Write a Flier A famous scientist is speaking at your next science club meeting. Write a flier announcing the talk. Include a headline, and summarize what the scientist will say. Note the meeting's date, time, and location. Try to use five spelling words.

Proofreading Marks

¶ Indent
∧ Add
⩘ Add a comma
⌄⌄ Add quotation marks
⊙ Add a period
⌐ Delete
≡ Capital letter
/ Small letter
∼ Reverse order

Expanding Vocabulary

**Spelling
Word Link**

criterion

The Greek Word Part *cris/crit* Several English words contain *cris* or *crit*, forms of the same word part meaning "to decide, judge, or separate." One is *criterion*, meaning "something upon which a decision is based." Other words that contain this word part also have to do with judging or deciding.

critic   crisis   criticize   hypocrisy

Write the word from the list above that completes each sentence. Use your Spelling Dictionary.

1. If you do not practice what you preach, you may be guilty of _____.
2. Julia Finch is a theater _____ for the local newspaper.
3. Try to _____ one another's work in a positive and helpful way.
4. The argument caused a _____ in the boys' friendship.

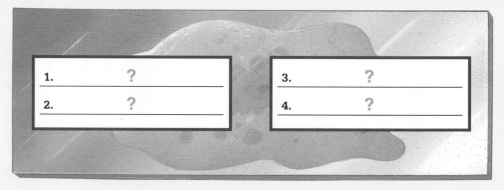

1.	?	3.	?
2.	?	4.	?

Now look up each of these words in your Spelling Dictionary: *critical*, *critique*, *hypocrite*, *hypocritical*. Write a sentence for each word.

5. _____ ? _____

_____ ? _____

6. _____ ? _____

_____ ? _____

7. _____ ? _____

_____ ? _____

8. _____ ? _____

_____ ? _____

Real-World Connection

Science: The Study of Cells All the words in the box relate to the study of cells. Look up these words in your Spelling Dictionary. Then write the words to complete this paragraph.

Spelling Word Link

nucleus

membrane
diffusion
mutation
cellular
molecule
tissue
chromosome
neuron

Each part of your body is made of a different kind of __(1)__, which in turn is made up of certain kinds of cells. For example, the basic __(2)__ unit of the nervous system is the __(3)__. Each cell is covered by a __(4)__ that controls what enters and leaves the cell through the process of __(5)__. In the nucleus of the cell is a set of rodlike structures. Each structure, or __(6)__, is composed mainly of a __(7)__ called DNA. DNA determines a person's height, hair and eye color, and many other characteristics. A tiny __(8)__, or change in the DNA, would produce a change in one of the characteristics.

TRY THIS!

Yes or No? Write *yes* or *no* to answer each question.

9. Is a mutation a type of change?
10. Does a cell surround its membrane?
11. Is a tissue part of a cell?
12. Can substances leave a cell by diffusion?

Fact File

In 1953, James D. Watson and Francis H. C. Crick discovered that a DNA molecule is shaped somewhat like a twisted ladder. This shape is called a "double helix." Watson and Crick won a Nobel Prize for their important discovery.

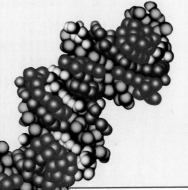

18 Review: Units 13–17

Unit 13 Vowel Changes I
pages 84–89

| flame | ignite | microscope | grateful | athlete |
| flammable | ignition | microscopic | gratitude | athletic |

 Spelling Strategy Remember that words can be related in spelling and meaning even though they have different vowel sounds.

Write the word that completes each sentence.
1. Roger put the key in the _____ to start the car.
2. Nancy was _____ for the surprise birthday party.
3. As a professional _____, Juanita won many sports awards.
4. The candle _____ flickered before it died.

Write the word that matches each definition.
5. thankfulness
6. very small
7. having to do with sports
8. easily burnt
9. to set fire to something
10. an instrument that magnifies

Unit 14 Latin Roots I
pages 90–95

| eruption | spectacular | abrupt | description | specimen |
| speculate | manuscript | rupture | transcribe | inspector |

 Spelling Strategy Knowing the Latin roots *spect/spec* ("to look at"), *scrib/scrip/script* ("to write"), and *rupt* ("to break; burst") can help you spell and understand words with these roots.

Write the words that complete the paragraph.
    The city of Pompeii came to an __(11)__ and violent end in A.D. 79. The explosive __(12)__ of Mt. Vesuvius must have been a __(13)__ event. Pliny the Younger, a Roman writer, left us a vivid __(14)__ of how the earth trembled and the sky was filled with black clouds.

Write the word that fits each clue.
15. something that can be examined
16. to make a copy the slow way
17. a process of breaking
18. think deeply
19. someone who examines
20. an early form of a book

Unit 15 The Suffixes *-ary*, *-ery*, and *-ory*   pages 96–101

mystery	literary	treachery	theory	elementary
boundary	machinery	imaginary	satisfactory	observatory

Spelling Strategy   When you hear the final |ə rē| sounds in a word, think of the spelling patterns *ary*, *ery*, and *ory*. When you hear the final |ĕr′ē| sounds, think of the patterns *ary* and *ery*.

Write the words that complete the paragraph.

Everyone has heard of King Arthur, betrayed by the __(21)__ of his friends. But did Arthur really exist? For centuries, this was a __(22)__ without a __(23)__ explanation. Many believed him to be an __(24)__ figure from literature. Today, the __(25)__ that he was a fifth-century British warrior is widely accepted.

Write the word that is associated with each profession.

26. grade-school teacher   28. surveyor   30. writer
27. mechanic   29. astronomer

Unit 16 Words from French   pages 102–107

technique	fatigue	amateur	bouquet	vague
boulevard	portrait	debris	plaque	depot

Spelling Strategy   Remember that words from French often contain silent letters, spell the |ē| sound with *i*, and spell the |k| sound with *que*.

Write the word that completes each sentence.

31. Through the fog, he saw the _____ outline of the house.
32. The winner of the competition received an engraved _____.
33. Although he is only an _____, critics loved his performance.
34. The Chinese first developed the _____ for making porcelain.
35. The island was covered in _____ left by the hurricane.

Write the word that completes each phrase.

36. smell a _____   39. wait for a train at the _____
37. paint someone's _____ 40. a feeling of _____
38. drive down the _____

Unit 17	Unusual Plurals			pages 108–113

nucleus	analysis	diagnosis	fungus	oasis
nuclei	analyses	diagnoses	fungi	oases

💡 Spelling Strategy

SINGULAR: bacter**ium**, criter**ion**, nucle**us**, analys**is**

PLURAL: bacter**ia**, criter**ia**, nucle**i**, analys**es**

Write the word that completes each sentence.

41. Ted's _____ of Fido's behavior told him the dog was hungry.

42. Ben looked at a map of all the _____ along the desert route.

43. Many kinds of _____ grow in the forest.

44. The two doctors presented conflicting _____ of the illness.

Write the word that fits each clue.

45. detailed studies

46. a core

47. a plant without green

48. many centers

49. a medical conclusion

50. a welcome spot of water

Challenge Words	Units 13–17			pages 84–113

impede	conspicuous	contemporary	naive	curriculum
impediment	retrospect	surveillance	itinerary	curricula

Write the word that completes each analogy.

51. outgoing : shy :: sophisticated : _____

52. transport : carry :: obstruct : _____

53. restaurants : menus :: schools : _____

54. near : far :: hidden : _____

55. school day : schedule :: journey : _____

56. aide : helper :: obstacle : _____

Write the word that matches each definition.

57. close observation

58. a review, survey, or contemplation of the past

59. a school's course of study

60. current; modern

Spelling-Meaning Strategy

The Latin Root *cis*

The word *precise* means "exact," as in "a precise definition." The meaning of the word comes from the Latin root *cis*, meaning "to cut." In order to make a definition precise, all vague or unnecessary information must be cut out. The word *scissors*, which names a cutting tool, also contains the root *cis*. Because they share the same root, *precise* and *scissors* are related in spelling and meaning.

Below are more words that contain the root *cis*.

de**cis**ion	con**cis**e	in**cis**ion
de**cis**ive	in**cis**or	in**cis**ive

precise
scissors

Think

- How does the root *cis* contribute to the meaning of each word? Look up the words in your Spelling Dictionary.
- In Unit 13, you learned that words can be related in spelling and meaning even though they share a vowel that has a different sound in each word. What vowel sound does the root *cis* have in each of the words above?

Apply and Extend

Complete these activities on a separate piece of paper.

1. Write six sentences. Use one word from the box above in each sentence.
2. What other words can you think of that belong to the same family as *precise* and *scissors*? Work with a partner to make a list of related words. Then look up the Latin root *cis* in your Spelling-Meaning Index. Add to your list any other related words that you find.

Summing Up

The Latin root *cis* means "to cut." Words that contain the same root are often related in spelling and meaning. Knowing some of the words in a family can help you to use and spell the others correctly.

Fishing is a kind of contest between human and fish. Some people find the contest exciting. Does Spinner?

from

Hook a Fish, Catch a Mountain

by Jean Craighead George

A skinny girl in mountain boots and bulky clothes stood on the bank of the river. She looked like a glass figurine wrapped for shipment. In one hand she held a fishing rod. With the other she pushed the long black hair from her face. It swept below her waist, a gleaming, well-groomed pyramid of lights.

Suddenly the fishing rod bowed like a question mark, and the girl braced as a fish took her line. The stones of the gravel bar rolled under her feet, and she was pulled into the icy Snake River. The water seeped through the eyelets of her mountain boots. She glanced around desperately. The entire valley of Jackson Hole, Wyoming—its sky and saw-blade mountains, its people and wild things—was conspiring against her. She, Spinner Shafter, age thirteen, a dancer in the Roundelay Dance Company, was about to be drowned by a fish.

"Get in here!" she screamed to the creature pulling her. She dug in her heels, gained a better footing, and yanked.

"Get in here—this minute—so that I never have to fish again . . . ever. . . ."

Think and Discuss

1. How does Spinner feel about fishing? How do you know? What else do you know about Spinner?

2. Where does the story take place? What details does the author provide to help you picture the setting?

3. What can you tell about the plot of this story from reading the story's beginning?

The Writing Process
Story

Do you have a great idea for a story? What events would make up your story's plot? What would the story's setting and characters be like? Write a short story. Use the guidelines, and follow the Writing Process.

1 ▶ Prewriting
- For story ideas, think of what might happen in a setting such as a bus, concert, spaceship, storm, or restaurant.
- Staple together three sheets of paper labeled *Plot*, *Setting*, and *Characters*. Make notes on them about your story ideas.

2 ▶ Draft
- Put your story down on paper. Don't worry about mistakes now.
- Include details and dialogue to let readers "see" your setting and characters.

3 ▶ Revise
- If necessary, revise your opening so that it will grab readers' attention.
- Add details and dialogue to make your setting and characters seem real.
- Have a writing conference.

4 ▶ Proofread
- Did you spell each word correctly?
- Did you avoid using double negatives?
- Did you use adjectives and adverbs correctly?
- Did you capitalize proper nouns and proper adjectives?

5 ▶ Publish
- Copy your story neatly. Add a catchy title.
- Share your story. Choose an exciting scene and act it out.

Guidelines for Writing a Story

✓ Organize story events in this order: rising action, climax, resolution.
✓ Use direct statements and vivid details to show readers what the setting and characters are like.
✓ Use dialogue to bring the characters to life.

Composition Words

athletic
spectacular
imaginary
depot
suspect
mystery
amateur
oasis

Vowel Changes II

Read and Say

Basic	READ the sentences. SAY each bold word.
1. harmony	The voices joined in sweet **harmony**.
2. harmonious	Your good will made it a **harmonious** meeting.
3. adapt	Did your pets **adapt** well to your new home?
4. adaptation	This movie is an **adaptation** of a play.
5. inspiration	Was the sunset the **inspiration** for your poem?
6. inspire	A great speech can **inspire** a crowd.
7. excellence	Good students strive for **excellence**.
8. excel	Studying will help you **excel** in spelling.
9. imposition	Vote no on the **imposition** of a sales tax!
10. impose	Don't **impose** on him by asking for a favor.
11. genetic	Hair color is a **genetic** trait.
12. gene	Your eye color is determined by a **gene**.
13. academy	The riding **academy** has students of all ages.
14. academic	The **academic** year ends in June.
15. variety	Those shoes come in a **variety** of colors.
16. various	We used **various** kinds of fruit in this pie.
17. narrative	We listened to a **narrative** of the tale.
18. narrate	The drama club needs you to **narrate** the play.
19. disposition	A gentle smile revealed her kind **disposition**.
20. dispose	Please **dispose** of your trash in that can.

Spelling Strategy   To remember the spelling of |ə| in some words, think of a related word in which the same vowel has the long or short vowel sound.

Think and Write   Write the pairs of Basic Words. In each pair, underline the vowels that change from |ə| to the long or short vowel sound.

Review	23. admiration
21. combination	24. admire
22. combine	

Challenge	27. derivation
25. triumph	28. derive
26. triumphant	

Independent Practice

Vocabulary: Using Context Write the Basic Word that completes each sentence. Use your Spelling Dictionary.

1. Songwriters often _____ familiar old songs by writing modern musical arrangements for them.
2. The _____ for "The Star-Spangled Banner," by Francis Scott Key, was a battle that Key witnessed during the War of 1812.
3. To _____ as a songwriter, you must be able to create words and music that the listener will want to hear again and again.
4. Many rock bands include backup singers who sing _____.
5. Jan dislikes rock music but plays it at her parties because she does not want to _____ her musical tastes on her guests.
6. Can children inherit musical ability through a _____?
7. Our school issues awards for musical and _____ achievements.
8. Cy has written songs in _____ styles, including jazz and pop.
9. For our school concert, Mrs. Novak will _____ the story of *Peter and the Wolf* while the students play the music.
10. The _____ sounds of the four voices filled the room.
11. Musical ability seems to be a _____ trait in our family.
12. Ted hoped his walk in the woods would _____ an idea for a new melody.

Vocabulary: Word Clues Write the Basic Word that fits each clue. Use your Spelling Dictionary.

13. You do this when you throw something away.
14. This helps people and animals adjust to new environments.
15. This is a kind of school.
16. This is a mix of different things.
17. This is hard to beat.
18. This might be throwing things away or changing their owners.
19. This has characters, a setting, and action.
20. This puts a burden on another person.

Challenge Words Write the Challenge Word that matches each definition. Use your Spelling Dictionary.

21. to win or succeed
22. to obtain from a source
23. victorious or successful
24. something taken from a source

Review: Spelling Spree

Meaning Match Add the letters and clues to write a Basic or Review Word.

Example: *in* + the pointed top of a steeple   *inspire*

1. a notice of something for sale + *mire*
2. *im* + to place or arrange
3. *h* + the limb connecting the hand to the shoulder + *ony*
4. *ex* + a room where prisoners are kept + *ence*
5. hereditary material + *tic*
6. *narr* + past tense of *eat*
7. a tool used to untangle hair + *ine*
8. *dis* + a place or location
9. *a* + an ungentlemanly man + *emy*
10. a mischievous creature + *osition*
11. to hurt + *onious*
12. *ad* + a synonym for *appropriate*
13. *combi* + a country and its people
14. *dis* + to model for a portrait or photograph
15. *nar* + a rodent + *ive*
16. *inspi* + to give out in limited amounts

 **+ *ine* =**

Letter Exchange Replace the underlined letters with the same number of letters to write a Basic or Review Word.

17. <u>ex</u>piration
18. <u>so</u>ciety
19. <u>g</u>ave
20. <u>tem</u>ptation
21. expe<u>l</u>
22. epi<u>d</u>emic
23. <u>cu</u>rious
24. ins<u>pe</u>ct

✓ How Are You Doing?
Write each spelling word in a sentence. Practice any misspelled spelling words with a partner.

Proofreading and Writing

Proofread: Spelling, Commas in a Series and with Interrupters Use commas to separate three or more items in a series. Also use them to set off words or phrases that interrupt the flow of a sentence.

> Estelle is a songwriter, pianist, and singer.
> Songwriting, however, is her favorite activity.

Find five misspelled Basic or Review Words and three missing commas in this song. Write the song correctly.

Jesse has as they say a golden dispisition.

And his varius charms inspire my awe.

His many virtues combine in perfect harmeny.

Could this excallence, I wonder, hide a flaw?

What habit, manner, or feature have I not seen

That could cause me to admier him less—

A certain mood a fault, or an imperfect gene

That could take away my happiness?

Basic
1. harmony
2. harmonious
3. adapt
4. adaptation
5. inspiration
6. inspire
7. excellence
8. excel
9. imposition
10. impose
11. genetic
12. gene
13. academy
14. academic
15. variety
16. various
17. narrative
18. narrate
19. disposition
20. dispose

Review
21. combination
22. combine
23. admiration
24. admire

Challenge
25. triumph
26. triumphant
27. derivation
28. derive

Write a Fan Letter Your favorite musical group has just released a song that you think is great. Write a fan letter to tell the group how you feel about the song. Try to use five spelling words and at least one series of three or more items or an interrupter.

Proofreading Marks
¶ Indent
∧ Add
⩘ Add a comma
ⱽⱽ Add quotation marks
⊙ Add a period
ꞷ Delete
≡ Capital letter
／ Small letter
∿ Reverse order

Expanding Vocabulary

Spelling Word Link

harmony

Jargon *Harmony* is a musical term used by musicians and non-musicians alike to mean "a pleasing combination of sounds." Some musical terms, however, are used mostly by people in the music world. For example, to musicians, a *cut* is a song recorded on a record, disc, or tape. This specialized language of a trade or profession is called **jargon**.

For each underlined jargon word in the paragraph, write the word below that has the same meaning. Use your Spelling Dictionary.

> well-rehearsed   adaptation   engagement   sample

The **(1)** gig at the Arrow Cafe was a big break for the Nice Boys. After the show, a talent scout asked them to record a **(2)** demo for Crystal Records. The next day, the group rehearsed their **(3)** cover of the Beatles song "Love Me Do." By evening, they sounded **(4)** tight and ready to record.

TEST-TAKING TACTICS

Vocabulary-in-Context Read the following sample passage and question.

Sample passage excerpt and question:

(20) Leila, the songwriter for Every Time, is talented but quite egotistical. When interviewed on "Top Ten Friday," she talked only about herself. The interviewer occasionally tried to slip in a question about the rest of the group, but Leila stubbornly brought the conversation back to her favorite topic: herself!

The word "egotistical" in line 20 means

(A) wealthy   (B) self-important   (C) ignorant
(D) argumentative   (E) not confident

To answer a question like this one, find the tested word in the passage and use context clues to make a guess about the word's meaning. Then find the answer choice that is closest to the meaning you figured out.

Now write the answers to these questions.

5.   What is the meaning of "egotistical"? Write its letter. _____?_____

6.   What context clues helped you figure out the meaning of "egotistical"?

_____?_____

_____?_____

_____?_____

Vocabulary Enrichment

Real-World Connection

Performing Arts: Songwriting All the words in the box relate to songwriting. Look up these words in your Spelling Dictionary. Then write the words to complete this paragraph.

Marc and Rena's songwriting __(1)__ was not going well. Marc didn't like the __(2)__ Rena had composed. He thought it was a boring tune. Rena, meanwhile, claimed that Marc's __(3)__ were meaningless. Marc finally agreed to reword the __(4)__ that was repeated after each __(5)__. To compromise, Rena wrote an __(6)__ part for the piano and changed a harsh six-note __(7)__. Then she jazzed up the beginning. As she hummed a few new opening bars, she quickly scribbled the __(8)__ for the music on the lines and spaces of the staff.

Spelling Word Link

harmonious

lyrics
instrumental
melody
refrain
notation
verse
chord
collaboration

TRY THIS!

Yes or No? Write *yes* or *no* to answer each question.

9. Are musical symbols used to write song lyrics?
10. Can a refrain be sung?
11. Can one person create a musical collaboration?
12. Are all the notes of a chord played at the same time?

Fact File

From 1915 to 1925, composer Eubie Blake and lyrics writer Noble Sissle comprised one of the most successful songwriting teams in the country. They wrote in the musical style known as ragtime. In 1921 their New York show, *Shuffle Along*, was such a hit that it set the style for some Broadway shows up until the 1930s.

Latin Roots II

Read and Say

Basic

READ the sentences. SAY each bold word.

1. contrast — How would you **contrast** frogs and toads?
2. institute — She takes classes at the art **institute**.
3. statue — A marble **statue** of a lion is at the entrance.
4. projector — Start the **projector** for the slide show.
5. reject — We can **reject** the offer if it is too low.
6. portable — Carry the **portable** computer by its handle.
7. objective — My **objective** is to finish the job by noon.
8. obstacle — The fallen tree was an **obstacle** in the road.
9. superstition — Is that **superstition** about black cats true?
10. transport — Many ranchers **transport** their cattle by rail.
11. reporter — Which newspaper **reporter** wrote that story?
12. inject — Use a pump to **inject** air into a flat tire.
13. circumstance — What **circumstance** made you change your mind?
14. stanza — He knew every **stanza** of the poem by heart.
15. interjection — Her loud **interjection** broke the silence.
16. porter — A **porter** carried our bags into the station.
17. adjective — More than one **adjective** can modify a noun.
18. deport — Will they **deport** him to his native country?
19. subjective — A person's taste in music is **subjective**.
20. statute — The senators voted on the proposed **statute**.

Spelling Strategy   Knowing the Latin roots *sta/sti/st* ("to stand"), *port* ("to carry"), and *ject* ("to throw") can help you spell and understand words with these roots.

Think and Write   Write each Basic Word under its root.

sta/sti/st	port	ject

Review		**Challenge**	
21. standard	23. import	26. portfolio	28. rapport
22. establish	24. export	27. abject	29. conjecture
	25. constitution		30. constituent

Independent Practice

Vocabulary: Definitions Write the Basic Word that matches each definition. Use your Spelling Dictionary.

1. not influenced by emotion
2. a machine that transmits an image onto a surface
3. to carry from one place to another
4. a condition, fact, or event
5. an educational organization
6. to force or drive into something
7. an illogical belief in magic or chance
8. something that stands in the way of a goal
9. to expel from a country
10. a law passed by a legislative body
11. an exclamation
12. based on personal opinion or experience

Vocabulary: Analogies Write the Basic Word that completes each analogy. Use your Spelling Dictionary.

Example: scissors : cut :: truck : _____   *transport*
13. composer : symphony :: sculptor : _____
14. similar : different :: compare : _____
15. essay : paragraph :: poem : _____
16. raise : lower :: accept : _____
17. food : waiter :: luggage : _____
18. verb : adverb :: noun : _____
19. lesson : teacher :: news : _____
20. heavy : light :: immovable : _____

Challenge Words Write the Challenge Word that fits each clue. Use your Spelling Dictionary.

21. This kind of situation or circumstance is likely to make a person miserable.
22. You can have this with someone you find easy to talk to and get along with.
23. Artwork travels neatly in this.
24. You engage in this when you form an opinion without having all the facts.
25. This person is represented by an elected official.

Dictionary

Stress In the phonetic respelling next to a dictionary entry word, a stress mark (´) follows the syllable that should be accented. If more than one syllable is stressed, a regular stress mark indicates the stronger, or **primary**, stress, and a lighter stress mark indicates **secondary** stress.

su·per·sti·tion |so͞o´ pər **stĭsh´** ən|

Practice Write each word below in syllables. Underline the syllable with primary stress. Circle the syllable with secondary stress. Use your Spelling Dictionary.

1. constitution
2. institute
3. interjection
4. circumstance

Review: Spelling Spree

Word Art 5–22. Find the Basic and Review Words hidden in the word below. Write the words in the order in which you find them.

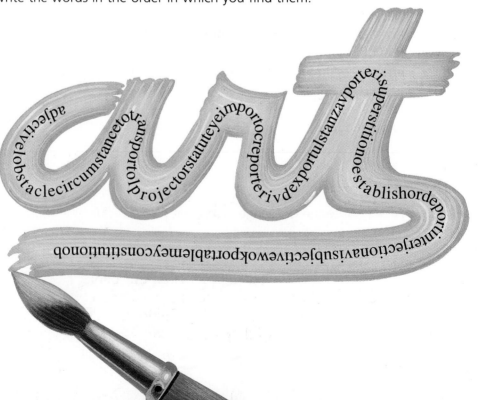

Proofreading and Writing

Proofread for Spelling Find six misspelled Basic or Review Words in this notice for a design contest. Write each word correctly.

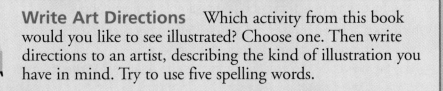

Attention students of the design instatute! Help us

establish a new image for Madison City. Our

objectiv is to enject color into Constitution Plaza

with a mural that will cover the wall behind the

stachue of James Madison. Submit your design on

standerd poster board. Meg O'Neil, arts reporter for

Madison City News, will select the winning design.

Entries must be in the mayor's office by May 24.

We will regect all late entries, so start now!

Write Art Directions Which activity from this book would you like to see illustrated? Choose one. Then write directions to an artist, describing the kind of illustration you have in mind. Try to use five spelling words.

Basic

1. contrast
2. institute
3. statue
4. projector
5. reject
6. portable
7. objective
8. obstacle
9. superstition
10. transport
11. reporter
12. inject
13. circumstance
14. stanza
15. interjection
16. porter
17. adjective
18. deport
19. subjective
20. statute

Review
21. standard
22. establish
23. import
24. export
25. constitution

Challenge
26. portfolio
27. abject
28. rapport
29. conjecture
30. constituent

Proofreading Marks
¶ Indent
∧ Add
⹁ Add a comma
⌄⌄ Add quotation marks
⊙ Add a period
͜ Delete
≡ Capital letter
／ Small letter
∽ Reverse order

Expanding Vocabulary

Spelling
Word Link

reject

Context Clues Like a synonym, an antonym can provide an excellent context clue to the meaning of an unfamiliar word. Suppose you did not know the word *reject*. The antonym in this sentence would give you a clue.

Jo hated to reject the offer, but she could not **accept** its terms.

Words such as *but*, *however*, *except*, *not*, *although*, and *rather than* can help you identify antonyms in a sentence.

Write the meaning of each underlined word. Then write the antonym that gave you the clue to the meaning of the underlined word.

1. Meg used paper with a <u>matte</u> finish rather than a glossy one.
2. Judy liked the unusual effect of the <u>asymmetrical</u> design, but her art director preferred a more balanced approach.
3. Although the boldly colored letters make the heading more <u>dynamic</u>, the rest of the page still looks lifeless.
4. Pat expected to be rewarded, not <u>chastised</u>, for her artwork.

TEST-TAKING TACTICS

Analogies When you analyze the relationship between the stem words in an analogy test question, pay careful attention to the meanings of the words. For example, at first glance you might think that the stem words in the sample analogy question below are synonyms. However, after studying the stem words, you'll notice that their meanings differ in degree of intensity. The paired words in the correct answer choice will also differ in degree of intensity.

ASK : BEG ::

(A) answer : respond
(B) glance : stare
(C) scribble : scrawl
(D) raise : lift
(E) finish : complete

Answer the following questions about the sample analogy above.

5. Which four answer choices can you eliminate because the paired words are simple synonyms? Write their letters.
6. Which answer choice correctly completes the analogy? Write its letter.

Real-World Connection

Art: Graphic Arts All the words in the box relate to graphic arts. Look up these words in your Spelling Dictionary. Then write the words to complete this paragraph.

As a __(1)__ advertising designer, I work for many companies. My job is to present a __(2)__, or idea, in a way that is visually powerful and appealing. With the client, I determine what __(3)__, such as photography or computer-generated art, to use for any artwork or __(4)__. I also choose an appropriate __(5)__ in which to print each piece of text. Then I draw a __(6)__, which is a precise plan or diagram, for the ad. I use a __(7)__ and other tools to __(8)__ all the graphic elements perfectly. It's exciting to see my designs become billboards and pages in magazines!

Spelling Word Link

portfolio

typeface
concept
medium
layout
align
T-square
illustration
freelance

TRY THIS!

Yes or No? Write *yes* if the underlined word is used correctly. Write *no* if it is not.

9. Use this <u>T-square</u> to draw the circles.
10. As a <u>freelance</u> artist, I can set my own work hours.
11. This painting suggests a <u>medium</u> of quiet and calm.
12. Let's pick an <u>illustration</u> to use on the book cover.

Fact File

If you were to examine the print in fifty books, you might find fifty different styles of type. Each typeface is designed to have a certain effect: plain or fancy, humorous or serious, old-fashioned or modern. Designers can choose from among thousands of typefaces.

Greek and Latin Prefixes

Read and Say

Basic

READ the sentences. **SAY** each bold word.

1. antiseptic   An **antiseptic** will kill the germs in a cut.
2. adhesive   Stick on the bandage with **adhesive** tape.
3. administer   Who can **administer** first aid to the injured?
4. absorb   This sponge can **absorb** a lot of water.
5. adequate   The campers had an **adequate** supply of food.
6. adept   She is quite **adept** at public speaking.
7. abnormal   Snow is **abnormal** in warm climates.
8. postpone   Let's **postpone** the game until the rain stops.
9. admission   The **admission** to the theme park is expensive!
10. postscript   Put a **postscript** at the end of your letter.
11. adviser   My **adviser** urged me to take this math course.
12. administration   All managers must be good at **administration**.
13. abuse   The ruler was overthrown for **abuse** of power.
14. absolve   The judge will **absolve** him and set him free.
15. absolute   Witnesses promise to tell the **absolute** truth.
16. antonym   List an **antonym** for each spelling word.
17. adjustment   A simple **adjustment** will fix the printer.
18. antifreeze   A car needs **antifreeze** in cold weather.
19. postgraduate   Sam took a **postgraduate** class after college.
20. postdate   I had to **postdate** the check for the next day.

Spelling Strategy   Remember the meanings of the prefixes *ab-* ("away from"), *ad-* ("to; at; near"), *post-* ("after"), and *anti-/ant-* ("opposite; against").

Think and Write   Write each Basic Word under its prefix.

ab-	ad-	post-	anti-/ant-

Review
21. advanced
22. admit
23. absence
24. advantage
25. adopt

Challenge
26. antibody
27. antagonize
28. abhor
29. adjacent
30. Antarctic

Independent Practice

Vocabulary: Word Clues Write the Basic Word that fits each clue. Use your Spelling Dictionary.

1. This may be *good* or *bad*, *up* or *down*, *hot* or *cold*.
2. This keeps things running smoothly.
3. This type of school is for people who are already well educated.
4. This prevents ice.
5. This is complete and without a doubt.
6. This is an afterthought.
7. A court does this to an accused person when it declares him or her not guilty.
8. This wears things out fast.
9. A person might do this to a check.
10. People listen to what this person has to say.
11. Things that do this leave nothing on the surface.
12. Moving to a new town might require this.
13. If you've gotten this, you're in.

Vocabulary: Replacing Words Write the Basic Word that means the same thing as the underlined word or words in each sentence. Use your Spelling Dictionary.

14. The kit has <u>enough</u> supplies for most first-aid situations.
15. After an accident, an emergency medical technician determines which injuries to treat immediately and which to <u>put off</u>.
16. Only trained personnel should <u>give</u> first aid in an emergency.
17. The accident victim's breathing was <u>unnatural</u>.
18. The teacher of the first-aid class is <u>highly skilled</u> at all types of emergency medical procedures.
19. We used the <u>substance that destroys germs</u> to wash out the inside of the ambulance.
20. Use <u>self-sticking</u> bandages to cover minor wounds.

Challenge Words Write the Challenge Word that matches each definition. Use your Spelling Dictionary.

21. next to; adjoining
22. to earn the dislike of
23. to regard with horror; hate
24. the region surrounding the South Pole
25. a substance in the blood that acts against foreign substances

Review: Spelling Spree

Invisible Letters Decide which letters should be added to complete each Basic or Review Word. Write the words correctly.

1. a _ s _ l _ t _
2. _ d _ i _ _ s t _ a _ _ _ n
3. p _ s _ g _ a _ _ _ t e
4. _ n t _ _ r _ _ z e
5. a _ v _ t _ _ _ _
6. _ b _ o _ m _ l
7. a _ _ u s _ m _ _ t
8. _ d _ i _ s _ _ n
9. a _ t _ s _ p t _ _
10. _ n _ _ n _ m
11. a _ m _ n _ s _ _ r
12. _ d _ i _ _ r
13. _ d o _ _
14. a d _ _ _ a t e

How Are You Doing?

List the spelling words that are difficult for you. Practice them with a partner.

Vocabulary: Coded Clues Write the Basic or Review Word that fits each clue. Circle the letter that would appear in the box.

Example: just enough _ _ _ _ _ _ ☐ _   adequa(t)e
15. to clear of blame _ _ _ _ ☐ _ _
16. something that sticks _ _ ☐ _ _ _ _ _
17. beyond beginner or intermediate _ _ ☐ _ _ _ _ _ _
18. the lack of something _ _ _ _ _ ☐ _
19. to confess a mistake _ _ ☐ _ _
20. harmful treatment _ _ ☐ _ _
21. to put off until a later time _ _ _ _ _ _ _ ☐ _
22. skillful or accomplished _ _ ☐ _ _
23. a thought added to a letter _ _ _ _ _ _ _ ☐ _ _
24. to write a future month and day _ _ _ _ _ ☐ _ _ _
25. what sponges do to liquids _ _ _ _ ☐ _

Now decode the Mystery Words. Below the lines are item numbers. Write the circled letters from those items to spell a first-aid procedure.

Mystery Words:

_ _ _ _?_ _ _ _   _ _ _ _?_ _ _ _
16 22 23 19 15 23 18 16   19 24 21 22 20 17 22 25

Proofreading and Writing

Proofread: Spelling, Dates and Addresses Capitalize proper nouns in dates and addresses. In a date, use a comma between the day and the year. In an address, use a comma between a city and a state or country, but not between a state and a ZIP Code.

   June 6, 1998   Chicago, Illinois 60611

Find five misspelled Basic or Review Words and three errors in dates and addresses in this excerpt from an ambulance log. Write the log entry correctly.

Address: *45 Oak Street*   Date: *July 19 1999*

        ware NH 00021   Time: *10:23 a.m.*

Patient: *Robert Wood*   Destination: *City Hospital*

Symptoms: *Patient appeared to be in advansed state of shock. Breathing abnormal— rapid and shallow, but with adequit airway.*

Action: *Began to adminster oxygen. Emergency room physician, Dr. E. Cooper, decided to admitt patient.*

Time of admision: *10:40 a.m.*

Basic

1. antiseptic
2. adhesive
3. administer
4. absorb
5. adequate
6. adept
7. abnormal
8. postpone
9. admission
10. postscript
11. adviser
12. administration
13. abuse
14. absolve
15. absolute
16. antonym
17. adjustment
18. antifreeze
19. postgraduate
20. postdate

Review

21. advanced
22. admit
23. absence
24. advantage
25. adopt

Challenge

26. antibody
27. antagonize
28. abhor
29. adjacent
30. Antarctic

Proofreading Marks

¶ Indent
∧ Add
⩜ Add a comma
ᰪ ᰪ Add quotation marks
⊙ Add a period
ᵍ Delete
≡ Capital letter
/ Small letter
∿ Reverse order

Write an Announcement Write an announcement of a first-aid course. Include a description of the procedures that will be taught. Also note the date of the course and the address at which it will be held. Try to use five spelling words.

Expanding Vocabulary

Spelling
Word Link

abnormal

Exact Words Which sentence is more precise?

The accident victim's breathing was **abnormal**.

The accident victim's breathing was **shallow**.

Vague words, such as *abnormal*, do not give a reader as much information as more precise or exact words. A thesaurus can help you choose the exact words to express your thoughts.

Write the word from the list below that best replaces *unusual* in each sentence. Use your Thesaurus.

rare   inappropriate   eccentric   monstrous

1. A misprinted stamp is valuable because it is <u>unusual</u>.
2. Wearing mismatched socks is one of Ann's <u>unusual</u> habits.
3. Is it <u>unusual</u> to eat chicken with your fingers?
4. Bulging eyes and fangs made the actor look <u>unusual</u>.

| 1. | ? | 3. | ? |
| 2. | ? | 4. | ? |

Now write four sentences of your own. In each sentence, use a different exact word for *unusual*.

5.   ?

       ?

6.   ?

       ?

7.   ?

       ?

8.   ?

       ?

Real-World Connection

Health: First Aid All the words in the box relate to first aid. Look up these words in your Spelling Dictionary. Then write the words to complete this paragraph.

A victim of severe physical __(1)__ requires immediate attention. The most important thing is to check the victim's __(2)__ and to __(3)__ the person if he or she is not breathing. Next, check for __(4)__, or severe bleeding. To stop the bleeding in an arm or leg, apply pressure to the wound or to the artery above the wound and __(5)__ the limb. As a last resort, use a belt, a piece of cloth, or something similar as a __(6)__. Almost all injuries produce shock, which is characterized by faintness and __(7)__; rapid, shallow breathing; and a weak or unsteady __(8)__. The best way to treat shock is to keep the victim still, warm, and comfortable until medical help arrives.

Spelling Word Link

| antiseptic |

trauma
respiration
pulse
hemorrhage
resuscitate
elevate
nausea
tourniquet

TRY THIS!

Yes or No? Write *yes* if the underlined word is used correctly. Write *no* if it is not.

9. To <u>elevate</u> your leg, put several pillows under it.
10. After the race, Tina's <u>respiration</u> was fast and deep.
11. Seth wore a <u>tourniquet</u> around his sprained knee.
12. Every first-aid kit should have a supply of <u>trauma</u>.

Fact File

Cardiopulmonary resuscitation (CPR) is a technique used when a person's heart has stopped beating. CPR combines artificial respiration with chest compressions that pump blood through the body. Many lives have been saved by people who knew CPR.

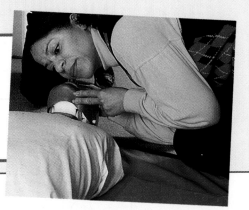

Words from Other Languages

Read and Say

Basic	READ the sentences. SAY each bold word.
1. igloo	Each family lived in an **igloo** made of ice.
2. parka	The girl wore a heavy **parka** with a hood.
3. tundra	It was bitterly cold on the treeless **tundra**.
4. walrus	Our zoo has both a **walrus** and a sea lion.
5. landscape	Rolling hills stretched across the **landscape**.
6. kayak	May we paddle our **kayak** across the lake?
7. sleigh	A horse pulled the **sleigh** across the snow.
8. moccasin	Wear a soft **moccasin** to ease your sore foot.
9. sketch	Can you draw a quick **sketch** of the house?
10. hickory	We gathered nuts from the **hickory** tree.
11. raccoon	That crafty **raccoon** got into the garbage!
12. skunk	The bad smell from the **skunk** lasted for days.
13. easel	He displayed his painting on a tall **easel**.
14. waffle	Would you like jam or honey on your **waffle**?
15. mammoth	The **mammoth** building took up a whole block.
16. coleslaw	Please chop some cabbage for the **coleslaw**.
17. chipmunk	I saw the striped back of a baby **chipmunk**.
18. decoy	Is that a real duck or a **decoy**?
19. squash	Pick some **squash** from the garden for dinner.
20. monsoon	The **monsoon** brought days of rain to the area.

Spelling Strategy Remember that English has borrowed words from many languages.

Think and Write Write the Basic Words.

Review	
21. iceberg	23. pianos
22. solos	24. altos
	25. cellos

Challenge	
26. steppe	28. yacht
27. caucus	29. persimmon
	30. caftan

Independent Practice

Vocabulary: Definitions Write the Basic Word that matches each definition.
Use your Spelling Dictionary.

1. a light, crisp cake
2. a salad of shredded raw cabbage with a dressing
3. a furry black and white animal that is capable of spraying a bad-smelling liquid
4. a scene formed by a stretch of countryside
5. huge; gigantic
6. a model of a bird, used by hunters to attract real birds

7. a cold, treeless region having only sparse, low-growing types of plant life
8. a furry animal with black masklike face markings and a ringed tail
9. a system of winds that affects the climate of a large area and changes direction with the season
10. a North American tree that has hard wood and bears edible nuts
11. a light vehicle with low runners for use on snow or ice
12. a small, squirrel-like animal with a striped back

Vocabulary: Classifying Write the Basic Word that fits each group. Use your Spelling Dictionary.

13. cabin, tent, hut, _____
14. jacket, coat, sweater, _____
15. porpoise, seal, whale, _____
16. rowboat, raft, canoe, _____
17. sandal, boot, sneaker, _____
18. canvas, paintbrush, palette, _____
19. cucumber, eggplant, pumpkin, _____
20. drawing, painting, photograph, _____

Challenge Words Write the Challenge Word that completes each analogy.
Use your Spelling Dictionary.

21. vegetable : broccoli :: fruit : _____
22. head : turban :: body : _____
23. air : jet :: water : _____
24. sand : desert :: grass : _____
25. business : conference :: politics : _____

Dictionary

Pronunciation Next to each dictionary entry is a phonetic respelling that tells you how to pronounce the word. If you do not understand a symbol used in the respelling, look it up in the pronunciation key, which appears regularly through the dictionary. The key shows what sound each symbol stands for by giving an example of a familiar word that contains the sound.

ă	pat	ŏ	pot	û	fur
ā	pay	ō	go	*th*	the
â	care	ô	paw, for	th	thin
ä	father	oi	oil	hw	which
ĕ	pet	ŏŏ	book	zh	usual
ē	be	ōō	boot	ə	ago, item,
ĭ	pit	yōō	cute		pencil, atom,
ī	ice	ou	out		circus
î	near	ŭ	cut	ər	butter

Practice Look at the underlined symbol in each phonetic respelling. Write the word from the pronunciation key that shows how that symbol is pronounced.

1. kayak |kī´ ăk´|
2. boutique |bōō tēk´|
3. altos |ăl´ tōz|
4. enchilada |ĕn´ chə lä´ də|

Review: Spelling Spree

Code Breaker Use the code key below to figure out the coded Basic and Review Words. Write the words correctly.

CODE:	n	o	p	q	r	s	t	u	v	w	x	y	z	a	b	c	d	e	f	g	h	i	j	k	l	m
LETTER:	a	b	c	d	e	f	g	h	i	j	k	l	m	n	o	p	q	r	s	t	u	v	w	x	y	z

Example: ynaqfpncr   *landscape*

5. fxrgpu
6. nygbf
7. enppbba
8. qrpbl
9. jnssyr
10. cnexn

11. fyrvtu
12. cvnabf
13. zbppnfva
14. fxhax
15. zbafbba
16. fbybf

17. fdhnfu
18. pryybf
19. puvczhax
20. pbyrfynj
21. rnfry
22. znzzbgu

Proofreading and Writing

Proofread for Spelling Find seven misspelled Basic or Review Words in this excerpt from a book report. Write each word correctly.

<u>Land of the Icicles</u>, by Jane Frost, describes the author's adventures in northern Alaska. Jane gave up her job making oak and hickery furniture, bought a parka, and headed for the frontier to live for a year. She settled on the tondra, near the Bering Sea. There she learned to fish from a kiyak and build an iglue. The frozen landskape provided the setting for many new experiences, some frightening and some funny. Jane's description of the walris that passed by on an iceburg is especially comic.

Write a Poster You have a summer job at a science museum. This July, the museum will open a new exhibit on the Arctic. Create a poster advertising the new exhibit. Describe some of the displays visitors will see. Try to use five spelling words.

Basic

1. igloo
2. parka
3. tundra
4. walrus
5. landscape
6. kayak
7. sleigh
8. moccasin
9. sketch
10. hickory
11. raccoon
12. skunk
13. easel
14. waffle
15. mammoth
16. coleslaw
17. chipmunk
18. decoy
19. squash
20. monsoon

Review
21. iceberg
22. solos
23. pianos
24. altos
25. cellos

Challenge
26. steppe
27. caucus
28. yacht
29. persimmon
30. caftan

Proofreading Marks
¶ Indent
∧ Add
⅄ Add a comma
♥♥ Add quotation marks
⊙ Add a period
⤷ Delete
≡ Capital letter
/ Small letter
∿ Reverse order

Expanding Vocabulary

Slang If you were playing a game and your opponent said, "I'm going to skunk you," that person would probably mean that he or she was going to beat you badly. This use of *skunk* is called slang. **Slang** is our most casual kind of language. Slang words often originate in particular groups within a culture.

Write the word below that can be used in place of the underlined slang word or expression in each sentence. Use your Spelling Dictionary.

failure   scold   betrayed   crazy

1. Kurt and I made a deal, but he <u>double-crossed</u> me.
2. Delia has some <u>wacky</u> ideas for new inventions.
3. The last movie this actor starred in was a <u>bomb</u>.
4. The teacher will <u>chew out</u> anyone who is late to class.

1. _____?_____
2. _____?_____

3. _____?_____
4. _____?_____

Now edit the following story to make it more casual. Replace each underlined word or phrase with a slang term. Write the slang terms.

The day Sam had to give his oral report on penguins, he came to school wearing a **(5)** <u>crazy</u> penguin costume. To his surprise, his teacher began to **(6)** <u>scold him</u>. Poor Sam felt that he had been **(7)** <u>betrayed</u>. Teachers were always telling Sam to be creative. He had tried, but the result had been a complete **(8)** <u>failure</u>!

5. _____?_____   7. _____?_____
6. _____?_____   8. _____?_____

Real-World Connection

Social Studies: The Arctic All the words in the box relate to the Arctic. Look up these words in your Spelling Dictionary. Then write the words to complete this paragraph.

Spelling Word Link

steppe

caribou
wolverine
permafrost
lichen
sable
ermine
Siberia
frigid

Snow and ice cover the Arctic for most of the year. The region's coldest weather occurs in __(1)__, in Russia, where January temperatures average –40°F. Even in midsummer, when the snow disappears in most places, the ground retains a thick layer of __(2)__. Despite its __(3)__ climate, the Arctic supports herds of __(4)__, which graze on a __(5)__ called reindeer moss. For centuries, trappers here have pursued the __(6)__ for its valuable dark fur and the __(7)__, whose fur coat whitens in winter. The vicious, bushy-tailed __(8)__ also makes its home in the cold north.

TRY THIS!

Yes or No? Write *yes* if the underlined word is used correctly. Write *no* if it is not.

9. Because of its color, the <u>ermine</u> blends into the snow.
10. They walked across <u>Siberia</u> in a day.
11. The fur of a <u>lichen</u> is very valuable.
12. The <u>permafrost</u> makes digging difficult.

Fact File

The aurora borealis, also called the northern lights, is a fantastic light display that stretches across the night sky of the Arctic. An aurora is formed when electrically charged particles from the sun interact with Earth's upper atmosphere.

Words Often Misspelled

Read and Say

Basic	READ the sentences. SAY each bold word.
1. cylinder	A soup can is shaped like a **cylinder**.
2. gauge	Does the fuel **gauge** show that we need gas?
3. circuit	There are too many lamps on this **circuit**.
4. guarantee	Her camera came with a lifetime **guarantee**.
5. vacuum	Please **vacuum** the crumbs from the carpet.
6. livelihood	Farming as a **livelihood** is hard work.
7. nuisance	Picking up my brother's toys is a **nuisance**.
8. prior	Let's buy our tickets **prior** to the show.
9. consequence	Being late was a **consequence** of oversleeping.
10. tongue	The cat licked its fur with its tiny **tongue**.
11. asthma	A bad cough can bring on an attack of **asthma**.
12. tortoise	Is a **tortoise** a kind of turtle?
13. biscuit	A hot **biscuit** spread with jam tastes great!
14. beige	This shade of **beige** has a lot of gray in it.
15. scholar	A **scholar** studies for years to gain knowledge.
16. campaign	Our **campaign** to end all homework failed.
17. bureau	I keep socks in the top drawer of my **bureau**.
18. bough	A **bough** of the tree tapped against my window.
19. emperor	Is that country ruled by an **emperor**?
20. raspberry	The seeds of the **raspberry** stuck in my teeth.

Spelling Strategy   Knowing the origin of a word with an odd spelling can often help you spell the word correctly.

Think and Write   Write the Basic Words. Underline any parts that you have trouble spelling.

Review		Challenge	
21. foreign	23. rhythm	26. carburetor	28. gaiety
22. separate	24. mileage	27. quandary	29. meringue
	25. similar		30. bayou

Independent Practice

Vocabulary: Definitions Write the Basic Word that matches each definition. Use your Spelling Dictionary.

1. a land turtle
2. the organ of taste
3. a result
4. the ruler of an empire
5. the way in which a person earns an income
6. a small purplish-red fruit with many seeds
7. a small flaky cake or cracker
8. a large tree branch
9. a chest of drawers
10. a circular chamber in a car engine
11. a person of great learning
12. an organized effort made in the attempt to win a political office
13. a chronic ailment whose symptoms include coughing and difficulty in breathing

Vocabulary: Using Context Write the Basic Word that completes each sentence. Use your Spelling Dictionary.

14. The new car comes with a two-year _____ on all major parts.
15. Once a month, I wash the exterior of our car and _____ the interior.
16. Have a used car inspected by a mechanic _____ to buying it.
17. The service station owner had confused the _____ car with the tan one because their colors were so similar.
18. As he drove across the desert, Kip checked the temperature _____ regularly to make sure the car was not overheating.
19. A faulty electrical _____ may cause the headlights to dim.
20. Emily groaned about what a _____ it was to start her old car on cold mornings.

Challenge Words Write the Challenge Word that fits each group. Use your Spelling Dictionary.

21. inlet, creek, cove, _____
22. icing, glaze, whipped cream, _____
23. accelerator, clutch, muffler, _____
24. happiness, joy, merriment, _____
25. predicament, problem, difficulty, _____

Review: Spelling Spree

Word Forms Write the Basic or Review Word that is the base word of each word below.

1. campaigner
2. rhythmic
3. asthmatic
4. circuitry
5. foreigner
6. scholarly
7. dissimilar
8. priority

> **How Are You Doing?**
> Write the spelling words in alphabetical order. Practice any misspelled words with a partner.

Letter Math Add and subtract letters from the words below to make Basic or Review Words. Write the new words.

Example: ask – k + signal – al = *assign*

9. consent – nt + quench – h + e =
10. icy – i + blinders – b – s =
11. hem – h + per + for – f =
12. step – t + a + rate =
13. torn – n + t + poise – p =
14. b + cure – c + auto – to =
15. alive – a + lie – e + hood =
16. b + cough – c =
17. nut – t + is + dance – d =
18. guard – d + an + tee =
19. smile – s + rage – r =
20. b + eight – ht + e =
21. grasp – g + b + merry – m =
22. vacate – ate + u + sum – s =
23. gauze – ze + page – pa =
24. ton + guest – st =
25. b + disc – d + quit – q =

Proofreading and Writing

Proofread: Spelling, Capitalizing and Punctuating Letters

When writing a letter, capitalize the greeting and the first word of the closing. Follow the greeting with a colon in a business letter and a comma in a friendly letter. Use a comma after the closing.

Dear Owen**,**   **D**ear **S**ir**:**   **S**incerely yours**,**

Find five misspelled Basic or Review Words and two errors in punctuation and capitalization in this excerpt from a letter. Write the letter correctly.

---

dear Mr. Thornhill:

    Last month I bought a baige Prego. Because the Prego

has the best reputation for quality of any foreign car, I did

not test-drive it prier to purchase. Now I find that the engine

rythm is irregular, and the car crawls up hills at the pace of

a tortoise. I have tried twice, without success, to have these

problems fixed. Since your guaruntee ensures satisfaction, I

am asking you to replace this car with a similer model.

    Sincerely

    Ronald Stankewicz

    Ronald Stankewicz

Write a Friendly Letter   What is your concept of the car of the future? Write a letter to a friend, sharing your ideas. Describe the car and its special features. Tell why the car will be superior to today's cars. Try to use five spelling words, and include a greeting and a closing.

Basic

1. cylinder
2. gauge
3. circuit
4. guarantee
5. vacuum
6. livelihood
7. nuisance
8. prior
9. consequence
10. tongue
11. asthma
12. tortoise
13. biscuit
14. beige
15. scholar
16. campaign
17. bureau
18. bough
19. emperor
20. raspberry

Review

21. foreign
22. separate
23. rhythm
24. mileage
25. similar

Challenge

26. carburetor
27. quandary
28. gaiety
29. meringue
30. bayou

Proofreading Marks

¶ Indent
∧ Add
⩑ Add a comma
⩔⩔ Add quotation marks
⊙ Add a period
⌐ Delete
≡ Capital letter
/ Small letter
∿ Reverse order

147

Thornhill
Avenue   02052

Unit 23 BONUS

Expanding Vocabulary

Spelling Word Link

tongue

Idioms If someone tells you to hold your tongue, don't reach for your mouth. *Hold your tongue* is an idiom meaning "be quiet." An **idiom** is an expression that has a meaning different from the combined meanings of its individual words. An idiom is usually listed in the dictionary under one of its main words.

Write a word or words that mean the same as each underlined idiom. Use your Spelling Dictionary.

1. Tell the children to <u>make haste</u>, or we will be late.
2. The game was cancelled <u>on account of</u> bad weather.
3. My teacher and I talked <u>at length</u> about my project.
4. The name of the car model was <u>on the tip of my tongue</u>.

1.	?	3.	?
2.	?	4.	?

Now write two sentences of your own for two of the idioms above. Use the idiom in the first sentence. Then rewrite the sentence, using words that express the meaning of the idiom.

5.   ?

     ?

     ?

     ?

6.   ?

     ?

     ?

     ?

Real-World Connection

Industrial Arts: Auto Mechanics All the words in the box relate to auto mechanics. Look up these words in your Spelling Dictionary. Then write the words to complete this paragraph.

Spelling Word Link

cylinder

mechanic
combustion
transmission
battery
radiator
valve
piston
lubricate

A car engine has many parts. In the center of the engine is a metal block containing several cylindrical holes. In each cylinder, a __(1)__ moves down, pulling fuel and air through an intake __(2)__ and back up, compressing the mixture. Then the __(3)__ provides a surge of electrical energy to the spark plug, causing the fuel and air mixture to burn. This process is called __(4)__. The burning gases expand and generate power. The __(5)__ controls the transfer of power from the engine to the wheels. Oil is used to __(6)__ the moving parts of the engine. Water circulating from the __(7)__ keeps the engine from overheating. A good __(8)__ can keep the whole system running smoothly.

TRY THIS!

Yes or No? Write *yes* or *no* to answer each question.

9. Is water necessary for combustion to occur?
10. Does a piston stay in the same position all the time?
11. Is a battery part of a car's electrical system?
12. Does a valve open and close?

Fact File

In 1901 the first automobile assembly line was created in Detroit, Michigan. Today, Detroit is known as "Motor City" because more automobiles are produced there than anywhere else in the United States.

24 Review: Units 19–23

Unit 19 Vowel Changes II pages 120–125

harmony	adapt	excellence	narrative	variety
harmonious	adaptation	excel	narrate	various

💡 **Spelling Strategy** To remember the spelling of |ə| in some words, think of a related word in which the same vowel has the long or short vowel sound.

Write the word that completes each sentence.
1. On the continent of Europe, _____ languages are spoken.
2. The film was an _____ of a novel by Emily Brontë.
3. The choral group sang a song in four-part _____.
4. As people gathered round, the storyteller began his _____.

Write the word that matches each definition.
5. to adjust
6. in agreement
7. to tell
8. several kinds
9. to be better than
10. the highest quality

Unit 20 Latin Roots II pages 126–131

reject	obstacle	projector	transport	superstition
inject	statute	stanza	porter	interjection

💡 **Spelling Strategy** Knowing the Latin roots *sta/sti/st* ("to stand"), *port* ("to carry"), and *ject* ("to throw") can help you spell and understand words with these roots.

Write the word that fits each clue.
11. move
12. a poetic paragraph
13. a picture machine
14. a legal rule

Write the word that completes each analogy.
15. question : inquiry :: exclamation : _____
16. pen : write :: needle : _____
17. decoration : ornament :: barrier : _____
18. letters : mail carrier :: baggage : _____
19. invitation : refuse :: offer : _____
20. logical : science :: unreasonable : _____

Unit 21 Greek and Latin Prefixes   pages 132–137

| antiseptic | absorb | adequate | adept | postpone |
| antifreeze | postgraduate | administration | abuse | adjustment |

💡 **Spelling Strategy**   Remember the meanings of the prefixes *ab-* ("away from"), *ad-* ("to; at; near"), *post-* ("after"), and *anti-/ant-* ("opposite; against").

Write the word that completes each sentence.

21. After much practice, Moira became _____ at glass blowing.
22. We bought sturdy boots that could take a lot of _____.
23. The new rules were made by the school _____.
24. A year after Rufus finished college, he began _____ work.

Write the word that fits each clue.

25. gather moisture
26. enough
27. decide to do later

28. an enemy of germs
29. something that follows change
30. a liquid for cold cars

Unit 22 Words from Other Languages   pages 138–143

| igloo | parka | landscape | moccasin | sketch |
| easel | squash | monsoon | mammoth | decoy |

💡 **Spelling Strategy**   Remember that English has borrowed words from many languages.

Write the words that complete the paragraph.

   Mark Mattus traveled north in order to paint the rocky Alaskan __(31)__ . The local people gave him a __(32)__ to wear and showed him how to make an __(33)__ from blocks of ice. Every morning Mark would set up his __(34)__ and make a rough __(35)__ of the scenic hills and mountains.

Write the word that fits each group.

36. breeze, gust, gale, _____
37. potato, turnip, cabbage, _____
38. enormous, huge, gigantic, _____

39. trap, bait, lure, _____
40. boot, sandal, shoe, _____

Unit 23	Words Often Misspelled	pages 144–149

guarantee	vacuum	nuisance	prior	tongue
biscuit	bureau	campaign	beige	bough

 Spelling Strategy   Knowing the origin of a word with an odd spelling can often help you spell the word correctly.

Write the word that completes each sentence.
41. I have searched through every drawer of the _____.
42. The _____ of the cherry tree was covered in blossoms.
43. Rob dusted the furniture before he began to _____ the rug.
44. Becky joined the _____ to elect Berta Martinez.

Write the word that matches each definition.
45. a bother
46. a promise
47. the main organ of taste
48. a small roll
49. grayish brown
50. earlier

Challenge Words	Units 19–23	pages 120–149

triumph	rapport	antagonize	caftan	quandary
triumphant	portfolio	adjacent	yacht	bayou

Write the words that complete the paragraph.

The team's _(51)_ was followed by a celebration in the field _(52)_ to the soccer grounds. The defeated team exhibited good sportsmanship by joining in the fun, while the _(53)_ team were careful not to _(54)_ their opponents by boasting of victory. In fact, by the end of the day, a delightful _(55)_ had developed between members of the opposing teams.

Write the word that fits each clue.
56. something an artist might carry
57. an uncertain state
58. a wet place favored by alligators
59. a water vehicle
60. a cloaklike robe

Spelling-Meaning Strategy

The Latin Root *solv*

Among the words you learned in Unit 21 were *absolve* and *absolute*. Did you know that these two words are related in meaning? Both come from the Latin word *solvere*, meaning "to loosen" or "to free." *Absolve* means "to free from guilt or blame," and *absolute* means "complete or perfect"—in other words, free from any kind of flaw.

The words below also contain the root *solv*. Notice that *solv* is sometimes spelled *solu*, as it is in *absolute*.

> ab**solve**
>
> ab**solu**te

dis**solve**	re**solve**	**solv**ent
solution	re**solu**tion	**solu**ble

Think

- How does the root *solv* contribute to the meaning of each word? Look up the words in your Spelling Dictionary.
- In Unit 19, you learned that a vowel can have a schwa sound in one word, yet have a long or short vowel sound in a related word. Thinking of the related word can help you remember the spelling of the schwa. What vowel sound does *solv* have in each of the words above?

Apply and Extend

Complete these activities on a separate piece of paper.

1. Write six sentences. Use one word from the box above in each sentence.
2. Can you think of other words that belong to the same family as *absolve* and *absolute*? With a partner, make a list of related words. Then look up the Latin root *solv* in your Spelling-Meaning Index. Add to your list any other related words that you find.

Summing Up

The Latin root *solv* means "to loosen" or "to free." Words that contain the same root are often related in spelling and meaning. Knowing some of the words in a family can help you to use and spell the others correctly.

What if one dinosaur had survived—not on land, but at the bottom of the sea? What would it look like?

from

"Up from the Deep"
by Ray Bradbury

Something was swimming toward the lighthouse tower.

It was a cold night, as I have said; the high tower was cold, the light coming and going and the foghorn calling and calling through the raveling mist. You couldn't see far and you couldn't see plain, but there was the deep sea moving on its way about the night earth, flat and quiet, the color of gray mud. Here were the two of us alone in the high tower, and there, far out at first, was a ripple, followed by a wave, a rising, a bubble, a bit of froth. Then, from the surface of the cold sea came a head, a large head, dark-colored, with immense eyes, and then a neck. And then—not a body, but more neck and more! The head rose a full forty feet above the water on a slender and beautiful dark neck. Only then did the body, like a little island of black coral and shells and crayfish, drip up from the subterranean. There was a flicker of tail. In all, from head to tip of tail, I estimated the monster at ninety or a hundred feet. . . .

It swam slowly and with a great dark majesty out in the icy waters, far away. The fog came and went about it, momentarily erasing its shape. One of the monster eyes caught and held and flashed back our immense light, red, white, red, white, like a disk, held high and sending a message in primeval code. It was as silent as the fog through which it swam.

Think and Discuss

1. What details does the author give to describe what the sea monster looked like?

2. What senses besides sight does the author appeal to? What words does he use to describe information taken in by these other senses?

The Writing Process
Description

Write a description of an interesting person, place, or thing. Choose details that help to plant a vivid image in your reader's mind. Use the guidelines, and follow the Writing Process.

1 Prewriting
- For topic ideas, list familiar people, places, and things. Select the one you would most enjoy writing about and could describe in the most detail.
- Make a cluster of sense words that you could use to describe your topic.

2 Draft
- Focus on your purpose, your audience, and the point of view you want to present about your subject.
- Include details as you write. Don't worry about errors now.

3 Revise
- Add sense words and figurative language to let your reader see, hear, smell, taste, or feel your subject.
- Change details that don't fit the purpose of your description.
- Replace vague terms with exact words.
- Have a writing conference.

4 Proofread
- Did you spell each word correctly?
- Did you use commas in a series and with interrupters correctly?

5 Publish
- Copy your description neatly. Add a suitable title.
- Share your description. Can your readers illustrate your subject?

Guidelines for Writing a Description

✓ Include details that suit your purpose and point of view.
✓ Use sense words, figurative language, and exact words to create a vivid picture.
✓ Choose a logical method of organizing your details.

Composition Words

harmonious
statue
cylinder
landscape
raspberry
adept
mammoth
beige

Absorbed Prefixes I

Read and Say

Basic

READ the sentences. **SAY** each bold word.

1. correspond — She and I **correspond** by mail.
2. arrangement — The **arrangement** of books was by subject.
3. illegible — The old map was torn and **illegible**.
4. assortment — Our store sells a wide **assortment** of goods.
5. irregular — An **irregular** heartbeat is not normal.
6. illiterate — He teaches **illiterate** adults to read.
7. attempt — My first **attempt** at cooking was a disaster.
8. accustomed — We sat in our **accustomed** places on the bus.
9. immature — The green berries are too **immature** to pick.
10. irresponsible — Their **irresponsible** acts caused much harm.
11. arrest — The police hope to **arrest** a suspect soon.
12. illogical — It is **illogical** to wear shorts in the snow.
13. irreparable — Is the crack in the vase **irreparable**?
14. immeasurable — The long distance seemed **immeasurable**.
15. irresistible — I must have more of that **irresistible** pie!
16. accompany — Will you **accompany** me to the dance?
17. immobilize — Casts **immobilize** bones so they can heal.
18. irreplaceable — The fire destroyed **irreplaceable** paintings.
19. assignment — Your **assignment** is to write a book report.
20. illegal — Mom was fined for parking in an **illegal** space.

Spelling Strategy   Remember that *ad-* ("to"), *in-* ("not; without"), and *con-* ("with; together") can be **absorbed prefixes** when their last letter changes to match the beginning consonant of the base word to which they are added.

Think and Write   Write each Basic Word under the heading that shows how its original prefix can be spelled when the prefix is absorbed.

ad- (ar-, as-, at-, ac-)   *in-* (il-, ir-, im-)   *con-* (cor-)

Review		**Challenge**	
21. account	23. approve	26. correlation	28. allocate
22. assure	24. immovable	27. attribute	29. immaterial
	25. immigrant		30. irrational

Independent Practice

Vocabulary: Replacing Words Write the Basic Word that means the same thing as the underlined word or words in each sentence. Use your Spelling Dictionary.

1. Barnes Museum has a wide <u>variety</u> of old manuscripts.
2. A library employee must <u>go along with</u> visitors to the rare book room.
3. Police hope to <u>apprehend</u> the thief who took the ancient book.
4. Ms. Rigby will make another <u>try</u> at translating the tablet's message.
5. The archaeologist studied the <u>order</u> of the strange letters.
6. Our class's <u>task</u> is to write reports about the history of various alphabets.
7. Professor Woo is <u>used to</u> reading ancient Chinese writing.
8. The scholars decided that their translation of the ancient writing was <u>not reasonable</u>.
9. Jeb plans to <u>communicate by letter</u> with a rare book dealer.
10. The damage to the manuscript was <u>not fixable</u>.
11. The destruction of the great library at Alexandria was a loss that was <u>beyond calculation</u>.
12. The writing on the clay tablet was <u>unreadable</u>.

Vocabulary: Definitions Write the Basic Word that matches each definition. Use your Spelling Dictionary.

13. to make incapable of moving
14. prohibited by law
15. not standard or usual
16. not fully grown or developed
17. unable to read and write
18. impossible to find a substitute for; unique
19. extremely tempting; impossible to hold out against
20. not dependable or accountable

Challenge Words Write the Challenge Word that fits each clue. Use your Spelling Dictionary.

21. This kind of fact is of no importance.
22. When you compare two facts, you might find this.
23. This kind of thought is beyond all reason.
24. You do this with money when you save for something special.
25. You do this by giving credit where credit is due.

Dictionary

Etymology Many dictionaries give the **etymology**, or origin and history, of an entry word. The etymology often appears after the definition and is usually enclosed in brackets.

The etymology of a word with a prefix or a suffix can often be found in the entry for the base word. For example, the etymology shown below for *legal*, the base word of *illegal*, also applies to *illegal*.

le·gal |lē´ gəl| *adj.* **1.** Authorized or set down by law: *the legal heir.* **2.** Permitted by law: *legal activities.* [Old French, from Latin *lēgālis*, from *lēx*, law.]

Practice Write the answer to each question. Use your Spelling Dictionary.

1. What language did the word *beige* most recently come from?
2. What Latin word did *primary* first come from?
3. What language did *illogical* originally come from?
4. What is the meaning of the Latin word that *corps* came from?
5. What is the meaning of the Latin word that *doubt* came from?

Review: Spelling Spree

Syllable Scramble Rearrange the syllables in each item to form a Basic or Review Word. Write the word correctly.

6. place ir ble re a
7. pa com ac ny
8. mi grant im
9. le gal il
10. a ra rep ble ir
11. ble si re spon ir
12. cus ac tomed
13. ble re i ir sist
14. ble mov im a
15. rest ar

16. ma im ture
17. prove ap
18. ment sign as
19. i il cal log
20. er ate il lit
21. bi im lize mo
22. u reg ir lar
23. ble i leg il
24. sure as
25. im ble meas a ur

Proofreading and Writing

Proofread for Spelling Find five misspelled Basic or Review Words in this paragraph. Write each word correctly.

English speakers are accustomed to an alphabetical writing system in which letters corespond to sounds, and an arangement of letters forms a word. Alphabetical systems acount for many of the world's writing systems. Some languages, however, have no alphabet. Chinese, for instance, uses characters to stand for ideas. The characters may be simple or compound. A compound character consists of an asortment of simple characters. For example, the compound character meaning "to bark" combines the simple characters for "mouth" and "dog." Chinese has about 50,000 characters in all. A person must know several thousand to even attemt to read a newspaper!

Write a Story What would we do without signs, newspapers, or books? Imagine that every written, typed, or printed word has suddenly disappeared. Write a story about something that might happen in such a situation. Try to use five spelling words.

Basic

1. correspond
2. arrangement
3. illegible
4. assortment
5. irregular
6. illiterate
7. attempt
8. accustomed
9. immature
10. irresponsible
11. arrest
12. illogical
13. irreparable
14. immeasurable
15. irresistible
16. accompany
17. immobilize
18. irreplaceable
19. assignment
20. illegal

Review

21. account
22. assure
23. approve
24. immovable
25. immigrant

Challenge

26. correlation
27. attribute
28. allocate
29. immaterial
30. irrational

Proofreading Marks

- ¶ Indent
- ∧ Add
- ∧ Add a comma
- “ ” Add quotation marks
- ⊙ Add a period
- Delete
- ≡ Capital letter
- / Small letter
- ∽ Reverse order

Expanding Vocabulary

Spelling Word Link

immature

Connotation Do *immature* and *youthful* mean the same thing? Their **denotations**, or dictionary meanings, are similar, but their **connotations** are very different. The connotation of a word is the feeling or attitude that people usually associate with it. A connotation is often either positive or negative.

POSITIVE: The boys' behavior was **youthful**.
NEGATIVE: The boys' behavior was **immature**.

Write each of the following pairs of words. Label each word *positive* or *negative* to describe its connotation.

1. irresponsible, carefree
2. unique, bizarre
3. detect, snoop
4. argument, debate

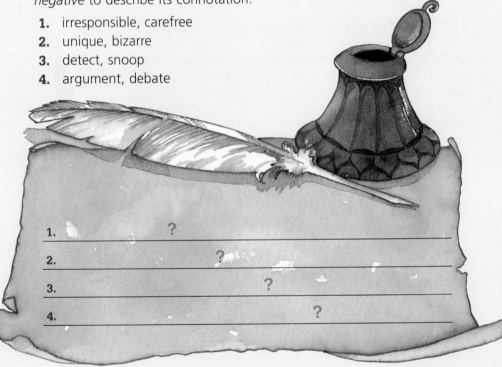

1. _____?_____
2. _____?_____
3. _____?_____
4. _____?_____

Now pick one of the word pairs from items 1–4. Write a sentence for each word in the pair.

5. _____?_____
_____?_____
6. _____?_____
_____?_____

Real-World Connection

Language Arts: History of Writing All the words in the box relate to the history of writing. Look up these words in your Spelling Dictionary. Then write the words to complete this paragraph.

> The earliest form of Egyptian writing was called __(1)__. Each character was a __(2)__, or picture symbol, that stood for a sound or an idea. At first, these symbols were carved in or written on stone. Later, the Egyptians developed a paperlike material called __(3)__. A person called a __(4)__ would write on a long __(5)__ made of this material, using a sharp instrument called a __(6)__, which was dipped in ink made of soot and water. Eventually, a flowing, __(7)__ style of writing was developed. Later, a phonetic alphabet replaced the ancient Egyptian writing, which was soon forgotten. About 1,500 years passed before anyone learned to __(8)__ its symbols.

Spelling Word Link

correspond

scribe
papyrus
stylus
scroll
hieroglyphics
decipher
pictograph
cursive

TRY THIS!

True or False? Write *T* if a sentence is true and *F* if it is false.

9. Cursive writing is another name for printing.
10. We learn to decipher writing when we learn to read.
11. Stylus is a type of paper.
12. A scribe was a person who made paper.

Fact File

In 1799 an odd stone was found in Rosetta, Egypt. On it was the same text carved in three languages: Greek, which was known to scholars, and two types of Egyptian writing. By comparing the languages, scholars were able to decipher the Egyptian hieroglyphics.

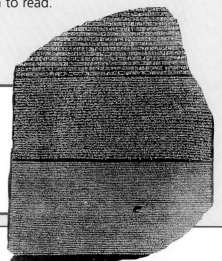

Latin Roots III

Read and Say

Basic

READ the sentences. **SAY** each bold word.

1. dictionary   Check the meaning of the word in a **dictionary**.
2. appendix   Find the **appendix** at the back of your book.
3. dependable   Is he **dependable** enough to care for the dog?
4. contradict   Mom says I must never **contradict** my teacher.
5. expense   Buying the tickets will be a big **expense**.
6. pendulum   Will a clock work if its **pendulum** is stuck?
7. prediction   The weather **prediction** called for snow.
8. suspense   I love the **suspense** of a good spy story.
9. compensation   What **compensation** will I receive for the job?
10. dictation   Always speak clearly when you give **dictation**.
11. suspend   Can we **suspend** the lamp from that hook?
12. diction   Actors need good **diction** to be understood.
13. dictator   The **dictator** ruled with an iron hand.
14. verdict   Has the jury reached a **verdict**?
15. impending   A dark sky is a sign of an **impending** storm.
16. dispense   Please **dispense** the food in equal servings.
17. predicament   Getting lost is a serious **predicament**.
18. pension   Will he receive a **pension** when he retires?
19. pendant   She wore a gold **pendant** around her neck.
20. penthouse   The hotel **penthouse** overlooks the city.

Spelling Strategy   Knowing the Latin roots *dict/dic* ("to say") and *pend/pens/pent* ("to hang; weigh") can help you spell and understand words with these roots.

Think and Write   Write each Basic Word under its root.

dict/dic   *pend/pens/pent*

Review
21. dedicate
22. edition
23. information
24. usage
25. determine

Challenge
26. pensive
27. indictment
28. jurisdiction
29. appendage
30. valedictorian

Independent Practice

Vocabulary: Analogies Write the Basic Word that completes each analogy. Use your Spelling Dictionary.

Example: vehicle : truck :: home : _____   *penthouse*

 1. work : labor :: payment : _____
 2. clothing : shirt :: jewelry : _____
 3. entertainer : actor :: ruler : _____
 4. tardy : prompt :: unreliable : _____
 5. maps : atlas :: words : _____
 6. support : oppose :: confirm : _____
 7. gain : profit :: cost : _____
 8. roll : wheel :: swing : _____
 9. grief : tragedy :: tension : _____
10. raise : elevate :: hang : _____
11. gather : collect :: distribute : _____
12. examination : diagnosis :: trial : _____

Vocabulary: Definitions Write the Basic Word that matches each definition. Use your Spelling Dictionary.

13. information that is said aloud so that another person can write or type it
14. a difficult or embarrassing situation
15. clarity of pronunciation
16. about to take place
17. the act of telling about an occurrence before it happens
18. an amount of money paid on a regular basis as a retirement benefit
19. a section at the end of a book containing additional information, such as tables and charts
20. an apartment that takes up the top floor of an apartment building

Challenge Words Write the Challenge Word that fits each clue. Use your Spelling Dictionary.

21. This might describe someone who is lost in thought.
22. This graduating student is tops in the class.
23. This can be an arm or a hand.
24. This accusation is serious.
25. This authority is completely legal.

Review: Spelling Spree

Puzzle Play Write the Basic Word that fits each clue. Circle the letter that would appear in the box.

Example: something that takes money _ _ ☐ _ _ _ _   ex(p)ense

1. part of a clock ☐ _ _ _ _ _ _ _
2. a look at what lies ahead _ ☐ _ _ _ _ _ _ _ _ _
3. a ruler whose word is law _ _ _ _ _ _ ☐ _
4. to give out _ _ _ _ _ ☐ _ _
5. a cause of tension _ ☐ _ _ _ _ _ _
6. the purpose of a paycheck _ _ _ _ _ _ _ _ _ _ _ _ ☐
7. to oppose an idea ☐ _ _ _ _ _ _ _ _ _
8. a jury's decision _ _ _ _ ☐ _ _
9. a sticky situation _ _ _ _ _ _ ☐ _ _ _ _
10. a characteristic of speech _ _ _ ☐ _ _ _
11. a retirement benefit _ _ _ _ ☐ _ _
12. an apartment that is tip-top _ _ _ _ _ ☐ _ _ _
13. words to be copied down _ _ _ _ _ _ _ _ ☐

Now write the circled letters in sequence. They will spell a mystery word that names a type of information found in a dictionary.

Mystery Word:

_ _ _ _ _ _ ? _ _ _ _ _ _

Invisible Letters Decide which letters should be added to complete each Basic or Review Word. Write the words correctly.

14. d _ _ e r _ i _ e
15. _ p _ e n _ _ x
16. e d _ t _ o _
17. s _ s p _ n _
18. _ e d _ _ a t e
19. p _ n d _ _ t
20. d _ _ e _ d a _ l e
21. u s _ _ e
22. d _ c t _ _ n _ r y
23. _ n f _ r m a _ _ o n
24. _ m p e _ d _ _ g
25. _ x _ e n _ e

How Are
You Doing?
List the spelling
words that are
difficult for you.
Practice them with
a partner.

Proofreading and Writing

Proofread: Spelling and Direct Quotations Use quotation marks and commas to set off a **direct quotation**—a speaker's exact words—from other words in a sentence. Place a comma before the opening quotation marks if the other words begin the sentence, and before the closing quotation marks if the quotation begins the sentence.

> Jamie said, "Mr. Salvatore edits dictionaries."
> "He works for a publishing company in Boston," she added.

Find five misspelled Basic or Review Words, one missing comma, and one error with quotation marks in this journal entry. Write the journal entry correctly.

Ahmad tried to contradik me today when I used the word _gobbledygook_. "There's no such word" he said. I pulled out my dependible dictionary to ditermine who was right. I was. "Maybe it is a word, but your ussage was wrong, insisted Ahmad. "It says here that _gobbledygook_ is a noun meaning unclear language," I said. For once, Ahmad had no infomation to add.

Write a Dictionary Entry Make up a word and create a complete dictionary entry for it. Include the phonetic respelling, the part of speech, at least one definition, and an example sentence to show how the word is used in context. Your example sentence should contain a direct quotation. Try to use five spelling words.

Basic

1. dictionary
2. appendix
3. dependable
4. contradict
5. expense
6. pendulum
7. prediction
8. suspense
9. compensation
10. dictation
11. suspend
12. diction
13. dictator
14. verdict
15. impending
16. dispense
17. predicament
18. pension
19. pendant
20. penthouse

Review

21. dedicate
22. edition
23. information
24. usage
25. determine

Challenge

26. pensive
27. indictment
28. jurisdiction
29. appendage
30. valedictorian

Proofreading Marks

¶ Indent
∧ Add
⅄ Add a comma
ᦐ ᦐ Add quotation marks
⊙ Add a period
⌇ Delete
≡ Capital letter
/ Small letter
∿ Reverse order

Expanding Vocabulary

**Spelling
Word Link**

dictionary

Context Clues If you come across an unfamiliar word in a list, the other words in the list might provide useful clues to its meaning. The words in a list can also help you determine the general meaning of a word that summarizes the list. Suppose you did not know the words *dictionary* and *compensation*. The lists in these sentences would provide context clues.

We used a dictionary, an **atlas**, and an **almanac**.

My compensation was **applause**, a **prize**, and an **A+**.

Use context clues to figure out the general meaning of each underlined word. Write your answers.

1. Should I use a comma, a hyphen, or a <u>virgule</u>?
2. <u>Components</u> of an entry include parts of speech, definitions, and origins.
3. I have French, Russian, and even <u>Estonian</u> dictionaries.
4. *Bologna*, *baloney*, and *boloney* are <u>variants</u> of the same word.

1.	?	3.	?
2.	?	4.	?

TEST-TAKING TACTICS

Analogies Being familiar with common types of relationships found in analogy test questions can help you complete the questions quickly and correctly. Some types of relationships to look for are *item* and *category*, *worker* and *workplace*, and *part* and *whole*. Study this sample analogy question.

INSTRUCTOR : SCHOOL ::

(A) chemist : laboratory   (B) handlebar : bicycle   (C) knife : cutlery

(D) sole : shoe   (E) biology : science

Now write the answers to these questions about the sample analogy.

5. What type of relationship exists between the stem words?
6. Which two answer choices can you eliminate because their relationship is that of *item* and *category*? Write their letters.
7. Which two answer choices can you eliminate because their relationship is that of *part* and *whole*? Write their letters.
8. Which answer choice correctly completes the analogy? Write its letter.

Real-World Connection

Language Arts: Dictionary All the words in the box relate to the dictionary. Look up these words in your Spelling Dictionary. Then write the words to complete this paragraph.

REFERENCE

A dictionary is a terrific word reference. An __(1)__ dictionary gives the meaning, or __(2)__, of nearly every word in the language. Dictionaries also provide other information about words. The phonetic respelling after an entry word shows how to pronounce the word. An accent mark tells which __(3)__ gets the greatest __(4)__. Some dictionaries include entries for __(5)__, or words used in casual speech. An __(6)__, which has a meaning different from the meanings of its individual words, may appear in the entry for one of its main words. Also often included in an entry is the history, or __(7)__, of the word, and sometimes a __(8)__, or word that has a similar meaning.

Spelling Word Link

dictionary

definition
stress
synonym
syllable
origin
slang
idiom
unabridged

TRY THIS!

Yes or No? Write *yes* or *no* to answer each question.

9. Is slang a formal way of speaking?
10. Are unabridged dictionaries shorter than other kinds?
11. Could a word's origin be Greek or Italian?
12. Does an idiom help you to pronounce a word?

Fact File

In 1828 Noah Webster published his *American Dictionary of the English Language*. This dictionary was the first to record American spellings, meanings, and pronunciations of English words, as well as words that originated in the United States.

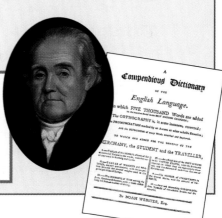

The Suffixes *-able* and *-ible*

Read and Say

Basic	READ the sentences. SAY each bold word.

1. *probable* — Speeding is the **probable** cause of the crash.
2. *reliable* — It takes a **reliable** person to care for a pet.
3. *available* — Is the new video game **available** yet?
4. *incredible* — His story about flying cows is **incredible**!
5. *desirable* — The most **desirable** seats are in the first row.
6. *divisible* — Is an odd number **divisible** by ten?
7. *flexible* — A **flexible** straw is better than a stiff one.
8. *knowledgeable* — Let a **knowledgeable** person explain the rules.
9. *miserable* — I felt **miserable** when my best friend moved.
10. *edible* — A carrot is an **edible** root.
11. *audible* — Her soft voice was barely **audible**.
12. *eligible* — Only students are **eligible** for the low price.
13. *memorable* — Our class trip was a **memorable** event.
14. *perishable* — Put the **perishable** food in the cooler.
15. *believable* — His excuse about a traffic jam is **believable**.
16. *durable* — Order a **durable** carpet for the hallway.
17. *permissible* — Is it **permissible** to chew gum in class?
18. *adjustable* — The **adjustable** belt fits all sizes.
19. *indestructible* — This **indestructible** plastic will last forever.
20. *acceptable* — Both written and typed reports are **acceptable**.

Spelling Strategy   Remember the spelling of the adjective suffixes *-able* and *-ible* ("able to be; worthy of; having").

Think and Write   Write each Basic Word under its suffix.

-able	*-ible*

Review		Challenge	
21. visible	23. changeable	26. negotiable	28. vulnerable
22. capable	24. impossible	27. plausible	29. compatible
	25. considerable		30. tangible

Independent Practice

Vocabulary: Question Clues Write the Basic Word that answers each question. Use your Spelling Dictionary.

1. What kind of object can be separated into parts or groups?
2. What kind of chair can be raised and lowered?
3. What kind of rug holds up well under years of heavy use?
4. What kind of products appeal to you when you are hungry?
5. What kind of thing is there if you want it?
6. What kind of object cannot be destroyed?
7. What kind of food is likely to spoil in a short time if it is not refrigerated?
8. What kind of object is one that everybody wants?
9. What kind of vibration is one you can hear?
10. What kind of explanation is a satisfactory one?
11. What kind of experience is one that you will keep in mind for a long time?
12. What kind of story tells about something amazing?

Vocabulary: Antonyms Write the Basic Word that is an antonym for each word below. Use your Spelling Dictionary.

13. unlikely
14. happy
15. undependable
16. unqualified
17. rigid
18. uninformed
19. forbidden
20. doubtful

Challenge Words Write the Challenge Word that matches each definition. Use your Spelling Dictionary.

21. appearing to be true or reasonable; possible
22. capable of being touched; real
23. capable of being harmed; open to danger or attack; unprotected
24. capable of being discussed in order to come to terms or reach an agreement
25. able to live or perform in harmony with another

Review: Spelling Spree

Code Breaker The Basic and Review Words below have been written in code. Use the following code key to figure out each word. Write the decoded words correctly.

CODE:	K	M	W	R	N	O	Z	L	P	D	Y	F	B	S	C	G	J	E	Q	H	T	A	X	U	V	I
LETTER:	a	b	c	d	e	f	g	h	i	j	k	l	m	n	o	p	q	r	s	t	u	v	w	x	y	z

Example: KRDTQHKMFN *adjustable*

1. KAKPFKMFN
2. RTEKMFN
3. GECMKMFN
4. PSRNQHETWHPMFN
5. PBGCQQPMFN
6. NRPMFN
7. RPAPQPMFN
8. BNBCEKMFN
9. NFPZPMFN
10. KTRPMFN
11. APQPMFN
12. GNEBPQQPMFN
13. PSWENRPMFN
14. WKGKMFN

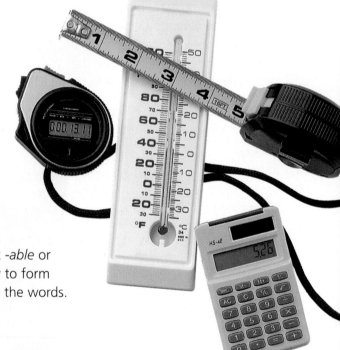

Word Forms Add the suffix *-able* or *-ible* to each base word below to form a Basic or Review Word. Write the words.

15. believe
16. misery
17. rely
18. desire
19. knowledge
20. consider
21. adjust
22. flex
23. perish
24. accept
25. change

✓ **How Are You Doing?**
Write each spelling word as a partner reads it aloud. Did you misspell any words?

Proofreading and Writing

Proofread: Spelling and Titles Capitalize the first word and all important words in a title. Underline the titles of long works, such as books, newspapers, and magazines. Enclose the titles of short works, such as poems, articles, and short stories, in quotation marks.

<u>To Kill a Mockingbird</u> *(book)*   "The Bear" *(short story)*

<u>The Wizard of Oz</u> *(movie)*   "On Silent Wings" *(article)*

Find five misspelled Basic and Review Words and two incorrectly written titles in this excerpt from a report. Write the report correctly.

According to an article entitled "A Race to the finish,"

a poll conducted by the "Daily Times" showed Ann

Goss leading Jon Wolk 52% to 47% in the race for

mayor. When asked how capabel they felt each

candidate was, 8% of those polled said that both are

knowledgable and that it is probable that either could

do a good job. While 38% find Wolk's vow not to

raise taxes belevable, 60% find it incredable and

think he should be more flexable. This

promises to be a memorable election.

Write a Statistical Report Write a statistical report about yourself. Your report might answer questions such as these: What is your age in days or minutes? How many miles do you walk in a week? How many hours of television have you watched? Include a report title, and check that it is written correctly. Try to use five spelling words.

Basic

1. probable
2. reliable
3. available
4. incredible
5. desirable
6. divisible
7. flexible
8. knowledgeable
9. miserable
10. edible
11. audible
12. eligible
13. memorable
14. perishable
15. believable
16. durable
17. permissible
18. adjustable
19. indestructible
20. acceptable

Review

21. visible
22. capable
23. changeable
24. impossible
25. considerable

Challenge

26. negotiable
27. plausible
28. vulnerable
29. compatible
30. tangible

Proofreading Marks

¶ Indent
∧ Add
⋏ Add a comma
Ꝟ Ꝟ Add quotation marks
⊙ Add a period
⌐ Delete
≡ Capital letter
/ Small letter
∩ Reverse order

Unit 27
BONUS

Expanding Vocabulary

Spelling Word Link

probable

Synonyms You know that synonyms are words with the same or nearly the same meaning.

probable = likely   incredible = unbelievable

Write the word in parentheses that is a synonym for the key word. Use your Thesaurus.

1. permissible (allowable, required)
2. durable (hard, sturdy)
3. acceptable (valuable, satisfactory)
4. miserable (unhappy, annoyed)

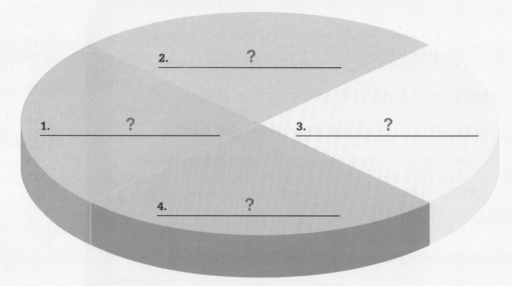

Now review the Thesaurus entries for the key words *permissible*, *durable*, *acceptable*, and *miserable*. Then read the following survey results. In each item, find a synonym of one of the key words. Write the synonym and the key word.

5. Sixty-one percent of the workers surveyed were able to buy indestructible goods during the past year.
6. Forty-six percent of those surveyed were discontented because they felt that their wages were too low.
7. Fifty-four percent of respondents believed that their current incomes were sufficient.
8. Eighty-seven percent of the people surveyed felt that it is legitimate to protest unfairly low wages.

Real-World Connection

Math: Statistics All the words in the box relate to statistics. Look up these words in your Spelling Dictionary. Then write the words to complete this paragraph.

Spelling Word Link

probable

frequency
distribution
mean
median
mode
range
tabulate
interpret

Mr. Huy's math class did two experiments. First the students tossed a coin 100 times. One person was assigned to __(1)__ , or count and arrange, the results. The coin turned up heads 51 times and tails 49 times. When asked to __(2)__ those results, the student decided that a coin will land on each side with equal __(3)__ . Next, the class conducted a survey of the ages of the students. The average age, or arithmetic __(4)__ , was 12.3 years. The middle, or __(5)__ , age was 12.2 years. Because 12.4 years came up most often, it was found to be the __(6)__ . The __(7)__ of ages went from 11.9 to 12.8 years. The __(8)__ of birthdays showed that more students had been born in the summer than in the winter.

TRY THIS!

Yes or No? Write *yes* if the underlined word is used correctly. Write *no* if it is not.

9. The <u>median</u> age of my 4- and 8-year-old brothers is 6.
10. The store wanted to <u>tabulate</u> customers for a poll.
11. Ms. Dey helped us understand and <u>interpret</u> the data.
12. Ken used a <u>mode</u> to add up the results of the survey.

Fact File

Most governments conduct a regular census, or count, of their populations. The United States conducts a census every five or ten years. The data gathered include the age, education, occupation, income, race, and sex of each person.

Words from Places

Read and Say

Basic	READ the sentences. SAY each bold word.
1. Cheddar	Do you like mild or sharp **Cheddar** on crackers?
2. cantaloupe	A sweet **cantaloupe** is my favorite melon.
3. tangerine	A **tangerine** is easier to peel than an orange.
4. mayonnaise	Spread **mayonnaise** on each slice of bread.
5. sardine	A **sardine** is a small but tasty fish.
6. scallion	The **scallion** has a mild taste for an onion.
7. currant	A **currant** can be a black or a red berry.
8. copper	Some fine cooking pots are made of **copper**.
9. attic	Can you help haul the trunks up to the **attic**?
10. magnet	What metals can a **magnet** attract?
11. seltzer	She prefers bubbly **seltzer** to plain water.
12. bologna	I like sandwiches made with ham or **bologna**.
13. frankfurter	I'll have a **frankfurter** on a bun for lunch.
14. pheasant	A colorful **pheasant** flew across the field.
15. badminton	Set up the net for a game of **badminton**.
16. limerick	Your funny poem is too long to be a **limerick**.
17. cologne	This bottle of **cologne** smells like roses.
18. bronze	The medal for third place is made of **bronze**.
19. mall	The **mall** is a good place to shop and walk.
20. spruce	The needles of the **spruce** are green all year.

Spelling Strategy   Knowing the origin of words that come from the names of places can help you spell and understand the meanings of the words.

Think and Write   Write the Basic Words.

Review		Challenge	
21. preparation	23. disease	26. Parmesan	28. meander
22. product	24. storage	27. stoic	29. labyrinth
	25. exercise		30. tarantula

Independent Practice

Vocabulary: Word Clues Write the Basic Word that fits each clue. Use your Spelling Dictionary.

1. This long, red sausage is often eaten in a roll at a baseball game.
2. This young vegetable has long green leaves and a white bulb.
3. This dressing most often makes its appearance in salads and sandwiches.
4. This is one of the smallest fruits you can find.
5. This metal can take the heat.
6. This short poem is good for a laugh.
7. This might contain shops, restaurants, and movie theaters.
8. This sausage is usually sliced and used in sandwiches.
9. This melon has a rough, dull skin but a sweet-smelling, orange heart.
10. This cheese, born in an English village, later traveled around the world.
11. This can hold your grocery list to the refrigerator door.
12. This metal is made up of a mixture of other metals.

Vocabulary: Classifying Write the Basic Word that fits each group. Use your Spelling Dictionary.

13. salmon, tuna, trout, _____
14. milk, water, juice, _____
15. grapefruit, orange, lemon, _____
16. tennis, volleyball, Ping-Pong, _____
17. pine, fir, redwood, _____
18. turkey, duck, quail, _____
19. basement, den, bedroom, _____
20. perfume, after-shave, lotion, _____

Challenge Words Write the Challenge Word that completes each analogy. Use your Spelling Dictionary.

21. riddle : puzzle :: maze : _____
22. violent : peaceful :: emotional : _____
23. bird : eagle :: spider : _____
24. stay : remain :: wander : _____
25. pasta : spaghetti :: cheese : _____

Dictionary

Variations in Spelling and Pronunciation If there is more than one acceptable way to spell or pronounce a word, the dictionary entry for the word will show the variations.

bo·lo·gna, also **ba·lo·ney** |bə lō´ nē| *or* |-nə| *or* |-nyə|

Although each spelling and pronunciation shown is acceptable, the one listed first is usually the preferred or most common one.

Practice Write the other acceptable spelling for each word below. Underline the syllable that is spelled differently. Use your Spelling Dictionary.

1. cantaloupe   **2.** encyclopedia   **3.** judgment   **4.** adviser

1. _____?_____   3. _____?_____

2. _____?_____   4. _____?_____

Write the number of acceptable pronunciations for each word below. Use your Spelling Dictionary.

5. burro   **7.** advertisement   **9.** attitude   **11.** data
6. plaza   **8.** chocolate   **10.** salve   **12.** licorice

5. __?__   8. __?__   11. __?__

6. __?__   9. __?__   12. __?__

7. __?__   10. __?__

Review: Spelling Spree

Letter Math Add and subtract letters from the words below to make Basic or Review Words. Write the new words.

Example: store – e + age = *storage*

13. malt – t + l =
14. spray – ay + truce – tr =
15. tsar – t + diner – r =
16. rascal – ra + lion =
17. ph + easy – y + ant =
18. occur – oc + grant – g =
19. lime + trick – t =
20. bad + mine – e + ton =
21. brown – w + haze – ha =

22. scant – s + aloud – d + pe =
23. rat – r + antic – an =
24. magic – ic + n + wet – w =
25. mayor – r + nn + raise – r =
26. proof – of + conduct – con =
27. crop – r + perk – k =
28. t + anger + mine – m =
29. co + logic – ic + ne =
30. dis + please – pl =

Proofreading and Writing

Proofread for Spelling Find seven misspelled Basic or Review Words in this advertisement for a book. Write each word correctly.

Why are Chedder and other hard cheeses better for you than soft cheeses? Why is turkey a healthier sandwich meat than balogna or a frankferter? Why is seltser a healthy beverage choice? Which food preperation methods destroy valuable nutrients? Is freezing the safest food storege method? These questions and many others are answered in <u>Eat for Fitness</u>, the new book by Amanda Roy, author of the best-selling <u>Exerxize for Fitness</u>.

On sale now at Bookworm's at the Village Mall.

EAT *for* FITNESS

by Amanda Roy

Basic

1. Cheddar
2. cantaloupe
3. tangerine
4. mayonnaise
5. sardine
6. scallion
7. currant
8. copper
9. attic
10. magnet
11. seltzer
12. bologna
13. frankfurter
14. pheasant
15. badminton
16. limerick
17. cologne
18. bronze
19. mall
20. spruce

Review

21. preparation
22. product
23. disease
24. storage
25. exercise

Challenge

26. Parmesan
27. stoic
28. meander
29. labyrinth
30. tarantula

Proofreading Marks

¶ Indent
∧ Add
⅄ Add a comma
Ꙫ Ꙫ Add quotation marks
⊙ Add a period
⌐ Delete
≡ Capital letter
/ Small letter
∩ Reverse order

Write a Menu Your school's clubs are putting on a festival to raise money for their projects. You will work in a food stand. Write a menu for the food stand. Give each menu item an appealing name, and include a descriptive sentence about each item. Try to use five spelling words.

Unit 28 BONUS

Expanding Vocabulary

Spelling Word Link

seltzer

Regional Differences Do the people where you live drink seltzer, soda water, or mineral water? Although the three names refer to the same thing, each comes from a different dialect. A **dialect** is the form of a language spoken in a particular region. The English language has many dialects.

From each list, write the word or words that are commonly used where you live.

1. peanut, goober, ground pea
2. soda, pop, tonic, soft drink
3. flannel cakes, griddle cakes, flapjacks, pancakes
4. firebug, firefly, glowworm, lightning bug
5. green beans, snap beans, string beans
6. faucet, spigot, tap

1. ____?____

4. ____?____

2. ____?____

5. ____?____

3. ____?____

6. ____?____

Now write a conversation between two people from different regions of the country. Each person uses and has to explain one regional term from items 1–6 that the other person does not understand.

____?____

____?____

____?____

____?____

____?____

Real-World Connection

Health: Nutrition All the words in the box relate to nutrition. Look up these words in your Spelling Dictionary. Then write the words to complete this paragraph.

Spelling Word Link

cantaloupe

nutrition
carbohydrate
protein
cholesterol
vitamin
mineral
dehydration
calorie

Good __(1)__ requires a balance of many nutrients, all performing important functions. Every __(2)__, from A to K, helps regulate a body process, and each __(3)__, such as iron or calcium, is needed for tissue growth. Several nutrients provide the body with energy. The amount of energy is measured in a unit of heat called a __(4)__. A __(5)__, such as starch or sugar, is a high-energy nutrient. The others are __(6)__, which helps to build and repair body tissues, and fats. Many fats contain __(7)__, however, which can build up in the arteries and cause heart disease. The most important dietary element is water because it carries the nutrients through the body. Lack of water, called __(8)__, can be a serious health problem.

TRY THIS!

True or False? Write *T* if the sentence is true and *F* if it is false.
9. Starch is a type of carbohydrate.
10. Too much water causes dehydration.
11. A calorie is used to measure weight.
12. Nutrition is the study of foods people eat and need.

Fact File

In the early 1900s, many food processing plants were unsanitary, and their products often contained harmful chemicals. In 1927 the Food and Drug Administration (FDA) was created to ensure that foods were processed safely.

Single or Double Consonants

Read and Say

Basic

READ the sentences. SAY each bold word.

1. *blizzard* — The **blizzard** brought three feet of snow.
2. *hurricane* — The flooding from the **hurricane** was terrible.
3. *satellite* — How long will the **satellite** stay in orbit?
4. *bulletin* — A news **bulletin** interrupted my favorite show.
5. *cancellation* — Heavy snow forced the **cancellation** of school.
6. *possibility* — Be prepared for the **possibility** of rain.
7. *forbidding* — Dark woods seem **forbidding** at night.
8. *allotted* — Each worker was **allotted** ten shares of stock.
9. *misspell* — How could I **misspell** such an easy word?
10. *credited* — I was **credited** with finding the missing cat.
11. *professor* — Isn't that college **professor** a famous poet?
12. *exaggerate* — Did he **exaggerate** the tale to make it scarier?
13. *medallion* — She won that gold **medallion** for bravery.
14. *villain* — Who saved the princess from the evil **villain**?
15. *gossiping* — Harmful rumors can spread through **gossiping**.
16. *challenge* — Climbing a mountain is an awesome **challenge**.
17. *equipped* — Are you **equipped** for camping in cold weather?
18. *necessary* — Plenty of sleep is **necessary** for good health.
19. *abbreviate* — We **abbreviate** words to save time and space.
20. *dissimilar* — A rabbit and a turtle are very **dissimilar**.

Spelling Strategy   Remember that double consonants can occur before the ending *-ed* or *-ing* and usually occur when a prefix ends with the same letter that begins the base word or root or is absorbed. Double consonants in other words must be remembered.

Think and Write   Write the Basic Words.

Review	23. tennis
21. permitting	24. appoint
22. channel	25. modeling

Challenge	28. remittance
26. pavilion	29. penicillin
27. miscellaneous	30. battalion

Independent Practice

Vocabulary: Question Clues Write the Basic Word that answers each question. Use your Spelling Dictionary.

1. Who usually opposes the hero in a movie?
2. What do people do when they tell tall tales?
3. What does a difficult task present?
4. What is often round or oval and might be worn around the neck?
5. What keeps a planned activity from taking place?
6. Who is the center of attention in a university lecture?
7. What are you if you have everything you need for a camping trip you are planning?
8. What might you do less often by using a dictionary more often?
9. What kind of things are unlike one another?
10. What could you do to shorten *road*, *pound*, or *post office*?
11. What did you do if you distributed something among several people?
12. What are you doing if you are spreading rumors?
13. What did you do if you gave someone recognition for good work?

Vocabulary: Using Context Write the Basic Word that completes each sentence. Use your Spelling Dictionary.

14. The _____ left a thick blanket of snow over the village.
15. The sky filled with dark, _____ storm clouds.
16. The _____ pictures showed clear skies over most of the state.
17. The tree was blown over by the winds of the _____.
18. Weather reports indicate a _____ of rain today.
19. The television program was interrupted by a weather _____ warning of an approaching storm.
20. Snow tires are _____ on these icy roads.

Challenge Words Write the Challenge Word that completes each analogy. Use your Spelling Dictionary.

21. house : mansion :: tent : _____
22. disease : pneumonia :: medication : _____
23. donation : contribution :: payment : _____
24. unique : exceptional :: various : _____
25. book : library :: soldier : _____

Review: Spelling Spree

Word Forms Add each base word and word part to write a Basic or Review Word.

1. equip + ed
2. permit + ing
3. credit + ed
4. dis + similar
5. forbid + ing
6. model + ing
7. allot + ed
8. gossip + ing
9. mis + spell

Word Cloud 10–25. Find the Basic and Review Words that are hidden in the storm cloud. Write the words correctly in the order in which you find them.

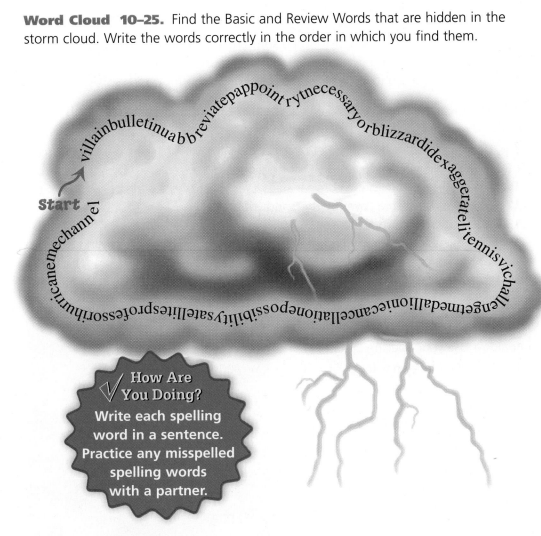

Start

villainbulletinuabbreviatepappointrytnecessaryorblizzardidexaggerateli tennisvichall engetmedallionecancellationepossibilitysatelliteprofessorihuricanememechannel

How Are You Doing?
Write each spelling word in a sentence. Practice any misspelled spelling words with a partner.

Proofreading and Writing

Proofread: Spelling, Subject and Object Pronouns Use a **subject pronoun** as the subject of a sentence or, after a linking verb, as a predicate pronoun. Use an **object pronoun** as a direct or an indirect object.

SUBJECT:	**He** forecasted a snowstorm.
PREDICATE PRONOUN:	A great weather forecaster is **he**.
DIRECT OBJECT:	The heavy downpour surprised **him**.
INDIRECT OBJECT:	The thunderstorm gave **him** a fright.

Find five misspelled Basic or Review Words and one incorrect pronoun in this television weather report. Write the report correctly.

Special Weather Buletin

Huricane Ben is moving our way. Satelite photos show the storm passing Bear Island. Although there is a posibility that it will move out to sea, officials are asking people not to travel. The people in most danger are them who live along the coast. Dover Airport has announced the cancelation of all flights.

Basic
1. blizzard
2. hurricane
3. satellite
4. bulletin
5. cancellation
6. possibility
7. forbidding
8. allotted
9. misspell
10. credited
11. professor
12. exaggerate
13. medallion
14. villain
15. gossiping
16. challenge
17. equipped
18. necessary
19. abbreviate
20. dissimilar

Review
21. permitting
22. channel
23. tennis
24. appoint
25. modeling

Challenge
26. pavilion
27. miscellaneous
28. remittance
29. penicillin
30. battalion

Write a Personal Narrative Has severe weather ever put you in an unusual situation? Have you been stranded in a blizzard, or blasted by a hurricane? Was it exciting or frightening? Write a personal narrative about your experience. Try to use five spelling words and at least one subject or object pronoun.

Proofreading Marks
¶   Indent
∧   Add
⋏   Add a comma
ᵛᵛ ᵛᵛ   Add quotation marks
⊙   Add a period
⌐   Delete
≡   Capital letter
/   Small letter
∿   Reverse order

Expanding Vocabulary

Spelling Word Link

credited

The Latin Root _cred_ The root _cred_ means "to believe" or "to trust." When a purchase is _credited_ to a person's account, the seller is trusting the buyer to pay the debt. Other English words also contain the root _cred_.

credentials   credibility   discredit   incredible

Write the word from the list above that completes each sentence. Use your Spelling Dictionary.

1. Jason lost his _____ after telling too many tall tales.
2. The political candidate tried to _____ her opponent.
3. Mia showed her press _____ at the gate.
4. The boys told a truly _____ story about a lake monster.

1. _____ ?   3. _____ ?

2. _____ ?   4. _____ ?

··

TEST-TAKING TACTICS

Sentence Completion When trying to answer a sentence completion question, always look for signal words in the incomplete sentence. Signal words help you understand the meaning of the sentence and provide useful clues to the missing word. Words such as _although_, _despite_, _but_, and _however_ indicate a contrast between elements within the sentence. Look at this example.

Sophie looked _____, despite the joyous occasion.

(A) magnificent   (B) surprised   (C) jolly

(D) gloomy   (E) childish

The word _despite_ signals that one sentence element is being contrasted with another. Since the missing word must be an adjective that describes Sophie, look for an adjective in the second part of the sentence. Then find the answer choice that contrasts with the given adjective.

5. What is the adjective in the second part of the sentence?
6. Which answer choice contrasts with the given adjective? Write its letter.

Real-World Connection

Science: Meteorology All the words in the box relate to meteorology. Look up these words in your Spelling Dictionary. Then write the words to complete this paragraph.

The science of __(1)__ focuses on the conditions of the __(2)__ , and is most visible in the form of the daily weather __(3)__ . Accurate predictions help us prepare for storms ranging from a minor __(4)__ to a major blizzard. Predictions of __(5)__ tell farmers when to harvest and how much to irrigate. Other predictable weather factors include __(6)__ , or dampness in the air, and air temperature. Temperature is measured on two scales. On the __(7)__ scale, water freezes at 32 degrees, while on the __(8)__ scale, water freezes at 0 degrees.

Spelling Word Link

satellite

meteorology
atmosphere
forecast
precipitation
humidity
squall
Fahrenheit
centigrade

TRY THIS!

Yes or No? Write *yes* if the underlined word is used correctly. Write *no* if it is not.

9. They expected <u>precipitation</u> in the form of snow.
10. After the calm of the <u>squall</u>, it began to rain.
11. Everything remained damp because of the high <u>humidity</u>.
12. Future weather forecasters must study <u>meteorology</u>.

Fact File

Have you ever awoken after a clear night to see dew shining on the grass? Dew forms when the night air cools, and the moisture in it begins to condense, or turn to liquid. The temperature at which this condensation begins is called the dew point. The dew point varies depending upon the amount of humidity in the air.

30 Review: Units 25–29

| Unit 25 | Absorbed Prefixes I | pages 156–161 |

correspond	assortment	illiterate	accustomed	immature
irreplaceable	accompany	assignment	immeasurable	irresistible

💡 **Spelling Strategy**   Remember that *ad-* ("to"), *in-* ("not; without"), and *con-* ("with; together") can be **absorbed prefixes** when their last letter changes to match the beginning consonant of the base word to which they are added.

Write the word that completes each analogy.

1. fragile : brittle :: usual : _____
2. hungry : starving :: tempting : _____
3. near : distant :: limited : _____
4. train : travel :: letter : _____

Write the word that fits each clue.

5. a task
6. unique
7. just starting out
8. having trouble with written words
9. to join someone
10. a collection of things

| Unit 26 | Latin Roots III | pages 162–167 |

dictionary	dependable	prediction	suspense	dictation
suspend	verdict	predicament	dispense	penthouse

💡 **Spelling Strategy**   Knowing the Latin roots *dict/dic* ("to say") and *pend/pens/pent* ("to hang; weigh") can help you spell and understand words with these roots.

Write the word associated with each of the following words.

11. secretary
12. apartment
13. guilty
14. mystery
15. meteorologist

Write the word that completes each sentence.

16. Mrs. Valdez will _____ vitamins to her children each morning.
17. Brian and Jim tried to _____ the hammock between two trees.
18. Julia bought a car that was _____ in all kinds of weather.
19. Terence looked up the word in the _____.
20. After a week, they found a way out of their terrible _____.

Unit 27 The Suffixes -able and -ible pages 168–173

probable	incredible	flexible	knowledgeable	miserable
memorable	perishable	durable	indestructible	acceptable

Spelling Strategy Remember the spelling of the adjective suffixes -able and -ible ("able to be; worthy of; having").

Write the word that is a synonym for each of the following words.

21. adaptable
22. informed
23. sturdy
24. unforgettable
25. unbelievable
26. unhappy

Write the word that completes each sentence.

27. Since Gary is trying hard, it is _____ that he will do well.
28. With its _____ cargo of fruit, the ship sailed as quickly as possible to its destination.
29. Ms. Smart said that messy papers were not _____.
30. No matter how well it is built, no building is _____.

Unit 28 Words from Places pages 174–179

Cheddar	magnet	sardine	attic	cantaloupe
pheasant	spruce	cologne	bronze	badminton

Spelling Strategy Knowing the origin of words that come from the names of places can help you spell and understand the meanings of the words.

Write the word that belongs in each group.

31. cod, minnow, catfish, _____
32. gold, iron, silver, _____
33. apple, grape, pear, _____
34. soccer, polo, tennis, _____
35. duck, chicken, goose, _____
36. cellar, stair, hall, _____

Write the word that completes each sentence.

37. Amelia ate a delicious sandwich of _____ cheese.
38. We went to the nursery to buy some shrubs and a _____.
39. The strong scent of the _____ that had spilled drifted out of the bathroom.
40. Dirk used a _____ to quickly pick up all the pins he'd dropped.

Unit 29   Single or Double Consonants   pages 180–185

blizzard	satellite	bulletin	possibility	hurricane
villain	medallion	necessary	abbreviate	professor

 Spelling Strategy   Remember that double consonants can occur before the ending *-ed* or *-ing* and usually occur when a prefix ends with the same letter that begins the base word or root or is absorbed. Double consonants in other words must be remembered.

Write the words that complete the paragraph.

A weather _(41)_ warning of heavy snow and high winds was aired repeatedly this morning. Pictures taken from a weather _(42)_ showed the _(43)_ moving our way. There is a _(44)_ that the storm will head out to sea, but authorities are preparing for the worst.

Write the word that fits each clue.

45. not extra

46. a wind storm

47. something decorative

48. to shorten

49. a knowledgeable person

50. someone with bad intentions

Challenge Words   Units 25–29   pages 156–185

allocate	irrational	pensive	jurisdiction	plausible
pavilion	labyrinth	meander	vulnerable	battalion

Write the words that complete the paragraph.

During the Middle Ages, much of Europe was _(51)_ to attack by the swift sailing ships of the Vikings. In many countries, the Vikings did terrible damage to towns and villages. Lawless and beyond the _(52)_ of any government, these raiders terrorized Europe for three centuries.

Write the word that matches each definition.

53. a maze

54. to wander

55. a fancy tent

56. seemingly reasonable

57. unable to think clearly

58. to set aside

59. a large body of troops

60. deeply thoughtful

Spelling-Meaning Strategy

The Latin Root *mem*

Someone or something that is memorable is unforgettable or easy to remember. One way to help people remember an exceptional person or event is to establish a memorial, which serves as a reminder. The words *memorable*, *remember*, and *memorial* are all related in spelling and meaning. Each comes from the Latin word *memor*, meaning "mindful."

Below are some additional words containing the root *mem*.

memorable
remember
memorial

memory	com**mem**orate	**mem**oir
memorandum	**mem**orabilia	im**mem**orial

Think

- How does the root *mem* contribute to the meaning of each word? Look up the words in your Spelling Dictionary.
- In Unit 25, you learned that an absorbed prefix is one that changes spelling so that its last letter matches the first consonant of the base word to which it is added. Which of the words in the box above contain absorbed prefixes?

Apply and Extend

Complete these activities on a separate piece of paper.

1. Write a short paragraph about a memorable person, place, or event. In your paragraph, use as many of the six words from the box above as you can.
2. Can you think of other words that belong to the same family as *memorable*, *remember*, and *memorial*? Work with a partner to make a list of related words. Then look up the Latin root *mem* in your Spelling-Meaning Index. Add to your list any other related words that you find.

Summing Up

The Latin root *mem* means "mindful." Words that contain the same root are often related in spelling and meaning. Knowing some of the words in a family can help you to use and spell the others correctly.

Persuasive Letter

Dear Mr. Otero:

Along with others at our school, I believe we should have a soccer team. Soccer is an exciting game. In "The History of Soccer," the sportswriter and soccer referee Ross R. Olney says, "In no other game is every player so important, and in no other game does every player get to control the ball so often."

Soccer is now very popular in this country. Mr. Olney states that by 1977 "soccer had become the 'in' sport," and "more and more high school and college teams were being formed." The other middle school in our county has a team, and so does the high school. The games attract a lot of students and some parents.

Most important of all, our school wants a team. I drew up a petition asking for a team and got a hundred students' signatures in three days. Fifteen teachers also signed. The petition is enclosed. Thirty students have checked the column, "Want to try out for team." Mr. Cargill, the physical education teacher, has even agreed to coach. The team is almost ready to go!

We hope that you and the school board will support our request for a soccer team that, in Mr. Olney's words, will have "parents and friends cheering from the grandstands and touchlines."

Sincerely,

Teresa Kelly

Think and Discuss

1. Do you think the letter is persuasive? Why or why not?
2. What reasons does the writer give to support her opinion?
3. What objections might the principal raise? Has the writer answered them? If so, how?

The Writing Process
Persuasive Letter

What opinion would you like to persuade another person to share? Write a persuasive letter to that person. Use the Guidelines for Persuading, and follow the Writing Process.

1 ▶ Prewriting
- For topic ideas, ask yourself questions like these: What does my community need? What would I like to save? What isn't fair?
- After choosing a subject, list the reasons why you feel the way you do about it. Decide which reasons will be important to your audience.

2 ▶ Draft
- Write a draft of your letter. Correct any errors later.
- Express your opinion clearly in a topic sentence. Support it with reasons, and back up your reasons with examples. Answer any possible objections your reader might have.

3 ▶ Revise
- Strengthen your reasons and add more examples, if necessary.
- Arrange your topic sentence, reasons, examples, and answers to objections in a sensible order.
- Have a writing conference. Did you succeed in convincing your listener?

4 ▶ Proofread
- Did you spell each word correctly?
- Did you use capital letters, punctuation marks, and pronouns correctly?

5 ▶ Publish
- Copy your letter neatly, using the letter form on page 256.
- Address an envelope and mail your letter.

Guidelines for Persuading

✓ State your opinion on the issue.

✓ Support your opinion with strong reasons and factual examples. Answer objections.

✓ End by restating your opinion and making a final appeal.

Composition Words

contradict
reliable
necessary
attempt
expense
challenge
available
equipped

Absorbed Prefixes II

Read and Say

Basic	READ the sentences. SAY each bold word.

1. *application* — Her **application** for college was accepted.
2. *appropriate* — Jeans are not **appropriate** at most weddings.
3. *arrival* — Do you know the **arrival** time of his plane?
4. *attitude* — A cheerful **attitude** makes life more pleasant.
5. *opportunity* — This is your **opportunity** to learn to spell.
6. *commute* — Does she **commute** to work by bus?
7. *accusation* — Is the **accusation** that he cheated true?
8. *irritate* — Poison ivy will **irritate** your skin.
9. *allergy* — Sometimes my **allergy** makes me sneeze.
10. *corrupt* — The **corrupt** officials stole our tax money.
11. *approximate* — Try an **approximate** answer if you are unsure.
12. *appetite* — Stomach flu kills your **appetite** for food.
13. *attach* — You can **attach** the boards with nails.
14. *attire* — Is the proper **attire** a suit and tie?
15. *opponent* — My **opponent** played well against me.
16. *commercial* — The **commercial** district has many shops.
17. *attain* — She hopes to **attain** her goal in the end.
18. *irrigate* — Long pipes are used to **irrigate** the fields.
19. *alliance* — Our countries have joined in an **alliance**.
20. *corrode* — Some metals become rusty when they **corrode**.

Spelling Strategy Knowing that the prefixes *ad-*, *in-*, *con-*, and *ob-* ("to or against") can be absorbed when added to word roots will help you remember to double the root's beginning consonant when one of these prefixes has been added.

Think and Write Write each Basic Word under the heading that shows how its original prefix can be spelled when the prefix is absorbed.

ad- (ap-, ar-, at-, ac-, al-)   *in- (ir-)*   *con- (com-, cor-)*   *ob- (op-)*

Review		Challenge	
	23. accurate		28. accomplice
21. appreciate	24. attract	26. accentuate	29. apparatus
22. comment	25. community	27. alleviate	30. apprehensive

Independent Practice

Vocabulary: Definitions Write the Basic Word that fits each definition. Use your Spelling Dictionary.

1. a request, as for a job or admittance to a school
2. a time or an occasion that is suitable for a certain purpose
3. clothing; the dress typically worn for a particular activity
4. to travel back and forth regularly between home and work
5. a charge brought against a person, stating that the person is guilty of wrongdoing
6. involving business or a profit-making activity
7. a formal agreement or union between nations, organizations, or individuals
8. a state of mind regarding someone or something
9. to dissolve or wear away (a material, structure, etc.), especially by chemical action
10. a disorder in which exposure to a particular substance produces a physical reaction such as sneezing or swelling
11. to supply with water by means of streams, ditches, pipes, canals, or other methods
12. a desire for food
13. to gain, accomplish, or achieve by effort

Vocabulary: Antonyms Write the Basic Word that is an antonym for each word below. Use your Spelling Dictionary.

14. honest
15. soothe
16. unsuitable
17. teammate
18. exact
19. departure
20. disconnect

Challenge Words Write the Challenge Word that is a synonym for the underlined word. Use your Spelling Dictionary.

21. to <u>relieve</u> the pain
22. a <u>partner</u> in crime
23. gymnastic <u>equipment</u>
24. <u>anxious</u> about upcoming surgery
25. to <u>emphasize</u> the color in the room

Review: Spelling Spree

Code Breaker The Basic and Review Words below are written in code. Use the following code key to figure out each word. Write the decoded words correctly.

CODE:	#	a	2	$	f	@	&	3	e	4	*	g	=	h	[	)	c	?	d	!	+	/	:	b	%	–
LETTER:	a	b	c	d	e	f	g	h	i	j	k	l	m	n	o	p	q	r	s	t	u	v	w	x	y	z

Example: #22+?#!f   *accurate*

1. #!!e?f
2. 2[??[$f
3. #!!?#2!
4. #gge#h2f
5. e??e&#!f
6. #))?[)?e#!f
7. #))?[be=#!f
8. [))[?!+he!%

Word Combination Add the beginning letters of the first word to the last letters of the second to write a Basic or Review Word.

Example: attack + retire   *attire*

9. command + immunity
10. appliance + vacation
11. correct + erupt
12. approach + depreciate
13. arrow + survival
14. alley + energy
15. common + flute
16. accuse + crate
17. appendix + petite
18. commerce + social
19. irregular + imitate
20. atmosphere + gratitude
21. accurate + sensation
22. opposite + continent
23. attend + brain
24. commotion + absent
25. attorney + detach

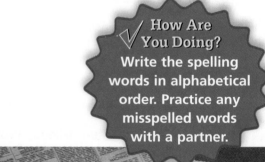

How Are You Doing? Write the spelling words in alphabetical order. Practice any misspelled words with a partner.

Proofreading and Writing

Proofread: Spelling, Pronouns in Compound Subjects and Objects Be careful to use the correct form of a pronoun in a compound subject or compound object. If you are uncertain which to choose, try separating the parts of the compound.

Mark and **I** applied. (*Mark applied. I applied.*)
He called Mark and **me**. (*He called Mark. He called me.*)

Find five misspelled Basic or Review Words and two incorrect pronouns in this excerpt from a letter of application. Write the excerpt correctly.

Please accept my applacation for the position of accountant with Beal Associates. My family and me have lived in this comunity for ten years. I know of your fine reputation in commersial real estate. I, too, have a good reputation—for being accurite with figures. I would apreciate the opportunity for an interview. That would give you and I a chance to discuss the job and how my experience suits it.

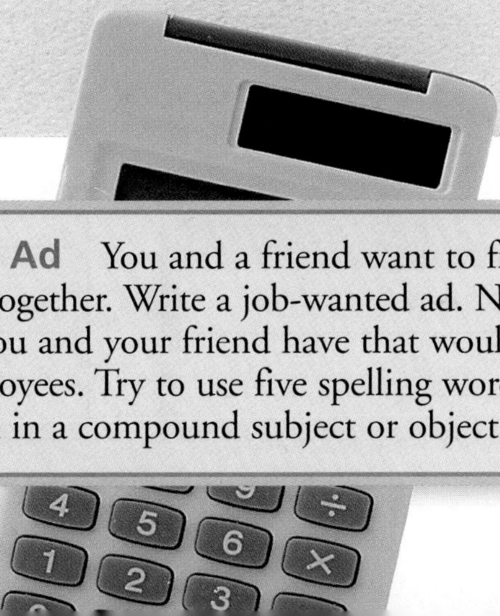

Write a Job-Wanted Ad You and a friend want to find part-time jobs, working together. Write a job-wanted ad. Note any qualities and skills you and your friend have that would make you desirable employees. Try to use five spelling words and at least one pronoun in a compound subject or object.

Basic

1. application
2. appropriate
3. arrival
4. attitude
5. opportunity
6. commute
7. accusation
8. irritate
9. allergy
10. corrupt
11. approximate
12. appetite
13. attach
14. attire
15. opponent
16. commercial
17. attain
18. irrigate
19. alliance
20. corrode

Review

21. appreciate
22. comment
23. accurate
24. attract
25. community

Challenge

26. accentuate
27. alleviate
28. accomplice
29. apparatus
30. apprehensive

Proofreading Marks

¶	Indent
∧	Add
∧,	Add a comma
∨ ∨	Add quotation marks
⊙	Add a period
℘	Delete
≡	Capital letter
/	Small letter
∿	Reverse order

Expanding Vocabulary

Context Clues You have learned about several types of context clues.

Spelling
Word Link

commute

attire
commute
appetite
opponent

APPOSITIVE: The <u>commute</u>, **a daily trip from home to work and back**, was exhausting.

SYNONYM: Her strongest <u>appetite</u> was a **desire** for power.

ANTONYM: I look upon my boss as an **ally**, not an <u>opponent</u>.

LIST: His interview <u>attire</u> included a **suit**, a **tie**, and **dress shoes**.

Write the meaning of each underlined word. Then write the other words in the sentence that are context clues.

1. Jim is working for a <u>linguist</u>, or language specialist.
2. The zoo job involves feeding peacocks, parrots, and <u>emus</u>.
3. Although Tia is usually silent, she is <u>loquacious</u> in interviews.
4. That last <u>gaffe</u> was a serious blunder that cost him his job.

1. ?	3. ?
2. ?	4. ?

Now choose the word from the box that belongs in each sentence. Then write the type of context clue that led you to your answer.

5. This applicant seems to have a strong _____ for hard work, rather than a distaste for it.
6. The mayor's _____, the person running against him for office, has promised to help young people find jobs that pay well.
7. The appealing aspects of this job are the work itself, the good pay, and the short _____ by bus.
8. Beth looked carefully through all of the clothing in her closet before choosing her _____ for the job interview.

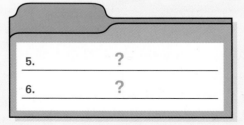

5. ?	7. ?
6. ?	8. ?

Vocabulary Enrichment

Real-World Connection

Life Skills: Job Interviews All the words in the box relate to job interviews. Look up these words in your Spelling Dictionary. Then write the words to complete this paragraph.

What would you do if you saw a newspaper __(1)__ describing your dream job? The first step in applying for a job usually is to send a letter of application along with a __(2)__ , which lists your skills and work experience, as well as the names of references, or people who will give you good __(3)__ . With luck, this will lead to an interview. At the interview, you must try to convince the __(4)__ that you are the best __(5)__ for the position. Show that you __(6)__ for the job and can handle the __(7)__ . Point out the kinds of experience and training you have had that fit each job __(8)__ .

Spelling Word Link

application

advertisement
requirement
résumé
candidate
employer
qualify
recommendations
responsibility

TRY THIS!

True or False? Write *T* if a sentence is true and *F* if it is false.

9. A job applicant is a candidate.
10. A résumé is a letter.
11. To qualify is to hire.
12. Recommendations come from people who know you.

Fact File

The Equal Employment Opportunity Commission, an agency of the United States government, ensures that employers treat workers equally, regardless of their race, religion, or national origin. The agency was established under the Civil Rights Act of 1964.

Suffixes *-ant/-ance, -ent/-ence*

Read and Say

Basic

READ the sentences. SAY each bold word.

1. *assistant* — My **assistant** handles many tasks for me.
2. *assistance* — Do you need **assistance** changing the tire?
3. *independent* — Our **independent** cat roams the neighborhood.
4. *independence* — The war for **independence** lasted for years.
5. *patient* — The **patient** child quietly waited her turn.
6. *patience* — Making fine lace takes **patience** and skill.
7. *confident* — He plays well and is **confident** of winning.
8. *confidence* — My belief and **confidence** in you will last.
9. *significant* — Losing his money was a **significant** problem.
10. *significance* — Did you grasp the **significance** of his words?
11. *competent* — A **competent** worker knows what to do.
12. *competence* — Her **competence** shows in her excellent work.
13. *attendant* — May I ask the flight **attendant** for a pillow?
14. *attendance* — My perfect **attendance** shows I am never ill.
15. *intelligent* — Even very **intelligent** students must study.
16. *intelligence* — The brain is the center of **intelligence**.
17. *elegant* — The **elegant** gown was made of fine silk.
18. *elegance* — Some rooms are fancy but have no **elegance**.
19. *magnificent* — The **magnificent** sunset took my breath away.
20. *magnificence* — We were awed by the **magnificence** of the gems.

Spelling Strategy Thinking of related words can help you remember how to spell the suffixes *-ant*, *-ance*, *-ent*, and *-ence* in particular words.

Think and Write   Write the pairs of Basic Words under their suffixes.

-ant/-ance   *-ent/-ence*

Review	23. permanent
21. instant	24. importance
22. instance	25. difference

Challenge	28. relevant
26. adolescent	29. relevance
27. adolescence	

Independent Practice

Vocabulary: Definitions Write the Basic Word that matches each definition.
Use your Spelling Dictionary.

1. the ability to calmly endure a difficult or annoying situation
2. the condition of being free and self-governing
3. the act or practice of being present
4. skill; the ability to do what is required
5. marked by good taste and refinement
6. a person who waits on another person
7. enduring trouble, hardship, annoyance, delay, etc., without complaint or anger
8. refinement and grace in appearance or manner
9. the ability to learn, think, understand, and know
10. grand; remarkable
11. sure of oneself
12. the meaning or sense of something; the state or quality of being important

Vocabulary: Synonyms
Write the Basic Word that
has the same meaning as
each word below. Use your
Spelling Dictionary.

13. self-reliant
14. smart
15. self-assurance
16. greatness
17. helper
18. important
19. able
20. help

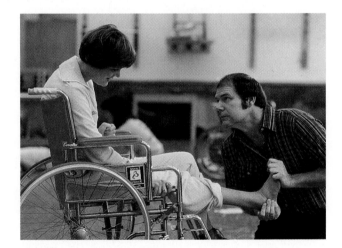

Challenge Words Write the Challenge Word that fits each clue. Use your
Spelling Dictionary.

21. Points that are raised by participants in a discussion usually have this.
22. This is a time of much growth and change.
23. This kind of person is not yet an adult but is no longer a child.
24. This type of idea is related to the matter under consideration.

Dictionary

Prefixes and Suffixes Dictionaries have separate entries for many prefixes and suffixes.

> **in-.** Also **il-** (before *l*) or **im-** (before *b*, *m*, and *p*) or **ir-** (before *r*). A prefix meaning "not or without": **independent**. [Middle English, from Old French, from Latin.]
>
> **-ence** or **-ency.** A suffix meaning "action, state, quality, or condition": **reference**. [From Latin *-entia*, from *-ens*.]

Practice Write the answer to each question. Use your Spelling Dictionary.

1. Which definition of *sub-* is used in the sentence *We went down the steps to the subway station?*
2. What language did the prefix *re-* most recently come from?
3. Which of these suffixes can be used to form nouns: *-ian, -ness, -ize, -dom?*
4. What does the prefix *inter-* mean in the word *intercity?*

1.	?	3.	?
2.	?	4.	?

Review: Spelling Spree

Whirlpool of Words 5–22. Find the Basic and Review Words that are hidden in the whirlpool. Write the words correctly in the order in which you find them.

Proofreading and Writing

Proofread for Spelling Find seven misspelled Basic or Review Words in this paragraph. Write each word correctly.

Liz Rook knew that she would need pateince while waiting for her injuries to heal. After the accident, the loss of her independance was worse than any physical pain. Slowly, however, she regained confidence in her abilities. Her physical therapist guided her through exercises with competense and inteligence. It wasn't long before Liz decided that physical therapy would be a magnaficent occupation. Daily more confadent, she began planning her career. The accident that had once seemed a tragedy began to take on a whole new significence.

Basic

1. assistant
2. assistance
3. independent
4. independence
5. patient
6. patience
7. confident
8. confidence
9. significant
10. significance
11. competent
12. competence
13. attendant
14. attendance
15. intelligent
16. intelligence
17. elegant
18. elegance
19. magnificent
20. magnificence

Review

21. instant
22. instance
23. permanent
24. importance
25. difference

Challenge

26. adolescent
27. adolescence
28. relevant
29. relevance

Proofreading Marks
¶ Indent
∧ Add
⩘ Add a comma
⌄⌄ ⌄⌄ Add quotation marks
⊙ Add a period
ℐ Delete
≡ Capital letter
/ Small letter
∾ Reverse order

Write a Summary of Your Career Plans What career would you like to pursue when your schooling is completed? Write a summary of your career plans. Tell why you have chosen that career and why it is an appropriate career for you. Try to use five spelling words.

Unit 32 BONUS

Expanding Vocabulary

The Latin Root *sist* You have already learned that the Latin root *sta* means "to stand." The root *sist* is another form of *sta* and has the same meaning. A number of English words contain the root *sist*. One such word is *assistant*, meaning "one who assists; a helper." An assistant is a person who, in a sense, "stands nearby."

subsist   resistance   persistent   insist

Write a word from the list above to complete each sentence. Use your Spelling Dictionary.

1. A healthy diet helps maintain your _____ to colds.
2. If you are _____, you can solve most problems.
3. Mia stubbornly continued to _____ that her way was the right way.
4. Can a person _____ on water alone?

TEST-TAKING TACTICS

Sentence Completion Some sentence completion test questions have two blanks. Each answer choice will contain a pair of words, and you must choose the pair in which BOTH words fit the sentence context. Look at this sample sentence and its answer choices.

Physical therapists must be very aware of their patients' _____, as some patients may be too _____ to complete certain exercises.

(A) strengths...stubborn
(B) limitations...strong
(C) conditions...frail
(D) attitudes...miserable
(E) moods...weak

To tackle a sentence with two blanks, start by trying the first word in each answer pair. If that word makes no sense, eliminate that answer. Next, check both words of the remaining answer choices, and eliminate choices as you go. Then, to verify that your answer choice makes sense, say the sentence to yourself with your chosen word pair in place.

Write *A, B, C, D,* or *E* to answer the following question.

5. Which answer choice *best* fits the sample sentence's meaning?

Real-World Connection

Careers: Physical Therapy All the words in the box relate to physical therapy. Look up these words in your Spelling Dictionary. Then write the words to complete this paragraph.

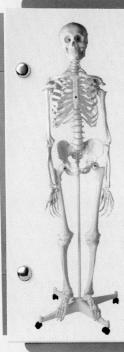

Physical therapists plan and administer treatments to __(1)__ people who are suffering from a __(2)__ due to injury or disease. Among the most common __(3)__ procedures are exercise, massage, and applications of heat, cold, water, or electricity. These help to relieve pain and to restore strength and __(4)__, or movement, to muscles and joints. They also help patients improve the __(5)__ of a limb over which they have lost some control or prevent __(6)__ in muscles that they are not using at all. Although physical therapists work most directly on the muscular and __(7)__ systems, they must have a detailed knowledge of all parts of the human __(8)__.

Spelling Word Link

assistance

therapeutic
rehabilitate
anatomy
skeletal
disability
atrophy
mobility
coordination

TRY THIS!

Yes or No? Write *yes* or *no* to answer each question.

9. Can you invent anatomy?
10. Can a massage be therapeutic?
11. Does atrophy occur in well-exercised muscles?
12. Are bones part of the skeletal system?

Fact File

Ultrasound, or sound waves with frequencies beyond the range of human hearing, is often used in physical therapy. With a special device, beams of ultrasound can be focused on joints or muscles to produce penetrating heat that promotes healing.

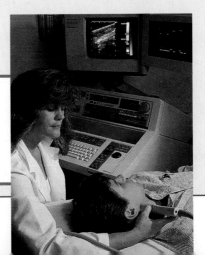

Verb Suffixes

Read and Say

Basic

READ the sentences. SAY each bold word.

1. analyze — The lab will **analyze** the blood sample.
2. summarize — Just **summarize** the most important points.
3. memorize — Will I have to recite the poem I **memorize**?
4. alphabetize — Did you **alphabetize** the list of names?
5. generalize — Try not to **generalize** about people.
6. visualize — Close your eyes and **visualize** the scene.
7. devise — We must **devise** a plan that will work.
8. compromise — You can settle the dispute if you **compromise**.
9. utilize — I **utilize** my cooking skills in the kitchen.
10. capitalize — Always **capitalize** proper nouns.
11. penalize — Will they **penalize** the team for bad behavior?
12. paralyze — Heavy snow can **paralyze** a city.
13. despise — Enemies often **despise** one another.
14. harmonize — The voices of the two singers **harmonize** well.
15. merchandise — Winter **merchandise** is on sale in the spring.
16. sterilize — Use boiling water to **sterilize** the bottle.
17. legalize — The town will **legalize** swimming in the pond.
18. authorize — Did the principal **authorize** your absence?
19. improvise — That comic can **improvise** a joke on the spot.
20. specialize — My store will **specialize** in rare glass.

Spelling Strategy When you hear the final |īz| sounds in a word, think of the spelling patterns **ize**, **ise**, and **yze**.

Think and Write Write each Basic Word under its suffix.

-ize   *-ise*   *-yze*

Review
21. organize
22. criticize
23. recognize
24. surprise
25. modernize

Challenge
26. symbolize
27. maximize
28. minimize
29. surmise
30. comprise

Independent Practice

Vocabulary: Word Clues Write the Basic Word that fits each clue. Use your
Spelling Dictionary.

1. When you do this, you make a long story short.
2. When you do this, you see with your imagination.
3. When you do this, you meet someone halfway.
4. You do this when you write the beginning of a sentence.
5. When people do this, they make something lawful.
6. To do this, you have to know your ABCs.
7. When you do this, you have not rehearsed.
8. If you do this, you will not forget.
9. When you do this, you get very good at one thing.
10. When you do this, you kill germs.
11. When you do this, you give someone power to do something.
12. When you do this, you are not being specific.

Vocabulary: Analogies Write the Basic Word that completes each analogy.
Use your Spelling Dictionary.

Example: prohibit : forbid :: approve : _____   *authorize*
13. example : demonstrate :: punishment : _____
14. needles : sew :: advertisement : _____
15. conflict : clash :: blend : _____
16. teach : instruct :: employ : _____
17. need : require :: invent : _____
18. like : adore :: dislike : _____
19. increase : decrease :: activate : _____
20. look : observe :: think : _____

Challenge Words Write the Challenge
Word that completes each sentence. Use
your Spelling Dictionary.

21. During her research about the American flag, Cheryl discovered that the
    stripes _____ the thirteen original colonies.
22. Because the index lists so few articles on Peruvian music, I _____ that little
    research has been done on the topic.
23. To _____ research time, limit your topic before you begin.
24. Our reference sources _____ the card catalog, almanacs, encyclopedias, and
    dictionaries, as well as other books.
25. To _____ your knowledge of a topic, explore as many sources of information
    as possible in your research.

Dictionary

Word Forms After the part of speech label in a dictionary entry, you might find the *-ed* and *-ing* forms of the entry word if it is a verb, the *-er* and *-est* forms if it is an adjective, or the plural form if it is a noun. These appear when the endings cause a change in the spelling of the base word. At the end of an entry, you might find a **run-on**, a word formed by adding a suffix to the entry word.

> **u·til·ize** |yo͞ot′l īz| *v.* **u·til·ized, u·til·iz·ing.** To use for a certain purpose: *utilizing the stream's water to run the mill.* —**u′til·i·za′tion** *n.*

Practice For each word, write the forms of the word that follow the part of speech label in your Spelling Dictionary.

1. abuse _____?_____

2. symphony _____?_____

3. panic _____?_____

4. vague _____?_____

Look up each word in your Spelling Dictionary. Write a run-on from the entry for each word.

| 5. attain | 6. duplicate | 7. desirable | 8. participate |

5. _____?_____   7. _____?_____

6. _____?_____   8. _____?_____

Modular Words Write a Basic or Review Word by adding the suffix *-ize, -ise,* or *-yze* to each group of letters that begins a word.

9. legal ___
10. capital ___
11. improv ___
12. harmon ___
13. critic ___
14. memor ___
15. author ___
16. merchand ___
17. steril ___

18. recogn ___
19. special ___
20. alphabet ___
21. comprom ___
22. visual ___
23. general ___
24. penal ___
25. desp ___
26. paral ___

Proofreading and Writing

Proofread for Spelling Find seven misspelled Basic or Review words in this paragraph. Write each word correctly.

Conducting surveys is an effective means of research. It should come as no surprize that many companies depend on surveys to determine the needs and wants of their customers. Surveys help companies modernise and improve their merchandise. You might want to devize and organise your own survey about a subject that interests you. First, write a list of questions. Then make copies of your questionnaire and hand them out to your classmates to complete. Finally, analyse the information you have gathered. How would you summarise your findings? How might you utilise the results of your survey?

Write a Brochure You are starting a business that will do research for anyone on any subject. Exactly what services do you provide? What might you do and where might you go to get information for a client? Write a brochure to hand out to your potential clients. Try to use five spelling words.

Basic

1. analyze
2. summarize
3. memorize
4. alphabetize
5. generalize
6. visualize
7. devise
8. compromise
9. utilize
10. capitalize
11. penalize
12. paralyze
13. despise
14. harmonize
15. merchandise
16. sterilize
17. legalize
18. authorize
19. improvise
20. specialize

Review
21. organize
22. criticize
23. recognize
24. surprise
25. modernize

Challenge
26. symbolize
27. maximize
28. minimize
29. surmise
30. comprise

Proofreading Marks
¶ Indent
∧ Add
⩓ Add a comma
ᱽ ᱽ Add quotation marks
⊙ Add a period
⤴ Delete
☰ Capital letter
/ Small letter
∩ Reverse order

Expanding Vocabulary

Spelling Word Link

despise

Synonyms and Antonyms You know that **synonyms** are words that have the same or nearly the same meaning. *Despise* and *hate* are synonyms. **Antonyms**, such as *despise* and *adore*, are words with opposite meanings.

Choose and write the synonym for each underlined word. Use your Thesaurus.

1.	utilize	improve	borrow	use
2.	sterilize	scrub	cure	disinfect
3.	organize	mix	arrange	adjust

Choose and write the antonym for each underlined word. Use your Thesaurus.

4.	penalize	win	honor	reward
5.	criticize	compliment	accept	understand
6.	harmonize	blend	divide	clash

TEST-TAKING TACTICS

Analogies Because words often have more than one meaning, it is important to carefully define each word in an analogy test question. Using an incorrect meaning for a word in a given word pair will change the relationship you define between those words. Look at this example.

REFUSE : ACCEPT ::

(A) contact : reach   (B) smile : joke   (C) scream : yell

(D) capture : release   (E) saddle : ride

To answer this question correctly, begin by thinking carefully about the different meanings of the stem word *refuse*. If you think of it as a noun meaning "garbage," you'll see that it has no clear relationship to *accept*. If you think of *refuse* as a verb meaning "to be unwilling to do, accept, or give," you can see that *accept* is its antonym. Therefore, the relationship between the words is that they are opposites.

Answer these questions about the example given above.

7. Which answer choices contain words with multiple meanings?
8. Which answer choice correctly completes the analogy? Write its letter.

Vocabulary Enrichment

Real-World Connection

Language Arts: Research Skills All the words in the box relate to research skills. Look up these words in your Spelling Dictionary. Then write the words to complete this paragraph.

Spelling Word Link

analyze

librarian
article
abstract
journal
issue
atlas
reference
almanac

When researching a topic, a good place to start is the __(1)__ department of the library. Whether you need information from an encyclopedia; an __(2)__, which is a book of maps; or the collection of facts in an __(3)__, you will find it in this department. You will also find help in locating sources of information. For instance, if you need to find an __(4)__ in a newspaper, magazine, or __(5)__, an index can help you. It will give you the name of the publication and the __(6)__ in which the piece appeared. It may even contain an __(7)__, or brief summary, of the report or story. If you need further assistance, a __(8)__ is always available.

TRY THIS!

Yes or No? Write *yes* or *no* to answer each question.

9. Can you read an abstract from cover to cover?
10. Can you find novels in the reference department?
11. Is a journal published regularly?
12. Can an almanac tell you who won the 1952 World Series?

Fact File

How do you find one particular book among the thousands in a library? Under the Dewey decimal system, a widely used classification system, books are grouped and numbered by subject. They are shelved in a numbered order, allowing you to find any book with ease.

Words New to English

Read and Say

Basic

READ the sentences. SAY each bold word.

1. telecast — The moon landing was **telecast** everywhere.
2. anchorperson — An **anchorperson** presents the news.
3. cablevision — Those programs are on **cablevision** only.
4. sitcom — I watch this **sitcom** whenever I need a laugh.
5. miniseries — The **miniseries** is on every night this week.
6. video — Neither the sound nor the **video** is working.
7. telethon — How much money did the **telethon** raise?
8. remote control — Use the **remote control** to change channels.
9. day care — The baby goes to **day care** when my mom works.
10. skateboard — I often ride my **skateboard** to school.
11. cassette — Do you have a **cassette** of their new album?
12. audio-visual — A television is an **audio-visual** device.
13. aerobics — I increase my heart rate in **aerobics** class.
14. granola — This box of **granola** contains oats and fruit.
15. racquetball — Is handball similar to **racquetball**?
16. Velcro — Some shoes have **Velcro** tabs instead of laces.
17. condominium — We moved from a **condominium** to a house.
18. contact lens — I can't see well with only one **contact lens**.
19. paramedic — A **paramedic** gave me first aid.
20. snowmobile — A **snowmobile** travels well on ice and snow.

Spelling Strategy   Knowing whether a word new to English was formed by creating a **compound word** or **blend** or by combining Greek or Latin word parts can help you spell the word correctly.

Think and Write   Write the Basic Words.

Review
21. computer
22. stereos
23. ambulance
24. hangar
25. campus

Challenge
26. simulcast
27. demographics
28. triathlon
29. biodegradable
30. discotheque

Independent Practice

Vocabulary: Definitions Write the Basic Word that matches each definition. Use your Spelling Dictionary.

1. a sequence of episodes that together make up a dramatic television production
2. a humorous television series
3. to broadcast by television
4. daytime supervision for children of preschool age
5. direction of an activity or machine from a distance, especially by radio or by coded signals
6. a system of exercises that condition the lungs and heart
7. a small cartridge containing tape or film
8. a television system that delivers signals to the sets of subscribers
9. audible as well as visible
10. the visual part of a television broadcast
11. a short, narrow stand mounted on wheels and ridden
12. a racket game played on a walled court

Vocabulary: Classifying Write the Basic Word that fits each group. Use your Spelling Dictionary.

13. reporter, meteorologist, producer, _____
14. raffle, bake sale, auction, _____
15. skis, sleigh, toboggan, _____
16. doctor, nurse, orderly, _____
17. binoculars, monocle, glasses, _____
18. penthouse, apartment, duplex, _____
19. zipper, snap, button, _____
20. muffin, oatmeal, corn flakes, _____

Challenge Words Write the Challenge Word that fits each clue. Use your Spelling Dictionary.

21. If you tune in to both parts of this, you will be hearing double.
22. This is the kind of place that can get your feet moving in record time.
23. This is three races in one.
24. This kind of breakdown is perfectly natural.
25. These statistics tell you a lot about people.

Review: Spelling Spree

Compound Clues Each item includes two definitions, one for each part of a Basic Word. Write the Basic Word.

Example: small + several related things in a row = *miniseries*

1. faraway + to direct =
2. a 24-hour period + to look after =
3. a heavy object that keeps a ship in place + an individual =
4. a bunch of electric wires wrapped together + sight =
5. ice crystals that fall from the sky + able to move =
6. having to do with hearing + having to do with seeing =
7. get in touch with + a transparent object that focuses light =
8. to glide across ice on blades + a plank =
9. a kind of paddle + a small, round object =

Word Riddles Write a Basic or Review Word for each riddle.

10. I am the part of a televised show that you can see.
11. Airplanes take shelter in me.
12. I am grounds for learning.
13. I am good for breakfast.
14. I work like a brain but can't think for myself.
15. We have speakers but cannot talk.
16. I am good for a laugh.
17. I keep you jumping to get your heart pumping.
18. I am light material with a strong hold.
19. I am a little box that holds many things to see and/or hear.
20. I am programmed to appear on a screen.
21. When my siren sounds, other vehicles get out of my way.
22. I am a televised call for help.
23. I am trained to help when help is needed in a hurry.
24. I can't be seen all at once, but I'm viewed in a short time.
25. I am a home, though I don't have a roof all to myself.

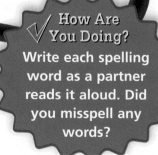

✓ **How Are You Doing?**
Write each spelling word as a partner reads it aloud. Did you misspell any words?

Proofreading and Writing

Proofread: Spelling and Agreement with Indefinite Pronouns An **indefinite pronoun** refers to a person or thing that is not identified. When an indefinite pronoun acts as a subject, the verb must agree with it in number.

SINGULAR: **Each** of the miniseries **has** three episodes.
PLURAL: **All** of the networks **begin** the new season in October.

Find five misspelled Basic or Review Words and two errors in agreement with indefinite pronouns in this television listing. Write the listing correctly.

8:00 PM   9 56   Roomies—Comedy

In this new sitcom, Chas (John Newman), is a gronola-crunching airobics instructor and raquetball enthusiast. He shares a condaminium with Ted (Burt Low), a computer wiz and vidio fan. Peace is threatened when each of the roommates try to inflict his lifestyle on the other. Neither of them are skilled at compromise. In the end, both learn a startling lesson.

Basic

1. telecast
2. anchorperson
3. cablevision
4. sitcom
5. miniseries
6. video
7. telethon
8. remote control
9. day care
10. skateboard
11. cassette
12. audio-visual
13. aerobics
14. granola
15. racquetball
16. Velcro
17. condominium
18. contact lens
19. paramedic
20. snowmobile

Review
21. computer
22. stereos
23. ambulance
24. hangar
25. campus

Challenge
26. simulcast
27. demographics
28. triathlon
29. biodegradable
30. discotheque

Proofreading Marks
¶ Indent
∧ Add
⋏ Add a comma
⌄⌄ ⌄⌄ Add quotation marks
⊙ Add a period
⌐ Delete
≡ Capital letter
／ Small letter
∪ Reverse order

Write a Proposal   Write a proposal for a television show that you think would be popular. Try to use five spelling words and at least one indefinite pronoun that acts as a subject.

Expanding Vocabulary

**Spelling
Word Link**

sitcom

Blends and Clipped Forms You know that a blend is formed by joining, or "blending," parts of existing words. *Sitcom* is a blend created from *situation comedy*. A **clipped form** is created by shortening, or "clipping," an existing word. For example, *condo* is the clipped form of *condominium*.

Write the long version of each clipped form below.

1. photo   **2.** sax   **3.** phone

1.	?
2.	?
3.	?

Write the words from which each blend is formed.
Use your Spelling Dictionary.

4. Velcro   **5.** brunch   **6.** motel

4.	?
5.	?
6.	?

Now write two sentences. In each one, use a clipped form from items 1–3 above and a blended form from items 4–6.

7.   ?

     ?

8.   ?

     ?

Real-World Connection

Performing Arts: Television All the words in the box relate to television. Look up these words in your Spelling Dictionary. Then write the words to complete this paragraph.

Spelling
Word Link

telecast

prime time
ratings
entertainment
educational
soap opera
docudrama
nonprofit
affiliate

Television stations fall into two categories: commercial stations, which are supported by advertising, and public, or __(1)__ stations, which are paid for by viewers. Both provide news and __(2)__ . Although commercial television offers some informational shows, public television offers more __(3)__ programs. Two popular types of commercial shows are the __(4)__ , a dramatic series about fictional characters, and the __(5)__ , a story based on real events. Each commercial station is an __(6)__ , or member, of a network. The networks use viewer surveys to produce __(7)__ , which tell them how popular each of their programs is. They air the most popular shows at __(8)__ , when most people watch.

TRY THIS!

Yes or No? Write *yes* or *no* to answer each question.

9. Can you watch commercials on nonprofit stations?
10. Do high ratings mean that a show is popular?
11. Is midday prime time?
12. Is a soap opera a musical program?

Fact File

The Emmy awards are honors given annually within the television industry for outstanding achievement in various categories. These include acting, writing, producing, and directing, as well as different types of programs.

215

Words Often Mispronounced

Read and Say

Basic

READ the sentences. SAY each bold word.

1. prescription — Please fill this **prescription** for my pills.
2. aspirin — Take an **aspirin** to ease the pain.
3. quantity — This box will hold a large **quantity** of pears.
4. arthritis — Is **arthritis** the cause of his sore joints?
5. jewelry — Her **jewelry** includes a pearl necklace.
6. handkerchief — I use a **handkerchief** instead of a tissue.
7. restaurant — Does that **restaurant** serve fresh fish?
8. sherbet — Ice cream contains more fat than **sherbet**.
9. governor — The **governor** enjoys running the state.
10. miniature — His **miniature** cars are only an inch long.
11. veterinarian — Did the **veterinarian** give the dog her shots?
12. glimpse — I caught a **glimpse** of him as he ran by.
13. licorice — Do you like the taste of **licorice** candy?
14. environment — A quiet **environment** aids studying.
15. chasm — A canyon is actually a deep **chasm**.
16. incidentally — She is, **incidentally**, my cousin.
17. comparable — The two pagers are **comparable** in price.
18. particularly — I **particularly** like this one of the five.
19. lightning — A bolt of **lightning** lit up the sky.
20. fulfill — I pledge to **fulfill** all of my duties.

Spelling Strategy Knowing the correct pronunciation of a word will help you spell it correctly.

Think and Write Write the Basic Words. Underline the parts of the words whose pronunciation you find troublesome.

Review		Challenge	
	23. obvious		28. haphazard
21. prompt	24. length	26. diphtheria	29. auxiliary
22. desperate	25. discovery	27. err	30. boisterous

Independent Practice

Vocabulary: Definitions Write the Basic Word that matches each definition. Use your Spelling Dictionary.

1. a written instruction from a doctor telling a pharmacist what medicine to prepare for a patient
2. a drug used to relieve fever and pain, usually taken in tablet form
3. a painful condition caused by inflammation and stiffness of a joint or joints in the body
4. a person trained to give medical care to animals
5. the chief executive of a state in the United States
6. ornaments, made of gems or other materials, that are made to be worn
7. a brilliant flash in the sky that results from a powerful discharge of electricity
8. a small square of cloth usually carried in a pocket
9. a place where food is served to the public
10. a sweet frozen dessert
11. a chewy candy, usually black or red
12. apart from the main subject; by the way

Vocabulary: Synonyms Write the Basic Word that has the same meaning as each word below. Use your Spelling Dictionary.

13. surroundings
14. similar
15. especially
16. satisfy
17. gorge
18. glance
19. amount
20. tiny

Challenge Words Write the Challenge Word that fits each clue. Use your Spelling Dictionary.

21. Though we try not to, we all do this sometimes.
22. This type of arrangement is due more to chance than to plan.
23. People who catch this do not feel at all well.
24. This type of person or thing is extra.
25. People who behave in this way are impossible to ignore.

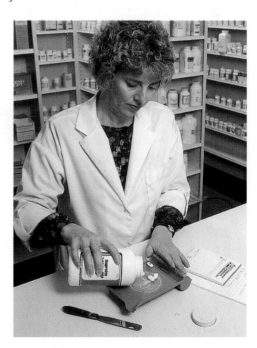

Review: Spelling Spree

Puzzle Play Write the Basic or Review Word that fits each clue. Circle the letter that would appear in the box.

Example: cold treat _ ☐ _ _ _ _ _   s(h)erbet

1. a deep crack ☐ _ _ _ _
2. a cloth square _ _ _ _ _ _ _ _ ☐ _ _ _
3. an animal doctor _ ☐ _ _ _ _ _ _ _ _ _ _
4. a quick look _ _ _ ☐ _ _ _ _
5. evident _ _ _ ☐ _ _ _ _
6. a dining site _ _ ☐ _ _ _ _ _ _ _ _
7. on time _ _ _ _ _ ☐
8. a body decoration _ _ _ _ _ ☐ _
9. by the way _ _ _ _ _ _ _ _ _ _ _ ☐

Now write the circled letters in sequence. They will spell a mystery word that names a subject related to pharmacy.

Mystery Word: __ __ __ __ __ __ __ __ __
                                    ?

Letter Math Add and subtract letters from the words below to make Basic or Review Words. Write the new words.

Example: glimmer – mer + lapse – la =   *glimpse*

10. let – t + ring – ri + th =
11. quaint – i + ity =
12. aspire – e + pin – p =
13. awful – aw + fill =
14. lick – k + or + ice =
15. light + inning – in =
16. disc + to – t + very =
17. usher – u + bet =
18. envy – y + iron + ment =
19. desk – k + pear – a + ate =
20. part + vehicular – veh + ly =
21. clomp – l + wearable – we =
22. pry – y + description – d =
23. glove – l + earn – ea + or =
24. car – c + thrift – f + is =
25. minus – us + i + mature – m =

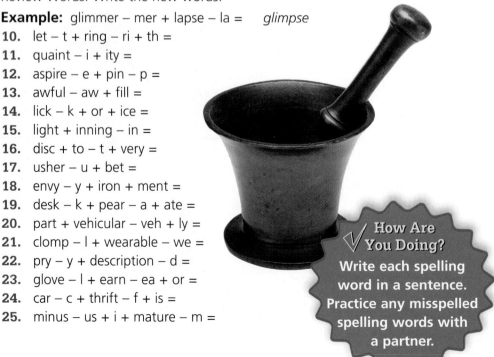

✓ **How Are You Doing?**
Write each spelling word in a sentence. Practice any misspelled spelling words with a partner.

Proofreading and Writing

Proofread: Spelling and Pronouns after Prepositions
When a pronoun is the object of a preposition, use the object form of the pronoun. Be especially careful when the pronoun is part of a compound object.

Dr. MacIntosh gave some multivitamins to Rita and **me**.

Find five misspelled Basic or Review Words and two incorrect pronouns in this dialogue. Write the dialogue correctly.

Mr. Klein: Good morning, Ms. Brown. I need Sylvia's arthritis perscription refilled. Incidently, could you recommend something for my wife and I? We are desparate to get rid of these colds, particlarly since we're going on vacation next week.

Ms. Brown: Well, we're still waiting for the discovry of a cure for colds. Between you and I, the best treatment is to rest and drink plenty of liquids.

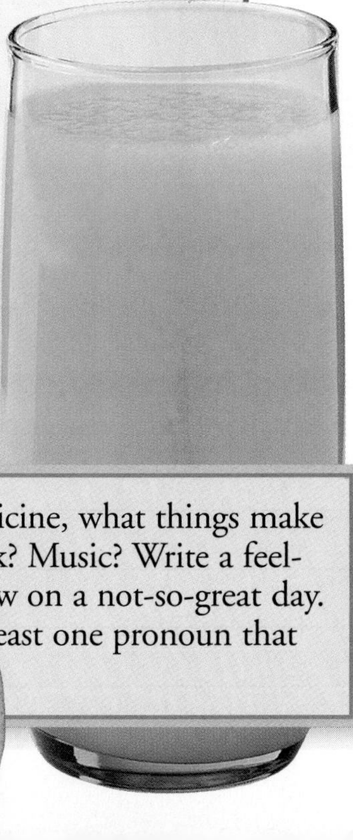

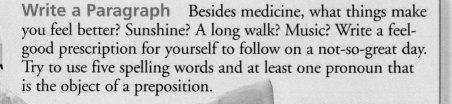

Write a Paragraph Besides medicine, what things make you feel better? Sunshine? A long walk? Music? Write a feel-good prescription for yourself to follow on a not-so-great day. Try to use five spelling words and at least one pronoun that is the object of a preposition.

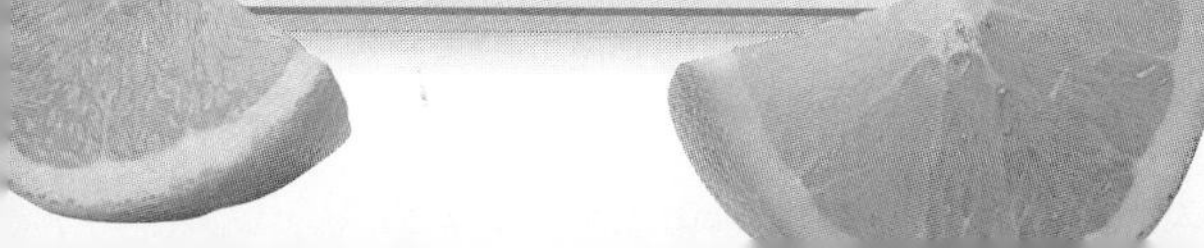

Basic

1. prescription
2. aspirin
3. quantity
4. arthritis
5. jewelry
6. handkerchief
7. restaurant
8. sherbet
9. governor
10. miniature
11. veterinarian
12. glimpse
13. licorice
14. environment
15. chasm
16. incidentally
17. comparable
18. particularly
19. lightning
20. fulfill

Review

21. prompt
22. desperate
23. obvious
24. length
25. discovery

Challenge

26. diphtheria
27. err
28. haphazard
29. auxiliary
30. boisterous

Proofreading Marks

¶	Indent
∧	Add
∧,	Add a comma
∨ ∨	Add quotation marks
⊙	Add a period
✓	Delete
≡	Capital letter
/	Small letter
∿	Reverse order

Unit 35 BONUS

Expanding Vocabulary

Spelling Word Link

governor

British English Some words have different meanings in Britain than they do in the United States. For example, in Britain some people use *governor* to mean *sir*. Other words have the same meanings but different spellings in each country. *Labor* is spelled *labour* in Britain. Still other British words are not used at all by speakers of American English. For instance, *waistcoat*, meaning *vest*, is not used in the United States.

Write the American word that means the same as each underlined British word. Use your Spelling Dictionary.

1. Mr. Pim is a <u>chemist</u>.
2. The child ate a <u>biscuit</u>.
3. Ms. Kay will <u>stand</u> for mayor.
4. A huge <u>lorry</u> rumbled by.

1. ?
2. ?
3. ?
4. ?

Write the American spelling of the underlined British word in each sentence. Use your Spelling Dictionary.

5. The crowd heard a musical <u>programme</u>.
6. A healthy diet includes plenty of <u>fibre</u>.

Now choose one of the pairs of words from items 1–4. Write one sentence for the British word and a second sentence for the American word.

7. ?

?

8. ?

?

Real-World Connection

Careers: Pharmacy All the words in the box relate to pharmacy. Look up these words in your Spelling Dictionary. Then write the words to complete this paragraph.

℞

When a doctor prescribes a __(1)__ , whether an __(2)__ to fight an infection or a __(3)__ to put on a burn, you go to a __(4)__ to have the prescription filled. It's a good idea to ask the pharmacist if there is a __(5)__ brand of the product, which is less expensive than name brands. You should also get the answers to some important questions. What __(6)__ , or amount, should you take, and how often? Could the medicine cause a __(7)__ of any kind? What is the __(8)__ date of the medicine? This information will enable you to use the drug safely and effectively.

Spelling Word Link

prescription

pharmacy
medication
dosage
side effect
expiration
antibiotic
salve
generic

TRY THIS!

Yes or No? Write *yes* or *no* to answer each question.

9. Is a dosage an amount?
10. Is an antibiotic a drug?
11. Is a salve a pill?
12. Is a pharmacy a store?

Fact File

Penicillin, which is produced from a mold, is a powerful bacteria-killing drug. As the first antibiotic successfully used to treat serious infectious diseases, it revolutionized medicine. Various forms of penicillin have been in use since the mid-1940s.

36 Review: Units 31–35

Unit 31   Absorbed Prefixes II
pages 192–197

appropriate	arrival	opportunity	commute	irritate
approximate	corrode	opponent	attach	irrigate

Spelling Strategy   Knowing that the prefixes *ad-*, *in-*, *con-*, and *ob-* ("to or against") can be absorbed when added to word roots will help you remember to double the root's beginning consonant when one of these prefixes has been added.

Write the word that completes each analogy.
1. fruit : rot :: metal : _____
2. tighten : loosen :: remove : _____
3. feed : fertilize :: water : _____
4. letter : communicate :: train : _____

Write the word that matches each definition.
5. estimated
6. a competitor
7. suitable
8. the act of reaching a destination
9. a chance
10. to annoy

Unit 32   Suffixes *-ant/-ance*, *-ent/-ence*   pages 198–203

assistant	patient	confident	magnificent	elegant
assistance	patience	confidence	magnificence	elegance

Spelling Strategy   Thinking of related words can help you remember how to spell the suffixes *-ant*, *-ance*, *-ent*, and *-ence* in particular words.

Write the word that completes each sentence.
11. Melissa was _____ that she would win the race.
12. The tailor's _____ finishes hems and presses the clothes.
13. Luis tried to be _____ as he waited in the long line.
14. The _____ restaurant used linen tablecloths and real crystal.

Write the word that fits each clue.
15. This is great.
16. This includes fine manners.
17. A great waterfall is this.
18. This removes fear and doubt.
19. You need this for a long wait.
20. A helpful person gives this.

Unit 33   Verb Suffixes

pages 204–209

analyze	memorize	visualize	devise	compromise
despise	harmonize	improvise	sterilize	merchandise

 Spelling Strategy   When you hear the final |īz| sounds in a word, think of the spelling patterns **ize**, **ise**, and **yze**.

Write the word that completes each sentence.

21. Jazz musicians often _____, instead of playing composed music.
22. In the days before writing, people had to _____ information.
23. Una longed for warmer days and began to _____ the long winter.
24. The math class worked to _____ the complicated word problem.
25. Theo tried to _____ the scenery described in the story.
26. Their argument ended when they agreed to _____.

Write the word associated with each of the following.

27. quartet
28. shopkeeper
29. scalpel
30. inventor

Unit 34   Words New to English

pages 210–215

day care	anchorperson	miniseries	remote control	skateboard
cassette	racquetball	paramedic	contact lens	Velcro

 Spelling Strategy   Knowing whether a word new to English was formed by creating a **compound word** or **blend** or by combining Greek or Latin word parts can help you spell the word correctly.

Write the word that fits each clue.

31. This game is played on a court.
32. This kind of program is not shown in one day.
33. This is good for working parents.
34. This provides a ride for one person.

Write the word associated with each of the following.

35. vision
36. emergency
37. news
38. fastening
39. recording
40. distance

Unit 35 Words Often Mispronounced pages 216–221

prescription	quantity	jewelry	handkerchief	restaurant
veterinarian	glimpse	chasm	environment	lightning

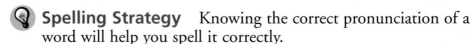 **Spelling Strategy** Knowing the correct pronunciation of a word will help you spell it correctly.

Write the word that fits each clue.
41. A doctor writes this.
42. This place has a kitchen and a dining room.
43. This person helps animals.
44. This often catches a sneeze.
45. This is uncontrollable electricity.
46. This decorates people.

Write the word that matches each definition.
47. amount
48. a gorge
49. a brief look
50. surroundings

Challenge Words	Units 31–35	pages 192–221

alleviate	relevant	symbolize	simulcast	haphazard
accomplice	relevance	comprise	triathlon	boisterous

Write the word that completes each phrase.
51. a _____ crowd
52. _____ the pain
53. an _____ in crime
54. a _____ point

Write the word that completes each sentence.
55. The concert was _____ in stereo on radio and television.
56. The gardens _____ rose bushes, flower-lined paths, beds of herbs, and fruit trees.
57. To train for the _____, Tom ran, swam, and cycled each day.
58. In ancient Rome, the eagle was used to _____ the government.
59. The _____ placement of objects made the room look messy.
60. What _____ does that comment have to this discussion?

Spelling-Meaning Strategy

The Latin Root *pet*

You have learned that *competent* means "capable" and that *competence* means "the state of being capable." You also know that *appetite* means "a desire," but did you know that the three words are related in spelling and meaning? Each contains the Latin root *pet*, meaning "go toward, seek, or strive for." A person who has an appetite seeks food, and a competent person strives to do things correctly, or to attain competence.

Here are some additional words that contain the root *pet*.

petition	com**pet**ition	im**pet**us
re**pet**ition	ap**pet**izer	per**pet**ual

com**pet**ent
com**pet**ence
ap**pet**ite

Think

- How does the root *pet* contribute to the meaning of each word? Look up the words in your Spelling Dictionary.
- In Unit 31, you learned that identifying absorbed prefixes can help you remember certain double consonants. Which of the words in the box above contains an absorbed prefix?

Apply and Extend

Complete these activities on a separate piece of paper.

1. Write a short paragraph about a goal that you or somebody else is striving for or has strived to achieve. In your paragraph, use as many of the six words from the box above as you can.
2. What other words belong to the same family as *competent*, *competence*, and *appetite*? Work with a partner to make a list of related words. Then look up the Latin root *pet* in your Spelling-Meaning Index. Add to your list any other related words that you find.

Summing Up

The Latin root *pet* means "to go toward, seek, or strive for." Words that contain the same root are often related in spelling and meaning. Knowing some of the words in a family can help you to use and spell the others correctly.

Can animals help scientists predict earthquakes? How?

from

"If Pandas Scream . . . an Earthquake Is Coming!"

by Phylis Magida

No matter how their actions are interpreted, animals do behave in many different ways before storms or frosts. Before earthquakes, however, they all tend to behave in more or less the *same* way. Some scientists call it restlessness, but an observer might call it panic. Before a 373 B.C. quake in Italy, mice, moles, and weasels came out of the ground in swarms. Before an 1868 quake in Chile, hundreds of sea birds cried and flew inland. Before a 1969 quake in China, zoo keepers noticed that the tigers were unhappy, the yak had rolled over and refused to eat, and the pandas had held their heads and "screamed."

But what are the animals responding to? At a United States Geological Survey conference, scientists came up with such things as changes in air pressure, in the electric field, in gases given off from the ground, in the electric charging of certain particles, in sound waves, and in the magnetic field.

Think and Discuss

1. What is the topic of each paragraph in the excerpt above?
2. How do animals behave before an earthquake? What details does the writer give?

The Writing Process
Research Report

What might be an interesting topic for a research report? Choose a topic that you can research easily, and write a brief report. Use the guidelines, and follow the Writing Process.

1 ▶ Prewriting
- Jot down topic ideas about one of these subjects: *people, places, animals, sports, history*.
- Pick a topic. Then list the questions that your report will answer. Do your research, taking notes to record facts that answer your questions.
- Organize your notes into an outline.

2 ▶ Draft
- Write your draft, following your outline. Don't worry about mistakes now.
- Write a paragraph for each main outline section.
- Include an introduction that identifies the topic and a conclusion that summarizes the main ideas.

3 ▶ Revise
- If necessary, reword your introduction so that it identifies your topic clearly.
- Add facts and details. Organize them logically.
- Check that your conclusion ties together the main ideas. Revise it if necessary.
- Have a writing conference.

4 ▶ Proofread
- Did you spell each word correctly?
- Did you use pronouns correctly in compound subjects and objects and after prepositions?
- Do indefinite pronouns used as subjects agree with their verbs?

5 ▶ Publish
- Copy your report neatly. Add an interesting title.
- Share your report. Present it as a speech.

Guidelines for Writing a Research Report

✓ Expand your notes into paragraphs. State the main idea of each paragraph in a topic sentence.
✓ Support each main idea with facts and details.
✓ Arrange paragraphs in a logical order.
✓ Include a clear introduction and a conclusion that sums up your main ideas.

Composition Words

approximate
significance
environment
independent
analyze
devise
comparable
particularly

Student's Handbook

Extra Practice and Review   229

Writer's Resources

Capitalization and Punctuation Guide
Abbreviations   247
Bibliography   248
Titles   249
Quotations   250
Capitalization   250
Punctuation   252

Letter Models
Friendly Letter   255
Business Letter   256

Thesaurus

Using the Thesaurus   257
Thesaurus Index   259
Thesaurus   263

Spelling-Meaning Index

Consonant Changes   271
Vowel Changes   271
Absorbed Prefixes   272
Word Parts   274

Spelling Dictionary

Spelling Table   279
How to Use a Dictionary   281
Spelling Dictionary   282

Handwriting Models   356

Extra Practice and Review

Unit 1   Silent/Sounded Consonants   pages 12–17

debt	heir	autumn	doubt	vehicle
debit	inherit	autumnal	dubious	vehicular

 Spelling Strategy   To spell a word with a silent consonant, think of a related word in which the consonant is sounded.

Write the word that completes each sentence.
1. He felt relieved when he had paid off his _____.
2. Cara used _____ reds, golds, and oranges in her painting.
3. According to the will, the niece will _____ the entire estate.
4. If you commit a _____ violation, you will probably get a ticket.

Write the word that matches each definition.
5. someone who benefits from a will
6. something that transports
7. a debt charged to an account
8. the season before winter
9. to be unsure of
10. doubtful

Unit 2   Greek Word Parts I   pages 18–23

phonograph	xylophone	choreography	telephone	homograph
graphic	paragraph	calligraphy	telegraph	homophone

 Spelling Strategy   Knowing the Greek word parts *phon* ("sound"), *auto* ("self"), and *graph* ("writing") can help you spell and understand words with these parts.

Write the word associated with each item.
11. penmanship
12. disc jockey
13. dance
14. sentences
15. musical instrument
16. dial tone

Write the word that fits each clue.
17. This kind of word has a twin in sound but not in spelling.
18. This kind of word has a twin in spelling but not in meaning.
19. This is one way to describe an illustration or a diagram.
20. This system sends messages in code.

Unit 3   Number Prefixes   pages 24–29

billion	tripod	unison	bicycle	triangle
triplets	unify	bimonthly	university	semifinals

 Spelling Strategy   Remember that *uni-* ("one"), *bi-* ("two; twice"), *tri-* ("three"), and *semi-* ("half") are number prefixes.

Write the word that completes each analogy.

21. two : twins :: three : _____
22. runners : sled :: wheels : _____
23. entertainment : theater :: education : _____
24. four : rectangle :: three : _____

Write the word that matches each definition.

25. notes sounded together
26. every two months
27. one thousand million
28. games in a tournament
29. a three-legged stand
30. to join together

Unit 4   Words from Names   pages 30–35

gardenia	zinnia	guy	leotard	graham cracker
sideburns	mackintosh	derby	derrick	Ferris wheel

 Spelling Strategy   Knowing the origin of words that come from names can help you spell and understand the meanings of the words.

Write the words that complete the paragraph.

The stranger had bushy __(31)__ that grew halfway down his cheeks. He was dressed in a suit and carried a __(32)__ in case of rain. When he tipped his round-topped __(33)__ to me, he revealed curly black hair. As he walked on down the road, I saw him pause to pick a white __(34)__ from a shrub and put it in his buttonhole.

Write the word that fits each clue.

35. a crunchy munch
36. a fair ride
37. any fellow
38. part of many dance costumes
39. a machine for moving things
40. a colorful flower

Cycle 1

border	colonel	council	bail	compliment
boarder	kernel	counsel	bale	complement

💡 **Spelling Strategy**   Remember to think about meaning when using a **homophone**, a word that sounds like another but has a different spelling and meaning.

Write the word that is a synonym for each of the following words.

41. boundary   **42.** advise   **43.** lodger   **44.** match   **45.** flatter

Write the word that completes each sentence.

46. I could tell from his uniform that he was an army _____.

47. Each _____ of cotton will be shipped to a cloth factory.

48. The teacher showed us how the wheat husk protected the _____.

49. The mayor called a meeting of the town _____.

50. If the accused's _____ is paid, she is free until her trial.

Challenge Words   Units 1–5   pages 12–41

condemn	bicentennial	cacophony	fuchsia	trivet
condemnation	topography	autonomy	illicit	
trigonometry	poinsettia	sequoia	elicit	

Write the word that matches each definition.

51. to call forth

52. harsh, unpleasant sound

53. self-government

54. unlawful

55. to strongly disapprove of

56. purplish-red

57. a 200th anniversary

58. a tropical plant

Write the word that completes each analogy.

59. face : features :: land : _____

60. science : biology :: mathematics : _____

61. glass : coaster :: casserole : _____

62. acceptance : rejection :: approval : _____

63. animal : whale :: tree : _____

Unit 7 Consonant Changes

pages 48–53

violate	exhibit	duplicate	evaluate	congratulate
violation	exhibition	duplication	evaluation	congratulations

💡 **Spelling Strategy** To remember the spelling of the |sh| sound in words such as *detection* and *operation*, think of a word that is related in spelling and meaning.

Write the word that matches each definition.

1. to judge **2.** to display **3.** to break **4.** best wishes

Write the world that completes each analogy.

5. confusion : order :: obedience : _____
6. expose : reveal :: reproduce : _____
7. test : examination :: judgment : _____
8. sorrow : joy :: sympathize : _____
9. ballroom : party :: gallery : _____
10. change : transformation :: copying : _____

Unit 8 Greek Word Parts II

pages 54–59

geometry	diameter	centimeter	kilogram	cyclone
thermometer	physics	grammatical	cyclical	thermal

💡 **Spelling Strategy** Knowing the Greek word parts *cycl* ("circle"), *phys* ("nature"), *gram* ("something written"), *therm* ("heat"), and *meter/metry* ("measure") can help you spell and understand words with these parts.

Write the word that fits each clue.

11. This measures temperature.
12. This kind of sentence follows the rules.
13. This line always passes through the middle.
14. This is a light weight.

Write the word that belongs in each group.

15. tornado, wind, _____
16. geology, astronomy, _____
17. yard, foot, _____
18. repeated, returning, _____
19. arithmetic, algebra, _____
20. warm, insulating, _____

Cycle 2

Unit 9 Noun Suffixes

pages 60–65

ornament	sculpture	fragment	texture	freedom
argument	legislature	fracture	tournament	kingdom

 Spelling Strategy The suffixes *-ure, -ment,* and *-dom* form nouns when added to base words or roots. Remember the spelling patterns for these suffixes.

Write the word that is a synonym for each of the following words.

21. quarrel
22. piece
23. crack
24. decoration
25. contest
26. liberty

Write the word that completes each analogy.

27. soldiers : army :: lawmakers : _____
28. piano : music :: clay : _____
29. president : democracy :: ruler : _____
30. red : color :: smooth : _____

Unit 10 Words from Spanish

pages 66–71

tomato	siesta	burro	poncho	chocolate
enchilada	iguana	chili	vanilla	burrito

 Spelling Strategy Knowing how to pronounce a word from Spanish will often help you spell it.

Write the words that complete the paragraph.

Lucia finished her bowl of __(31)__ , slipped her warm __(32)__ over her head, and hopped onto her __(33)__ , Pedro, to buy some sweet, dark __(34)__ in the market. Pedro, however, was drowsy and wanted to take a __(35)__ . Just as he was closing his eyes, an __(36)__ ran past, and Pedro, who was afraid of lizards, awoke with a start.

Write the word that fits each clue.

37. flavoring from orchid seeds
38. rolled tortilla with filling and sauce
39. a tortilla-wrapped sandwich
40. a fruit used in salads

233

Unit 11 Words Often Confused

pages 72–77

continual	reality	bizarre	formally	prescribe
continuous	realty	bazaar	formerly	proscribe

Spelling Strategy To avoid confusing words with similar spellings and pronunciations, think of the meanings of the words.

Write the word that completes each analogy.

41. familiar : ordinary :: strange : _____
42. fiction : nonfiction :: fantasy : _____
43. blue jeans : casually :: tuxedo : _____
44. homework : assign :: medicine : _____

Write the word that matches each definition.

45. real estate
46. to make unlawful
47. at an earlier time

48. repeated regularly and often
49. a kind of fair
50. continuing without interruption

Challenge Words   Units 7–11

pages 48–77

implicate	parallelogram	hacienda	ellipse	platinum
implication	acknowledgment	anagram	eclipse	
guacamole	caricature	fissure	isometric	

Write the word associated with each of the following words.

51. exercise
52. metal

53. exaggeration
54. avocado

55. oval
56. sun

Write the word that completes each sentence.

57. The word *stone* is an _____ for *notes*.
58. The poem conveyed the idea by _____, rather than directly.
59. Roberto Sanchez, a wealthy rancher, owns a _____ in Argentina.
60. The earthquake created a deep _____ in the land.
61. The accused tried to _____ as many other people as he could.
62. Samantha longed for praise and the _____ of her talents.
63. A rectangle is a kind of _____.

Cycle 3

Unit 13 Vowel Changes I   pages 84–89

precise	meter	grave	revise	humane
precision	metric	gravity	revision	humanity

 Spelling Strategy Remember that words can be related in spelling and meaning even though they have different vowel sounds.

Write the word that is an antonym for each word below.

1. cruel
2. humorous
3. inaccuracy
4. gaiety
5. indefinite
6. brutality

Write the word that fits each clue.

7. This describes a system of measurement.
8. This act can lead to improvement.
9. You do this when you edit something you have written.
10. This is a little more than a yard.

Unit 14 Latin Roots I   pages 90–95

spectator	spectacle	interruption	subscribe	disrupt
bankrupt	respect	inscription	suspect	aspect

 Spelling Strategy Knowing the Latin roots *spect/spec* ("to look at"), *scrib/scrip/script* ("to write"), and *rupt* ("to break; burst") can help you spell and understand words with these roots.

Write the word that is a synonym for each of the following words.

11. element
12. disturb
13. display
14. onlooker
15. honor
16. interference

Write the word that completes each analogy.

17. rich : poor :: prosperous : _____
18. bottle : label :: trophy : _____
19. certainty : know :: uncertainty : _____
20. club : join :: magazine : _____

Unit 15 The Suffixes *-ary*, *-ery*, and *-ory* pages 96–101

bravery	primary	legendary	forgery	cemetery
secretary	nursery	vocabulary	ordinary	temporary

 Spelling Strategy When you hear the final |ə rē| sounds in a word, think of the spelling patterns **ary**, **ery**, and **ory**. When you hear the final |ĕr′ē| sounds, think of the patterns **ary** and **ery**.

Write the word that matches each definition.

21. graveyard

22. not permanent

23. courage

24. a baby's room

25. talked about frequently; famous

26. first in time or sequence

Write the word that completes each sentence.

27. The twenty-dollar bill was worthless because it was a _____.

28. The boss asked my _____ to write and distribute a memo.

29. A dictionary can help you expand your _____.

30. The surprise visit turned an _____ day into a family reunion.

Unit 16 Words from French pages 102–107

ballet	debut	petite	massage	antique
reservoir	boutique	plateau	coupon	crochet

Spelling Strategy Remember that words from French often contain silent letters, spell the |ē| sound with *i*, and spell the |k| sound with *que*.

Write the words that complete the paragraph.

Jesse, a young dancer, is preparing for his __(31)__ as the new co-star of a __(32)__ company. As part of his exercise program, he lifts weights. Although his partner, Liz, is __(33)__, he still needs a good deal of strength to lift her over his shoulder. After each rehearsal, his muscles need a soothing __(34)__.

Write the word associated with each of the following words.

35. water

36. flatness

37. yarn

38. shopping

39. age

40. savings

Cycle 3

Unit 17 Unusual Plurals

pages 108–113

bacterium	criterion	datum	thesis	cactus
bacteria	criteria	data	theses	cacti

Spelling Strategy

SINGULAR: bacteri**um**, criteri**on**, nucle**us**, analys**is**

PLURAL: bacteri**a**, criteri**a**, nucle**i**, analys**es**

Write the word that completes each phrase.

41. a _____ for judgment

42. two prickly desert _____

43. gather _____ for a report

44. millions of microscopic _____

45. present a _____

46. base a judgment on sound _____

Write the word that completes each sentence.

47. Each _____ is enclosed by its cell wall.

48. One _____ conflicted with all the other information.

49. He argued several _____ in his long research paper.

50. Stephanie pricked her finger on a small _____.

Challenge Words   Units 13–17   pages 84–113

suffice	introspection	derogatory	porcelain	coup
sufficient	discriminatory	phenomenon	ensemble	
nondescript	preliminary	phenomena	spectrum	

Write the word that is a synonym or an antonym for each word.

51. occurrences   **53.** flattering   **55.** enough   **57.** extraordinary

52. final   **54.** china   **56.** fair

Write a word to replace the underlined word or words in each sentence below.

58. This group of musicians will perform at the wedding.

59. Her purchase of the bankrupt firm is quite a brilliant move.

60. I needed some time alone for self-examination.

61. Several people witnessed the strange occurrence.

62. Jim experienced a wide range of emotions during the crisis.

63. Our water supply will be enough for another few days.

Unit 19 Vowel Changes II
pages 120–125

inspiration	imposition	genetic	academy	disposition
inspire	impose	gene	academic	dispose

💡 **Spelling Strategy** To remember the spelling of |ə| in some words, think of a related word in which the same vowel has the long or short vowel sound.

Write the word that completes each sentence.
1. We acquire _____ traits, such as eye color, from our parents.
2. Shani decided to _____ of all the clothes she'd outgrown.
3. I did not want to _____ on their hospitality.
4. Dwight takes flute lessons at a music _____.

Write the word that matches each definition.
5. the act of discarding
6. of a school
7. an unfair demand
8. to stimulate to creativity
9. a sudden, original idea
10. the cell part that controls heredity

Unit 20 Latin Roots II
pages 126–131

contrast	objective	statue	portable	institute
reporter	subjective	deport	adjective	circumstance

💡 **Spelling Strategy** Knowing the Latin roots *sta/sti/st* ("to stand"), *port* ("to carry"), and *ject* ("to throw") can help you spell and understand words with these roots.

Write the word that belongs in each group.
11. expel, exile, _____
12. painting, mobile, _____
13. situation, condition, _____
14. editor, columnist, _____
15. noun, verb, _____

Write the word that completes each analogy.
16. health care : hospital :: research : _____
17. article : factual :: editorial : _____
18. truthful : honest :: fair : _____
19. house : stationary :: tent : _____
20. likeness : resemblance :: difference : _____

Cycle 4

pages 132–137

Unit 21   Greek and Latin Prefixes

adhesive	administer	abnormal	admission	postscript
adviser	absolve	absolute	antonym	postdate

 Spelling Strategy   Remember the meanings of the prefixes *ab-* ("away from"), *ad-* ("to; at; near"), *post-* ("after"), and *anti-/ant-* ("opposite; against").

Write the word formed by adding a prefix to each word below.

21. solve
22. script
23. normal
24. date
25. mission
26. minister

Write the word formed by adding a prefix to each word below.

27. This sticks.
28. This person offers guidance.
29. This always has an opposite.
30. This is nothing less than total.

Unit 22   Words from Other Languages

pages 138–143

tundra	walrus	kayak	sleigh	hickory
raccoon	skunk	waffle	coleslaw	chipmunk

 Spelling Strategy   Remember that English has borrowed words from many languages.

Write the word that belongs in each group.

31. canoe, surfboard, _____
32. forest, desert, _____
33. oak, maple, _____
34. muffin, pancake, _____

Write the word that fits each clue.

35. This animal has a strange perfume.
36. This moves on runners.
37. This animal is small, brown, and striped.
38. This salad relies on cabbage.
39. This has large tusks.
40. This wears a furry mask.

Unit 23 Words Often Misspelled

pages 144–149

cylinder	gauge	circuit	livelihood	consequence
asthma	tortoise	scholar	emperor	raspberry

Spelling Strategy Knowing the origin of a word with an odd spelling can often help you spell the word correctly.

Write the word that fits each group.

41. result, effect, _____
42. cone, cube, _____
43. scale, meter, _____
44. czar, king, _____

Write the word associated with each of the following things.

45. job
46. jam
47. breathing

48. shell
49. electricity
50. knowledge

Challenge Words   Units 19–23   pages 120–149

derive	constituent	antibody	gaiety	abhor
derivation	carburetor	meringue	caucus	abject
conjecture	Antarctic	persimmon	steppe	

Write the word that is a synonym for each word below.

51. merriment   **52.** obtain   **53.** guess   **54.** voter   **55.** miserable

Write the word that completes each sentence.

56. The word *planet* is a _____ from Greek.
57. The _____ was not ripe enough to eat.
58. Due to a faulty _____, the engine would not burn fuel properly.
59. She whipped the egg whites and sugar into a fluffy _____.
60. They journeyed across the cold _____ to the South Pole.
61. The body produces a different kind of _____ for each virus.
62. The party members held a _____ to discuss campaign tactics.
63. The Russian shepherd grazed his flock on the grassy _____.
64. Many people _____ spiders and snakes.

Cycle 5

Unit 25   Absorbed Prefixes I   pages 156–161

arrangement	illegible	irregular	attempt	irresponsible
irreparable	illogical	immobilize	arrest	illegal

 Spelling Strategy   Remember that *ad-* ("to"), *in-* ("not; without"), and *con-* ("with; together") can be **absorbed prefixes** when their last letter changes to match the beginning consonant of the base word to which they are added.

Write the word that matches each definition below.

1. not rational
2. not usual
3. not mendable
4. not lawful
5. not readable
6. not reliable

Write the word that fits each clue.

7. You must do this to a broken leg.
8. This is the order of things.
9. This is a good try.
10. The police do this.

Unit 26   Latin Roots III   pages 162–167

appendix	contradict	expense	pendulum	compensation
diction	dictator	pension	pendant	impending

 Spelling Strategy   Knowing the Latin roots *dict/dic* ("to say") and *pend/pens/pent* ("to hang; weigh") can help you spell and understand words with these roots.

Write the word that completes each analogy.

11. employment : salary :: retirement : _____
12. present : current :: approaching : _____
13. agree : support :: disagree : _____
14. writing : penmanship :: speech : _____

Write the word that matches each definition.

15. a hanging ornament
16. a cost
17. something given as payment
18. a ruler with unlimited power
19. a weight that swings freely
20. a section of a book

Unit 27　The Suffixes -*able* and -*ible*　pages 168–173

reliable	available	desirable	divisible	edible
audible	eligible	believable	permissible	adjustable

Spelling Strategy　Remember the spelling of the adjective suffixes -*able* and -*ible* ("able to be; worthy of; having").

Write the word that is a synonym for each of the following words.

21. allowable

22. appealing

23. dependable

24. qualified

25. obtainable

Write the word that completes each sentence.

26. The _____ strap could be shortened or lengthened.

27. The number sixteen is evenly _____ by four.

28. Can you distinguish _____ mushrooms from poisonous ones?

29. Our neighbors' conversations were _____ through the thin walls.

30. The novel had a good plot and realistic, _____ characters.

Unit 28　Words from Places　pages 174–179

tangerine	mayonnaise	scallion	currant	copper
seltzer	frankfurter	limerick	bologna	mall

Spelling Strategy　Knowing the origin of words that come from the names of places can help you spell and understand the meanings of the words.

Write the words that complete the paragraph.

　　Tom spread a spoonful of creamy white __(31)__ on two slices of bread. He added some lettuce and tomatoes and several slices of __(32)__ , his favorite kind of cold cuts. Then he poured himself a tall glass of clear, sparkling __(33)__ . For dessert, he peeled a sweet, juicy __(34)__ .

Write the word that fits each group.

35. sausage, hot dog, _____

36. garlic, onion, _____

37. tin, lead, _____

38. shopping center, market, _____

39. berry, raisin, _____

40. poem, nursery rhyme, _____

Unit 29   Single or Double Consonants   pages 180–185

cancellation	forbidding	allotted	misspell	credited
exaggerate	gossiping	challenge	equipped	dissimilar

💡 **Spelling Strategy**   Remember that double consonants can occur before the ending *-ed* or *-ing* and usually occur when a prefix ends with the same letter that begins the base word or root or is absorbed. Double consonants in other words must be remembered.

Write the word associated with each of the following words.

41. contest
42. plans
43. writing

44. contrast
45. acknowledgment
46. rumors

Write the word that is a synonym for each word below.

47. overstate
48. supplied

49. frightening
50. distributed

Challenge Words   Units 25–29   pages 156–185

valedictorian	immaterial	attribute	indictment	tangible
miscellaneous	penicillin	tarantula	remittance	Parmesan
correlation	negotiable	appendage	compatible	stoic

Write the word that matches each definition.

51. unemotional
52. a body part
53. a kind of cheese
54. a kind of spider
55. unimportant
56. the top student in a class

57. relationship
58. payment
59. to give credit or blame
60. real
61. able to be worked out
62. assorted

Write the word that completes each analogy.

63. tree : oak :: antibiotic : _____
64. guilty : conviction :: accused : _____
65. conflicting : clashing :: harmonious : _____

Extra Practice and Review

Unit 31 Absorbed Prefixes II

pages 192–197

application	attitude	accusation	allergy	corrupt
appetite	attire	commercial	attain	alliance

💡 **Spelling Strategy** Knowing that the prefixes *ad-, in-, con-,* and *ob-* ("to or against") can be absorbed when added to word roots will help you remember to double the root's beginning consonant when one of these prefixes has been added.

Write a word by changing each underlined prefix below.

1. <u>re</u>liance 2. <u>con</u>tain 3. <u>com</u>plication 4. <u>dis</u>rupt 5. <u>re</u>tire

Write the word that fits each clue.

6. This is often made in court.
7. The longer you go without eating, the larger this grows.
8. This might cause you to sneeze.
9. This type of endeavor is concerned with making money.
10. If this is positive, your life will be brighter.

Unit 32 Suffixes *-ant/-ance, -ent/-ence*

pages 198–203

independent	significant	competent	attendant	intelligent
independence	significance	competence	attendance	intelligence

💡 **Spelling Strategy** Thinking of related words can help you remember how to spell the suffixes *-ant, -ance, -ent,* and *-ence* in particular words.

Write the word that is an antonym for each word below.

11. stupid
12. incapable
13. inability
14. meaningless
15. absence
16. unimportance

Write the word that completes each sentence.

17. A gas station _____ checked the oil and wiped the windshield.
18. The American colonies declared their _____ from Britain.
19. Her eagerness to learn is a sign of _____.
20. In order to become _____, he had to earn his own living.

Cycle 6

Unit 33   Verb Suffixes   pages 204–209

summarize	alphabetize	generalize	utilize	capitalize
penalize	paralyze	legalize	authorize	specialize

 Spelling Strategy   When you hear the final |īz| sounds in a word, think of the spelling patterns **ize**, **ise**, and **yze**.

Write the word that completes each analogy.

21. food : consume :: tools : _____

22. create : destroy :: outlaw : _____

23. motion : mobilize :: stillness : _____

24. narrow : specify :: broad : _____

Write the word that completes each phrase.

25. to _____ books by author   **28.** to _____ for breaking a rule

26. to _____ a movie plot   **29.** to _____ someone to take charge

27. to _____ a proper noun   **30.** to _____ in a field of study

Unit 34   Words New to English   pages 210–215

cablevision	sitcom	video	telethon	telecast
audio-visual	aerobics	granola	snowmobile	condominium

 Spelling Strategy   Knowing whether a word new to English was formed by creating a **compound word** or **blend** or by combining Greek or Latin word parts can help you spell the word correctly.

Write the words to complete the paragraph.

    Julie was hungry after her vigorous __(31)__ class. She ate a bowl of crunchy __(32)__ and turned on the television. She was glad that she had begun subscribing to __(33)__ because now she could watch her favorite show—a zany __(34)__ about a young couple living in New York.

Write the word that fits each clue.

35. This is real estate.   **38.** This part of a broadcast is seen.

36. This can outrun a sled.   **39.** This is for the ears and eyes.

37. This raises funds.   **40.** Television stations do this.

Unit 35   Words Often Mispronounced   pages 216–221

aspirin	arthritis	sherbet	governor	miniature
licorice	incidentally	comparable	particularly	fulfill

Spelling Strategy   Knowing the correct pronunciation of a word will help you spell it correctly.

Write the word that fits each group.

41. mayor, senator, _____

42. tiny, small, _____

43. rheumatism, allergy, _____

44. peppermint, lemon, _____

45. ice cream, custard, _____

46. cough syrup, antacid, _____

Write the word that can replace the underlined word or words.

47. Do my qualifications <u>satisfy</u> the job requirements?

48. Martha, <u>by the way</u>, may join us at the movies.

49. The fish is <u>especially</u> good at this restaurant.

50. The two dancers have <u>similar</u> qualities.

Challenge Words   Units 31–35   pages 192–221

adolescent	biodegradable	accentuate	apparatus	surmise
adolescence	demographics	auxiliary	maximize	err
apprehensive	diphtheria	discotheque	minimize	

Write the word that matches each definition.

51. held in reserve

52. a dance club

53. a teenager

54. to make a mistake

55. suppose

56. make the greatest

57. make the least

58. highlight

59. a contagious disease

60. able to decompose

Write the word that completes each sentence.

61. People's ages and incomes are included in _____.

62. Cindy felt _____ about going to the party alone.

63. Matt seems to have gone from childhood to _____ overnight.

64. The gym was filled with all kinds of exercise _____.

Writer's Resources

Capitalization and Punctuation Guide

Abbreviations

Abbreviations are shortened forms of words. Most abbreviations begin with a capital letter and end with a period.

Titles	Mr. *(Mister)* Mr. Juan Albano	Sr. *(Senior)* John Helt, Sr.
	Mrs. *(Mistress)* Mrs. Frances Wong	Jr. *(Junior)* John Helt, Jr.
	Ms. Susan Clark	Dr. *(Doctor)* Dr. Janice Dodd

Note: *Miss* is not an abbreviation and does not end with a period.

Words used in addresses	St. *(Street)*	Blvd. *(Boulevard)*	Mt. *(Mount or Mountain)*
	Rd. *(Road)*	Rte. *(Route)*	Expy. *(Expressway)*
	Ave. *(Avenue)*	Apt. *(Apartment)*	Pkwy. *(Parkway)*
	Dr. *(Drive)*		

Words used in business	Co. *(Company)*	Corp. *(Corporation)*
	Ltd. *(Limited)*	Inc. *(Incorporated)*

Other abbreviations

Some abbreviations are written in all capital letters, with a letter standing for each important word.

P.D. *(Police Department)*	P.O. *(Post Office)*
R.N. *(Registered Nurse)*	M.A. *(Master of Arts)*

Some abbreviations do not have capital letters or periods.

mph *(miles per hour)*   hp *(horsepower)*   km *(kilometer)*

Some abbreviations begin with a small letter and end with a period.

gal. *(gallon)*   p. *(page)*   min. *(minute)*

Abbreviations of government agencies or national organizations usually do not have periods.

IRS *(Internal Revenue Service)*   NBA *(National Basketball Association)*

Days of the week	Mon. *(Monday)*	Fri. *(Friday)*
	Tues. *(Tuesday)*	Sat. *(Saturday)*
	Wed. *(Wednesday)*	Sun. *(Sunday)*
	Thurs. *(Thursday)*	

Months of the year			
	Jan. *(January)*	Apr. *(April)*	Oct. *(October)*
	Feb. *(February)*	Aug. *(August)*	Nov. *(November)*
	Mar. *(March)*	Sept. *(September)*	Dec. *(December)*

Note: *May, June,* and *July* are not abbreviated.

States

The United States Postal Service uses two capital letters and no period in each of its state abbreviations

AL *(Alabama)*	LA *(Louisiana)*	OH *(Ohio)*
AK *(Alaska)*	ME *(Maine)*	OK *(Oklahoma)*
AZ *(Arizona)*	MD *(Maryland)*	OR *(Oregon)*
AR *(Arkansas)*	MA *(Massachussetts)*	PA *(Pennsylvania)*
CA *(California)*	MI *(Michigan)*	RI *(Rhode Island)*
CO *(Colorado)*	MN *(Minnesota)*	SC *(South Carolina)*
CT *(Connecticut)*	MS *(Mississippi)*	SD *(South Dakota)*
DE *(Delaware)*	MO *(Missouri)*	TN *(Tennessee)*
FL *(Florida)*	MT *(Montana)*	TX *(Texas)*
GA *(Georgia)*	NE *(Nebraska)*	UT *(Utah)*
HI *(Hawaii)*	NV *(Nevada)*	VT *(Vermont)*
ID *(Idaho)*	NH *(New Hampshire)*	VA *(Virginia)*
IL *(Illinois)*	NJ *(New Jersey)*	WA *(Washington)*
IN *(Indiana)*	NM *(New Mexico)*	WV *(West Virginia)*
IA *(Iowa)*	NY *(New York)*	WI *(Wisconsin)*
KS *(Kansas)*	NC *(North Carolina)*	WY *(Wyoming)*
KY *(Kentucky)*	ND *(North Dakota)*	

Bibliography

The basic organization of a bibliography is alphabetical, although entries can be grouped by the type of reference materials used: books, encyclopedias, magazines. If the author's name is not given, list the title first and alphabetize it by the first important word of the title.

Books

List the author's name (last name first), the book title (underlined), the city where the publisher is located, the publisher's name, and the year of publication. Note the punctuation.

Katan, Norma Jean. Hieroglyphs: The Writing of Ancient Egypt.
　　New York: Simon & Schuster, 1981.

Encyclopedia article	**List the author's name (last name first), then the title of the article (in quotation marks). Next, give the title of the encyclopedia (underlined), and the year of publication of the edition that you are using. Note the punctuation.** Mann, Alan E. "Prehistoric People." The World Book Encyclopedia. 1997 ed. **If the author of the article is not given, begin your listing with the title of the article.** "Charles River." Collier's Encyclopedia. 1997 ed.
Magazine or newspaper article	**List the author's name (last name first), the title of the article (in quotation marks), the name of the magazine or newspaper (underlined), the date of publication, the section in which the article appears (for newspaper articles only), and the page number of the article.** MAGAZINE: Kirschner, Suzanne. "From School to Space." Popular Science, June 1998, pp. 56–57. NEWSPAPER: "Storms and Low Prices Jeopardize Apple Farms." The New York Times, Nov. 2, 1998, Sec. A, p. 23. **Here is another way you can write these entries:** MAGAZINE: Kirschner, Suzanne. "From School to Space." Popular Science June 1998: 56–57. NEWSPAPER: "Storms and Low Prices Jeopardize Apple Farms." The New York Times 2 Nov. 1998, sec. A:23.

Titles

Underlining	**Titles of books, magazines, newspapers, plays, movies, television series, works of art, musical compositions, planes, trains, ships, and spacecraft are underlined.** The Giver *(book)* Nova *(TV series)* New Moon *(magazine)* Waterlilies *(painting)* Chicago Tribune *(newspaper)* Discovery *(spacecraft)*
Quotation marks	**Titles of short stories, articles, songs, book chapters, and most poems are enclosed in quotation marks.** "The Fox" *(short story)* "America" *(song)* "If" *(poem)* "Sand Skiing" *(article)* "Celtic Art" *(chapter)*

Quotations

Quotation marks with commas and end marks

Quotation marks are used to set off a speaker's exact words. Commas separate a quotation from the rest of the sentence. The first word begins with a capital letter.

"Please put away your books," said Mr. Emory.

Lisa asked, "When is the report due?"

Quotation marks with divided quotations

Sometimes a quotation is divided into two parts. Enclose each part in quotation marks. If the second part of the divided quotation continues the original sentence, begin it with a small letter. If it starts a new sentence, begin it with a capital letter.

"Where," asked the visitor, "is the post office?"

"I must mail a letter," he added. "It is urgent."

Always place a period inside closing quotation marks. Place a question mark or an exclamation point outside closing quotation marks unless the quotation itself is a question or an exclamation.

Did the stranger really say, "This is top secret"?

Kate exclaimed, "Look at that beautiful baby!"

Dialogue

In dialogue, begin a new paragraph whenever the speaker changes.

"Where is Bangladesh?" asked our history teacher, Ms. Flores.

"I think it is in India," said Scott.

"No," said Angela. "It used to be part of Pakistan, but now it is an independent nation."

Indirect quotations

An indirect quotation tells what a person has said without using that person's exact words. Do not use quotation marks to set off indirect quotations.

Avram mentioned that he had to go to the library.

Capitalization

Rules for capitalization

Capitalize the first word of every sentence.

What an unusual color the roses are!

Capitalize the pronoun *I*.

What should I do next?

Rules for capitalization

(continued)

Capitalize every important word in the names of particular people, places, or things.

Emily G. Hesse   District of Columbia   Lincoln Memorial

Capitalize titles or their abbreviations when used with a person's name.

Governor Bradford   Senator Smith   Dr. Lin

Capitalize proper adjectives.

We ate at a Chinese restaurant.   He is French.

Capitalize the names of months and days.

My birthday is not on the last Monday in March.

Capitalize the names of organizations, businesses, institutions, and agencies.

National Hockey League   The Status Company

Capitalize the names of periods, holidays, and other special events.

Bronze Age   Industrial Revolution   Labor Day

Capitalize the first and last words and all important words in the titles of books, newspapers, magazines, stories, songs, poems, reports, and outlines. (Articles, short conjunctions, and short prepositions are not capitalized unless they are the first or last word.)

Julie of the Wolves   "Over the Rainbow"
The New York Times   "The Road Not Taken"
Farm Journal   "Canadian National Parks"
"Up from the Deep"   "The Exports of Italy"

Capitalize the first word of each main topic and subtopic in an outline.

I. Types of libraries
    A. Large public library
    B. Bookmobile

Capitalize the first word in the greeting and the closing of a letter.

Dear Marcia,   Yours truly,

Capitalize nationalities, languages, religions, and religious terms.

Chinese   Spanish   American   Buddhism

Capitalize words showing family relationships only when they are used before a name or when they take the place of a name.

Today, Uncle Jerry is coming.   My uncle and I are good friends.

Rules for capitalization
(continued)

Capitalize cities, counties, states, countries, continents, and regions of the United States.

London	Iowa	Asia
Essex County	Canada	the South

Capitalize streets, highways, buildings, bridges, and monuments.

Fifth Avenue	Empire State Building	Statue of Liberty
Interstate 90	Golden Gate Bridge	

Capitalize planets, bodies of water, and geographic features.

Saturn	Indian Ocean	Andes Mountains	Sahara Desert

Capitalize the names of documents.

Declaration of Independence   Atomic Energy Act

Punctuation

End marks

There are three end marks. A *period (.)* ends a declarative or imperative sentence. A *question mark (?)* follows an interrogative sentence. An *exclamation point (!)* follows an exclamatory sentence.

The scissors are on my desk. *(declarative)*
Look up the spelling of that word. *(imperative)*
How is the word spelled? *(interrogative)*
This is your best poem so far! *(exclamatory)*

Interjections

An *interjection* is a word or group of words that expresses feeling. It is followed by a comma or an exclamation point.

My goodness, this tastes terrible.
Hurray! The field goal counts.

Apostrophe

To form the possessive of a singular noun, use an apostrophe and *s*.

sister's	family's	Tess's	Jim Dodge's

For a plural noun that ends in *s*, add an apostrophe only.

sisters'	families'	Smiths'	Evanses'

For a plural noun that does not end in *s*, add an apostrophe and *s*.

women's	alumni's	mice's	brothers-in-law's

Use an apostrophe in contractions in place of the dropped letters.

isn't *(is not)*	wasn't *(was not)*	I'm *(I am)*
can't *(cannot)*	we're *(we are)*	they've *(they have)*
won't *(will not)*	it's *(it is)*	they'll *(they will)*

| **Colon** | **Use a colon in the greeting of a business letter.** |
| | Dear Mrs. Trimby: Dear Realty Homes: |

Use a colon to introduce a list.
I like the following foods: fish, peas, and pears.

Use a colon when writing the time of day.
They came back from lunch at 1:04 P.M.

Comma

Use commas to separate words in a series.
We bought apples, peaches, and grapes.

Use a comma to separate the simple sentences in a compound sentence.
Some students were at lunch, but others were studying.

Use commas to set off an appositive from the rest of the sentence when the appositive is not necessary to the meaning of the sentence.
The poet Emily Dickinson lived a quiet life.
(The appositive is necessary to the meaning.)
Massachusetts, the Bay State, has lovely beaches.
(The appositive is not necessary to the meaning.)

Use commas after introductory words such as *yes*, *no*, *oh*, and *well*.
Well, it's just too cold out.   No, it isn't six yet.

Use commas to set off interrupters such as *however*, *for example*, *in my opinion*, and *as a matter of fact*.
London, however, never bored him.

Use a comma to set off a noun in direct address.
Jean, help me fix this tire.   How was your trip, Grandpa?

Use a comma to separate the month and day from the year. Use a comma to separate the year from the rest of the sentence.
My sister was born on April 9, 1984, in Detroit.
July 4, 1776, is the birthday of our nation.

Use a comma between the names of a city and a state or a city and a country.
Los Angeles, California   Caracas, Venezuela

Use a comma between a street and a city when they appear in a sentence but not between the state and the ZIP Code.
I live at 29 Bear Brook Lane, Provo, Utah 84604.

Comma
(continued)

Use a comma after the greeting in a friendly letter and after the closing in all letters.

Dear Selena,   Sincerely yours,

Use a comma following an introductory prepositional phrase.

Inside the top drawer, you will find a ruler.

Semicolon

A semicolon can be used to separate the parts of a compound sentence.

It was very late; we decided to go to bed.

Hyphens, dashes, and parentheses

Use a hyphen to join the parts of compound numbers, to join two or more words that work together as one adjective before a noun, or to divide a word at the end of a line.

sixty-one   well-developed paragraph
Raphael is known as one of Italy's many magnif-
icent painters.

Use dashes to show a break of thought in a sentence.

The paintings—curiously enough—are done in oil.

Use parentheses to enclose an explanation that is not of major importance to a sentence.

Read Chapter 2 (page 67) for more information.

Letter Models

Friendly Letter

Use correct letter format, capitalization, and punctuation in a friendly letter. A friendly letter has **five** parts.

1. The **heading** contains your complete address and the date.
2. The **greeting**, or salutation, usually includes the word *Dear* and the name of the person to whom you are writing.
3. The **body** of the letter is your message. Indent each paragraph.
4. The **closing** appears under the last paragraph and lines up with the heading. Some common closings are *Your friend, Love,* and *So long.*
5. The **signature** is your first name. Sign it below the closing.

Study this model.

Heading ⟶
42 Pheasant Lane
Reading, MA 01867
April 12, 1999

Greeting ⟶ Dear Sue,

Body ⟶
How are things in Detroit? Is it finally getting warm there?

You must be looking forward to baseball season! It will be great when the Tigers come to play in Boston. Dad bought tickets for the first game! We'll be in Fenway Park, cheering for the Red Sox. You'll be in Detroit, watching the game on TV and cheering for the Tigers. Who do you think will win?

When are you going to a game in Tiger Stadium? Write and tell me!

Closing ⟶ Your cousin,

Signature ⟶ Andy

985003 ADMIT ONE 985003

255

Letter Models

Business Letter

Use correct letter format, capitalization, and punctuation in a business letter. A business letter has **six** parts.

1. The **heading** is the same as in a friendly letter.
2. The **inside address** includes the name and address of the person or business that will receive the letter.
3. The **greeting** follows the inside address. If you do not know whom to address, use *Dear Sir or Madam* or the company's name. Use a colon (:) after the greeting.
4. The **body** is your message. Be direct and polite.
5. The **closing** is formal. Use such closings as *Yours truly* or *Sincerely*.
6. The **signature** is your full name. Write it under the closing. Print or type your name under your signature.

Study this model

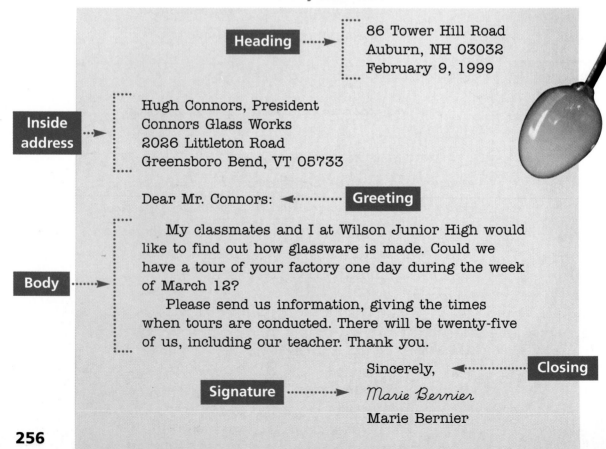

Heading ......▶
86 Tower Hill Road
Auburn, NH 03032
February 9, 1999

Inside address ...▶
Hugh Connors, President
Connors Glass Works
2026 Littleton Road
Greensboro Bend, VT 05733

Dear Mr. Connors: ◀·········· **Greeting**

Body ·······▶
   My classmates and I at Wilson Junior High would like to find out how glassware is made. Could we have a tour of your factory one day during the week of March 12?
   Please send us information, giving the times when tours are conducted. There will be twenty-five of us, including our teacher. Thank you.

                              Sincerely, ◀········· **Closing**

Signature ··········▶ *Marie Bernier*
                              Marie Bernier

Using the Thesaurus

Why Use a Thesaurus?

A **thesaurus** is a reference that can help you make your writing clearer and more interesting. Use it to find a word to replace an overused word or to find an exact word to say what you mean.

How to Use This Thesaurus

This thesaurus includes main entries for words you often use. The **main entry words** appear in blue and are in alphabetical order. The main entry for *important* is shown below. Each main entry includes

- the **part of speech**, a **definition**, and a **sample sentence** for the main entry word;
- several **subentry words** that could be used in place of the main entry word, with a definition and a sample sentence for each one;
- **antonyms**, or opposites, for the main entry word.

For example How would you decide which subentry to use to replace *important* in this sentence?

*Allyson gave an **important** speech on graduation day.*

1 Find each subentry word given for *important*. They are *memorable, notable,* and *significant*.

2 Read the definition and the sample sentence for each subentry. Decide which subentry fits the meaning of the sentence most closely.

*Allyson gave a **memorable** speech on graduation day.*

Part of speech

Main entry word

harmonize

Definition

me or during the same period of time.
an our vacations so that they **coincide**.

pond to be in agreement; match or
re closely. *Each number **corresponds** to a
n on the test.*

rate to combine into a whole. *Many*
nt ideas were **integ** **Subentries**
ation speech.

to make into a unit. *A disaster tends to*
the people it affects.

yms: clash *v.,* conflict *v.*

important *adj.* able to determine or
change the course of events or nature of
things. *Gettysburg was the site of an **important**
Civil War battle.*

memorable remarkable; unforgettable.
*Martin Luther King, Jr.'s "I Have a Dream"
speech is **memorable**.*

notable worthy of notice or comment.
*There is one **notable** exception to this rule.*

significant having a great deal of meaning.
*The footprints provided a **significant** clue to the
detective.*

antonyms: frivolous, incidental, petty, trivial

Sample sentence

Antonyms

ten *v.* to move or act swiftly. *Jim
ned to get to school on time.*
to race or rush with sudden speed. *Lee*

257

Using the Thesaurus

Using the Thesaurus Index

The Thesaurus Index will help you find a word in this Thesaurus. The Thesaurus Index lists **all** of the main entry words, the subentries, and any antonyms included in the Thesaurus. The words in the Thesaurus Index are in alphabetical order.

When you look in the Thesaurus Index, you will see that words are shown in three ways.

Main entry words are shown in blue. For example, the word *important* is a main entry.

Antonyms are shown in regular print. For example, *imprecise* is an antonym.

Subentries are shown in dark print. For example, *inactive* is a subentry.

> ## I
>
> **idle** *adj.*
> **illustration picture** *n.*
> **image picture** *n.*
> **immediate near** *adj.*
> **immobilized idle** *adj.*
> **impending near** *adj.*
> **important** *adj.*
> **impose fix** *v.*
> imprecise **definite** *adj.*
> **imprison penalize** *v.*
> inaccurate **definite** *adj.*
> **inactive idle** *adj.*
> inadequate **acceptable** *adj.*
> **inappropriate unusual** *adj.*

Practice Look up each word below in the Thesaurus Index. Write the main entry word for each word.

1. little 2. repair 3. associate 4. remote 5. chief

Use the Thesaurus to choose a more exact word to replace each underlined word. Rewrite each sentence, using the new word.

6. At our next meeting, we will <u>question</u> our club rules.
7. I <u>guess</u> that most of the discussion will be about one rule.
8. Some members have <u>questioned</u> the rule about attendance.
9. They feel that we should <u>penalize</u> people who are late.
10. I hope that the discussion will not be <u>unfriendly</u>.

Thesaurus Index

A

ability **knack** *n.*
abnormal **strange** *adj.*
absolute **definite** *adj.*
acceptable *adj.*
accessible **near** *adj.*
acclaim **compliment** *n.*
accompany **join** *v.*
adapt **fix** *v.*
adeptness **knack** *n.*
adequate **acceptable** *adj.*
adjacent **near** *adj.*
adjust **fix** *v.*
admissible **permissible** *adj.*
advise *v.*
affiliate **join** *v.*
affix **fix** *v.*
affront **compliment** *n.*
allowable **permissible** *adj.*
always *adv.*
amiable **unfriendly** *adj.*
analyze **question** *v.*
anchor **fix** *v.*
animated **idle** *adj.*
answer **question** *v.*
applause **compliment** *n.*
apprise **advise** *v.*
appropriate **unusual** *adj.*
arrange **fix** *v.*
arrange **organize** *v.*
assemble **fix** *v.*
assign **fix** *v.*
associate **join** *v.*
assume **guess** *v.*
attach **fix** *v.*
attend **join** *v.*

B

banned **permissible** *adj.*
begonia **flower** *n.*
belittle **talk** *v.*
belligerent **unfriendly** *adj.*
berate **talk** *v.*
big **little** *adj.*
bizarre **strange** *adj.*
blend **harmonize** *v.*
boarder *n.*
border *n.*
boundary **border** *n.*
break **fix** *v.*

C

canvass **question** *v.*
categorize **organize** *v.*
cause **effect** *n.*
caution **advise** *v.*
ceaselessly **always** *adv.*
cement **fix** *v.*
censure **criticize** *v.*
challenge **question** *v.*
chasten **penalize** *v.*
chastise **penalize** *v.*
cheerful **miserable** *adj.*
chief **principal** *adj.*
clash **harmonize** *v.*
classify **organize** *v.*
cleanse **sterilize** *v.*
coincide **harmonize** *v.*
command **fix** *v.*
commendation **compliment** *n.*
commonplace **strange** *adj.*
compensate **penalize** *v.*
competence **knack** *n.*
compliment **criticize** *v.*
compliment *n.*
compose **fix** *v.*
condemn **criticize** *v.*

conflict **harmonize** *v.*
congenial **unfriendly** *adj.*
congratulate **talk** *v.*
connect **fix** *v.*
consequence **effect** *n.*
constantly **always** *adv.*
contest **question** *v.*
continually **always** *adv.*
continuously **always** *adv.*
contrary **unfriendly** *adj.*
correspond **harmonize** *v.*
counsel **advise** *v.*
criticize *v.*

D

dash **hasten** *v.*
dawdle **hasten** *v.*
deceive **advise** *v.*
decontaminate **sterilize** *v.*
decree **fix** *v.*
deficient **acceptable** *adj.*
definite *adj.*
delay **hasten** *v.*
delicate **durable** *adj.*
delude **advise** *v.*
demand **question** *v.*
denounce **criticize** *v.*
depressed **miserable** *adj.*
describe **talk** *v.*
desolate **miserable** *adj.*
despondent **miserable** *adj.*
detach **fix** *v.*
dictate **fix** *v.*
dictator **ruler** *n.*
diligent **idle** *adj.*
discipline **penalize** *v.*
discontented **miserable** *adj.*
disinfect **sterilize** *v.*
dismantle **fix** *v.*
dispose **organize** *v.*
dispute **question** *v.*

disrupt **fix** *v.*
disrupt **organize** *v.*
distant **near** *adj.*
disturb **organize** *v.*
dominant principal *adj.*
doubt question *v.*
durable *adj.*

E

eccentric unusual *adj.*
effect *n.*
emperor ruler *n.*
employ utilize *v.*
employed **idle** *adj.*
encourage talk *v.*
end effect *n.*
endlessly always *adv.*
enlighten advise *v.*
escort join *v.*
eternally always *adv.*
everlastingly always *adv.*
examine question *v.*
exercise utilize *v.*
expertise knack *n.*
explain talk *v.*
explicit definite *adj.*
explore question *v.*

F

fix *v.*
flattery compliment *n.*
fleetingly **always** *adv.*
flower *n.*
forbidden **permissible** *adj.*
foreign strange *adj.*
fracture **fix** *v.*
fragile **durable** *adj.*
free **fix** *v.*
fringe border *n.*
frivolous **important** *adj.*

G

gardenia flower *n.*
generalize talk *v.*
governor ruler *n.*
guess *v.*

H

handle utilize *v.*
hardy durable *adj.*
harmonize *v.*
hasten *v.*
hostile unfriendly *adj.*

I

idle *adj.*
illustration picture *n.*
image picture *n.*
immediate near *adj.*
immobilized idle *adj.*
impending near *adj.*
important *adj.*
impose fix *v.*
imprecise **definite** *adj.*
imprison penalize *v.*
inaccurate **definite** *adj.*
inactive idle *adj.*
inadequate **acceptable** *adj.*
inappropriate unusual *adj.*
incessantly always *adv.*
incidental **important** *adj.*
incompetence **knack** *n.*
inconsolable miserable *adj.*
incredible unbelievable *adj.*
indestructible durable *adj.*
indestructibly always *adv.*
indolent idle *adj.*
industrious **idle** *adj.*

inefficiency **knack** *n.*
inert idle *adj.*
infinitely always *adv.*
inform advise *v.*
inform talk *v.*
inhabitant boarder *n.*
inquire question *v.*
insignificant **principal** *adj.*
inspire **talk** *v.*
insufficient acceptable *adj.*
insult **compliment** *n.*
integrate harmonize *v.*
interior **border** *n.*
interminably always *adv.*
interrogate question *v.*
interview question *v.*
investigate question *v.*
irregular strange *adj.*
irregularly **always** *adv.*

J

join *v.*
joyous **miserable** *adj.*

K

knack *n.*

L

legalized permissible *adj.*
legitimate permissible *adj.*
liberate **fix** *v.*
little *adj.*
lodger boarder *n.*

M

magnolia flower *n.*
malign talk *v.*
mammoth **little** *adj.*
margin border *n.*

meager **little** *adj.*
memorable **important** *adj.*
mend **fix** *v.*
microscopic **little** *adj.*
miniature **little** *adj.*
minor **principal** *adj.*
miserable *adj.*
misinform **advise** *v.*
mislead **advise** *v.*
monarch **ruler** *n.*
monstrous **unusual** *adj.*
moor **fix** *v.*

N

narrate **talk** *v.*
near *adj.*
normal **unusual** *adj.*
notable **important** *adj.*

O

occasionally **always** *adv.*
occupant **boarder** *n.*
ordain **fix** *v.*
organize *v.*
outcome **effect** *n.*
overhaul **fix** *v.*

P

patch **fix** *v.*
penalize *v.*
perennially **always** *adv.*
perimeter **border** *n.*
permanently **always** *adv.*
permissible *adj.*
perpetually **always** *adv.*
petite **little** *adj.*
petty **important** *adj.*
phenomenal **unbelievable** *adj.*
photograph **picture** *n.*
picture *n.*

plausible **unbelievable** *adj.*
portrait **picture** *n.*
positive **definite** *adj.*
praise **compliment** *n.*
praise **criticize** *v.*
praise **talk** *v.*
precise **definite** *adj.*
predict **guess** *v.*
premier **ruler** *n.*
prepare **fix** *v.*
preposterous **unbelievable** *adj.*
president **ruler** *n.*
presume **guess** *v.*
primary **principal** *adj.*
principal *adj.*
probe **question** *v.*
proficiency **knack** *n.*
punish **penalize** *v.*
purify **sterilize** *v.*

Q

query **question** *v.*
question *v.*
quiz **question** *v.*

R

rare **unusual** *adj.*
ready **fix** *v.*
reason **effect** *n.*
reassure **talk** *v.*
rebuke **talk** *v.*
recite **talk** *v.*
recommend **advise** *v.*
recommend **talk** *v.*
reconcile **fix** *v.*
recondition **fix** *v.*
recount **talk** *v.*
regularly **always** *adv.*
relate **talk** *v.*
relentlessly **always** *adv.*
remote **near** *adj.*

repair **fix** *v.*
reply **question** *v.*
reprehend **criticize** *v.*
reproach **criticize** *v.*
resident **boarder** *n.*
respectable **acceptable** *adj.*
respond **question** *v.*
result **effect** *n.*
revise **fix** *v.*
reward **penalize** *v.*
ridicule **talk** *v.*
robust **durable** *adj.*
ruler *n.*
rupture **fix** *v.*

S

sanitize **sterilize** *v.*
satisfactory **acceptable** *adj.*
scant **little** *adj.*
scuttle **hasten** *v.*
secure **fix** *v.*
settle **fix** *v.*
significant **important** *adj.*
sketch **picture** *n.*
slander **talk** *v.*
slight **little** *adj.*
slothful **idle** *adj.*
sort **organize** *v.*
specific **definite** *adj.*
specify **fix** *v.*
speculate **guess** *v.*
sprint **hasten** *v.*
steadily **always** *adv.*
sterilize *v.*
stipulate **fix** *v.*
stout **durable** *adj.*
strange *adj.*
sturdy **durable** *adj.*
sufficient **acceptable** *adj.*
summarize **talk** *v.*
suspect **guess** *v.*

Thesaurus Index

T

talk *v.*
temporarily **always** *adv.*
tenant boarder *n.*
test question *v.*
tighten fix *v.*
tiny little *adj.*
tolerable acceptable *adj.*
tribute compliment *n.*
trivial **important** *adj.*

U

unbelievable *adj.*
unceasingly always *adv.*
undo **fix** *v.*
unemployed idle *adj.*
unfriendly *adj.*
unhappy miserable *adj.*
unify harmonize *v.*
unique strange *adj.*
unusual *adj.*
unvaryingly always *adv.*
use utilize *v.*
usual **unusual** *adj.*
utilize *v.*

V

verge **border** *n.*
violet **flower** *n.*

W

weak **durable** *adj.*

Thesaurus

A

acceptable *adj.* fitting; suitable. *Our English teacher said that only typed reports will be acceptable.*

adequate good, large, rich, or full enough. *We have an **adequate** amount of money to cover our vacation expenses.*

respectable proper in behavior, character, or appearance. *A **respectable** person would never throw food in a restaurant.*

satisfactory sufficient to meet a demand or requirement; adequate. *After her mother made sure that Lorna had done a **satisfactory** job of cleaning her room, Lorna was allowed to go out to the movies.*

sufficient as much as is needed. *This row has a **sufficient** number of seats for us to sit together.*

tolerable passable. *The food in this restaurant is barely **tolerable**.*

antonyms: deficient, inadequate, insufficient

---

advise *v.* to give advice to or to offer advice. *The car mechanic **advised** Andre to buy a new car soon because his old one needed too many expensive repairs.*

apprise to cause to know. *At next week's meeting, the treasurer will **apprise** us of the status of our budget.*

caution to warn against possible trouble or danger. *The forecaster **cautioned** people to avoid driving in the city during the snowstorm.*

counsel to give advice or guidance. *The lawyer **counseled** her client to plead guilty to all the charges.*

enlighten to give knowledge or insight to; instruct. *This lecture will **enlighten** you about the dangers of hazardous waste.*

inform to give information to; notify. *The letter **informed** the Cohens that their rent was going up.*

recommend to offer a suggestion. *The doctor **recommended** that Santos stay home from work after he hurt his back.*

antonyms: deceive, delude, misinform, mislead

Word Bank

always *adv.* for all time; without interruption or end.

ceaselessly	interminably
constantly	perennially
continually	permanently
continuously	perpetually
endlessly	regularly
eternally	relentlessly
everlastingly	steadily
incessantly	unceasingly
indestructibly	unvaryingly
infinitely	

antonyms: fleetingly, irregularly, occasionally, temporarily

B

boarder *n.* a person who pays for and receives meals and lodging at another person's home. *The new **boarder** comes out of his room only for meals.*

inhabitant a permanent resident of a particular place. *Mr. Suarez has been an **inhabitant** of Hale Street his whole life.*

lodger a person who rents a room or rooms in another person's house. *The last **lodger** who rented this room was a student.*

occupant someone or something occupying a place or position. *The **occupants** of apartment 3G are in France for two weeks.*

resident a person who makes his or her home in a particular place. *All town **residents** are encouraged to vote in the election.*

tenant a person who pays rent to use or occupy the property of another. *The **tenant's** rent was raised.*

---

border *n.* the line where one country, area, or region ends and another begins. *The French guard stamped our passports at the **border**.*

263

boundary an edge or dividing line marking a place where a country, state, or other region ends. *The Ohio River marks the Ohio and Kentucky boundary.*

fringe an outer part. *At dawn, we saw deer standing on the fringe of the open field.*

margin the blank space bordering the written or printed area on a page. *Cassie jotted notes in the margin after she filled the page.*

perimeter the outer limits of an area. *Mr. Sacco fenced off the perimeter of his vegetable garden.*

verge the extreme edge, rim, or margin of something. *The new shopping center is on the verge of an agricultural area.*
antonym: interior

C

compliment *n.* an expression of praise or admiration. *Tessa paid Joan a compliment on her new hairdo.*

acclaim loud or enthusiastic praise. *The prince enjoyed widespread public acclaim.*

applause praise or approval expressed by clapping hands. *Thunderous applause shook the playhouse as the curtain came down.*

commendation recommendation or praise. *The young lieutenant received a commendation for his bravery in battle.*

flattery excessive and insincere praise. *Justin's flattery did not influence the coach's decision.*

praise an expression of warm approval. *Her father's praise meant more to her than winning the game.*

tribute a gift or some other acknowledgment of gratitude, respect, or admiration. *We paid tribute to the Teacher of the Year.*
antonyms: affront, insult *n.*

criticize *v.* to judge the merits and faults of; evaluate. *The restaurant reviewer criticized the café's poor service.*

censure to express strong disapproval. *The Senate censured two of its members for their misconduct.*

condemn to pronounce judgment against. *The criminal was condemned to life in prison.*

denounce to express very strong disapproval. *Congress denounced the budget cuts.*

reprehend to show disapproval. *The coach reprehended the actions of the players.*

reproach to criticize severely or sternly. *Ms. Loo reproached her noisy students.*
antonyms: compliment *v.*, praise *v.*

D

definite *adj.* certain, sure. *It is definite that we're moving to Florida.*

absolute without reservation; unqualified. *I have absolute faith in Jed's word.*

explicit clearly defined; specific. *Ruth gave us explicit directions to her house.*

positive absolutely certain. *Jackie was positive that she would be able to find the way to the little pond in the woods.*

precise definite; not vague. *The witness gave a precise account of the accident.*

specific explicitly set forth. *Each customer had a specific complaint to discuss.*
antonyms: imprecise, inaccurate

durable *adj.* able to withstand wear and tear; sturdy. *Denim is a good fabric for jeans because it is so durable.*

hardy able to withstand unfavorable conditions. *St. Bernards are hardy dogs that can survive severely cold temperatures.*

indestructible not capable of being destroyed. *Since I travel so much, I need luggage that is practically indestructible.*

robust full of health and strength; vigorous. *Katherine is a descendant of robust pioneers.*

stout strong or solid. *The stout sailor did not hesitate to lift the massive oar.*

sturdy strong; durable; substantial. *The inspector said that the house beams were sturdy.*
antonyms: delicate, fragile, weak

E

effect *n.* something brought about by a cause. *Music has a relaxing **effect** on me.*
consequence something that follows from an action or condition. *Hillary's poor grades were the **consequence** of her failure to study.*
end the finish. *By March we are always ready for the **end** of winter.*
outcome the final result. *I could not stay to see the **outcome** of the game.*
result something that is produced by an action or happening. *The power failure was a **result** of the storm.*
antonyms: cause, reason

F

Shades of Meaning

fix *v.*

1. to restore to good working condition:

adapt	overhaul	recondition
adjust	patch	repair
mend	reconcile	revise

2. to put together:

arrange	compose	ready
assemble	prepare	settle

3. to place or fasten securely:

affix	cement	secure
anchor	connect	tighten
attach	moor	

4. to establish definitely:

assign	dictate	specify
command	impose	stipulate
decree	ordain	

antonyms: 1. break, disrupt, fracture *v.,* rupture *v.* **2.** dismantle, undo **3.** detach, free, liberate

flower *n.* the colorful, showy petals of a plant. *Anna wore a red **flower** in her hair.*
begonia any of several plants often grown for their showy flowers or colorfully marked leaves. *Mr. Amata planted **begonias** in his window boxes.*
gardenia large, fragrant white flower of a shrub with glossy evergreen leaves. *The sweet fragrance of **gardenias** perfumed the summer night.*
magnolia large, showy white or pink flowers of a tree or shrub. *The delicate pink petals of **magnolia** blossoms litter the green lawn in late spring.*
violet bluish purple or white flower of a low-growing plant. *The young boy handed his mother a small bouquet of **violets**.*

G

guess *v.* to estimate, judge, or surmise by intuition or hunch. *Jody **guessed** that Leo would win the grand prize.*
assume to take for granted. *Let us **assume** that it will take a week to do this job.*
predict to tell about or make known in advance. *The meteorologist **predicted** heavy snow.*
presume to assume to be true in the absence of anything to the contrary. *Since Jay did not call, I **presume** he is on his way.*
speculate to use the powers of the mind to conceive ideas. *Scientists **speculate** that there could be some form of life on Mars.*
suspect to believe without being sure. *Kim **suspected** that Patty would do better if she studied more.*

H

harmonize *v.* to be in or bring into agreement or harmony. *The costumes* **harmonize** *with the scenery.*

blend to mingle or shade in as a part of. *The color of the woodwork* **blends** *well with the blue in the wallpaper.*

coincide to occur at the same time or during the same period of time. *Let's plan our vacations so that they* **coincide**.

correspond to be in agreement; match or compare closely. *Each number* **corresponds** *to a question on the test.*

integrate to combine into a whole. *Many different ideas were* **integrated** *into Tony's nomination speech.*

unify to make into a unit. *A disaster tends to* **unify** *the people it affects.*

antonyms: clash *v.*, conflict *v.*

hasten *v.* to move or act swiftly. *Jim* **hastened** *to get to school on time.*

dash to race or rush with sudden speed. *Lee* **dashed** *after the runaway dog.*

scuttle to move with quick, small steps. *The spider* **scuttled** *along the floor.*

sprint to run at top speed. *Pam* **sprinted** *toward the goal.*

antonyms: dawdle, delay *v.*

I

idle *adj.* not working or devoted to working or producing. *The trains were* **idle** *during the railway workers' strike.*

immobilized incapable of moving. *Our car was* **immobilized** *along with others involved in the lengthy traffic jam.*

inactive not active or not tending to be active. *Even the bees seemed to be* **inactive** *during the humid summer days.*

indolent disinclined to work; habitually lazy. *Jerome wasn't* **indolent**; *he just couldn't find a job that challenged him.*

inert unable to move or act. *Paralyzed with fear, Lois stood* **inert** *on stage and tried in vain to remember her next line.*

slothful lazy. *Karen's* **slothful** *habits annoyed her parents.*

unemployed out of work; jobless. *The* **unemployed** *pilot missed flying every day.*

antonyms: animated, diligent, employed, industrious

important *adj.* able to determine or change the course of events or nature of things. *Gettysburg was the site of an* **important** *Civil War battle.*

memorable remarkable; unforgettable. *Martin Luther King, Jr.'s "I Have a Dream" speech is* **memorable**.

notable worthy of notice or comment. *There is one* **notable** *exception to this rule.*

significant having a great deal of meaning. *The footprints provided a* **significant** *clue to the detective.*

antonyms: frivolous, incidental, petty, trivial

J

join *v.* to enter into the company of. *Ellie will* **join** *us later at the restaurant.*

accompany to go along with. *Mrs. Van Helm will* **accompany** *Mary to the train station.*

affiliate to associate or join, as with a larger or more important body. *Our club is* **affiliated** *with a state organization.*

associate to connect oneself with a cause or a group. *She won't* **associate** *with members of that club.*

attend to follow as a result or to accompany as a circumstance. *Fame and glory* **attended** *her throughout her life.*

escort to accompany someone, giving protection or guidance. *Armed guards* **escorted** *the train carrying supplies to the troops.*

K

knack *n.* a special talent or skill. *Georgia has a knack for arranging furniture.*

ability a natural or acquired skill or talent. *Harido has a keen ability in math.*

adeptness a skillfulness and effectiveness. *I admire her adeptness at fixing engines.*

competence ability to do what is required. *Kit landed the plane with the competence of an experienced pilot.*

expertise expert skill or knowledge. *Her field of expertise is solar energy.*

proficiency competence through training or practice. *Tom has proficiency in five foreign languages.*

antonyms: incompetence, inefficiency

L

little *adj.* small in size or quantity. *I'm full, so give me only a little piece of fruit.*

meager lacking in quantity. *They divided the meager bits of bread between them.*

microscopic very small; minute. *Thousands of microscopic bugs attacked our plants.*

miniature on a greatly reduced scale from the usual. *The doll house contains miniature furniture.*

petite small and slender; dainty. *The football player looked like a giant next to his petite mother.*

scant not enough in amount or size. *There is scant vegetation in the desert.*

slight small in size or proportion. *He is pale and slight, but he can run.*

tiny extremely small. *The baby kicked his tiny feet.*

antonyms: big, mammoth *adj.*

M

miserable *adj.* very unhappy; wretched. *Hay fever made her feel miserable.*

depressed gloomy; dejected. *The team was depressed after losing the championship.*

desolate lonely and sad. *His eyes told a desolate story of loneliness and despair.*

despondent in low spirits. *Lynda was despondent after losing her job.*

discontented restlessly unhappy. *Dan was discontented and bored with his life.*

inconsolable not able to be comforted. *He was inconsolable after his dog died.*

unhappy not happy; sad. *The unhappy child began to cry.*

antonyms: cheerful, joyous

N

near *adj.* close in space, time, position, or degree. *The library is near our house.*

accessible easy to reach. *A small airport is accessible from our town.*

adjacent next to; adjoining. *The four girls shared adjacent hotel rooms.*

immediate close at hand. *There are two malls in our immediate neighborhood.*

impending about to take place. *A sense of impending doom hung in the air.*

antonyms: distant, remote

O

organize *v.* to put together in an orderly, systematic way. *Before she began speaking, she organized her notes.*

arrange to put in a deliberate order. *Arrange the events in sequential order.*

categorize to put into a specifically defined division or class. *Categorize these animals as reptiles or amphibians.*

classify to arrange or organize according to a class or category. *We classify and file every document.*

dispose to place or set in a particular order. *She disposed the merchandise attractively.*

sort to arrange according to class, kind, or size. *Beth **sorted** her clothes into three piles— new, old, and very old.*
antonyms: disrupt, disturb

P

penalize *v.* to subject to a penalty, as for an offense or infringement of a rule. *The Tigers were **penalized** for pushing and shoving.*
chasten to punish in order to correct. *Mrs. Lin **chastened** Han for missing dinner.*
chastise to punish for wrongdoing. *Pioneer schoolteachers severely **chastised** students who misbehaved.*
discipline to punish in order to reform or train. *We had to **discipline** our puppy to keep him from running into the road.*
imprison to put in prison. *The thief was **imprisoned** for fifteen years.*
punish to cause to undergo a penalty for a crime, fault, or misbehavior. *Dad **punished** Sid for being rude to Mr. Greeley.*
antonyms: compensate, reward *v.*

permissible *adj.* such as can be permitted. *Fishing in the lake is **permissible** except during a drought.*
admissible accepted or permitted. *The evidence was not **admissible** because the judge thought the child giving the testimony was too young.*
allowable capable of being permitted. *Running in the halls is not **allowable** because it is dangerous both to the runner and to others.*
legalize to make legal. *Town officials decided to **legalize** the open burning of leaves.*
legitimate being or acting in accordance with the law; lawful. *The newborn child was the **legitimate** heir to the throne.*
antonyms: banned, forbidden

picture *n.* a visual representation or image. *Here is a **picture** of my younger sister.*
illustration a picture, diagram, or chart, serving to clarify, explain, or decorate. *This **illustration** shows exactly what the new mall will look like.*
image a mental picture of something not present or real. *His mind was filled with **images** of his hometown.*
photograph an image formed on a light-sensitive surface by a camera. *He admired her **photographs** of the countryside.*
portrait a painting, photograph, or other likeness of a person. *A famous artist was hired to paint a **portrait** of the king.*
sketch a rough preliminary drawing or painting. *Chuck made two **sketches** of the tree before he began to paint.*

principal *adj.* first or foremost in rank, degree, or importance. *All **principal** parts in the play have been cast.*
chief most important; main. *The town's **chief** industry was dairy farming.*
dominant having the most influence or control; governing. *The cello was the **dominant** instrument in the quartet.*
primary first in importance, degree, or quality. *His **primary** reason for joining the club was to make new friends.*
antonyms: insignificant, minor

Q

Word Bank

question *v.* to ask questions of.

analyze	doubt	investigate
canvass	examine	probe
challenge	explore	query
contest	inquire	quiz
demand	interrogate	test
dispute	interview	

antonyms answer *v.*, reply *v.*, respond

R

ruler *n.* a person, such as a queen, who governs a country. *The country enjoyed peace while the queen was ruler.*

dictator a ruler who has complete authority and unlimited power over the government of a country. *The people rebelled against the tyrannical dictator.*

emperor a male ruler of an empire. *The emperor waved to his subjects from the imperial palace.*

governor the person elected chief executive of a state in the United States. *The governor proposed the new state budget.*

monarch a ruler or sovereign, such as a king, queen, or emperor. *The people saw their monarch only during royal ceremonies.*

premier the chief minister or chief executive of a government. *The premier met with top leaders from around the world.*

president the chief executive of a republic, such as the United States. *The first President of the United States was George Washington.*

S

sterilize *v.* to free from living microorganisms, especially those that cause disease. *The doctor sterilizes his instruments after each use.*

cleanse to make clean and pure. *The nurse thoroughly cleansed the girl's cut.*

decontaminate to free of harmful substances, such as poisonous chemicals or radioactive materials. *They decontaminated the factory after the toxic chemical leak.*

disinfect to rid of microorganisms that are capable of causing diseases. *Alice disinfected the bandages by rinsing them in bleach.*

purify to free from anything harmful or undesirable. *A filter purifies the water from our well.*

sanitize to free from elements, such as filth or bacteria, that endanger health. *We sanitized everything that went into the baby's mouth.*

---

strange *adj.* not usual. *She had the strange sensation that she had been there before.*

abnormal not normal; unusual. *This amount of rain is abnormal for this time of year.*

bizarre very strange or odd. *The young girl dressed in a bizarre fashion.*

foreign not naturally or normally belonging. *Even the signs on the road were foreign to us.*

irregular unusual or improper. *His comments were highly irregular for one who had not participated in drafting the proposal.*

unique being the only one. *The research scientist had a unique relationship with the wolves.*

antonym: commonplace

T

Shades of Meaning

talk *v.* to use human speech

1. to speak favorably about or to:
congratulate	praise
encourage	reassure
inspire	recommend

2. to give a verbal account of:
describe	inform	recount
explain	narrate	relate
generalize	recite	summarize

3. to speak of or to in a disapproving manner:
belittle	malign	ridicule
berate	rebuke	slander

contrary stubbornly opposed to others. *She is so **contrary** that she'll never agree with our plan.*
hostile feeling or showing opposition. *He remained **hostile** despite my effort to forget the past and become friends.*
antonyms: amiable, congenial

unusual *adj.* not usual, common, or ordinary. *Sal has collected hundreds of **unusual** insects.*
eccentric odd or unusual in appearance or behavior. *Aunt Esther's big flowery hats and heavy hiking boots make her look rather **eccentric**.*
inappropriate not appropriate; unsuitable. *It was highly **inappropriate** for Thomas to walk out during the principal's talk.*
monstrous deviating greatly from the norm in appearance or structure. *The new town hall was a **monstrous** example of a bizarre trend in architecture.*
rare infrequently occurring. *Mr. Woolf grows **rare** orchids in his greenhouse.*
antonyms: appropriate, normal, usual

U

unbelievable *adj.* not to be believed. *The tale about UFO sightings was **unbelievable**.*
incredible unbelievable. *It was **incredible** that he survived against such odds.*
phenomenal extraordinary. *The **phenomenal** story of his success was in all the papers.*
preposterous completely unreasonable or absurd. *The story of the two-headed giraffe was **preposterous**.*
antonym: plausible

unfriendly *adj.* not friendly. *Their new neighbors were **unfriendly** and unpleasant.*
belligerent inclined to fight; quarrelsome. *People avoided him because of his angry, **belligerent** personality.*

utilize *v.* to put to use for a certain purpose. *We **utilized** the sun's energy to heat our house.*
employ to make use of or to put to use. *Tia **employed** her reasoning powers to solve the problem.*
exercise to put into play or operation; use. ***Exercise** your right to vote.*
handle to operate with the hands; manipulate. *Watch how Sumi **handles** a golf club.*
use to bring or put into service. *You can **use** this cloth to wipe up the spill.*

Spelling-Meaning Index

Phonics and Spelling

This Spelling-Meaning Index contains words related in spelling and meaning. The Index has four sections: Consonant Changes, Vowel Changes, Absorbed Prefixes, and Word Parts. The first two sections contain related word pairs and other words in the same word families. The last two sections contain a list of absorbed prefixes, Latin word roots and Greek word parts, and words that contain these word parts. The words in each section of this Index are in alphabetical order.

Consonant Changes
The letters in dark print show that the spelling stays the same even though the sound changes.

Consonant Changes:
Silent to Sounded

Sometimes you can remember how to spell a word with a silent consonant by thinking of a related word in which the letter is pronounced.

autum**n**-autum**n**al
colum**n**-colum**n**ist
condem**n**-condem**n**ation
de**b**t-de**b**it
desi**g**n-desi**g**nate
dou**b**t-du**b**ious
hasten-haste
heir-in**h**erit
mus**c**le-mus**c**ular
resi**g**n-resi**g**nation
solem**n**-solem**n**ity
ve**h**icle-ve**h**icular

Consonant Changes:
The Sound of *t*

The sound of a final *t* may change to the |sh| sound when the suffix *-ion* is added. Thinking of a related word can help you remember that the |sh| sound is spelled *t*.

congratula**t**e-congratula**t**ions
connec**t**-connec**t**ion

coopera**t**e-coopera**t**ion
detec**t**-detec**t**ion
duplica**t**e-duplica**t**ion
evalua**t**e-evalua**t**ion
exhibi**t**-exhibi**t**ion
implica**t**e-implica**t**ion
investiga**t**e-investiga**t**ion
opera**t**e-opera**t**ion
participa**t**e-participa**t**ion
prosecu**t**e-prosecu**t**ion
punctua**t**e-punctua**t**ion
viola**t**e-viola**t**ion

Vowel Changes
The letters in dark print show that the spelling stays the same even though the sound changes.

Vowel Changes:
Long to Short Vowel Sound

Words that are related in meaning are often related in spelling, even though one word has a long vowel sound and the other word has a short vowel sound.

athl**e**te-athl**e**tic
atr**o**cious-atr**o**city
fer**o**cious-fer**o**city
fl**a**me-fl**a**mmable
gr**a**teful-gr**a**titude
gr**a**ve-gr**a**vity
hum**a**ne-hum**a**nity
ign**i**te-ign**i**tion

impede-impediment
induce-induction
introduce-introduction
meter-metric
microscope-microscopic
precise-precision
produce-production
reduce-reduction
revise-revision
suffice-sufficient

Vowel Changes:
Schwa to Long Vowel Sound

You can remember how to spell the schwa sound in some words by thinking of a related word with a long vowel sound spelled the same way.

admiration-admire
alternative-alternate
combination-combine
definition-define
deprivation-deprive
derivation-derive
disposition-dispose
harmony-harmonious
immunize-immune
imposition-impose
indicative-indicate
infinite-finite
initiative-initiate
inspiration-inspire
mandatory-mandate
narrative-narrate
remedy-remedial
stability-stable
strategy-strategic
variety-various
vegetable-vegetation

Vowel Changes:
Schwa to Short Vowel Sound

You can remember how to spell the schwa sound in some words by thinking of a related word with a short vowel sound spelled the same way.

academy-academic
adapt-adaptation
economy-economics
emphasis-emphatic
excellence-excel
genetic-gene
illustrate-illustrative
neutral-neutrality
original-origin
punctual-punctuality
restoration-restore
sequence-sequential
syllable-syllabication
symbolism-symbolic
tranquil-tranquility
triumph-triumphant
trivial-triviality

Absorbed Prefixes

Some prefixes change their spellings to match the first letter or sound of the word roots or base words to which they are attached. Knowing this can help you remember to double the consonant in some words with these prefixes. The letters in dark print highlight the prefix.

ad- "to, toward"

accede
accent
accentuate
accept
acceptable
access
accessory
acclaim
acclamation
accommodate
accompany
accomplice
accordion
account
accountant
accumulate
accuracy
accurate
accusation
accustomed
affectionate
affiliate
aggravate
aggressive
allegiance
alleviate
alliance
alliteration
allocate
allotted
allude
announcer
apparatus
apparel
apparent
appendage

appendix
appetite
appetizer
appliance
applicable
applicant
application
appoint
appraisal
appreciate
apprehensive
apprentice
appropriate
approve
approximate
arrangement
arrest
arrival
assembly
assent
assign
assignment
assimilation
assistance
assistant
assortment
assure
attach
attain
attempt
attendance
attendant
attire
attitude
attract
attribute

con- "with, together"

accommodate
collaborate
collapse
collateral
commit
committee
communication
community
colleague
collision
commemorate
comment

commentary
commercial
commiserate
commission
commute
correlation
correspond
correspondent
corroborate
corrode
corrupt

in- "in, not, with, together"

illegal
illegible
illicit
illiterate
illogical
illuminate
illusion
illustrate
illustration
illustrative
immaculate
immaterial
immature
immeasurable
immemorial
immerse

immigrant
immigrate
immobilize
immortal
immovable
irrational
irregular
irrelevant
irreparable
irreplaceable
irresistible
irresponsible
irrevocable
irrigate
irritate

ob- "to; against"

occasional
occupation
occurrence

opponent
opportunity
opposite

Spelling-Meaning Index

Word Parts

Words with the same Latin word root or Greek word part are related in spelling and meaning. Knowing the meaning of a word part can help you understand and spell the words in that family. The letters in dark print highlight the word part.

Latin Word Roots

cis, "to cut"

con**cis**e	in**cis**ive
de**cis**ion	in**cis**or
de**cis**ive	pre**cis**e
ex**cis**e	pre**cis**ion
in**cis**ion	**scis**sors

cred, "to believe" or "to trust"

ac**cred**it	**cred**it
credence	dis**cred**it
credentials	in**cred**ible
credibility	in**cred**ulous

dict, "to say"

ab**dict**ate	in**dict**
contra**dict**	in**dict**ment
de**dic**ate	juris**dict**ion
dictate	pre**dic**ament
dictation	pre**dic**ate
dictator	pre**dict**
diction	pre**dict**ion
dictionary	vale**dict**orian
dictum	ver**dict**
e**dict**	

fract or **frag,** "to break"

fracas	**frag**ment
fraction	in**fract**ion
fracture	re**fract**
fragile	

gest, "to bear, carry, or bring"

con**gest**	**gest**ation
con**gest**ion	**gest**iculate
di**gest**	**gest**ure
di**gest**ion	in**gest**
di**gest**ive	sug**gest**
gestate	sug**gest**ion

ject, "to throw"

ab**ject**	ob**ject**ion
ad**ject**ive	ob**ject**ive
con**ject**ure	pro**ject**
de**ject**ed	pro**ject**ile
e**ject**	pro**ject**or
e**ject**ion	re**ject**
in**ject**	re**ject**ion
in**ject**ion	sub**ject**
inter**ject**	sub**ject**ive
inter**ject**ion	tra**ject**ory
ob**ject**	

mem, "mindful"

com**mem**orate	**mem**orandum
im**mem**orial	**mem**orial
memento	**mem**orize
memoir	**mem**ory
memorabilia	re**mem**ber
memorable	

pend, "to hang, weigh"

ap**pend**	im**pend**ing
ap**pend**age	**pend**ant
ap**pend**ix	**pend**ing
com**pens**ate	**pend**ulous
com**pens**ation	**pend**ulum
com**pens**atory	**pens**ion
de**pend**	**pens**ive
de**pend**able	**pent**house
de**pend**ent	per**pend**icular
dis**pens**e	pro**pens**ity
ex**pend**	sti**pend**
ex**pend**iture	sus**pend**
ex**pens**e	sus**pens**e
ex**pens**ive	sus**pens**ion

pet, "go toward, seek, strive for"

ap**pet**ite	im**pet**us
ap**pet**izer	per**pet**ual
com**pet**e	**pet**ition
com**pet**ence	**pet**ulant
com**pet**ent	re**peat**
com**pet**ition	re**pet**ition
com**pet**itive	re**pet**itive
com**pet**itor	

port, "to carry"

de**port**	**port**folio
ex**port**	pur**port**
im**port**	rap**port**
im**port**ance	re**port**
im**port**ant	re**port**er
pass**port**	sup**port**
portable	trans**port**
porter	trans**port**ation

rupt, "to break, burst"

ab**rupt**	e**rupt**
bank**rupt**	e**rupt**ion
cor**rupt**	inter**rupt**
cor**rupt**ion	inter**rupt**ion
dis**rupt**	**rupt**ure
dis**rupt**ion	

scrib, "to write"

a**scrib**e	pro**scrib**e
circum**scrib**e	**scrib**ble
de**scrib**e	**scrib**e
de**scrip**tion	**scrip**t
in**scrib**e	**scrip**ture
in**scrip**tion	sub**scrib**e
manu**scrip**t	sub**scrip**t
nonde**scrip**t	sub**scrip**tion
post**scrip**t	super**scrip**t
pre**scrib**e	tran**scrib**e
pre**scrip**tion	

sign, "mark or seal"

as**sign**	**sign**ature
as**sign**ment	**sign**et
con**sign**	**sign**ificance
de**sign**	**sign**ificant
de**sign**ate	**sign**ify
de**sign**ation	
en**sign**	
in**sign**ia	
re**sign**	
re**sign**ation	
signal	

Spelling-Meaning Index

sist, "to stand"

assist
assistance
assistant
coexist
consist
consistency
consistent
desist
exist
existence
insist
insistence
insistent
irresistible
persist
persistence
persistent
resist
resistance
resistant
subsist
subsistance
subsistant
transistor

solv, "to loosen or to free"

absolute
absolve
dissolve
resolute
resolution
resolve
soluble
solution
solve
solvent

spect, "to look at"

aspect
auspices
circumspect
conspicuous
disrespect
expect
expectation
inspect
inspection
inspector
introspection
perspective
prospect
prospector
respect
retrospect
specimen
specious
spectacle
spectacular
spectator
specter
spectral
spectrum
speculate
suspect
suspicion
suspicious

sta, "to stand"

circumstance
constant
constituent
constitute
constitution
contrast
destitute
distance
distant
establish
establishment
estate
instance
instant
institute
institution
obstacle
stability
stabilize
stable
stage
stalwart
stance
stand
standard
stanza
state
statement
static
station
stationary
stationery
statistic
statue
stature
status
statute
stay
substance
substantial
substantiate
substitute
superstition

Greek Word Parts

ast, "star"

aster
asterisk
asteroid
astral
astrodome
astrology
astronaut
astronomer
astronomical
astronomy
disaster

cris or **crit,** "to decide, judge, or separate"

crisis	**crit**icize
criteria	**crit**ique
criterion	dia**crit**ical
critic	hypo**crisy**
critical	hypo**crit**e
criticism	

cycl, "circle"

bi**cycl**e	en**cycl**opedia
cycle	motor**cycl**e
cyclical	re**cycl**e
cyclist	tri**cycl**e
cyclone	

gram, "something written"

ana**gram**	holo**gram**
cardio**gram**	kilo**gram**
dia**gram**	mono**gram**
epi**gram**	parallelo**gram**
grammar	pro**gram**
grammatical	tele**gram**

graph, "writing"

autobio**graph**y	icono**graph**y
auto**graph**	lexico**graph**er
biblio**graph**y	lexico**graph**y
bio**graph**y	litho**graph**
calli**graph**y	mimeo**graph**
cardio**graph**	oceano**graph**y
carto**graph**er	para**graph**
carto**graph**y	phono**graph**
choreo**graph**	photo**graph**
choreo**graph**y	photo**graph**y
cinemato**graph**er	picto**graph**
cinemato**graph**y	poly**graph**
di**graph**	seismo**graph**
geo**graph**y	steno**graph**er
graffiti	tele**graph**
graphic	topo**graph**y
graphite	typo**graph**y
homo**graph**	

meter, "measure"

baro**meter**	odo**meter**
baro**metr**ic	para**meter**
centi**meter**	peri**meter**
dia**meter**	speedo**meter**
geo**metr**ic	sym**metr**ical
geo**metr**y	sym**metr**y
iso**metr**ic	thermo**meter**
metric	trigono**metr**y
metronome	
micro**meter**	

Spelling-Meaning Index

phon, "sound"

cacophony
homophone
megaphone
microphone
phoneme
phonetic
phonics

phonograph
saxophone
symphonic
symphony
telephone
xylophone

phys, "nature"

physical
physician
physicist

physics
physiology
physique

scope, "to see"

gyroscope
horoscope
kaleidoscope
microscope

periscope
stethoscope
telescope

therm, "heat"

thermal
thermodynamic
thermometer

thermos
thermostat

Spelling Dictionary

Spelling Table

This Spelling Table shows many of the letter combinations that spell the same sounds in different words. Use this table for help in looking up words that you do not know how to spell.

Sounds	Spellings	Sample Words
|ă|	a, au	bat, have, laugh
|ā|	a, ai, ay, ea, ei, eigh, ey	made, later, rain, play, great, vein, eight, they
|âr|	air, are, ear, eir, ere	fair, care, bear, their, where
|ä|	a, al	father, calm
|är|	ar, ear	art, heart
|b|	b, bb	bus, rabbit
|ch|	c, ch, tch, tu	cello, chin, match, culture
|d|	d, dd	dark, sudden
|ĕ|	a, ai, ay, e, ea, ie	any, said, says, went, head, friend
|ē|	e, ea, ee, ei, ey, i, ie, y	these, we, beast, fleet, receive, honey, magazine, chief, bumpy
|f|	f, ff, gh, ph	funny, off, enough, physical
|g|	g, gg, gu	get, egg, guide
|h|	h, wh	hat, who
|hw|	wh	when
|ĭ|	a, e, ee, i, ia, u, ui, y	cottage, before, been, mix, give, carriage, busy, build, gym

Sounds	Spellings	Sample Words
|ī|	ei, i, ie, igh, uy, y, ye	height, time, mind, pie, fight, buy, try, dye, type
|îr|	ear, eer, eir, ere, ier	near, deer, weird, here, pier
|j|	dge, g, ge, j	judge, germ, orange, jump
|k|	c, cc, ch, ck, k, que	picnic, account, school, stick, keep, antique
|kw|	qu	quick
|l|	l, ll	last, all
|m|	m, mb, mm, mn	mop, bomb, summer, column
|n|	gn, kn, n, nn, pn	sign, knee, nine, banner, pneumonia
|ng|	n, ng	think, ring
|ŏ|	a, ho, o	was, honor, pond
|ō|	ew, o, oa, oe, ou, ough, ow	sew, most, hope, float, toe, shoulder, though, row
|ô|	a, al, au, aw, o, ough	walk, talk, haunt, lawn, soft, brought
|ôr|	oar, oor, or, ore, our	roar, door, storm, store, court
|oi|	oi, oy	join, toy

279

Sounds	Spellings	Sample Words	Sounds	Spellings	Sample Words
|ou|	ou, ough, ow	loud, bough, now	|th|	th	thin, teeth
|o͝o|	oo, ou, u	good, could, put	|ŭ|	o, oe, oo, ou, u	front, come, does, flood, tough, sun
|o͞o|	eu, ew, o, oe, oo, ou, ough, u, ue, ui	neutral, flew, do, lose, shoe, spoon, you, through, truth, blue, juice	|yo͞o|	eau, ew, iew, u, ue	beauty, few, view, use, cue, fuel
|p|	p, pp	paint, happen	|ûr|	ear, er, ir, or, our, ur	learn, herd, girl, word, journey, turn
|r|	r, rh, rr, wr	rub, rhyme, borrow, write	|v|	f, v	of, very
|s|	c, ce, ps, s, sc, ss	city, fence, psychology, same, scent, lesson	|w|	o, w	one, way
			|y|	i, y	million, yes
|sh|	ce, ch, ci, s, sh, ss, ti	ocean, machine, special, sure, sheep, mission, nation	|z|	s, ss, x, z, zz	please, dessert, xylophone, zoo, blizzard
			|zh|	ge, s	garage, usual
|t|	ed, t, tt	stopped, talk, button	|ə|	a, ai, e, eo, i, ie, o, ou, u	about, captain, silent, surgeon, pencil, ancient, lemon, famous, circus
|_th_|	th	they, other			

How to Use a Dictionary

Finding an Entry Word

Guide Words

The word you want to find in a dictionary is listed in alphabetical order. To find it quickly, use the guide words at the top of each page. The two guide words name the first and last entries on the page.

Base Words

To find a word ending in **-ed** or **-ing**, you usually must look up its base word. For example, to find **equipped** or **equipping**, look up the base word **equip**.

Homographs

Homographs have separate, numbered entries. For example, **desert** meaning "a dry, barren region" is listed as **desert¹**. **Desert** meaning "to forsake or leave" is listed as **desert²**.

Reading an Entry

Read the dictionary entry below. Note the purpose of each part.

The **pronunciation** shows you how to say the entry word.

The **part of speech** (verb) is identified by an abbreviation (*v.*).

The **-ed** and **-ing** forms of a verb are often shown.

The **entry word** is shown, separated into syllables.

The **definition** tells you what the word means.

adjective align

The **etymology** tells the history and origin of the word.

ad•mire |ăd mīr´| *v.* **ad•mired, ad•mir•ing.** To look at or regard with wonder or pleasure: *admire a mountain view.* [Latin *admīrārī*, to wonder at: *ad-*, to, at + *mīrārī*, to wonder.] —**ad•mir´er** *n.*

ad•mis•sion |ăd mĭsh´ən| *n.* A price charged or paid to enter a place: *Admiss the science museum is five dollars.* [Latin to + *mittere*, to send in.]

ad•mit |ăd mĭt´| *v.* **ad•mit•ted, ad•mit•ting.** To acknowledge or confess as a fact.

|ăd´l ĕs´əns| *n.* The

A **run-on entry** is shown in dark type at the end of the entry.

A **sample sentence** or **phrase** helps to make the meaning clear.

Spelling Dictionary

A

ab-. Also **a-** (before *m*, *p*, and *v*) or **au-** (before *f*) or **abs-** (before *t*). A prefix meaning "from, away, or off": **absent, abrupt.** [Latin, from *ab*, away from.]

ab·bre·vi·ate |ə brē´vē āt´| *v.* **ab·bre·vi·at·ed, ab·bre·vi·at·ing.** To reduce (a word or group of words) to a shorter form by leaving out some of the letters.

ab·hor |ăb hôr´| *v.* **ab·horred, ab·hor·ring.** To regard with horror or loathing: *abhor violence.* [Latin *ab-*, away from + *horrēre*, to shudder.]

ab·ject |ăb´jĕkt´| *or* |ăb jĕkt´| *adj.* Deeply hopeless and miserable: *abject poverty.* [Latin *ab-*, away from + *jacere*, to throw.]

-able. A suffix that forms adjectives and means: **1.** Capable or worthy of: **lovable.** **2.** Tending toward: **sizable.** [From Latin *-ābilis, -ībilis.*]

ab·nor·mal |ăb nôr´məl| *adj.* Not normal; unusual. [Latin *ab-*, away from + *norma*, rule.]

a·brupt |ə brŭpt´| *adj.* **1.** Unexpected; sudden. **2.** Short and brief so as to suggest rudeness or displeasure: *an abrupt answer.* [Latin *abruptus*, to break off: *ab-*, off + *rumpere*, to break.]

ab·sence |ăb´səns| *n.* A lack: *an absence of reliable information.*

ab·so·lute |ăb´sə lōōt´| *adj.* Complete; total: *absolute silence.* [Latin *ab-*, away from + *solvere*, to loosen.]

ab·solve |ăb zŏlv´| *or* |-sŏlv´| *v.* **ab·solved, ab·solv·ing.** To clear of blame or guilt: *The court absolved him of guilt.* [Latin *ab-*, away from + *solvere*, to loosen, free.]

ab·sorb |ăb sôrb´| *or* |-zôrb´| *v.* To take in; soak up: *A sponge absorbs moisture.* [Latin *ab-*, away from + *sorbēre*, to suck.]

ab·stract |ăb´străkt´| *or* |ăb străkt´| *n.* A brief summary of the main points of a text: *an abstract of a speech.*

Abbreviation Key

n.	noun	*prep.*	preposition
v.	verb	*interj.*	interjection
adj.	adjective	*sing.*	singular
adv.	adverb	*pl.*	plural
pron.	pronoun	*p.*	past
conj.	conjunction	*p. part.*	past participle

a·buse |ə byōōz´| *v.* **a·bused, a·bus·ing.** To use improperly; misuse: *The barons abused their privileges.* —*n.* |ə byōōs´|. **1.** Improper use; misuse: *the abuse of power.* **2.** Mistreatment. [From Latin *abūtī*, to use up: *ab-*, away from + *ūtī*, to use.]

ac·a·dem·ic |ăk´ə dĕm´ĭk| *adj.* Of a school or college: *an academic degree.*

a·cad·e·my |ə kăd´ə mē| *n., pl.* **a·cad·e·mies.** A school for a special field of study: *a naval academy.* [Latin, from Greek *Acadēmia*, name of the place in Athens where Plato taught.]

ac·cen·tu·ate |ăk sĕn´chōō āt´| *v.* **ac·cen·tu·at·ed, ac·cen·tu·at·ing.** To give prominence to; emphasize; point up. [Latin *accentus*, accent: *ad-*, to + *cantus*, song.]

ac·cept |ăk sĕpt´| *v.* **1.** To take (something offered): *accept an award.* **2.** To say yes to: *I accept your invitation.* **3.** To regard as true; believe in: *accept a theory.*

ac·cept·a·ble |ăk sĕp´tə bəl| *adj.* Proper; correct: *an acceptable pronunciation.*

ac·cess |ăk´sĕs´| *n.* **1.** The act of entering; entrance: *gain access through the basement.* **2.** Way of approaching or reaching: *a city with easy access to the sea.*

ac·com·pa·ny |ə kŭm´pə nē| *v.* **ac·com·pa·nied, ac·com·pa·ny·ing, ac·com·pa·nies.** To go along with: *I accompanied her to the store.* [Latin *ad-*, to + *compain(g)*, companion.]

ac·com·plice |ə kŏm´plĭs| *n.* Someone who aids a lawbreaker in a crime but is not necessarily present at the time of the crime. [Middle English, from *a complice,* an associate, or complice, from Latin *complex,* closely connected: *com-,* together + *-plex,* fold.]

ac·count |ə kount´| *n.* **1.** A written or spoken description of events; a narrative: *an account of his adventures.* **2.** A set of reasons; explanation: *Give an account of your odd behavior.* **Idiom. on account of** or **on (someone's) account.** Because of: *Cancelled on account of rain.*

ac·cu·rate |ăk´yər ĭt| *adj.* **1.** Free from errors or mistakes; correct: *accurate answers.* **2.** Exact; precise: *an accurate description.* [Latin *accūrāre,* to attend to carefully: *ad-,* to + *cūrāre,* to care for, attend to.]

ac·cu·sa·tion |ăk´yōō zā´shən| *n.* A statement or formal declaration that a person has been guilty of wrongdoing: *He vigorously denied the accusation.* [From Latin *accūsāre,* to accuse, "call to account": *ad-,* to + *causa,* cause.]

ac·cus·tomed |ə kŭs´təmd| *adj.* Usual; habitual; familiar: *The train left at the accustomed hour.* **Idiom. accustomed to.** Used to; familiar with: *He is accustomed to doing things his own way.* [Latin *ad-,* to + *costume,* custom.]

a·chieve·ment |ə chēv´mənt| *n.* The act or process of attaining or accomplishing something: *the achievement of their goals.*

ac·knowl·edg·ment, also **ac·knowl·edge·ment** |ăk nŏl´ĭj mənt| *n.* **1.** The act of acknowledging; recognition: *bowed his head in acknowledgment of guilt.* **2.** Something done or sent in answer to or recognition of another's action: *an acknowledgment of an invitation.*

a·cous·tics |ə kōō´stĭks| *n.* The overall effect of sound produced and heard in a particular place, especially an enclosed space. *The acoustics of a concert hall are poor for speech.*

Pronunciation Key					
ă	pat	ŏ	pot	û	fur
ā	pay	ō	go	*th*	the
â	care	ô	paw, for	th	thin
ä	father	oi	oil	hw	which
ĕ	pet	ōō	book	zh	usual
ē	be	ōō	boot	ə	ago, item
ĭ	pit	yōō	cute		pencil, atom
ī	ice	ou	out		circus
î	near	ŭ	cut	ər	butter

ac·quit·tal |ə kwĭt´l| *n.* The freeing of a person from an accusation of wrongdoing by the judgment of a court: *The lawyer worked for acquittal of her client.*

ad-. Also **ac-** (before *c*) or **af-** (before *f*) *or* **ag-** (before *g*) or **al-** (before *l*) *or* **an-** (before *n*) *or* **ar-** (before *r*) *or* **as-** (before *s*) or **at-** (before *t*). A prefix meaning "toward, to": **adhere.** [Latin, from *ad,* to, toward, or at.]

a·dapt |ə dăpt´| *v.* To change or adjust for a certain purpose: *adapt our methods to meet the new situation.* [Latin *adaptāre,* to fit: *ad-,* to + *aptāre,* to fit, from *aptus,* apt.]

ad·ap·ta·tion |ăd´əp tā´shən| *n.* The act or process of adapting; change or adjustment to meet new conditions: *adaptation to a new environment.*

a·dept |ə dĕpt´| *adj.* Skillful and effective: *adept at sewing.* [Latin *ad-,* to + *apīscī,* to reach for.]

ad·e·quate |ăd´ĭ kwĭt| *adj.* Sufficient; enough: *adequate supplies.* [Latin *ad-,* to + *aequāre,* to make equal.]

ad·he·sive |ăd hē´sĭv| *adj.* Tending to hold fast to another material; sticky: *adhesive tape.* [Latin *ad-,* to + *haerēre,* to stick.]

ad·ja·cent |ə jā´sənt | *adj.* Next to; adjoining: *the room adjacent to mine.* [Latin *ad-,* near to + *jacēre,* to lie.]

ad·jec·tive |ăj´ĭk tĭv| *n.* In grammar, a word used to describe a noun or to limit its meaning. [From Latin *adjectus*, added, from *adjacere*, to throw to, add: *ad-*, to + *jacere*, to throw.]

ad·just·a·ble |ə jŭs´tə bəl| *adj.* Capable of being adjusted: *an adjustable lens.*

ad·just·ment |ə jŭst´mənt| *n.* The act of adjusting. [Latin *ad-*, near to + *juxta*, close by.]

ad·min·i·ster |ăd mĭn´ĭ stər| *v.* To give as a remedy or treatment: *administer artificial respiration.* [Latin *ad-*, to + *ministrāre*, to serve.]

ad·min·is·tra·tion |ăd mĭn´ĭ strā´shən| *n.* **1.** The act of administering: *the administration of justice.* **2.** The officials who manage an institution or organization: *the school administration.* [Latin *ad-*, to + *ministrāre*, to serve.]

ad·mi·ra·tion |ăd´mə rā´shən| *n.* **1.** Pleasure, wonder, and delight in someone or something. **2.** A high opinion; respect; esteem: *the admiration of a son for his father.*

ad·mire |ăd mīr´| *v.* **ad·mired, ad·mir·ing.** To look at or regard with wonder or pleasure: *admire a mountain view.* [Latin *admīrārī*, to wonder at: *ad-*, to, at + *mīrārī*, to wonder.] —**ad·mir´er** *n.*

ad·mis·sion |ăd mĭsh´ən| *n.* A price charged or paid to enter a place: *Admission to the science museum is five dollars.* [Latin *ad-*, to + *mittere*, to send in.]

ad·mit |ăd mĭt´| *v.* **ad·mit·ted, ad·mit·ting.** To acknowledge or confess as a fact.

ad·o·les·cence |ăd´l ĕs´əns| *n.* The period of physical and psychological development that leads from childhood to adulthood.

ad·o·les·cent |ăd´l ĕs´ənt| *n.* A boy or girl, especially a teenager, in the stage of development between childhood and adulthood.

a·dopt |ə dŏpt´| *v.* To take (a new member) into one's family, tribe, or nation and treat as one's own: *adopt a child.*

ad·vanced |ăd vănst´| *or* |-vänst´| *adj.* **1.** At a higher level than others: *an advanced student; advanced courses.* **2.** Ahead of the times; progressive: *advanced ideas.*

ad·van·tage |ăd văn´tĭj| *or* |-vän´-| *n.* A good point or favorable feature: *the advantages of city life.*

ad·ver·tise·ment |ăd´vər tīz´mənt| *or* |ăd vûr´tĭs mənt| *or* |-tĭz-| *n.* A public notice, as in a newspaper or on the radio, to call attention to a product, a meeting, etc.

ad·vice |ăd vīs´| *n.* An opinion about how to solve a problem; guidance.

ad·vise |ăd vīz´| *v.* **ad·vised, ad·vis·ing.** To give advice to or offer advice; recommend: *I advise you to finish your project.*

ad·vi·ser, also **ad·vi·sor** |ăd vī´zər| *n.* A person who offers advice, especially officially or professionally. [Latin *ad-*, to, at + *visus*, to see.]

aer·o·bics |â rō´bĭks| *n.* (used with a sing. or pl. verb) A system of physical conditioning that involves vigorous exercise, as calisthenics, combined with dance routines. [From Greek: *aero-*, air + *bios*, life.]

af·fil·i·ate |ə fĭl´ē ĭt| *or* |-āt´| *n.* A person or company associated or joined with another; a member: *We have affiliates abroad as well as here.*

a·li·as |ā´lē əs| *n.* An assumed name used by a person wishing to conceal his or her identity: *John Smith is the alias of Harry Cromwell.*

al·i·bi |ăl´ə bī´| *n., pl.* **al·i·bis.** A legal defense whereby a defendant attempts to prove that he or she was not present at the scene of a crime when the crime was committed: *Her alibi is that she was out of town.*

a·lign |ə līn´| *v.* To arrange in a straight line: *The chairs were aligned in rows.*

al·ler·gy |ăl´ər jē| *n., pl.* **al·ler·gies.** A disorder in which exposure to a small amount of a substance, generally a protein, fat, or carbohydrate, or to an environmental influence, such as heat or cold, causes an abnormal and often violent reaction that may include difficulty in breathing, sneezing, watering of the eyes, and shock. [German *Allergie*, "altered reaction": *all(o)* + Greek *ergon*, work, effect.]

al·le·vi·ate |ə lē´vē āt´| *v.* **al·le·vi·at·ed, al·le·vi·at·ing.** To make more bearable; relieve; lessen: *alleviate pain.* [Late Latin *alleviāre*, to lighten: Latin *ad-*, toward + *levis*, light.]

al·li·ance |ə lī´əns| *n.* A formal agreement or union between nations, organizations, or individuals: *a treaty of alliance.* [Old French *alier*, to ally, from Latin *alligāre*, to bind to: *ad-*, to + *ligāre*, to bind.]

al·li·ga·tor |ăl´ĭ gā´tər| *n.* A large reptile with sharp teeth and powerful jaws. Its snout is blunter than that of the closely related crocodile. [From Spanish *el lagarto*: *el*, the + *lagarto*, lizard.]

al·lo·cate |ăl´ə kāt´| *v.* **al·lo·cat·ed, al·lo·cat·ing.** To set aside for a particular purpose; allot: *allocate funds.* [Latin *ad-*, toward + *locāre*, to place, from *locus*, place.]

al·lot |ə lŏt´| *v.* **al·lot·ted, al·lot·ting.** To distribute or parcel out: *allot portions of land.*

Pronunciation Key

ă	pat	ŏ	pot	û	fur
ā	pay	ō	go	*th*	the
â	care	ô	paw, for	th	thin
ä	father	oi	oil	hw	which
ě	pet	oͦo	book	zh	usual
ē	be	ōō	boot	ə	ago, item
ĭ	pit	yōō	cute		pencil, atom
ī	ice	ou	out		circus
î	near	ŭ	cut	ər	butter

al·ma·nac |ôl´mə năk´| *or* |ăl´-| *n.* A book published once a year containing calendars, statistics, and other information in many different fields.

al·pha·bet·ize |ăl´fə bĭ tīz´| *v.* **al·pha·bet·ized, al·pha·bet·iz·ing.** To arrange in alphabetical order.

al·to |ăl´tō| *n., pl.* **al·tos. 1.** A low singing voice of a woman or boy, or sometimes, a high singing voice of a man, lower than a soprano and higher than a tenor. **2.** A person having such a voice.

am·a·teur |ăm´ə cho͝or´| *or* |-chər| *or* |-tyo͝or´| *n.* **1.** A person who engages in an art, science, or sport for enjoyment rather than for money. **2.** A person who does something without professional skill. [French, from Latin *amātōr*, a lover, from *amāre*, to love.]

am·bu·lance |ăm´byə ləns| *n.* A large automobile specially equipped to rush sick and injured people to a hospital.

an·a·gram |ăn´ə gram´| *n.* A word or phrase formed by changing the order of the letters of another word or phrase: *Spin is an anagram of snip.* [From Latin *anagramma*: from Greek *ana*, up + *gramma*, letter.]

a·nal·y·sis |ə năl´ĭ sĭs| *n., pl.* **a·nal·y·ses** |ə năl´ĭ sēz´|. The process of separating a subject into its parts and studying them so as to determine its nature: *an analysis of the presidential election.*

an·a·lyze |ăn´ə līz´| *v.* **an·a·lyzed,
an·a·lyz·ing. 1.** To examine in detail:
analyze the test results. **2.** To make a
mathematical analysis of. [From Greek
analuein, to undo: *ana-,* back + *luein,* to
loosen.]

a·nat·o·my |ə năt´ə mē| *n., pl.*
a·nat·o·mies. The human body: *the anatomy
of an athlete.*

-ance. A suffix that forms nouns from
verbs: **resemblance.**

an·chor·per·son |ăng´kər pûr´sən| *n.*
In radio and television, the narrator of a news
broadcast in which several correspondents
give their reports. [Greek *ankýlos,* crooked,
curved + *person,* from Latin *persona,* mask.]

an·cient |ān´shənt| *adj.* Very old; aged.

Ang·kor Wat |ăng´kôr vät| Temple near
Angkor Thom, the ancient Khmer capital, in
northwestern Cambodia.

-ant. A suffix that forms nouns and
adjectives: **deodorant; resultant.** [From
Latin *-ans.*]

an·tag·o·nize |ăn tăg´ə nīz´| *v.*
an·tag·o·nized, an·tag·o·niz·ing. To earn
the dislike of: *He antagonized her by being
rude.* [Greek *anti-,* against + *agōnizesthai,* to
struggle.]

Ant·arc·tic |ănt ärk´tĭk| *or* |-är´tĭk| *n.*
Antarctica and its surrounding waters. [Greek
antarktikos: anti-, opposite + *arktikos,* from
arktos, bear.]

anti-. When *anti-* is followed by a capital
letter or the letter *i,* it appears with a hyphen:
anti-intellectual. A prefix meaning "opposed,
against, or counteracting": **antifreeze.** [Greek,
from *anti,* opposite.]

an·ti·bi·ot·ic |ăn´tē bī ŏt´ĭk| *n.* Any of a
group of substances such as penicillin and
streptomycin, produced by certain fungi,
bacteria, and other organisms, that are
capable of destroying microorganisms or
stopping their growth. They are widely used
in the treatment and prevention of diseases.

an·ti·bod·y |ăn´tĭ bŏd´ē| *n., pl.*
an·ti·bod·ies. Any of various proteins that
are found in the blood and that are generated
in reaction to foreign proteins or
carbohydrates. They are capable of acting
against these foreign substances and so give
immunity against certain microorganisms and
toxins. [Greek *anti-,* against + *body,* from Old
English *bodig,* from Germanic *bot-,* container.]

an·ti·freeze |ăn´tĭ frēz´| *n.* A liquid
added to another liquid, such as water, to
lower its freezing point. [Greek *anti-,* against
+ *freeze,* from Middle English *fresen.*]

an·tique |ăn tēk´| *n.* Something having
special value because of its age, especially a
work of art or handicraft that is over 100
years old. [French, from Latin *antīquus,*
ancient, former.]

an·ti·sep·tic |ăn´tĭ sĕp´tĭk| *n.* A drug or
agent capable of destroying microorganisms,
especially those germs that produce disease,
fermentation, or rot. [Greek *anti-,* against +
septic, from Greek *sēptos,* rotten.]

an·to·nym |ăn´tə nĭm´| *n.* A word having
a sense opposite to a sense of another word:
Fat is an antonym of skinny. [Greek *anti-,*
opposite, against + *onym,* from *onoma,* name.]

ap·pa·ra·tus |ăp´ə ră´təs| *or* |-răt´əs|
n., pl. **ap·pa·ra·tus** *or* **ap·pa·ra·tus·es.**
Equipment, especially laboratory
equipment: *a lab filled with apparatus.*
[Latin *apparātus,* equipment, from
apparāre, to prepare; *ad-,* to + *parāre,* to
make ready.]

ap·pend·age |ə pĕn´dĭj| *n.* Any part or organ of the body that hangs or projects from another part: *A finger is an appendage of the hand.* [Latin *appendere*: *ad-*, to + *pendere*, to hang.]

ap·pen·dix |ə pĕn´dĭks| *n., pl.* **ap·pen·dix·es** or **ap·pen·di·ces** |ə pĕn´di sēz´|. A section at the end of a book containing additional information, tables, etc. [From Latin *appendere*: *ad-*, to + *pendere*, to hang.]

ap·pe·tite |ăp´ĭ tīt´| *n.* **1.** The desire for food or drink. **2.** A strong desire for something: *an appetite for learning.* [From Latin *appetitus*, from *ad-*, toward + *petere*, to seek.]

ap·pe·tiz·er |ăp´ə tī´zər| *n.* A food or drink taken before a meal to arouse the appetite. [Latin *appetere*, to strive after, desire eagerly: *ad-*, toward + *petere*, to seek.]

ap·pli·ca·tion |ăp´lĭ kā´shən| *n.* A request, as for a job or admittance to a school. [From Latin *applicātiō*, from *applicāre*, apply.]

ap·point |ə point´| *v.* To select or designate for an office, position, or duty.

ap·pre·ci·ate |ə prē´shē āt´| *v.* **ap·pre·ci·at·ed, ap·pre·ci·at·ing.** To recognize the worth, quality, or importance of; value highly: *He appreciated the advice.* [Late Latin *appretiāre*, to set a value on: *ad-*, to + *pretiāre*, to value.]

ap·pre·hen·sive |ăp´rĭ hĕn´sĭv| *adj.* Anxious or fearful: *apprehensive about the future.*

ap·pro·pri·ate |ə prō´prē ĭt| *adj.* Suitable for a particular person, condition, occasion, or place; proper: *appropriate clothes.* —*v.* |ə prō´prē āt´| **ap·pro·pri·at·ed, ap·pro·pri·at·ing.** To set apart for a particular use: *Congress appropriated money for education.* [From Latin *appropriare*, to make one's own: Latin *ad-*, to + *proprius*, own.]

Pronunciation Key

ă	pat	ŏ	pot	û	fur
ā	pay	ō	go	*th*	**the**
â	care	ô	paw, for	th	**thin**
ä	father	oi	**oil**	hw	**which**
ĕ	pet	ŏŏ	**book**	zh	usual
ē	be	ōō	**boot**	ə	ago, item
ĭ	pit	yōō	cute		pencil, atom
ī	ice	ou	**out**		circus
î	near	ŭ	cut	ər	butter

ap·prove |ə prōōv´| *v.* **ap·proved, ap·prov·ing.** **1.** To think of favorably; consider right or good: *approve of the plan.* **2.** To confirm or consent to officially; sanction; ratify: *They approved the treaty.*

ap·prox·i·mate |ə prŏk´sə mĭt| *adj.* Almost exact or accurate: *the approximate height of a building.* [Late Latin *approximātus*, from *approximāre*, to come near to: Latin *ad-*, to + *proximāre*, to come near.]

arc |ärk| *n.* A portion of a curve, especially of a circle: *The rainbow was a bright arc in the sky.*

ar·chi·tec·ture |är´kĭ tĕk´chər| *n.* The art and occupation of designing and directing the construction of buildings and other structures.

ar·gu·ment |är´gyə mənt| *n.* A quarrel or dispute; disagreement.

ar·id |ăr´ĭd| *adj.* Having little or no rainfall; dry; parched: *an arid wasteland.*

ar·range·ment |ə rānj´mənt| *n.* The order in which things are arranged. [From the Old French *arengier*: *a-*, from *ad-*, to + *rengier*, to put in a line.]

ar·rest |ə rĕst´| *v.* To seize and hold under authority of law. [From Latin *arrestāre*, to cause to stop: Latin *ad-*, to + *restāre*, to stop, stay behind.]

ar·ri·val |ə rī´vəl| *n.* The act of arriving: *her arrival at the airport.* [From Vulgar Latin *arripāre*, to land, come to shore.]

ar·son |är´sən| *n.* The crime of intentionally setting fire to buildings or other property: *He was convicted of arson.*

ar·thri·tis |är thrī´tĭs| *n.* Inflammation and stiffness of a joint or joints in the body. [Latin from Greek *arthron,* joint + *-itis,* pertaining to, native.]

ar·ti·cle |är´tĭ kəl| *n.* A written piece that forms an independent part of a publication; a report; essay: *a magazine article.*

-ary. A suffix that forms adjectives from nouns: **budgetary; parliamentary.**

as·pect |ăs´pĕkt´| *n.* The appearance of an idea, situation, or plan, as viewed by the mind; an element or facet: *examine every aspect of the situation.* [Middle English from Latin *aspectus,* a view, past participle of *aspicere,* to look at: *ad-,* to + *specere,* to look.]

as·pi·rin |ăs´pə rĭn| *or* |-prĭn| *n.* **1.** A white, crystalline compound of carbon, hydrogen, and oxygen in the proportions $C_9H_8O_4$, commonly used as a drug to relieve fever and pain; acetylsalicylic acid. **2.** A tablet of aspirin.

as·sign |ə sīn´| *v.* To set apart for a particular purpose; designate: *Assign a day for the trial.* [Middle English from Old French from Latin *assignāre,* to mark out: *ad-,* to + *signāre,* to mark, from *signum,* sign.]

as·sign·ment |ə sīn´mənt| *n.* Something assigned, especially a task or job.

as·sis·tance |ə sĭs´təns| *n.* Help; aid: *financial assistance.*

as·sis·tant |ə sĭs´tənt| *n.* One who assists; a helper: *the president's special assistant.*

as·sort·ment |ə sôrt´mənt| *n.* A collection of various kinds; variety: *an assortment of vegetables.* [From Latin *ad-,* to + *sorte,* kind, + noun suffix *ment.*]

as·sure |ə shŏŏr´| *v.* **as·sured, as·sur·ing.** **1.** To declare confidently: *I can assure you that we shall take appropriate action.* **2.** To make certain; guarantee; ensure: *They helped assure Jefferson's election.*

Usage: **Assure, ensure,** and **insure** all mean "to make secure or certain." Only *assure* is used to mean "to set a person's mind at rest": *assured the teacher of his efforts to study.* Although *ensure* and *insure* are usually used the same ways, only *insure* is now widely used to mean "to guarantee property against risk": *to insure property.*

as·ter·oid |ăs´tə roid´| *n.* Any of numerous objects that orbit the sun, chiefly in the region between Mars and Jupiter. They range in size from about one to several hundred miles in diameter and are often irregular in shape.

asth·ma |ăz´mə| *or* |ăs´-| *n.* A chronic disease that is often allergy-related. Its chief symptom is tightness of the chest with coughing and difficulty in breathing.

as·tron·o·my |ə strŏn´ə mē| *n.* The scientific study of the part of the universe that lies beyond the Earth, especially the observation of stars, planets, comets, and galaxies.

-ate. A suffix that forms verbs and means "to become or cause to be": **laminate; pollinate.** [Middle English *-at,* from Latin *-atus.*]

ath·lete |ăth´lēt´| *n.* A person who competes or takes part in sports. [From Greek *athlētēs,* contestant, from *athlein,* to contend for an award, from *athlon,* award, prize.]

ath·let·ic |ăth lĕt´ĭk| *adj.* **1.** Of or for athletics: *athletic ability.* **2.** Of or for athletes: *athletic competition.* **3.** Physically strong; muscular: *an athletic build.*

at·las |ăt´ləs| *n.* A book or bound collection of maps: *Find South America in an atlas.*

at·mos·phere |ăt´mə sfîr´| *n.* **1.** The gas that surrounds a body in space and is held by the body's gravitation field: *Earth's atmosphere.* **2.** The air or climate of a place: *the desert atmosphere.*

at·ro·phy |ăt´rə fē| *n.* The wasting away of the body or any of its organs or tissues: *He experienced atrophy of the muscles in his legs.*

at·tach |ə tăch´| *v.* To fasten on or join; connect: *attach the wires.* [From Old French *attacher*, to fasten (with a stake).]

at·tain |ə tān´| *v.* To gain, accomplish, or achieve by effort: *attain victory.*
—**at·tain´a·ble** *adj.* [From Latin *attingere*: *ad-*, to + *tangere*, to touch.]

at·tempt |ə tĕmpt´| *n.* An effort or try: *my first attempt.* [From Latin *attemptāre*: *ad-*, to + *temptāre*, to try, tempt.]

at·ten·dance |ə tĕn´dəns| *n.* The act or practice of being present: *regular attendance.*

at·ten·dant |ə tĕn´dənt| *n.* A person who attends or waits on another.

at·tic |ăt´ĭk| *n.* The space in a house just under the roof; a garret. [From *Attic story*, originally a small top story having square columns in the Attic (of ancient Attica or Athens) style.]

at·tire |ə tīr´| *n.* Clothing, costume, or apparel: *tennis attire.* [From Old French *atirier*, to arrange into ranks, put in order: *a-*, from Latin *ad-*, to + *tire*, order, rank.]

at·ti·tude |ăt´ĭ tōōd´| *or* |-tyōōd´| *n.* A state of mind with regard to someone or something; a point of view: *a good attitude toward life.* [From Italian *attitudine*, from Late Latin *aptitūdō*, fitness, from Latin *aptus*, fit, apt.]

at·tract |ə trăkt´| *v.* To draw or direct to oneself or itself by some quality or action: *Sweet-smelling flowers attract bees.* [Latin *attrahere*: *ad-*, toward + *trahere*, to draw.]

at·trib·ute |ə trĭb´yōōt| *v.* **at·trib·ut·ed, at·trib·ut·ing.** To regard or consider as belonging to or resulting from someone or something; ascribe: *Air pollution has been partly attributed to cars.* [Latin *attribuēre*: *ad-*, to + *tribuēre*, to allot, grant.]

au·di·ble |ô´də bəl| *adj.* Capable of being heard: *an audible whisper.*

au·di·ence |ô´dē əns| *n.* The people gathered to see and hear a play, movie, concert, etc.

au·di·o·vis·u·al, *also* **au·di·o·vis·u·al** |ô´dē ō vĭzh´ōō əl| *adj.* **1.** Both audible and visible. **2.** Of or relating to materials, such as videotapes or compact disks, that use television and other electronic equipment to present information in both visible and audible form. [Latin *audīre*, to hear + *vīsus*, vision.]

au·thor·ize |ô´thə rīz´| *v.* **au·thor·ized, au·thor·iz·ing.** To grant authority or power to: *He is authorized to form a commission.*

auto-¹ A word part meaning "self" or "self-caused": **autobiography.** [Greek, from *autos*, self.]

auto-² A word part meaning "self-propelling": **automobile.**

au·to·bi·og·ra·phy |ô´tō bī ŏg´rə fē| *or* |-bē-| *n., pl.* **au·to·bi·og·ra·phies.** The story of a person's life written by that person. [From Greek *autos*, self + *bios*, life + *graphein*, to write.]

au·to·crat |ô´tə krăt´| *n.* A ruler having absolute power. [From Greek *autokratēs*, ruling by oneself: *autos*, self + *kratos*, power.]

au·to·graph |ô´tə grăf´| *or* |-gräf´| *n.* A signature, usually of a famous person, that is saved by an admirer or collector.

au·to·mat·ic |ô´tə măt´ĭk| *adj.* Capable of operating correctly without the control of a human being; self-operating or self-regulating. [From Greek *automatos*, acting by itself: *autos*, self + *matos*, willing.]

Pronunciation Key

ă	pat	ŏ	pot	û	fur
ā	pay	ō	go	*th*	the
â	care	ô	paw, for	th	thin
ä	father	oi	oil	hw	which
ĕ	pet	ōō	book	zh	usual
ē	be	ōō	boot	ə	ago, item
ĭ	pit	yōō	cute		pencil, atom
ī	ice	ou	out		circus
î	near	ŭ	cut	ər	butter

au·to·mo·bile |ô´tə mə **bēl**´| *or* |**-mō**´bēl´| *or* |ô´tə mə bēl´| *n.* A land vehicle equipped to carry a driver and several passengers, generally moving on four wheels and propelled by an engine that burns gasoline. [French from Greek *autos*, self + Latin *mōbilis*, to move.]

au·ton·o·my |ô tŏn´ə mē| *n.* Self-government. [From Greek *autonomos*, self-ruling: *autos*, self + *nomos*, law.]

au·tumn |ô´təm| *n.* The season between summer and winter, lasting from the autumnal equinox in late September to the winter solstice in late December.

au·tum·nal |ô tŭm´nəl| *adj.* Of autumn: *the autumnal reds and golds of the trees.*

aux·il·ia·ry |ôg zĭl´yə rē| *or* |-zĭl´ə-| *n., pl.* **aux·il·ia·ries.** One that helps; an assistant.

a·vail·a·ble |ə vā´lə bəl| *adj.* Obtainable.

B

bac·te·ri·a |băk tîr´ē ə| *pl. n.* The less frequently used singular is **bac·te·ri·um** |băk tîr´ē əm|. Very small one-celled organisms often considered to be plants, although they usually lack green coloring.

bad·min·ton |băd´mĭn´tən| *n.* A game in which players use a light, long-handled racket to hit a shuttlecock back and forth over a high net. [After *Badminton*, the country seat of the Duke of Beaufort in Gloucestershire, England.]

bail¹ |bāl| *n.* Money supplied for the temporary release of an arrested person and guaranteeing his or her appearance for trial.

bail² |bāl| *v.* To remove (water) from a boat by repeatedly filling a container and emptying it.

bale |bāl| *n.* A large bound package or bundle of raw or finished material: *a bale of hay.*

bal·le·ri·na |băl´ə **rē**´nə| *n.* A principal female dancer in a ballet company.

bal·let |bă lā´| *or* |băl´ā´| *n.* **1.** A form of artistic dance based on a technique composed of jumps, turns, and poses, all requiring great precision and grace. **2. a.** A theatrical dance form performed in costume and combining the arts of ballet dancing, music, painting, and drama to convey a story, a theme, or an atmosphere. **b.** A theatrical performance of this dance form. [French, from Italian *balletto*, a dance, from *ballare*, to dance.]

bank·rupt |băngk´rŭpt´| *or* |-rəpt| *adj.* Completely without money; financially ruined. [French *banqueroute,* from Italian *banca rotta*, "broken counter": *banca*, moneychanger's table + *rotta*, from *rumpere*, to break.]

ba·rom·e·ter |bə rŏm´ĭ tər| *n.* An instrument that measures and indicates atmospheric pressure and is widely used in the study and forecasting of weather. [From Greek *baros*, weight + *metron*, meter, measure.]

barre |bär| *n.* The wooden bar or railing fixed horizontally to the wall of a ballet classroom as a hand support: *limbered up at the barre.*

bar·ren |băr´ən| *adj.* Lacking or unable to produce growing plants or crops: *barren soil.*

ba·ton |bə tŏn´| *or* |băt´n| *n.* A thin, tapered stick often used by the conductor in leading a band, chorus, or orchestra.

bat·tal·ion |bə tăl´yən| *n.* A large group of soldiers organized as a unit, usually consisting of two or more companies.

bat·ter·y |băt´ə rē| *n., pl.* **bat·ter·ies.** A device that generates an electric current.

bay·ou |bī´o͞o| *or* |bī´ō| *n.* A sluggish, marshy body of water connected with a river or lake and common in the southern United States.

ba·zaar |bə zär´| *n.* **1.** An Oriental market, usually consisting of a street lined with shops and stalls. **2.** A fair or sale, usually to raise money for a charity: *a church bazaar.*

beat |bēt| *v.* **1.** To hit or strike. **2.** To defeat. **3.** Informal. To be better than: *This certainly beats working.*

be·go·nia |bĭ gōn´yə| *n.* Any of several plants often grown for their showy flowers or colorfully marked leaves. [After Michel *Bégon* (1638–1710), governor of Santo Domingo.]

beige |bāzh| *adj.* Light grayish or yellowish brown. [French, from Old French *bege*.]

Bei·jing |bā´jĭng´| The capital of China.

be·lieve |bĭ lēv´| *v.* **be·lieved, be·liev·ing.** To accept as true or real.
— **be·liev´a·ble** *adj.*: *a believable story.*

bi-. A prefix meaning "two" or "twice": **bi-monthly; bisect.** [Latin, from *bis-*, twice.]

Pronunciation Key

ă	pat	ŏ	pot	û	fur
ā	pay	ō	go	*th*	**the**
â	care	ô	paw, for	th	**thin**
ä	father	oi	**oil**	hw	**which**
ĕ	pet	o͝o	**book**	zh	usual
ē	be	o͞o	**boot**	ə	**ago, item**
ĭ	pit	yo͞o	**cute**		pencil, atom
ī	ice	ou	**out**		circus
î	near	ŭ	cut	ər	butter

bi·an·nu·al |bī ăn´yo͞o əl| *adj.* Happening twice each year; semiannual. [From Latin *bi-*, twice, + *annus*, year.]

bib·li·og·ra·phy |bĭb´lē ŏg´rə fē| *n., pl.* **bib·li·og·ra·phies. 1.** A list of the works of a specific author or publisher. **2.** A list of the books and other writings on a specific subject consulted by an author. [French *bibliographie*, from New Latin *bibliographia*: Greek *biblion*, book + *graphein*, to write.]

bi·cen·ten·ni·al |bī´sĕn tĕn´ē əl| *n.* A 200th anniversary or its celebration: *the bicentennial of American independence.* [*bi-*, + *centennial*, from Latin *bi-*, *bin-*, from *bis*, twice + Latin *centum*, hundred.]

bi·ceps |bī´sĕps´| *n., pl.* **bi·ceps.** Any muscle that has two points of attachment at one end, especially the large muscle at the front of the upper arm that bends the elbow. [Latin, "two-headed": *bi-*, from *bis*, twice + *-ceps*, from *caput*, head.]

bi·cy·cle |bī´sĭ kəl| *or* |-sĭk´əl| *n.* A light vehicle consisting of a metal frame on which two wheels are mounted, one behind the other. It has a seat for the rider, who steers the front wheel by means of handlebars and drives the rear wheel by means of pedals. [French, from Latin *bi-*, from *bis*, twice + Greek *kuklos*, circle, wheel.]

bi·lin·gual |bī lĭng´gwəl| *adj.* Able to speak two languages equally well. [Latin *bilinguis*: *bi-*, from *bis*, twice + *lingua*, tongue.]

bil·lion |bĭl´yən| *n.* In the United States, one thousand million; 1,000,000,000 or 10⁹. [French, from Latin *bi-*, from *bis*, twice + (m)illion.]

bi·month·ly |bī mŭnth´lē| *adv.* Once every two months: *Meetings are held bimonthly.* [From Latin *bi-*, from *bis*, twice + Middle English *mōneth*, from Old English *mōnath*.]

bin·oc·u·lar |bə nŏk´yə lər| *or* |bī-| *n.* Often **binoculars.** Any optical device, such as a microscope or a pair of field glasses, designed for use by both eyes at once and consisting of two small telescopes. [Latin *bin-*, from *bis*, twice + *ocular*, from *oculāris*, of the eyes, from *oculus*, eye.]

bi·o·de·grad·a·ble |bī´ō dĭ grā´də bəl| *adj.* Capable of being decomposed by natural biological processes: *a biodegradable substance.* [From bio(logically) + degrade + able.]

bis·cuit |bĭs´kĭt| *n.* **1.** A small, flaky cake of bread leavened with baking powder or soda. **2.** *British.* A cookie.

bi·zarre |bĭ zär´| *adj.* Very strange or odd; grotesque: *a bizarre hat; a bizarre idea.*

bliz·zard |blĭz´ərd| *n.* A very heavy snowstorm with strong winds.

board·er |bôr´dər| *or* |bōr´-| *n.* A person who pays for and receives both meals and lodging at another person's home.

bois·ter·ous |boi´stər əs| *or* |-strəs| *adj.* Noisy and lacking restraint or discipline: *a boisterous mob.*

bo·le·ro |bō lâr´ō| *n., pl.* **bo·le·ros.** A very short jacket of Spanish origin, worn open in the front.

bo·lo·gna, also **ba·lo·ney** |bə lō´nē| *or* |-nə| *or* |-nyə| *n.* A seasoned smoked sausage made of mixed meats. [After *Bologna,* Italy.]

bomb |bŏm| *n.* **1.** An explosive weapon constructed to go off upon striking a given object, area, or other target, or by another means, such as a timing mechanism. **2.** *Slang.* A failure.

bo·nan·za |bə năn´zə| *n.* **1.** A rich mine or vein of ore. **2.** Something that provides a large profit or great wealth: *That invention turned into a real bonanza.* [Spanish, fair weather, prosperity, from Latin *bonus,* good.]

bor·der |bôr´dər| *n.* **1.** The line where one country, state, or region ends and another begins; a boundary: *across the Canadian border.* **2.** An edge, margin, or rim: *the border of the photograph.*

bore·dom |bôr´dəm| *n.* Weariness of mind or spirit caused by lack or loss of interest.

bot·a·ny |bŏt´n ē| *n.* The scientific study of plants.

bough |bou| *n.* A large branch of a tree.

boul·e·vard |bool´ə värd´| *or* |boo´lə-| *n.* A broad city street, often lined with trees. [French, from *belouart,* rampart.]

bound·a·ry |boun´də rē| *or* |-drē| *n., pl.* **bound·a·ries.** An edge, limit, or dividing line marking the place where a country, state, or other region ends: *The Gulf of Mexico forms the southern boundary of Louisiana.*

bou·quet |bō kā´| *or* |boo-| *n.* A bunch of flowers. [French, from Old French *bosquet,* clump, from *bosc,* forest.]

bou·tique |boo tēk´| *n.* A small retail shop that sells gifts, fashionable clothes, etc. [French, from Greek *apothēkē,* storeroom.]

boy·cott |boi´kŏt´| *n.* An organized group refusal to use a product or service or to deal with a business or nation, as a means of protest. —*v.* To participate in an organized group refusal: *to boycott a store.* [After Charles C. *Boycott* (1832–1897), a British land agent who charged such high rents that people refused to deal with him.]

boy·sen·ber·ry |boi´zən bĕr´ē| *n., pl.* **-ber·ries.** A large, dark-red berry related to the loganberry, blackberry, and raspberry. [Developed by Rudolph *Boysen,* 20th-century American horticulturalist.]

Braille, *also* **braille** |brāl| *n.* A system of writing and printing for the blind, in which raised dots representing letters, numbers, and punctuation are read by feeling them with the fingers. [Invented by Louis *Braille* (1809–1852), a blind French musician and teacher of the blind.]

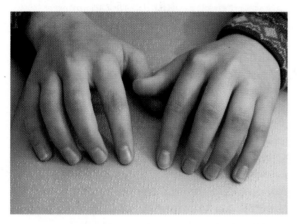

Pronunciation Key					
ă	pat	ŏ	pot	û	fur
ā	pay	ō	go	*th*	**the**
â	care	ô	paw, for	th	**thin**
ä	father	oi	**oil**	hw	**wh**ich
ĕ	pet	o͝o	book	zh	usual
ē	be	o͞o	boot	ə	**a**go, item
ĭ	pit	yo͞o	cute		penc**i**l, at**o**m
ī	ice	ou	**out**		circ**u**s
î	near	ŭ	cut	ər	butt**er**

brav·er·y |brā′və rē| *or* |brāv′rē| *n., pl.* **brav·er·ies.** The condition or quality of being brave; courage.

bril·liant |brĭl′yənt| *adj.* Shining brightly; glittering: *A brilliant sun blazed in the sky.*

bronze |brŏnz| *n.* Any of various alloys of copper that usually contain tin, sometimes with small amounts of other elements such as antimony and phosphorus. [Italian *bronzo,* bell metal, brass (possibly from Latin *aes Brundisium,* copper of Brundisium, ancient seaport in southeastern Italy).]

brunch |brŭnch| *n.* A meal eaten late in the morning as breakfast and lunch. [br(eakfast) + (l)unch.]

Bue·nos Ai·res |bwā′nəs âr′ēz| *or* |īr′ēz| *or* |bō′nəs| The capital of Argentina.

bul·le·tin |bo͝ol′ĭ tn| *or* |-tĭn| *n.* A statement on a matter of public interest, as in a newspaper, on television, or on the radio: *a weather bulletin.*

bu·reau |byo͝or′ō| *n., pl.* **bu·reaus** *or* **bu·reaux.** A chest of drawers.

bur·ri·to |bo͝o rē′tō| *or* |bə-| *n.* A flour tortilla wrapped around a filling, as beef, beans, or cheese. [American Spanish, from Spanish, little donkey, diminutive of *burro,* burro.]

bur·ro |bûr′ō| *or* |bo͝or′ō| *or* |bŭr′ō| *n., pl.* **bur·ros.** A small donkey, usually used for riding or for carrying loads. [Spanish, from *borrico,* donkey, from Late Latin *burricus,* small horse.]

by·line, *also* **by-line** |bī′līn′| *n.* A line at the head of a newspaper or magazine article giving the writer's name: *His story carried his by-line.*

C

ca·ble·vi·sion |kā′bəl vĭzh′ən| *n.* Cable television. [cable + (tele)vision.]

ca·coph·o·ny |kə kŏf′ə nē| *n., pl.* **ca·coph·o·nies.** Harsh, unpleasant sound; dissonance: *the untuned instruments created cacophony.* [From Greek, *kakophōnia,* from *kakos,* bad + *phōnē,* sound, voice.]

cac·tus |kăk′təs| *n., pl.* **cac·ti** |kăk′tī′| *or* **cac·tus·es.** One of many kinds of plants that have thick, leafless, often spiny stems and that grow in hot, dry places.

caf·tan |kăf´tən| *or* |käf tän´| *n.* A coatlike robe with long sleeves and sometimes tied with a sash, worn in the Near East. [Russian *kaftan*, from Turkish *qaftān*.]

Cai·ro |kī´rō|. The capital of Egypt and the largest city in Africa, on the Nile River.

cal·lig·ra·phy |kə lĭg´rə fē| *n.* Beautiful handwriting; fine penmanship. [From Greek *kalli-*, from *kallos*, beauty + *graphein*, to write.]

cal·o·rie |kăl´ə rē| *n.* A unit of heat used in physics, chemistry, and related sciences, equal to the amount of heat needed to raise one gram of water one degree Celsuis (centigrade).

cam·paign |kăm pān´| *n.* Organized activity to attain some political, social, or commercial goal: *campaign for justice.*

cam·pus |kăm´pəs| *n.* The grounds of a school, especially of a college or university.

can·cel·la·tion |kăn´sə lā´shən| *n.* The act of calling off or stopping: *cancellation of a date; cancellation of a subscription.*

can·di·date |kăn´dĭ dāt| *or* |-dĭt| *n.* A person who seeks or is nominated for an office, prize, honor, etc.: *job candidate.*

can·ta·loupe, also **can·ta·loup** |kăn´tl ōp´| *n.* A melon with a ribbed, rough rind and sweet-smelling orange flesh. [From Italian *cantalupo*, first grown at Cantalupo, a papal villa near Rome.]

ca·pa·ble |kā´pə bəl| *adj.* **1.** Able; skilled; competent: *a capable teacher.* **2.** —**capable of.** Having the ability or capacity for: *a boy capable of being a great athlete.*

cap·i·tal |kăp´ĭ tl| *n.* A city that is the seat of a state or national government. —*adj.* Excellent: *a capital fellow.*

cap·i·tal·ize |kăp´ĭ tl īz´| *v.* **cap·i·tal·ized, cap·i·tal·iz·ing.** To begin a word with a capital letter.

cap·i·tol |kăp´ĭ tl| *n.* The building in which a state legislature assembles: *The governor's office is in the capitol.*

car·a·van |kăr´ə văn´| *n.* An expedition of merchants, pilgrims, etc., traveling together, especially through desert regions: *The caravan stopped at an oasis.*

car·bo·hy·drate |kär´bō hī´drāt´| *or* |-bə-| *n.* Any of a group of chemical compounds, including sugars, starches, and cellulose, that are composed of carbon, hydrogen, and oxygen.

car·bu·re·tor |kär´bə rā´tər| *or* |-byə-| *n.* A part of a gasoline engine that vaporizes or atomizes the gasoline and mixes it with air in such a way that it will burn properly.

car·di·gan |kär´di gən| *n.* A sweater or knitted jacket without a collar, opening down the front and usually buttoning. [After James Thomas Brudenell, Seventh Earl of *Cardigan* (1797–1868).]

car·go |kär´gō| *n., pl.* **car·goes** or **car·gos.** The freight carried by a ship, airplane, etc. [From Spanish *cargar*, to load, from Latin *carrus*, a kind of vehicle.]

car·i·bou |kăr´ə boo´| *n., pl.* **car·i·bou** or **car·i·bous.** A deer of arctic regions of North America, with large, spreading antlers in both the males and females. [Canadian French, from Proto-Algonquian *mekālixpowa*, "snow shoveler."]

car·i·ca·ture |kăr´ĭ kə choor´| *or* |-chər´| *n.* A picture or description of a person or thing in which certain distinctive features are greatly exaggerated or distorted to produce a comic effect.

cas·sette |kə sĕt´| *or* |kă-| *n.* **1.** A lightproof case containing a roll of film that can be inserted directly into a camera. **2.** A small case containing magnetic tape for use in a tape recorder, in certain electric typewriters, etc. [French, small box, from Old French, diminutive of *casse*, case (box).]

cau·cus |kô´kəs| *n., pl.* **cau·cus·es** or **cau·cus·ses.** A meeting of members of a political party to decide on a question of policy or to choose a candidate for office. [Earlier *corcas*, probably of Algonquian origin, perhaps akin to *caucasasu* (Virginia Algonquian word for "counselor," recorded by Captain John Smith).]

cel·e·brate |sĕl´ə brāt´| *v.* **cel·e·brat·ed, cel·e·brat·ing.** To mark (a special occasion) with festive activity: *celebrate one's birthday.*

cel·lo |chĕl´ō| *n., pl.* **cel·los.** A musical instrument of the violin family, having four strings and a pitch an octave below that of the viola.

cel·lu·lar |sĕl´yə lər| *adj.* Of, like, or containing a cell or cells: *cellular structure.*

cem·e·ter·y |sĕm´ĭ tĕr´ē| *n., pl.* **cem·e·ter·ies.** A place for burying the dead; a graveyard.

cen·ti·grade |sĕn´tĭ grād´| *adj.* Of or relating to a temperature scale that divides the interval between the boiling and freezing points of water into 100°; Celsius.

cen·ti·me·ter |sĕn´tə mē´tər| *n.* A unit of length; 1/100 meter. [From Latin *centum*, hundred + Greek *metron*, meter, measure.]

ce·re·al |sîr´ē əl| *n.* **1.** The seeds of certain grasses, such as wheat, oats, or corn, used as food. **2.** A food, such as a breakfast food, made from such grain.

cer·e·mo·ny |sĕr´ə mō´nē| *n., pl.* **cer·e·mo·nies.** A formal act or set of acts performed in honor or celebration of an occasion, such as a wedding or funeral: *a wedding ceremony.*

Pronunciation Key

ă	pat	ŏ	pot	û	fur
ā	pay	ō	go	*th*	the
â	care	ô	paw, for	th	thin
ä	father	oi	oil	hw	which
ĕ	pet	ōō	book	zh	usual
ē	be	ōō	boot	ə	ago, item
ĭ	pit	yōō	cute		pencil, atom
ī	ice	ou	out		circus
î	near	ŭ	cut	ər	butter

chal·lenge |chăl´ənj| *n.* A special quality naturally belonging to something and requiring full use of one's abilities, energy, or resources: *the challenge of mountain climbing.*

change |chānj| *v.* **changed, chang·ing.** To make or become different; alter. —**change´a·ble** *adj.*: *changeable weather.*

chan·nel |chăn´əl| *n.* **1.** The depression or cut in the earth through which a river or stream passes. **2.** A part of a river or harbor deep enough to form a passage for ships.

chasm |kăz´əm| *n.* A deep crack or opening in the surface of the earth; a narrow gorge.

Ched·dar, also **ched·dar** |chĕd´ər| *n.* A firm, usually yellowish cheese. [First made in *Cheddar*, a village in Somerset, England.]

chem·ist |kĕm´ĭst| *n.* **1.** A scientist who specializes in chemistry. **2.** *British.* A pharmacist.

chew |chōō| *v.* To grind, crush, or gnaw with the teeth or jaws. —*phrasal verb.* **chew out.** *Slang.* To scold.

chief |chēf| *n., pl.* **chiefs.** A person with the highest rank or authority; a leader: *the chief of police.*

chil·i |chĭl´ē| *n., pl.* **chil·ies. 1.** The very sharp-tasting pod of a kind of red pepper. **2.** A seasoning made from the dried or ground pods of this pepper. **3.** A spicy dish made with chili, beans, and often meat. [Spanish *chile, chili,* from Nahuatl *chilli.*]

chip·munk |**chĭp´**mŭngk´| *n.* A small animal resembling a squirrel but smaller and having a striped back. [Variant of earlier *chitmunk*, from Algonquian.]

choc·o·late |**chô´**kə lĭt| *or* |**chŏk´**ə-| *or* |**chôk´**lĭt| *or* |**chŏk´**-| *n.* A sweet drink or candy made with ground, roasted cacao seeds. —*adj.* Having the flavor of chocolate: *chocolate milk.* [Spanish, from Aztec *xocolatl*: *xococ*, bitter + *atl*, water.]

cho·les·ter·ol |kə **lĕs´**tə rôl´| *or* |-rōl´| *or* |-rŏl´| *n.* A white, soapy compound of carbon, hydrogen, and oxygen ($C_{27}H_{46}O$) that occurs in many animal and plant tissues and substances, especially in bile, fats, the brain, the blood, egg yolk, and seeds. It sometimes collects on the inner walls of the arteries and causes them to harden.

chord |kôrd| *n.* A combination of three or more musical tones sounded at the same time.

cho·re·o·graph |**kôr´**ē ə grăph´| *or* |-gräf´| *or* |**kōr´**-| *v.* To create the choreography of (a ballet or other stage work).

cho·re·og·ra·phy |kôr´ē **ŏg´**rə fē| *or* |**kōr´**-| *n.* The art of creating and arranging ballet or dances. [From French *chorégraphie*: Greek *khoreios*, of a dance, from *khoros*, dance + *graphein*, to write.]

chro·mo·some |**krō´**mə sōm´| *n.* A genetic structure located in the nucleus of a cell. Chromosomes are composed mainly of DNA and transmit hereditary characteristics from parents to their offspring.

cir·cuit |**sûr´**kĭt| *n.* **1.** A closed path through which an electric current flows or may flow. **2.** A connection of electrical or electronic parts or devices intended to accomplish some purpose: *a radio circuit.*

cir·cum·fer·ence |sər **kŭm´**fər əns| *n.* The boundary line of a circle: *Can you determine the circumference of the hoop?*

cir·cum·stance |**sûr´**kəm stăns´| *n.* Often **circumstances.** One of the conditions, facts, or events connected with and usually affecting another event, a person, or a course of action: *She investigated the circumstances surrounding the accident.* [From Latin *circumstāntia*, accessory details, from *circumstāre*, to stand around, be accessory: *circum-*, around (from *circus*, circle) + *stāre*, to stand.]

clas·si·cal |**klăs´**ĭ kəl| *adj.* **1.** Of the musical style that prevailed in Europe in the late part of the 18th century. **2.** Pertaining to concert music or all music other than popular music and folk music. **3.** Standard or traditional rather than new or experimental: *classical methods of navigation.*

clas·si·fy |**klăs´**ə fī´| *v.* **clas·si·fied, clas·si·fy·ing, clas·si·fies.** To arrange in classes or assign to a class; sort; categorize: *A librarian classifies books.*

cli·mac·tic |klī **măk´**tĭk| *adj.* Of or forming a climax, or point of greatest intensity or effect in a series of events: *The climactic event was the rescue of the castaways.*

cli·mat·ic |klī **măt´**ĭk| *adj.* Of climate: *Climatic changes develop slowly.*

co·coa |**kō´**kō´| *n.* **1.** A powder made from roasted ground cacao seeds from which much of the fat has been removed. **2.** A sweet drink made with cocoa and milk or water. [Variant of *cacao*, Spanish, from Nahuatl *cacahuatl*, cacao beans.]

cole·slaw, also **cole slaw** |**kōl´**slô´| *n.* A salad of shredded raw cabbage with a dressing. [Dutch *koolsla*: *kool*, cabbage + *sla*, short for *salade*, salad.]

col·lab·o·rate |kə **lăb´**ə rāt´| *v.* **col·lab·o·rat·ed, col·lab·o·rat·ing.** To work together on a project: *They collaborated on the script.* —**col·lab´o·ra´tion** *n.*: *Their collaboration was such a success that they continued to work together.*

co·logne |kə **lōn´**| *n.* A scented liquid made of alcohol and fragrant oils. [French *eau de cologne*, "water of Cologne," from *Cologne*, Germany.]

colo·nel |kûr´nəl| *n.* An officer in the U.S. Army, Air Force, or Marine Corps ranking below a brigadier general.

Col·os·se·um |kôl´ə sē´əm| *n.* An arena in Rome, built by Vespasian and Titus (A.D. 75–80) and used for public entertainment.

col·umn |kŏl´əm| *n.* A feature article that appears regularly in a newspaper or magazine.

col·um·nist |kŏl´əm nĭst| *or* |-ə mĭst| *n.* A person who writes a column for a newspaper or magazine.

com·bi·na·tion |kŏm´bə nā´shən| *n.* **1.** The act or process of combining. **2.** The condition of being combined. **3.** Something that results from combining two or more things: *An alloy is a combination of metals.*

com·bine |kəm bīn´| *v.* **com·bined, com·bin·ing. 1.** To bring or come together; make or become united; join. **2.** To join or cause to join (two or more substances) to make a single substance, such as a chemical compound or an alloy. [Late Latin *combīnāre*: Latin *com-*, together + *bīnī*, two at a time.]

com·bus·tion |kəm bŭs´chən| *n.* A chemical reaction, especially a combination with oxygen, that goes on rapidly and produces light and heat.

com·et |kŏm ĭt| *n.* A mass of material that travels around the sun in an immense elongated orbit. When close enough to the sun to be visible, a comet usually appears as an object with a glowing head attached to a long, vaporous tail that always points away from the sun.

Pronunciation Key

ă	pat	ŏ	pot	û	fur
ā	pay	ō	go	*th*	the
â	care	ô	paw, for	th	thin
ä	father	oi	oil	hw	which
ĕ	pet	ŏŏ	book	zh	usual
ē	be	ōō	boot	ə	ago, item
ĭ	pit	yōō	cute		pencil, atom
ī	ice	ou	out		circus
î	near	ŭ	cut	ər	butter

com·mem·o·rate |kə mĕm´ə rāt´| *v.* **com·mem·o·rat·ed, com·mem·o·rat·ing.** To honor the memory of: *They commemorated the victory every year.* [Latin *commemorāre*, to call to mind clearly: *com-*, + *memorāre*, to remind, speak of, from *memor*, mindful.]

com·ment |kŏm´ĕnt´| *n.* A written note or a remark that explains, interprets, or gives an opinion on something: *a critic's comment.* [Latin *commentus*, to contrive by thought.]

com·mer·cial |kə mûr´shəl| *adj.* Of or engaged in commerce: *a commercial airport.* [Latin *commercium*: *com-*, + *merx*, merchandise.]

com·mu·ni·ty |kə myōō´nĭ tē| *n., pl.* **com·mu·ni·ties. 1. a.** A group of people living in the same locality and under the same government. **b.** The district or locality in which they live. **2.** A group of people who have close ties, as through common nationality or interests: *New York's Puerto Rican community.* [Latin *commūnis*, common.]

com·mute |kə myōōt´| *v.* **com·mut·ed, com·mut·ing, com·mutes.** To travel regularly between a home in one community and work or school in another. —*n.* A trip made by a commuter: *a commute of 15 miles to work.* [From Latin *commūtāre*, to exchange: *com-*, together + *mūtāre*, to change.]

com·pa·ra·ble |kŏm´pər ə bəl| *adj.* Capable of being compared; having like traits; similar or equivalent: *comparable in size.*

com·pat·i·ble |kəm păt´ə bəl| *adj.* Able to live or perform in agreement or harmony with another or others.

com·pen·sa·tion |kŏm´pən sā´shən| *n.* Something given as payment or amends, as for work, loss, or injury: *The bonus was compensation for her extra work.* [Latin *compensāre*, to weigh one thing against another: *com-*, together + *pensāre*, to weigh.]

com·pe·tence |kŏm´pĭ tns| *n.* Ability to do what is required; the state of being capable: skill: *I do not doubt his competence.*

com·pe·tent |kŏm´pĭ tnt| *adj.* Able to do what is required; capable: *a competent worker.*

com·pe·ti·tion |kŏm´pə tĭsh´ən| *n.* **1.** The act of competing as in a contest. **2.** A contest or similar test of skill or ability: *a baking competition.* **3.** Rivalry or struggle to win an advantage, success, or profit: *competition between the two teams.* [Late Latin *competitionem*, rivalry, from *competere*, strive in common.]

com·ple·ment |kŏm´plə mənt| *n.* Something that completes, makes up a whole, or brings to perfection: *An attractive table setting is a complement to a well-prepared meal.* —*v.* |kŏm´plə mĕnt´|. To make complete; add to the effect of; be a complement to: *That hat complements your dress perfectly.*

com·pli·ment |kŏm´plə mənt| *n.* An expression of praise or admiration: *Maria paid Tony a compliment on his cooking.*

com·prise |kəm prīz´| *v.* **com·prised, com·pris·ing.** To consist of; be composed of; include: *The union comprises fifty states.*

com·pro·mise |kŏm´prə mīz´| *v.* **com·pro·mised, com·pro·mis·ing.** To yield or make adjustments in certain demands, principles, details, etc.; settle by taking the middle way between extremes: *They decided to compromise.*

com·put·er |kəm pyōō´tər| *n.* A device that computes, especially one of many complex electronic devices that are capable of doing arithmetic at high speeds, of making certain decisions, of storing and analyzing data, and, often, of controlling machinery.

con-. Also **col-** (before *l*) or **cor-** (before *r*) or **com-** (before *p, b,* or *m*) or **co-** (before vowels, *h,* and *gn*). A prefix meaning "together, with": **compete.** [Old Latin preposition *con.*]

con·cept |kŏn´sĕpt´| *n.* A general idea or understanding: *the concept of gravity.*

con·cer·to |kən chĕr´tō| *n., pl.* **con·cer·tos** or **con·cer·ti** |kən chĕr´tē|. A musical composition written for one or more solo instruments and an orchestra: *a piano concerto.*

con·cise |kən sīs´| *adj.* Expressing much in a few words; brief and clear: *a concise paragraph.* [From Latin *concidere*, to cut up: *com-*, + *caedere*, to cut.]

con·demn |kən dĕm´| *v.* To express strong disapproval of; denounce: *The treaty condemned the use of war to solve problems.*

con·dem·na·tion |kŏn´dĕm nā´shən| *or* |-dəm-| *n.* **1. a.** The act of condemning. **b.** The condition or fact of being condemned. **2.** An expression of strong disapproval.

con·do·min·i·um |kŏn´də mĭn´ē əm| *n.* An apartment building in which the individual apartments are owned by the tenants. [New Latin: *con-*, together + *dominium*, property.]

con·duc·tor |kən dŭk´tər| *n.* The person who conducts, or leads, an orchestra, band, or other group of musical performers.

con·fi·dence |kŏn´fĭ dəns| *n.* A feeling of assurance, especially of self-assurance: *states his case with confidence. He lacks confidence in himself.*

con·fi·dent |kŏn´fĭ dənt| *adj.* Feeling or showing confidence; sure of oneself; certain: *The team is confident of victory.*

con·firm |kən fûrm´| *v.* To support or establish the validity of: *Experiments confirmed the theory.*

con·gest |kən jĕst´| *v.* To overfill; overcrowd. [Latin *congere,* to bring together, heap up: *com-,* together + *gerere,* to carry.]

con·ges·tion |kən jĕs´chən| *n.* A condition of overcrowding: *traffic congestion.*

con·grat·u·late |kən grăch´ə lāt´| *v.* **con·grat·u·lat·ed, con·grat·u·lat·ing.** To speak to (someone) with praise for an achievement or any good event. [Latin *congrātulārī,* to rejoice with someone: *com-,* with + *grātulārī,* to express one's joy, rejoice, from *grātus,* pleasing.]

con·grat·u·la·tion |kən grăch´ə lā´shən| *n.* **1.** The act of congratulating: *a few quiet words of congratulation.* **2. congratulations.** An expression used in congratulating someone.

con·jec·ture |kən jĕk´chər| *n.* The formation of an opinion or conclusion from incomplete or insufficient evidence; guesswork: *The origin of language is a matter of pure conjecture.* [Latin *com-,* together + *jacere,* to throw.]

con·nect |kə nĕkt´| *v.* To join or come together; link: *A new road connects the two towns.*

con·nec·tion |kə nĕk´shən| *n.* The act of connecting or condition of being connected.

con·science |kŏn´shəns| *n.* An inner sense in a person that distinguishes right from wrong: *My conscience is clear.*

Pronunciation Key

ă	pat	ŏ	pot	û	fur
ā	pay	ō	go	*th*	the
â	care	ô	paw, for	th	thin
ä	father	oi	oil	hw	which
ě	pet	ŏŏ	book	zh	usual
ē	be	ōō	boot	ə	ago, item
ĭ	pit	yōō	cute		pencil, atom
ī	ice	ou	out		circus
î	near	ŭ	cut	ər	butter

con·scious |kŏn´shəs| *adj.* **1.** Having or showing self-consciousness; aware: *He is conscious of his shortcomings.* **2.** Done with awareness; intentional; deliberate: *a conscious effort to speak more clearly.* —**con´scious·ly** *adv.*

con·se·quence |kŏn´sĭ kwĕns´| *or* |-kwəns| *n.* Something that follows from an action or condition; an effect; result: *the consequences of a decision.*

con·sid·er·a·ble |kən sĭd´ər ə bəl| *adj.* Fairly large or great in amount, extent, or degree: *a considerable income.*

con·spic·u·ous |kən spĭk´yōō əs| *adj.* Attracting attention; striking the eye: *a conspicuous error.*

con·stel·la·tion |kŏn´stə lā´shən| *n.* Any of 88 groups of stars that are thought to resemble objects, animals, and mythological characters, and that have been named after them.

con·stit·u·ent |kən stĭch´ōō ənt| *n.* Someone represented by an elected official; a voter. [Latin *com-,* + *statuere,* to set up.]

con·sti·tu·tion |kŏn´stĭ tōō´shən| *or* |-tyōō´-| *n.* The basic law of a politically organized body, such as a nation or state.

contact lens. A tiny lens designed to correct a defect in vision, worn directly on the cornea of the eye and practically invisible when in place. [Latin *contāctus,* from *contingere,* to touch: *com-,* together + *tangere,* to touch.]

con·tem·po·rar·y |kən **tĕm´**pə rĕr´ē| *adj.* Current; modern: *a contemporary composer.*

con·tin·u·al |kən **tĭn´**yōō əl| *adj.* Repeated regularly and frequently: *the continual banging of the shutters.*
Usage: **continual, continuous.** *Continual* means "over and over again." *Continuous* means "unbroken."

con·tin·u·ous |kən **tĭn´**yōō əs| *adj.* Continuing without interruption; unbroken: *Living cells must have a continuous supply of oxygen.* —See Usage note at **continual.**

con·tra·dict |kŏn´trə **dĭkt´**| *v.* **1.** To assert or express the opposite of (a statement): *The witness seemed to contradict his previous testimony.* **2.** To declare to be untrue: *She contradicted the statement.* [Latin *contrādīcere,* to speak against: *contrā,* against + *dīcere,* to speak.]

con·trast |kən **trăst´**| *v.* To compare in order to reveal differences: *to contrast good and evil.* [Latin *contrā,* against + *stāre,* to stand.]

co·op·er·ate |kō **ŏp´**ə rāt´| *v.* **co·op·er·at·ed, co·op·er·at·ing.** To work or act with another or others for a common purpose.

co·op·er·a·tion |kō ŏp´ə **rā´**shən| *n.* Joint action: *This treaty will promote international cooperation.*

co·or·di·na·tion |kō ôr´dn **ā´**shən| *n.* The organized action of muscles in the performance of complicated movements or tasks: *A juggler must have good coordination.*

cop·per |**kŏp´**ər| *n.* One of the elements, a reddish-brown metal that is an excellent conductor of heat and electricity. [Latin *Cyprium (aes),* "(copper) of Cyprus" (Cyprus was known in ancient times as the source of the best copper).]

core |kôr| *or* |kōr| *n.* **1.** The hard or stringy central part of certain fruits, such as an apple or pear, containing the seeds. **2.** The innermost or most important part of anything; heart; essence: *the core of the scientists' work.*

corps |kôr| *or* |kōr| *n., pl.* **corps** |kôrz| *or* |kōrz| **1.** A large army unit composed of two or more divisions. **2.** Any group of people acting together. [Latin *corpus,* body.]

cor·re·la·tion |kôr´ə **lā´**shən| *or* |kŏr´-| *n.* A relationship; systematic connection; correspondence: *The two sets of statistics show a direct correlation.* [Medieval Latin *correlātiō: con-,* together + *relātiō* relation.]

cor·re·spond |kôr´ĭ **spŏnd´**| *or* |kŏr´-| *v.* To communicate by letter, especially on a regular basis. [From Medieval Latin *correspondēre: con-,* together + *respondēre,* respond.]

cor·re·spond·ent |kôr´ĭ **spŏn´**dənt| *n.* Someone hired by a newspaper, radio station, etc., to report on news from faraway places: *The correspondent phoned in her story.*

cor·rode |kə **rōd´**| *v.* **cor·rod·ed, cor·rod·ing.** To dissolve or wear away (a material, structure, etc.), especially by chemical action: *Some metals corrode.* [From Latin *corrodere,* to gnaw to pieces: *con-,* + *rodere,* to gnaw.]

cor·rupt |kə **rŭpt´**| *adj.* Marked by or open to bribery, the selling of political favors, etc.; dishonest: *a corrupt government.* [From Latin *corruptus,* from *corrumpere,* destroy, ruin: *con-,* completely + *rumpere,* to break.]

coun·cil |**koun´**səl| *n.* **1.** A gathering of persons called together to discuss or settle a problem or question. **2.** A group of people chosen to make laws or rules governing something: *a city council; student council.*

coun·sel |**koun´**səl| *n.* **1.** Advice; guidance: *to offer counsel.* **2.** *pl.* **counsel.** A lawyer or group of lawyers giving legal advice. —*v.* **coun·seled** *or* **coun·selled, coun·sel·ing** *or* **coun·sel·ling.** To give advice: *She counsels students.*

coup |kōō| *n., pl.* **coups** |kōōz|. A brilliantly executed move or action that obtains the desired results: *Sam pulled off quite a coup in winning the match.* [French, from Latin *colaphus*, from Greek *kolaphos*, a blow.]

cou·pon |kōō´pŏn| *or* |kyōō´-| *n.* A detachable part of a ticket or advertisement that entitles the bearer to certain benefits, such as a cash refund or a gift. [French, from *couper*, to cut off, from *coup*, a blow.]

cov·er |kŭv´ər| *n.* Musical jargon for a recording or an adaptation of a song by anyone other than the original performer.

cre·den·tial |krĭ dĕn´shəl| *n.*
1. Something that entitles a person to confidence, credit, or authority. **2.** Often **credentials.** A letter or other written evidence of a person's qualifications or status. [Latin *crēdentia*, trust, credence, from *crēdere*, to believe.]

cred·i·bil·i·ty |krĕd´ə bĭl´ĭ tē| *n.* The condition or quality of being believable. [Latin *crēdibilis*, from *crēdere*, to believe.]

cred·it |krĕd´ĭt| *v.* **1.** To give honor to (a person) for something: *credit him with the discovery.* **2.** To attribute (something) to a person: *Some credit the song to Haydn.* [From Latin *crēditum*, "something entrusted," from *crēdere*, to believe, entrust.]

cri·sis |krī´sĭs| *n., pl.* **cri·ses** |krī´sēz|. A point or period of great difficulty during which change often occurs; a turning point. [From Greek *krisis*, turning point, from *krinein*, to separate, decide.]

cri·te·ri·on |krī tîr´ē ən| *n., pl.* **cri·te·ri·a** |krī tîr´ē ə| *or* **cri·te·ri·ons.** A rule or standard on which a judgment can be based: *What are your criteria for judging the work?* [From Greek *krites*, a judge, umpire, from *krinein*, to separate, choose.]

crit·ic |krĭt´ĭk| *n.* A person who forms and expresses judgments of the good and bad qualities of anything. [From Greek *kritikos*, able to discern, critical, from *kritos*, separated, chosen, from *krinein*, to separate, choose.]

Pronunciation Key

ă	pat	ŏ	pot	û	fur
ā	pay	ō	go	*th*	**the**
â	care	ô	paw, for	th	**thin**
ä	father	oi	**oil**	hw	**which**
ĕ	pet	ŏŏ	book	zh	usual
ē	be	ōō	boot	ə	**ago, item**
ĭ	pit	yōō	cute		pencil, atom
ī	ice	ou	**out**		circus
î	near	ŭ	cut	ər	butter

crit·i·cal |krĭt´ĭ kəl| *adj.* **1.** Inclined to judge severely; likely to find fault: *A critical person is seldom pleased with anything.*
2. Marked by or exercising careful evaluation and judgment: *critical analysis of a poem.*
3. Extremely important or decisive: *a critical point in the political campaign.*

crit·i·cize |krĭt´ĭ sīz´| *v.* **crit·i·cized, crit·i·ciz·ing. 1.** To judge the merits and faults of; evaluate: *criticize a play.* **2.** To judge severely; find fault with: *newspapers criticizing the mayor.* [From Greek *kritike*, the art of criticism, from *kritikos*, critical, from *kritos*, separated, from *krinein*, to separate, choose.]

cri·tique |krĭ tēk´| *n.* A critical review or commentary, such as an evaluation of an artistic work.

cro·chet |krō shā´| *v.* **cro·cheted** |krō shād´|, **cro·chet·ing** |krō shā´ĭng|. To make (a piece of needlework) by looping thread or yarn into connected links with a hooked needle called a **crochet hook.** [French, a hook.]

cur·rant |kûr´ənt| *or* |kŭr´-| *n.* The small, sour, usually red or blackish fruit of a prickly shrub, used for making jelly. [Middle English (raysons of) *coraunte*, (raisins of) Corinth, from Norman French *Corauntz*, from Old French *Corinthe*, Corinth.]

cur·ric·u·lum |kə rĭk´yə ləm| *n., pl.* **cur·ric·u·la** |kə rĭk´yə lə| *or* **cur·ric·u·lums.** All the courses of study offered at a particular educational institution.

cur·sive |kûr´sĭv| *adj.* Of or designating writing or printing in which the letters are joined together; flowing: *cursive writing.*

cus·tom |kŭs´təm| *n.* An accepted practice or convention followed by tradition: *Shaking hands is an ancient custom.*

cy·clic |sī´klĭk| *or* |sĭk´lĭk| *or* **cy·cli·cal** |sī´klĭ kəl| *or* |sĭk´lĭ-| *adj.* Of or occurring in cycles. [From Greek *kuklos*, circle, cycle.]

cy·clone |sī´klōn´| *n.* Any violent rotating windstorm, such as a tornado. [Probably from Greek *kukloma*, coil, wheel, from *kuklos*, circle, cycle.]

cyl·in·der |sĭl´ən dər| *n.* **1.** A hollow or solid object shaped like a tube or pipe. **2.** The chamber in which a piston moves back and forth, as in an engine or pump.

D

da·ta |dā´tə| *or* |dăt´ə| *or* |dä´tə| *pl. n.* The less frequently used singular is **da·tum** |dā´təm| *or* |dă´təm| *or* |dä´təm |. Information, especially when it is to be analyzed or used as the basis for a decision. *Usage:* **datum, data.** *Datum* is Latin for "a given fact," and *data* is its plural. Since *data* is often understood as "information" rather than "facts," it is commonly viewed as a collective noun and treated as singular. In formal writing, however, *data* is usually used as a plural: *Numerical data are obtained by counting and measuring.*

day care *n.* The providing of daytime supervision, training, or medical services for children of preschool age or for the elderly.

deb·it |dĕb´ĭt| *n.* A debt charged to and recorded in an account. —*v.* To charge with or as a debt: *Debit my account for $10.* [Middle English *debite*, from Latin *debitum*, debt.]

de·bris, also **dé·bris** |də brē´| *or* |dā´brē´| *n.* The scattered remains of something broken, destroyed, or discarded; fragments; rubble. [French, from *desbrisier*, to break to pieces.]

debt |dĕt| *n.* Something, such as money, owed by one person to another: *a $200 debt.* [From Latin *debita*, debt, from *debere*, to owe.]

de·but, also **dé·but** |dā byōō´| *or* |dĭ-| *or* |dā´byōō´| *n.* A first public appearance, as of an actor on the stage. [French, from *débuter*, to make one's debut, "give the first stroke in a game."]

de·ci·pher |dĭ sī´fər| *v.* To read or interpret (something hard to understand or illegible).

de·ci·sion |dĭ sĭzh´ən| *n.* A final or definite conclusion; a judgment: *made a decision.* [From Latin *decidere*, to cut off, determine: *de-*, off + *caedere*, to cut.]

de·ci·sive |dĭ sī´sĭv| *adj.* Having the power to settle something; conclusive: *a decisive move.* [From Latin *decidere*, to cut off, determine: *de-*, off + *caedere*, to cut.]

de·coy |dē´koi´| *or* |dĭ koi´| *n.* A model of a duck or other bird, used by hunters to attract wild birds or animals. [Possibly from Dutch *dekooi*, "the cage."]

ded·i·cate |dĕd´ĭ kāt´| *v.* **ded·i·cat·ed, ded·i·cat·ing.** To give or commit (oneself) fully to something, such as a course of action; devote: *He dedicated himself to research.*

de·duc·tion |dĭ dŭk´shən| *n.* **1.** The act or process of deducing. **2.** A method of logical reasoning in which each conclusion necessarily follows from the propositions stated. **3.** A conclusion reached by this method: *a brilliant deduction.*

de·fend·ant |dĭ **fĕn**´dənt| *n.* The person against whom a legal action is brought: *the defendant in the trial.*

def·i·ni·tion |dĕf´ə **nĭsh**´ən| *n.* A statement of the meaning of a word or phrase.

de·hy·dra·tion |dē´hī **drā**´shən| *n.* The act or process of losing water or moisture.

dem·o |**dĕm**´ō| *n., pl.* **dem·os.** A sample recording of a song, sent to recording companies or others to promote the music or performers.

dem·o·graph·ics |dĕm´ə **grăf**´ĭks| *or* |dē´mə-| *n. (used with a plural verb).* Data related to the characteristics of human populations, such as size, growth, density, distribution, and vital statistics, used especially to identify consumer markets. [French *démographie*: Greek *dēmos*, people + *-graphy*, from *graphein*, to write.]

de·pend·a·ble |dĭ **pĕn**´də bəl| *adj.* Reliable. [From Latin *dēpendēre*: *dē*, down + *pendēre*, to hang.]

de·port |dĭ **pôrt**´| *or* |-**pōrt**´| *v.* To expel (a foreigner) from a country: *He was deported for breaking the law.* [Latin *dēportāre*, carry off: *dē-*, away + *portāre*, carry.]

de·pot |**dē**´pō| *n.* A railroad or bus station. [French from Latin *dēpositum*, deposit.]

der·by |**dûr**´bē| *n., pl.* **der·bies.** A stiff felt hat with a round crown and a narrow, curved brim. [From the Earl of *Derby*, who founded the Derby, a yearly horse race in England, at which this type of hat was worn.]

der·i·va·tion |dĕr´ə **vā**´shən| *n.* Something that is derived.

de·rive |dĭ **rīv**´| *v.* **de·rived, de·riv·ing.** To obtain or originate from a source: *The word "algebra" derives from Arabic.* [Middle English *deriven*, spring from.]

de·rog·a·to·ry |dĭ **rŏg**´ə tôr´ē| *adj.* Tending to belittle; harshly critical: *a derogatory remark.*

Pronunciation Key

ă	pat	ŏ	pot	û	fur
ā	pay	ō	go	*th*	**the**
â	care	ô	paw, for	th	**thin**
ä	father	oi	**oil**	hw	**which**
ĕ	pet	ŏŏ	book	zh	usual
ē	be	ōō	boot	ə	ago, item
ĭ	pit	yōō	cute		pencil, atom
ī	ice	ou	**out**		circus
î	near	ŭ	cut	ər	butter

der·rick |**dĕr**´ĭk| *n.* A large crane for lifting and moving heavy objects. [Originally, a gallows, after *Derick*, noted hangman at Tyburn, England, around 1600.]

de·scribe |dĭ skrīb´| *v.* **de·scribed, de·scrib·ing.** To give a verbal account of; tell about in detail: *describe one's experiences.*

de·scrip·tion |dĭ skrĭp´shən| *n.* **1.** The act, process, or technique of describing; verbal representation. **2.** An account in words describing something. [From Latin *dēscrībere*, to copy off, write down: *dē-*, down + *scrībere*, to write.]

des·ert[1] |dĕz´ərt| *n.* A dry, barren region, often covered with sand.

de·sert[2] |dĭ zûrt´| *v.* To forsake or leave; to abandon.

de·sert[3] |dĭ zûrt´| *n.* Often **deserts.** Something that is deserved, especially punishment: *He received his just deserts.*

de·sign |dĭ zīn´| *v.* **1.** To draw up plans for (something), especially by means of sketches or drawings: *design a building; design dresses.* **2.** To plan or intend for a specific purpose: *This dictionary is especially designed for students.* —*n.* A drawing or sketch giving the details of how something is to be made. [Old French from Latin *dēsignāre*, designate, mark out: *dē-*, out + *signāre*, mark, from *signum*, sign.]

des·ig·nate |dĕz´ĭg nāt´| *v.* **des·ig·nat·ed, des·ig·nat·ing.** To indicate or specify; point out; show: *Markers designate the boundary.* [Latin *dēsignāre: dē-*, out + *signāre*, mark, from *signum*, sign.]

de·sir·a·ble |dĭ zīr´ə bəl| *adj.* Of such quality as to be desired; pleasing; fine: *The most desirable apartments in the building overlook the park.* —**de·sir´a·bil´i·ty** *n.* —**de·sir´a·bly** *adv.*

des·per·a·do |dĕs´pə rä´dō| *n., pl.* **des·per·a·does** or **des·per·a·dos.** A desperate or bold outlaw.

des·per·ate |dĕs´pər ĭt| *or* |-prĭt| *adj.* **1.** In a critical or hopeless situation and thus ready to do anything: *a desperate criminal.* **2.** Having an urgent or overwhelming need for something: *desperate for money.*

de·spise |dĭ spīz´| *v.* **de·spised, de·spis·ing.** To regard with contempt or scorn.

des·sert |dĭ zûrt´| *n.* The last course of a lunch or dinner, often consisting of fruit, ice cream, or pastry.

de·tect |dĭ tĕkt´| *v.* To discover or notice the existence, presence, or fact of: *I detected something strange in her silence.* —**de·tec´tion** *n.*: *early detection of an illness.* [Middle English from Latin *dētegere*, uncover: *dē-*, (reversal) + *tegere*, to cover.]

de·ter·mine |dĭ tûr´mĭn| *v.* **de·ter·mined, de·ter·min·ing. 1.** To fix, settle, or decide: *Determine whether each of the following is true or false.* **2.** To be the cause of; influence: *Climate helps determine where people live, how they dress, and what they eat.*

de·tour |dē´toor´| *or* |dĭ toor´| *n.* A road used temporarily instead of a main road. [Old French, from *destorner*, to turn away.]

de·vel·op·ment |dĭ vĕl´əp mənt| *n.* The act or process of developing or growing: *the development of industry.*

de·vise |dĭ vīz´| *v.* **de·vised, de·vis·ing.** To form or arrange in the mind; plan; invent; contrive: *devise a plan.*

di·ag·no·sis |dī´əg nō´sĭs| *n., pl.* **di·ag·no·ses** |dī´əg nō´sēz´|. **1.** The act or process of examining in order to identify or determine the nature of a disease or malfunction. **2.** The conclusion reached as a result of such an examination.

di·a·gram |dī´ə grăm´| *n.* A visual display, such as a drawing or sketch, that shows how something works or indicates the relationships between its parts. [Latin *diagramma*, from Greek *diagraphein*, to mark out: *dia-*, apart + *graphein*, to write.]

di·am·e·ter |dī ăm´ĭ tər| *n.* **1.** A straight line that passes through the center of a circle or sphere from a point on one side to a point on the other. **2.** The measure of such a line segment. [From Greek *diametros*, "line which measures through": *dia-*, through + *metron*, meter, measure.]

dic·ta·tion |dĭk tā´shən| *n.* **1.** The act of dictating material to another to be written down. **2.** The material dictated. [Latin *dictāre*, form of *dīcere*, to say, tell.]

dic·ta·tor |dĭk´tā´tər| *or* |dĭk tā´tər| *n.*
A ruler who has complete authority and unlimited power over the government of a country, especially a tyrant. [Latin, from *dictāre*, dictate.]

dic·tion |dĭk´shən| *n.* **1.** The choice and use of words in speaking or writing.
2. Distinctness of speech; clarity of pronunciation. [Latin *dictiō*, from *dictus,* past participle of *dīcere*, to say.]

dic·tion·ar·y |dĭk´shə nĕr´ē| *n., pl.*
dic·tion·ar·ies. A book containing an alphabetical list of words with information given for each word. Such information includes meaning, pronunciation, etymology, usage, and synonyms. [Latin *dictiō*, diction.]

die·sel |dē´zəl| *n.* Something powered by a diesel engine, especially a locomotive.
[After Rudolph *Diesel* (1858–1913), who invented the diesel engine.]

dif·fer·ence |dĭf´ər əns| *or* |dĭf´rəns| *n.*
1. The condition of being different; variation.

dif·fi·cult |dĭf´ĭ kŭlt´| *or* |-kəlt| *adj.*
Hard to do, accomplish, or perform: *a difficult task.*

dif·fu·sion |dĭ fyōō´zhən| *n.* **1.** The process of diffusing, or spreading, or the condition of being diffused; *the diffusion of liquids.* **2.** The gradual mixing of two or more substances as a result of random motion of their molecules.

di·gest |dĭ jĕst´| *or* |dī-| *v.* To change (food) or become changed into a form that is eaily absorbed into the body. [Middle English *digesten*, from Latin *dīgerere*, to divide, distribute, digest: *dī-*, apart + *gerere*, to carry.]

di·ges·tion |dĭ jĕs´chən| *or* |dī-| *n.*
1. The processes by which food is changed into simple substances that the body can absorb. **2.** The ability to carry on these processes.

diph·the·ri·a |dĭf thîr´ē ə| *or* |dĭp-| *n.*
A serious contagious disease caused by infection with certain bacilli. Its symptoms include high fever, weakness, and the formation in the throat

Pronunciation Key

ă	pat	ŏ	pot	û	fur
ā	pay	ō	go	*th*	*th*e
â	care	ô	paw, for	th	thin
ä	father	oi	oil	hw	which
ĕ	pet	ŏŏ	book	zh	usual
ē	be	ōō	boot	ə	ago, item
ĭ	pit	yōō	cute		pencil, atom
ī	ice	ou	out		circus
î	near	ŭ	cut	ər	butter

and other air passages of false membranes that cause difficulty in breathing.

dis·a·bil·i·ty |dĭs´ə bĭl´ĭ tē| *n., pl.*
dis·a·bil·i·ties. 1. The condition of lacking or losing a physical or mental capacity.
2. Something that disables; a handicap: *Being short is a disability for a basketball player.*

dis·ap·point·ment |dĭs´ə point´mənt| *n.* A feeling of unhappiness caused by unfulfilled hopes or expectations: *The cancelled field trip caused disappointment among the students.*

dis·clo·sure |dĭs klō´zhər| *n.* The act of disclosing, or uncovering: *disclosure of important information.*

dis·co·theque |dĭs´kə tĕk´| *or* |dĭs´kə tĕk´| *n.* A nightclub that offers dancing to amplified recorded music. [French, from Italian *discoteca*, record collection: *disco*, record + *-teca*, collection.]

dis·cov·er·y |dĭ skŭv´ə rē| *n., pl.*
dis·cov·er·ies. 1. The act or an example of discovering. **2.** Something discovered.

dis·cred·it |dĭs krĕd´ĭt| *v.* To damage in reputation; disgrace: *The report discredits him.* [English *dis-*, not + *credit*, from Latin *crēdere*, to believe.]

dis·creet |dĭ skrēt´| *adj.* Having or showing caution or self-restraint in one's speech or behavior; showing good judgment; prudent: *a polite and discreet person; keeping a discreet distance from a strange animal.*

dis·crete |dĭ **skrēt´**| *adj.* Being a separate thing; individual; distinct: *discrete items in a list.*

dis·crim·i·na·tor·y |dĭ **skrĭm´**ə nə tôr´ē| or |-tōr´ē| *adj.* Showing prejudice; biased.

dis·ease |dĭ **zēz´**| *n.* Any condition of an organism that makes it unable to function in the normal, proper way, especially a condition that results from infection, inherent weakness, or pressures of the environment.

dis·guise |dĭs **gīz´**| *n.* Clothes or other personal effects, such as make-up, worn to conceal one's true identity. —*v.* To conceal identity with clothes or other effects.

dis·patch·er |dĭ **spăch´**ər| *n.* A person employed to control the departure and movements of trains, taxicabs, delivery trucks, etc., or to route telegraph communications.

dis·pense |dĭ **spĕns´**| *v.* **dis•spensed, dis•pens•ing. 1.** To deal out or distribute in parts or portions. **2.** To prepare and give out (medicines). [Latin *dispendere*, to weigh out: *dis-*, away + *pendere*, to weigh.]

dis·pose |dĭ **spōz´**| *v.* **dis•posed, dis•pos•ing.** To place or set in a particular order; arrange. —**dispose of.** To get rid of, as by attending to or settling, giving or selling, destroying or throwing away, or eating or drinking: *They disposed of the garbage.* [Old French, *disposer*, reshaped, from Latin *dispōnere*, to place here and there.]

dis·po·si·tion |dĭs´pə **zĭsh´**ən| *n.* **1.** An act of disposing of, as by transferring ownership or throwing away. **2.** One's usual mood; temperament: *a grouchy disposition.*

dis·rupt |dĭs **rŭpt´**| *v.* To upset the order of; throw into confusion or disorder: *a storm that disrupted the lives of hundreds.* [Latin *disrumpere*, to break apart: *dis-*, apart + *rumpere*, to break.]

dis·sim·i·lar |dĭ **sĭm´**ə lər| or |dĭs **sĭm´-**| *adj.* Unlike; different; distinct.

dis·solve |dĭ **zŏlv´**| *v.* **dis•solved, dis•solv•ing. 1.** To absorb into a solution; to liquefy: *The tablet dissolved in water.* **2.** To bring to an end: *dissolve a partnership.* [Latin

dissolvere: *dis-*, apart + *solvere*, to loosen, untie.]

dis·tri·bu·tion |dĭs´trə **byoo´**shən| *n.* The way in which a thing is distributed: *the map showing the distribution of wildlife in America.*

di·vis·i·ble |dĭ **vĭz´**ə bəl| *adj.* Capable of being divided.

doc·u·dra·ma |dŏk´yə **drä´**mə| or |-drăm´ə| *n.* A television or motion-picture dramatization of events based on fact. [docu(mentary) + drama.]

doc·u·ment |dŏk´yə mənt| *n.* An official paper that can be used to furnish evidence or information.

-dom. A suffix that forms nouns: **freedom; kingdom.**

dor·mant |dôr´mənt| *adj.* Not active but capable of renewed activity: *a dormant volcano.*

dos·age |dō´sĭj| *n.* **1.** The administration or application of medicine or something that acts on living organisms in regulated amounts. **2.** The amount administered or applied: *the prescribed dosage.*

dou·ble-cross |dŭb´əl **krôs´**| or |-krŏs´|. *Slang v.* To betray (someone) by doing the opposite of what was agreed on.

doubt |dout| *v.* To be uncertain or unsure about: *I doubt that I can go.* —*n.* An uncertain condition or state of affairs: *When in doubt, ask.* [Middle English from Old French from Latin *dubitare*, to waver.]

draft |drăft| or |dräft| *n.* **1.** A current of air, especially in an enclosed area. **2.** A preliminary outline, plan, or picture; a version: *a rough draft of the paragraph.* —*v.* To select for a specific duty: *draft a new candidate.*

dra·mat·ic |drə **măt´**ĭk| *adj.* Striking in appearance or effect: *a dramatic sunset.*

drom·e·dar·y |drŏm´ĭ dĕr´ē| or |drŭm´-| *n., pl.* **drom•e•dar•ies.** The one-humped camel widely used for riding and carrying loads in northern Africa and southwestern Asia.

du·bi·ous |dōo'bē əs| *or* |dyōo'-| *adj.*
Doubtful; uncertain: *I am dubious about the outcome.* [Latin *dubius*, moving in two directions.]

du·pli·cate |dōo'plĭ kāt'| *or* |dyōo'-| *v.*
du·pli·cat·ed, du·pli·cat·ing. To make an exact copy of: *duplicate a key.* —**du'pli·ca'tion** *n.*: *duplication of the original document.* [Latin *duplicare*, to make twofold, from *duplex*, double.]

du·ra·ble |dōor'ə bəl| *or* |dyōor'-| *adj.*
Able to withstand wear and tear; sturdy; lasting: *a durable plastic raincoat.*

E

ea·sel |ē'zəl| *n.* An upright stand or rack used to support the canvas or other material painted on by an artist or to display a picture or sign. [Dutch *ezel*, "donkey."]

ech·o |ĕk'ō| *n., pl.* **ech·oes.** **1. a.** A reflected sound wave or series of reflected sound waves that reaches an observer with a long delay to be heard as distinct from the original direct sound wave. **b.** A sound produced in this way. **2.** Any repetition or imitation of something, as of the opinions, speech, or dress of another: *an echo of her mother's smile.*

e·clipse |ĭ klĭps'| *n.* The blocking by one celestial body of part or all of the light that reaches an observer from another celestial body.

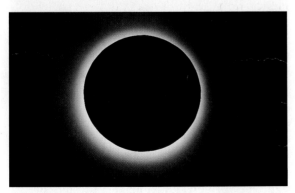

ed·i·ble |ĕd'ə bəl| *adj.* capable of being eaten; fit to eat: *edible mushrooms.*

Pronunciation Key

ă	pat	ŏ	pot	û	fur
ā	pay	ō	go	*th*	the
â	care	ô	paw, for	th	thin
ä	father	oi	oil	hw	which
ĕ	pet	ŏŏ	book	zh	usual
ē	be	ōō	boot	ə	ago, item
ĭ	pit	yōō	cute		pencil, atom
ī	ice	ou	out		circus
î	near	ŭ	cut	ər	butter

e·di·tion |ĭ dĭsh'ən| *n.* **1. a.** The entire number of copies of a book or newspaper printed at one time and having the same content. **b.** A single copy of such a number. **2.** Any of the various forms in which something is issued or produced: *I bought the paperback edition of that novel.*

ed·u·ca·tion·al |ĕj'ōo kā'shə nəl| *adj.*
1. Of education: *an educational system.*
2. Serving to give knowledge or skill; instructive: *an educational television program.*

Eif·fel Tower |ī'fəl| A tower 984 feet high, located in Paris, France. The tower was designed by A.G. *Eiffel* and originally erected for the Paris Exposition (1889).

el·e·gance |ĕl'ĭ gəns| *n.* Refinement and grace in appearance or manner: *the elegance of the dancer's performance.*

el·e·gant |ĕl'ĭ gənt| *adj.* Characterized by elegance; refined or tastefully lavish: *an elegant restaurant.*

el·e·men·ta·ry |ĕl'ə mĕn'tə rē| *or* |-trē| *adj.* Of, involving, or introducing the fundamental or simplest aspects of a subject: *an elementary textbook.*

el·e·vate |ĕl'ə vāt'| *v.* **el·e·vat·ed, el·e·vat·ing.** **1.** To raise to a higher place or position; lift up: *A nurse elevated the head of the bed.* **2.** To promote to a higher rank.

e·lic·it |ĭ lĭs'ĭt| *v.* To bring out; evoke: *He elicited the truth from the witness.*

el·i·gi·ble |ĕl´ĭ jə bəl| *adj.* Qualified for a group, position, privilege, etc.: *When you are eighteen years old, you will be eligible to vote.*

el·lipse |ĭ lĭps´| *n.* A closed curve shaped like an oval with identical ends: *Earth's orbit around the Sun is an ellipse.*

em·bar·go |ĕm bär´gō| *n., pl.* **em·bar·goes.** A suspension by a government of foreign trade or of foreign trade in a particular commodity: *an embargo on sugar.* [Spanish, from *embargar,* to impede, restrain, from Vulgar Latin *imbarricāre,* "to place behind bars": Latin *in-,* in + *barra,* bar.]

em·per·or |ĕm´pər ər| *n.* A male ruler of an empire.

em·ploy·er |ĕm ploi´ər| *n.* A person or corporation that employs people for wages or a salary: *hired by the employer.*

-en. A suffix that forms verbs and means "to become or cause to be": **hasten.** [Middle English *-nen,* from Old English *-nien.*]

-ence or **ency.** A suffix meaning "action, state, quality, or condition": **reference.** [From Latin *entia,* from *-ens.*]

en·chi·la·da |ĕn´chĭ lä´də| *n.* A rolled tortilla with a cheese or meat filling, served with a spicy sauce on top. [American Spanish, feminine past participle of *enchilar,* to put chili in.]

en·cy·clo·pe·di·a, also **en·cy·clo·pae·di·a** |ĕn sī´klə pē´dē ə| *n.* A book or set of books containing articles arranged in alphabetical order and covering one particular field or a wide variety of subjects. [Medieval Latin from Greek *enkuklios paideia,* general education: *enkuklios,* in a circle, general (*en-,* in + *kuklos,* circle) + *paideia,* education.]

en·dur·ance |ĕn dŏŏr´əns| *or* |-dyŏŏr´-| *n.* The ability to withstand strain, stress, hardship, use, etc.: *Climbing that mountain is a real test of a person's endurance.*

en·sem·ble |än säm´bəl| *n.* A group of musicians who perform together. [French, "together," from Latin *insimul,* at the same time.]

en·sign |ĕn´sən| *or* |ĕn´sīn| *n.* A national flag or banner, often having a special insignia, displayed on ships. [From Latin *insigne,* sign, mark, from *insignis,* marked: *in-,* in + *signum,* distinctive mark or figure, seal, signal.]

-ent. A suffix that forms adjectives and nouns: **resident.** [From Latin *-ens.*]

en·ter·tain·ment |ĕn´tər tān´mənt| *n.* Something intended to amuse or divert, as a show or nightclub act.

en·vi·ron·ment |ĕn vī´rən mənt| *or* |-vī´ərn-| *n.* Surroundings and conditions that affect natural processes and the growth and development of living things: *Fish are adapted to their environment; a loving environment.*

e·quip |ĭ kwĭp´| *v.* **e·quipped, e·quip·ping.** To supply with what is needed or wanted; provide: *We equipped ourselves for the long hike.*

e·quip·ment |ĭ kwĭp´mənt| *n.* The things needed or used for a particular purpose.

er·mine |ûr´mĭn| *n.* A weasel with brownish fur that in winter turns to white with a black tail tip.

e·ro·sion |ĭ rō´zhən| *n.* The process of eroding, or wearing away, or the condition of being eroded, especially by natural agents such as wind, water, and weather: *to prevent erosion.*

err |ûr| *or* |ĕr| *v.* To make a mistake or error; be incorrect: *We sometimes err.*

e·rup·tion |ĭ rŭp´shən| *n.* **1.** The fact or an example of erupting, or bursting forth: *The frequency of eruption varies among geysers.* **2.** A sudden, often violent outburst: *the eruption of a disease.* [Latin *ērumpere*, to break out, to burst: *ē-*, out, from *ex-*, + *rumpere*, to break.]

-ery. A suffix that forms nouns from verbs or other nouns: **bakery; greenery.**

es·tab·lish |ĭ stăb´lĭsh| *v.* To begin to set up, as a business; found; create: *His grandfather established the company in 1889.*

e·vac·u·ate |ĭ văk´yōo āt´| *v.* **e·vac·u·at·ed, e·vac·u·at·ing.** To send people away from or withdraw from an area: *evacuate a city.*

e·val·u·ate |ĭ văl´yōo āt´| *v.* **e·val·u·at·ed, e·val·u·at·ing.** To find out, judge, or estimate the value or worth of; examine and appraise: *evaluate a book.* [French from Old French *evaluer*: *e-*, out, from Latin *ex-*, + *valēre*, to be strong, be of value.]

e·val·u·a·tion |ĭ văl´yōo ā´shən| *n.* The act of evaluating or judging: *Evaluation requires you to use all of your thought processes.*

ex·ag·ger·ate |ĭg zăj´ə rāt´| *v.* **ex·ag·ger·at·ed, ex·ag·ger·at·ing.** To enlarge or magnify beyond the truth; overstate: *Often people will exaggerate a story.*

ex·am·ple |ĭg zăm´pəl| *or* |-zăm´-| *n.* One case, item, fact, or incident that is typical of a whole class or group; a sample or specimen.

ex·cel |ĭk sĕl´| *v.* **ex·celled, ex·cel·ling.** To be better than or superior to (others); surpass: *She excels in sports.* [Middle English *excellen*, from Latin *excellere*, to excel.]

ex·cel·lence |ĕk´sə ləns| *n.* The condition or quality of being excellent; superiority.

ex·cept |ĭk sĕpt´| *prep.* Other than; but.

ex·cess |ĭk sĕs´| *or* |ĕk´sĕs´| *n.* Something that exceeds, or goes beyond, what is normal or sufficient: *We had an excess of food.* —*adj.* Exceeding, or going beyond, what is normal or required: *Shake off the excess water.*

Pronunciation Key

ă	pat	ŏ	pot	û	fur
ā	pay	ō	go	*th*	**the**
â	care	ô	paw, for	th	thin
ä	father	oi	oil	hw	which
ĕ	pet	ōō	book	zh	usual
ē	be	ōō	boot	ə	ago, item
ĭ	pit	yōō	cute		pencil, atom
ī	ice	ou	out		circus
î	near	ŭ	cut	ər	butter

ex·er·cise |ĕk´sər sīz´| *n.* **1.** The fulfillment or performance of (a duty, office, or function): *the exercise of their official duties.* **2.** An activity requiring physical exertion, usually done to maintain or develop physical fitness.

ex·haust |ĭg zôst´| *v.* To wear out completely; tire: *She exhausts herself with work.*

ex·hib·it |ĭg zĭb´ĭt| *v.* To give evidence of; show; demonstrate: *exhibit your work.* [From Latin *exhibere*, to hold forth, exhibit: *ex-*, out + *habere*, to hold.]

ex·hi·bi·tion |ĕk´sə bĭsh´ən| *n.* An act or example of exhibiting; a display: *an exhibition of strength; the flying exhibition.*

ex·pense |ĭk spĕns´| *n.* The cost involved in some activity; a price. [From Late Latin *expensa*, from Latin *expendere*, to expend.]

ex·pi·ra·tion |ĕk´spə rā´shən| *n.* The process of coming to a close; termination: *the expiration of a lease.*

ex·plode |ĭk splōd´| *v.* **ex·plod·ed, ex·plod·ing.** To break apart and be destroyed by an explosion: *Suddenly the tank exploded.*

ex·plo·sion |ĭk splō´zhən| *n.* **1.** A sudden, violent release of energy from a confined space, especially with the production of a shock wave and a loud, sharp sound, as well as heat, light, flames, and flying debris. **2.** The loud, sharp sound made by such a release of energy. **3.** A sudden outbreak: *an explosion of laughter.*

ex·port |ĭk **spôrt´**| *or* |-**spōrt´**| *or* |ĕk **´spôrt´**| *or* |-**spōrt´**| *v.* To send or carry (goods or products) to another country for trade or sale: *America exports to many lands.* —*n.* |ĕk´spôrt´| *or* |-spōrt´| The act or process of exporting: *the export of raw materials.*

ex·tinct |ĭk **stĭngkt´**| *adj.* Not likely to erupt; inactive: *an extinct volcano.*

ex·tin·guish |ĭk **stĭng´gwĭsh**| *v.* To put out (a fire or flame); quench: *extinguish a candle.*

F

Fahr·en·heit |**făr´**ən hīt´| *adj.* Of or concerning a temperature scale that indicates the freezing point of water as 32° and the boiling point of water as 212° under normal atmospheric pressure.

fail·ure |**fāl´**yər| *n.* The condition or an example of failing; lack of success: *a crop failure.*

fa·tigue |fə **tēg´**| *n.* Physical or mental weariness or exhaustion resulting from hard work or strain. [French from Old French *fatiguer*, to fatigue, or tire.]

Ferris wheel |**fĕr´**ĭs| *n.* A large upright, rotating wheel with suspended seats on which people ride for amusement. [Designed by George W.G. *Ferris* (1859–1896), American engineer.]

fer·til·ize |**fûr´**tl īz´| *v.* **fer·til·ized, fer·til·iz·ing.** To cause (an egg cell, plant, etc.) to become capable of reproduction, such as by supplying a plant with pollen.

fi·ber |**fī´**bər| *n.* Also *chiefly British* **fi·bre.** **1.** A slender, threadlike strand, as of plant or animal tissue or of man-made material: *Cotton and nylon fibers.* **2.** A number of fibers forming a single substance: *muscle fiber.*

fier·y |**fīr´**ē| *or* |**fī´**ə rē| *adj.* **fier·i·er, fier·i·est.** Of, containing, consisting of, or like fire: *the fiery path of a comet across the sky.*

fi·es·ta |fē **ĕs´**tə| *n.* **1.** A religious feast or holiday, especially one celebrated in Spanish-speaking countries. **2.** Any celebration or festive occasion. [Spanish, from Latin *fĕsta*, joyous, festive.]

fi·na·le |fĭ **năl´**ē| *or* |-**nä´**lē| *n.* The final section of something that is performed, especially the ending of a musical composition.

fire·proof |**fīr´**prŏŏf| *adj.* Made of material or materials that do not burn or that do not crack or break when exposed to heat or fire.

fis·sure |**fĭsh´**ər| *n.* A long, narrow crack or opening, as in the face of a rock.

flame |flām| *n.* The often bright zone of burning gases and fine suspended particles that forms as a result of a fire. [From Latin *flamma*, to shine, flash, burn; fire.]

flam·ma·ble |**flăm´**ə bəl| *adj.* Easy to set fire to and capable of burning very rapidly: *Gasoline is very flammable.* [From Latin *flammāre*, to blaze, from *flamma*, to shine, flash, burn; fire.]

Usage: **flammable, inflammable.** *Flammable* and *inflammable* are identical in meaning. They both mean "easy to set fire to."

flex·i·ble |**flĕk´**sə bəl| *adj.* Capable of bending or being bent; supple; pliable.

for·bid·ding |fər **bĭd´**ĭng| *or* |fôr-| *adj.* Threatening, dangerous, or unfriendly in nature or appearance; frightening.

fore·cast |fôr´kăst´| *or* |-käst´| *or*
|fōr´-| *n.* A prediction, as of coming events
or conditions: *the weather forecast.*

for·eign |fôr´ĭn| *or* |fŏr´-| *adj.* **1.** Being
outside or different from one's own country:
a foreign country. **2.** Of, from, by, with, or for
another country or other countries: *a foreign
language.*

for·ger·y |fôr´jə rē| *or* |fōr´-| *n., pl.*
for·ger·ies. The act or crime of imitating a
signature, document, painting, etc., with the
intention of passing off the copy as the real
thing.

for·mal |fôr´məl| *adj.* **1.** Following
accepted forms, conventions, or rules: *formal
English.* **2.** Structured according to forms or
conventions: *a formal meeting of the
committee.* **3.** Officially made or stated: *a
formal wedding announcement.* **4.** Suitable for
occasions when elegant clothes and fine
manners are called for: *formal dress.* **5.** Stiff;
cold; ceremonious. —**for´mal·ly** *adv.*: *They
greeted the ambassador formally.*

for·mer·ly |fôr´mər lē| *adv.* At a former,
or earlier, time; once: *Machines are used for
work formerly done by people.*

frac·tion |frăk´shən| *n.* A part of a
whole, expressed as two numbers with a line
between them, such as 2/3. [From Late Latin
fractiō, act of breaking, from Latin *frangere*, to
break.]

frac·ture |frăk´chər| *v.* **frac·tured,
frac·tur·ing.** To break or cause to break.
[From Latin *fractūre*, from *frangere*, to break.]

frag·ile |frăj´əl| *or* |-īl´| *adj.* Easily
damaged or broken; brittle. [From Latin
fragilis, from *frangere*, to break.]

frag·ment |frăg´mənt| *n.* A piece or part
broken off or detached from a whole: *a
fragment of a china plate.* [From Latin
fragmentum, from *frangere*, to break.]

frank·fur·ter |frăngk´fər tər| *n.* A
smoked sausage of beef or of beef and pork.
[From *Frankfurt*, Germany.]

free·dom |frē´dəm| *n.* The condition of
being free: *The people fought for freedom.*

Pronunciation Key

ă	pat	ŏ	pot	û	fur
ā	pay	ō	go	*th*	the
â	care	ô	paw, for	th	thin
ä	father	oi	oil	hw	which
ĕ	pet	ŏŏ	book	zh	usual
ē	be	ōō	boot	ə	ago, item
ĭ	pit	yōō	cute		pencil, atom
ī	ice	ou	out		circus
î	near	ŭ	cut	ər	butter

free·lance |frē´lăns´| *or* |-läns´| *adj.*
Pertaining to or produced by a person,
especially a writer or an artist, who sells his or
her services to employers without a long-term
commitment to any one of them: *a freelance job.*

fre·quen·cy |frē´kwən sē| *n., pl.*
fre·quen·cies. The number of occurrences
of a specified event within a given interval:
*a machine that recorded the frequency of
earthquakes.*

frig·id |frĭj´ĭd| *adj.* Extremely cold.

fuch·sia |fyōō´shə| *n.* **1.** A plant grown
for its drooping, often red and purple flowers.
2. A bright purplish red. —*adj.* Bright
purplish red. [After Leonhard *Fuchs*
(1501–1566), German botanist.]

ful·fill |fōōl fĭl´| *v.* To measure up to;
satisfy: *fulfill all requirements.*

fume |fyōōm| *n.* Any smoke, vapor, or gas,
especially one that is irritating or has an
unpleasant odor: *the fumes from a smokestack.*

fun·gi |fŭn´jī| *n.* A plural of **fungus.**

fun·gus |fŭng´gəs| *n., pl.* **fun·gi**
|fŭn´jī| *or* **fun·gus·es.** Any of a group of
plants, such as a mushroom, mold, yeast, or
mildew, that have no green coloring and that
obtain their nourishment from living on dead
plant or animal substance.

fu·ri·ous |fyŏŏr´ē əs| *adj.* Full of or
marked by extreme anger; raging.

G

gab |găb| *v.* **gabbed, gab·bing.** *Informal.* To talk idly and often at length; chatter.

gai·e·ty |gā´ĭ tē| *n.* The condition of being gay or merry; cheerfulness: *the gaiety of the party.*

gar·de·nia |gär dē´nyə| *n.* **1.** A shrub with glossy evergreen leaves and large, fragrant white flowers. **2.** The flower of this shrub. [After Dr. Alexander *Garden* (1731–1790), Scottish naturalist.]

gauge |gāj| *n.* **1.** A standard or scale of measurement. **2.** Any of a large number of devices or instruments used in making measurements or indicating measured values: *a pressure gauge.* —*v.* **gauged, gaug·ing.** To measure precisely, especially by using a gauge: *gauge the depth of the ocean.*

gene |jēn| *n.* A unit, located at a particular point on a chromosome, that controls or acts in the transmission of a hereditary characteristic, such as hair color or eye color in human beings, from parents to offspring.

gen·er·al·ize |jĕn´ər ə līz´| *v.* **gen·er·al·ized, gen·er·al·iz·ing.** To make a general statement about a broad subject.

ge·ner·ic |jə nĕr´ĭk| *adj.* Not having a trademark or brand name; belonging to an entire class of products.

ge·net·ic |jə nĕt´ĭk| *or* **ge·net·i·cal** |jə nĕt´ĭ kəl| *adj.* Of, affecting, or affected by a gene or genes: *genetic traits.*

ge·og·ra·phy |jē ŏg´rə fē| *n., pl.* **ge·og·ra·phies.** The study of the earth and its features and the distribution on the earth of life, including the position of continents, mountains, oceans, and rivers, the arrangement and the boundaries of countries, states, and cities, and the effect of location on climate, resources, population, products, etc. [Latin *geōgraphia,* from Greek: *geō,* from *gē,* earth + *graphein,* to write.]

ge·om·e·try |jē ŏm´ĭ trē| *n., pl.* **ge·om·e·tries.** The mathematical study of the properties, measurement, and relationships of points, lines, planes, surfaces, and angles, and of figures composed of combinations of them. [From Greek *geōmetrein,* to measure land: *geo-,* from *gē,* earth + *metrein,* from *metron,* measure.]

ger·mi·nate |jûr´mə nāt´| *v.* **ger·mi·nat·ed, ger·mi·nat·ing.** To begin or cause to begin to grow; sprout: *Seeds need water to germinate.*

ges·ture |jĕs´chər| *n.* A motion of the hands, arms, head, or body used while speaking or in place of speech to help express one's meaning: *The speaker used dramatic gestures.* [From Latin *gerere,* to carry, act.]

gig |gĭg| *n.* To musicians, a job or paying engagement.

gi·gan·tic |jī găn´tĭk| *adj.* Of extraordinary strength, size, power, etc.; huge.

glimpse |glĭmps| *n.* A brief, incomplete view or look: *a glimpse of the town.* —*v.* **glimpsed, glimps·ing.** To obtain a brief, incomplete view of: *glimpsed a passing car.*

gos·sip |gŏs´əp| *v.* To engage in chatty conversation; to spread rumors.

gov·er·nor |gŭv´ər nər| *n.* The person elected chief executive of a state in the United States.

gra·ham crack·er |grā´əm| *n.* A slightly sweet, usually rectangular cracker made from whole-wheat flour. [After Sylvester *Graham* (1794–1851), an American promoter of better diet.]

-gram¹. A word part meaning "something written or drawn": **diagram; telegram.** [From Greek *gramma,* letter and *grammē,* line.]

-gram². A word part meaning "a metric unit, used to measure weight or mass, equal to about 1/28 ounce": **kilogram.** [From Late Latin *gramma,* a small unit, from Greek, letter.]

gram·mar |grăm´ər| *n.* The system of rules used by the speakers of a language for making sentences in that language.

gram·mat·i·cal |grə **măt´** ĭ kəl| *adj.*
Conforming to the rules of grammar: *a grammatical sentence.* [From Greek *grammatikos*, pertaining to letters, from *gramma*, letter.]

gra·no·la |grə **nō´**lə| *n.* Rolled oats mixed with various ingredients, such as dried fruit, brown sugar, and nuts, used especially as a breakfast cereal. [Originally a trademark.]

-graph. A word part meaning:
1. Something that writes or records: **seismograph; telegraph. 2.** Something written or drawn: **paragraph.** [From Greek *graphein*, to write.]

graph·ic |**grăf´**ĭk| *adj.* **1.** Of written or drawn representations: *a diagram is a graphic representation of something.* **2.** Described in vivid detail: *a graphic description.* [From Greek *graphien*, to write.]

-graphy. A word part meaning: **1.** The process or method of writing or representing in a certain way: **photography. 2.** Science of a specific subject: **oceanography.** [From Greek *graphein*, to write.]

grate·ful |**grāt´**fəl| *adj.* Appreciative; thankful: *He was grateful for the help.* [From Latin *grātus*, pleasing, favorable.]

grat·i·tude |**grăt´**ĭ tōod´| *or* |**-ty**ōōd´| *n.* Appreciation or thankfulness, as for something received or kindness shown. [From Latin *grātus*, favorable.]

grave |grāv| *adj.* **grav·er, grav·est.**
1. Extremely serious; critical: *a grave illness; grave danger.* **2.** *n.* A hole dug in the ground for the burial of a corpse. **3.** A place of burial. *The sea is the grave of many sailors.* [Old French, from Latin *gravis*, heavy.]

grav·i·ty |**grăv´**ĭ tē| *n.* Seriousness; importance: *It was then that we realized the gravity of the situation.* [Old French, from Latin *gravitās*, from *gravis*, heavy, serious.]

gua·ca·mo·le |gwä´kə **mō´**lē| *n.* A spread of mashed avocado, tomato pulp, mayonnaise, and seasonings. [Mexican Spanish from Nahuatl *ahuacomolli: ahuacatl*, avocado + *molli*, sauce.]

Pronunciation Key

ă	pat	ŏ	pot	û	fur
ā	pay	ō	go	*th*	**the**
â	care	ô	paw, for	th	**thin**
ä	father	oi	**oil**	hw	**which**
ĕ	pet	ŏŏ	book	zh	usual
ē	be	ōō	boot	ə	**ago, item**
ĭ	pit	yōō	cute		pencil, at**om**
ī	ice	ou	**out**		circus
î	near	ŭ	cut	ər	butt**er**

guar·an·tee |găr´ən tē´| *n.* A promise or assurance, such as one given by a manufacturer as to the quality or durability of a product.

guer·ril·la, also **gue·ril·la** |gə **rĭl´**ə| *n.* A member of an irregular military force that uses harassing tactics against an enemy army, usually with the support of the local population. [Spanish, diminutive of *guerra*, war.]

guy |gī| *n. Informal.* A man; fellow; chap. [Possibly after *Guy* Fawkes (1570–1606), leader of the Gunpowder Plot to blow up the British king and Parliament in 1605.]

H

ha·ci·en·da |hä´sē **ĕn´**də| *n.* In Spanish-speaking countries, a large estate; a plantation or large ranch. [Spanish, landed property, from Latin *facienda*, things to be done.]

half |hăf| *or* |häf| *n., pl.* **halves** |hăvz| *or* |hävz|. Either of two equal parts into which a thing can be divided.

halves |hăvz| *or* |hävz| *n.* Plural of **half.**

ham·mock |hăm´ək| *n.* A hanging bed or couch made of strong fabric supported by cords between two supports. [Spanish *hamaca*, from Taino.]

hand·ker·chief |hăng´kər chĭf| *or* |-chēf´| *n.* A small square of cloth used to wipe the nose, eyes, or brow, sometimes carried for decoration.

han·gar |hăng´ər| *n.* A building used for housing or repairing aircraft.

hap·haz·ard |hăp hăz´ərd| *adj.* Lacking any definite plan or order; left to chance; random: *haphazard selection.*

har·dy |här´dē| *adj.* **har·di·er, har·di·est. 1.** Strong; robust: *a hardy mountain climber.* **2.** Able to withstand unfavorable conditions, such as cold weather: *a hardy rosebush.*

har·mo·ni·ous |här mō´nē əs| *adj.* **1.** Marked by agreement and good will; friendly: *a harmonious meeting.* **2.** Pleasing to the ear; melodious: *harmonious sounds.*

har·mo·nize |här´mə nīz´| *v.* **har·mo·nized, har·mo·niz·ing. 1.** To sing or play in harmony. **2.** To be in or bring into agreement or harmony; be or make harmonious: *The tablecloth should harmonize with the dishes.*

har·mo·ny |här´mə nē| *n., pl.* **har·mo·nies.** A combination of musical sounds considered to be pleasing. [Old

French *(h)armonie*, from Latin *harmonia*, from Greek, agreement, means of joining, from *harmos*, joint.]

haste |hāst| *n.* Swiftness of motion or action; rapidity; a hurry. ***Idiom.* make haste.** To move or act swiftly; to hurry.

has·ten |hā´sən| *v.* To move or act swiftly; hurry: *He hastened home from school.*

Ha·wai·i |hə wä´ē| *or* |-wä´yə|. A state of the United States, consisting of a group of islands in the Pacific Ocean. Capital, Honolulu.

heart·y |här´tē| *adj.* **heart·i·er, heart·i·est. 1.** Giving much nourishment; substantial: *a hearty soup.* **2.** Openly and thoroughly sincere or enthusiastic: *our hearty congratulations.*

heir |âr| *n.* A person who inherits or is legally entitled to inherit the property, rank, title, or office of another.

hem·or·rhage |hĕm´ər ĭj| *n.* Bleeding, especially heavy bleeding: *The surgeon stopped the patient's hemorrhage.*

hep·ta·gon |hĕp´tə gŏn´| *n.* A geometric figure that lies in a plane and is bounded by seven line segments.

he·ro |hîr´ō| *n., pl.* **he·roes.** A man noted for his courage or special achievements.

hick·o·ry |hĭk´ə rē| *n., pl.* **hick·o·ries. 1.** Any of several North American trees that have hard wood and that bear edible nuts with a smooth, hard shell. **2.** The wood of such a tree. [Possibly Algonquian, shortening of *pohickery*, a species of walnut.]

hi·er·o·glyph·ics |hī´ər ə glĭf´ĭks| *or* |hī´rə-| *n.* A system of writing, used in ancient Egypt, in which pictures or symbols are used to represent words or sounds.

hom·o·graph |hŏm´ə grăf´| *or* |-grăf´| *or* |hō´mə-| *n.* A word that has the same spelling as one or more other words but differs in meaning, origin, and sometimes in pronunciation; for example, *bass* (fish) and *bass* (deep tone or voice) are homographs. [From Greek *homos*, same + *graphein*, to write.]

hom·o·phone |hŏm´ə fōn| *or*
|hō´mə-| *n.* A word that has the same sound
as one or more other words but differs in
spelling, meaning, and origin; for example,
for, *fore*, and *four* are homophones. [From
Greek *homos*, same + *phōnē*, sound, voice.]
hor·ror |hôr´ər| *or* |hŏr´-| *n.* **1.** A
feeling of repugnance and fear; terror.
2. Something that causes such a feeling: *the
horrors of war.*
hor·ti·cul·ture |hôr´tĭ kŭl´chər| *n.* The
science or art of raising and caring for plants,
especially garden plants.
hos·tel |hŏs´təl| *n.* An inexpensive
lodging house for travelers and tourists of
high-school or college age.
hos·tile |hŏs´təl| *or* |-tīl´| *adj.* **1.** Feeling
or showing opposition: *hostile to the
suggestion.* **2.** Unfavorable to health or well-
being: *a hostile climate.*
hu·mane |hyōō mān´| *adj.* Kind;
compassionate; merciful: *a doctor's humane
concern.* [Middle English *humaine*, from Old
French from Latin *hūmānus*, human, kind,
humane.]
hu·man·i·ty |hyōō mǎn´ĭ tē| *n., pl.*
hu·man·i·ties. Human beings in general;
humankind: *affecting all humanity.* [From
Latin *hūmānitās*, from *hūmānus*, human,
kind, humane.]
hu·mid·i·ty |hyōō mǐd´ĭ tē| *n.*
Dampness, especially of the air.
hur·dle |hûr´dl| *n.* **1.** A barrier used in
obstacle races, usually consisting of a
horizontal bar supported by two uprights.
2. An obstacle or problem that must be
overcome.
hur·ri·cane |hûr´ĭ kān´| *or* |hŭr´-| *n.*
A severe, swirling tropical storm with heavy
rains and winds exceeding 75 miles per hour,
originating in the tropical parts of the
Atlantic Ocean or the Caribbean Sea and
moving generally northward.
hur·tle |hûr´tl| *v.* **hur·tled, hur·tling.**
To move or cause to move with or as if with
great speed: *The ball hurtled toward the outfield.*

Pronunciation Key					
ă	pat	ŏ	pot	û	fur
ā	pay	ō	go	*th*	**the**
â	care	ô	paw, for	th	**thin**
ä	father	oi	**oil**	hw	**whi**ch
ě	pet	ōō	book	zh	usual
ē	be	ōō	boot	ə	**a**go, item
ĭ	pit	yōō	cute		pencil, at**o**m
ī	ice	ou	**out**		circus
î	near	ŭ	cut	ər	butt**er**

hy·drant |hī´drənt| *n.* A large upright
pipe, usually on a curb, from which water can
be drawn for fighting fires; a fireplug.
hy·poc·ri·sy |hĭ pŏk´rĭ sē| *n.* A show or
expression of feelings, beliefs, or qualities by a
person who actually does not hold or possess
them; insincerity. [From Greek *hupokrisis*,
playing of a part on the stage, from
hypokrinein: *hupo-*, under + *krinein*, to
separate.]
hyp·o·crite |hĭp´ə krĭt´| *n.* A person
who practices hypocrisy.
hyp·o·crit·i·cal |hĭp´ə krĭt´ĭ kəl| *adj.*
1. Characterized by hypocrisy: *hypocritical
praise.* **2.** Being a hypocrite: *a hypocritical
politician.*

I

-ian. A suffix that forms nouns or
adjectives: **Canadian, magician.**
-ible. A suffix that forms adjectives and
means: **1.** Capable or worthy of: **divisible.**
2. Tending toward. [From Latin *-ābilis*,
-ībilis.]
ice·berg |īs´bûrg´| *n.* A large, massive
body of floating ice that has broken away
from a glacier. [Probably partial translation of
Danish and Norwegian *is*, ice + *berg*,
mountain.]

i·den·ti·ty |ī dĕn´tĭ tē| *n., pl.*
i·den·ti·ties. The condition of being a certain person or thing and definitely recognizable as such.

id·i·om |ĭd´ē əm| *n.* An expression having a special meaning not obtainable or not clear from the usual meaning of the words in the expression; for example, *fly off the handle* (lose one's temper) and *on pins and needles* (in a condition of anxiety) are idioms.

i·dle |īd´l| *adj.* **i·dler, i·dlest. 1.** Not working or devoted to working or producing: *idle employees.* **2.** Avoiding work; lazy; shiftless: *idle boys who would do nothing but play.*

i·dol |īd´l| *n.* A person or thing that is adored or greatly admired.

ig·loo |ĭg´lōō| *n.* An Eskimo house, sometimes built of blocks of ice. [Eskimo *iglu*, *igdlu*, house.]

ig·nite |ĭg nīt´| *v.* **ig·nit·ed, ig·nit·ing.** To set fire to or catch fire. [Latin *ignīre*, to set on fire, from *ignis*, fire.]

ig·ni·tion |ĭg nĭsh´ən| *n.* **1.** The act or process of igniting, or starting a fire. **2.** An electrical system that provides the spark that ignites the fuel mixture of an internal-combustion engine. **3.** A switch that activates this system.

i·gua·na |ĭ gwä´nə| *n.* An often large tropical American lizard with a ridge of spines along the back. [Spanish from Arawak, *iwana*.]

il·le·gal |ĭ lē´gəl| *adj.* Prohibited by law or by official rules, as of a game. [Latin *in-*, not + *lēgālis*, from *lex*, law.]

il·leg·i·ble |ĭ lĕj´ə bəl| *adj.* Not capable of being deciphered; not readable: *an illegible scrawl.* [Latin *in-*, not + *legible*, from Late Latin *legibilis*, from Latin *legere*, to read.]

il·lic·it |ĭ lĭs´ĭt| *adj.* Not permitted by law or custom; illegal; unlawful: *an illicit activity.*

il·lit·er·ate |ĭ lĭt´ər ĭt| *adj.* **1.** Unable to read and write. **2.** Showing a lack of education. [Latin *illiterātus*: *in-*, not + *literātus*, literate.]

il·log·i·cal |ĭ lŏj´ĭ kəl| *adj.* Having or showing a lack of logic, or clear reasoning: *His argument was illogical.*

il·lus·tra·tion |ĭl´ə strā´shən| *n.* Something, such as a picture, diagram, or chart, serving to clarify, explain, or decorate.

i·mag·i·nar·y |ĭ măj´ə nĕr´ē| *adj.* Having existence only in the imagination; unreal; fictitious: *an imaginary illness.*

im·ma·te·ri·al |ĭm´ə tîr´ē əl| *adj.* Of no importance or relevance; unimportant: *The question is immaterial and no longer relevant.* [Latin *in-*, not + *material*, from Latin *materia*, matter.]

im·ma·ture |ĭm´ə tŏŏr´| *or* |-tyŏŏr´| *or* |-chŏŏr´| *adj.* Not fully grown or developed; in an early or unripe stage: *immature corn.* [Latin *immātūrus*: *in-*, not + *mātūrus*, mature.]

im·meas·ur·a·ble |ĭ mĕzh´ər ə bəl| *adj.* Not capable of being measured: *immeasurable distance.* [Latin *in-*, not + *measurable*, from Latin *mētrī*, to measure.]

im·me·mo·ri·al |ĭm´ə môr´ē əl| *or* |-mōr´-| *adj.* Reaching beyond the limits of memory, tradition, or recorded history: *since time immemorial.* [Medieval Latin *immemoriālis*: Latin *in-*, not + *memoriālis*, memorial, from *memoria*, memory.]

im·mi·grant |ĭm´ĭ grənt| *n.* A person who leaves his native country or region to settle in another.

im·mo·bi·lize |ĭ **mō´**bə līz| *v.*
im·mo·bi·lized, im·mo·bi·liz·ing. To make immobile; render incapable of moving: *She was immobilized while her broken leg healed.* [From Latin *immōbilis*: *in-*, not + *mobilis*, mobile.]

im·mov·a·ble |ĭ **mōō´**və bəl| *adj.* **1.** Not capable of moving or of being moved. **2.** Unyielding; steadfast: *an immovable purpose.*

im·pede |ĭm **pēd´**| *v.* **im·ped·ed, im·ped·ing.** To obstruct or slow down; block. [Latin *impedīre*, to entangle, fetter.]

im·ped·i·ment |ĭm **pĕd´**ə mənt| *n.* A hindrance; obstruction: *His youth was no impediment to his success.* [Latin *impedīmentum*, from *impedīre*, to entangle, fetter.]

im·pend |ĭm **pĕnd´**| *v.* To be about to take place; loom: *the impending storm.*
—im·pend´ing *adj.*: *impending peril.* [Latin *impendēre*: *in-*, against + *pendēre*, to hang.]

im·pe·tus |**ĭm´**pə təs| *n., pl.* **im·pe·tus·es** A driving force: *The promise of quick wealth was the impetus behind the gold rush.* [Latin, attack, from *impetere*, to assail, attack: *in-*, against + *petere*, to go toward, seek.]

im·pli·cate |**ĭm´**plĭ kāt| *v.* **im·pli·cat·ed, im·pli·cat·ing.** To involve or connect with a crime or other disapproved activity: *His testimony implicated two people.* [Latin *implicāre*: *in-*, in + *plicāre*, to fold.]

im·pli·ca·tion |**ĭm´**plĭ **kā´**shən| *n.* **1.** Something implied: *the cultural implications of satellite communications.* **2.** The act of implying or suggesting, without direct explanation: *The writer conveyed his idea by implication.* **3.** The act of implicating or condition of being implicated: *denying his implication in the affair.*

im·port |ĭm **pôrt´**| *or* |-**pōrt´**| *or* |**ĭm´**pôrt´| *or* |-pōrt´| *v.* To bring or carry in from an outside source, especially to bring in (goods) from another country for trade, sale, or use. —*n.* Something imported, as from another country.

Pronunciation Key

ă	pat	ŏ	pot	û	fur
ā	pay	ō	go	*th*	**the**
â	care	ô	paw, for	th	**thin**
ä	father	oi	**oil**	hw	**which**
ĕ	pet	ŏŏ	book	zh	usual
ē	be	ōō	boot	ə	**ago, item**
ĭ	pit	yōō	cute		pencil, atom
ī	ice	ou	**out**		circus
î	near	ŭ	cut	ər	butter

---

im·por·tance |ĭm **pôr´**tns| *n.* The condition or quality of being important; significance.

im·pose |ĭm **pōz´**| *v.* **im·posed, im·pos·ing.** To bring about by exercising authority; force to prevail: *impose a settlement.* *phrasal verb.* **impose on** (or **upon**). To take advantage of: *They did not wish to impose on us.* [From Latin *imponere*, to put on.]

im·po·si·tion |**ĭm´**pə **zĭsh´**ən| *n.* Something imposed, as a tax or burden: *The colonists resented the imposition of a tax on tea.*

im·pos·si·ble |ĭm **pŏs´**ə bəl| *adj.* Not capable of happening or existing.

im·pro·vise |**ĭm´**prə vīz´| *v.* **im·pro·vised, im·pro·vis·ing.** To invent or compose without preparation: *improvise a melody.*

in-. Also **il-** (before *l*) or **im-** (before *b*, *m*, and *p*) or **ir-** (before *r*). A prefix meaning "not or without": **independent.** [Middle English, from Old French, from Latin.]

in·ac·tive |ĭn **ăk´**tĭv| *adj.* Not active or not tending to be active: *an inactive volcano.*

in·ci·den·tal·ly |ĭn´sĭ **dĕn´**tl ē| *adv.* Apart from the main subject; by the way: *Incidentally, what time is it?*

in·ci·sion |ĭn **sĭzh´**n| *n.* A thin, clean cut, especially in surgery. [From Latin *incidere*: *in-*, into, in + *caedere*, to cut.]

in·ci·sive |ĭn sī′sĭv| *adj.* Sharp and clear; penetrating: *incisive comments; an incisive mind.* [From Latin *incidere*: *in-*, into, in + *caedere*, to cut.]

in·ci·sor |ĭn sī′zər| *n.* A tooth adapted for cutting, as one of the wedge-shaped teeth found in the front of the jaws of mammals. [From Latin *incidere*: *in-*, into, in + *caedere*, to cut.]

in·cred·i·ble |ĭn krĕd′ə bəl| *adj.*
1. Unbelievable: *an incredible excuse.*
2. Astonishing; amazing: *He lived to the incredible age of 125.* [Latin *incredibilis*: *in-*, not + *credibilis*, from *crēdere*, to believe.]

in·de·pend·ence |ĭn′dĭ pĕn′dəns| *n.* The condition or quality of being independent.

in·de·pend·ent |ĭn′dĭ pĕn′dənt| *adj.* Free from the influence, control, or government of others; self-reliant: *an independent mind; an independent country.*

in·de·struc·ti·ble |ĭn′dĭ strŭk′tə bəl| *adj.* Not capable of being destroyed.

in·dict·ment |ĭn dīt′mənt| *n.* A written statement, drawn up by the prosecuting attorney, listing the charges against an accused person. [From Middle English *enditen*, to accuse, from Norman French, from Latin *indīcere*, to proclaim: *in-*, toward + *dīcere*, to pronounce.]

in·flam·ma·ble |ĭn flăm′ə bəl| *adj.* Tending to catch fire easily and burn rapidly; flammable. —See Usage note at **flammable.**

in·for·ma·tion |ĭn′fər mā′shən| *n.*
1. Facts or data about a certain event or subject. **2.** The act or process of informing or the condition of being informed: *for your information.*

in·frac·tion |ĭn frăk′shən| *n.* A breach or violation of a law, rule, or regulation. [From Latin *infringere*, to destroy: *in-*, + *frangere*, to break.]

in·gest |ĭn jĕst′| *v.* To take in (food) by or as if by swallowing. [Latin *ingerere*, to carry in: *in-*, in + *gerere*, to carry.]

in·hale |ĭn hāl′| *v.* **in·haled, in·hal·ing.** To draw in (air or smoke) by breathing; breathe in: *inhale deeply.* —**in′ha·la′tion** |ĭn′hə lā′shən| *n.*: *inhalation of fresh air.*

in·her·it |ĭn hĕr′ĭt| *v.* To receive (property) from someone after he dies, usually as provided for in a will. [From Late Latin *inhereditare*, from *heres*, heir.]

in·ject |ĭn jĕkt′| *v.* To force or drive (a liquid or gas) into something: *inject fuel into a cylinder of an engine.* [From Latin *injicere*, to throw or put in: *in-*, in + *jacere*, to throw.]

in·no·cent |ĭn′ə sənt| *adj.* **1.** Not guilty of a specific crime or fault. **2.** Not experienced or worldly; naive: *an innocent child.*

in·scrip·tion |ĭn skrĭp′shən| *n.* **1.** The act or an example of writing or engraving: *the inscription of the plaque took two hours.* **2.** Something inscribed: *the inscription was hard to read.* [From Latin *inscriptiō*, a writing in or upon, from *inscrībere*: *in-*, in+ *scrībere*, to write.]

in·sig·ni·a |ĭn sĭg′nē ə| *n., pl.* **in·sig·ni·a** or **in·sig·ni·as.** A badge of office, rank, nationality, membership, etc.; an emblem. [Latin, plural of *insigne*, sign, mark, from *insignīs*, marked: *in-*, in + *signum*, distinctive mark or figure, seal, signal.]

in·sist |ĭn sĭst′| *v.* To be firm in one's demand; take a strong stand: *I insist on watching the ball game.* [Latin *insistere*, to stand on, persist: *in-*, on + *sistere*, to cause to stand.]

in·spec·tor |ĭn **spĕk´**tər| *n.* A person who inspects or examines. [From Latin *inspicere*, to look into: *in-*, in + *specere*, to look at.]

in·spi·ra·tion |ĭn´spə **rā´**shən| *n.*
1. Someone or something that inspires: *Bach was an inspiration to many other composers.*
2. Something that is inspired; a sudden, original idea.

in·spire |ĭn **spīr´**| *v.* **in·spired, in·spir·ing.** To stimulate to creativity or action: *Her words inspired me to get involved.* [Old French *inspirer*, from Latin *inspīrāre*, to breathe into.]

in·stance |ĭn´stəns| *n.* A case or example: *many instances of success.*

in·stant |ĭn´stənt| *n.* A period of time almost too brief to detect; a moment. —*adj.* Immediate: *an instant success.*

in·sti·tute |ĭn´stĭ tōōt´| *or* |-tyōōt´| *n.* An educational institution: *a research institute.* [From Latin *instituere*, to establish: *in-*, in + *statuere*, to set up, from *status,* to stand.]

in·stru·ment |ĭn´strə mənt| *n.* A device used by a musician in making music.

in·stru·men·tal |ĭn´strə **mĕn´**tl| *adj.* Performed on or written for musical instruments: *I prefer instrumental music to vocal music.*

in·tel·li·gence |ĭn **tĕl´**ə jəns| *n.* The capacity to learn, think, understand, and know; mental ability.

in·tel·li·gent |ĭn **tĕl´**ə jənt| *adj.*
1. Having intelligence. **2.** Showing intelligence; wise or thoughtful: *an intelligent decision.*

inter-. A prefix meaning: **1.** Between; among: **international. 2.** Mutually; together: **interact.**

in·ter·jec·tion |ĭn´tər **jĕk´**shən| *n.* Any exclamation: *His sudden interjection interrupted the discussion.* [Latin *interjicere*, to throw between: *inter-*, between + *jacere,* to throw.]

in·ter·mis·sion |ĭn´tər **mĭsh´**ən| *n.* An interruption or recess, as between the acts of a play.

Pronunciation Key

ă	pat	ŏ	pot	û	fur
ā	pay	ō	go	*th*	*th*e
â	care	ô	paw, for	th	thin
ä	father	oi	oil	hw	which
ĕ	pet	ŏŏ	book	zh	usual
ē	be	ōō	boot	ə	ago, item
ĭ	pit	yōō	cute		pencil, atom
ī	ice	ou	out		circus
î	near	ŭ	cut	ər	butter

---

in·ter·pret |ĭn **tûr´**prĭt| *v.* To explain or clarify the meaning or significance of: *interpret data.*

in·ter·rupt |ĭn tə **rŭpt´**| *v.* **1.** To break in upon: *interrupt a meeting.* **2.** To stop the conversation, speech, or action of (someone) by breaking in. **3.** To break the continuity of: *His father's illness interrupted his schooling.* — **in´ter·rup´tion** *n.: Please forgive the interruption.* [From Latin *interrumpere*, to break in: *inter-*, between + *rumpere*, to break.]

in·trigue |ĭn **trēg´**| *n.* **1.** Plotting or scheming carried on in secret. **2.** A secret plot or scheme: *the spy's intrigue.*

in·tro·spec·tion |ĭn´trə **spĕk´**shən| *n.* The act or practice of looking inward to examine one's own thoughts and feelings. [From Latin *introspicere*, to look into: *intrō-*, into + *specere*, to look at.]

in·ves·ti·gate |ĭn **vĕs´**tĭ gāt´| *v.* **in·ves·ti·gat·ed, in·ves·ti·gat·ing.** To look into or examine carefully in a search for facts, knowledge, or information: *investigate a burglary.* [Latin *investigere*, to search into: *in-*, in + *vestigare*, to trace, track.]

in·ves·ti·ga·tion |ĭn vĕs´tĭ **gā´**shən| *n.* An examination, study, search, or inquiry conducted for the purpose of discovering facts or getting information.

-ion. A suffix that forms nouns and means: **1.** An act or process or the outcome of an act or process: **fission. 2.** A state of being: **elation.**

ir·ra·tion·al |ĭ răsh´ə nəl| *adj.* Not based on or guided by reason; unreasonable; illogical: *an irrational fear.* [Latin *in-*, not + *rational*, from Latin *ratiō*, reason, ratio.]

ir·reg·u·lar |ĭ rĕg´yə lər| *adj.* Not standard or uniform, as in shape, size, or length: *an irregular coastline.* [Latin *in-*, not + *regular*, from Latin *rēgulāris*, containing rules.]

ir·rep·a·ra·ble |ĭ rĕp´ər ə bəl| *adj.* Not capable of being repaired, undone, or set right: *irreparable damage.* [Latin *in-*, not + *reparable*, from Latin *reparāre*: *re-*, back + *parāre*, to put in order, prepare.]

ir·re·place·a·ble |ĭr´ĭ plā´sə bəl| *adj.* Not capable of being replaced: *irreplaceable supplies of coal and oil.* [Latin *in-*, not + *placeable*, from Middle English, space, locality.]

ir·re·sist·i·ble |ĭr´ĭ zĭs´tə bəl| *adj.* Too strong, powerful, or compelling to be resisted: *an irresistible impulse.* [Latin *in-*, not + *resistible*, from Latin *resistere*, to stand back, resist: *re-*, back, against + *sistere*, to set, place.]

ir·re·spon·si·ble |ĭr´ĭ spŏn´sə bəl| *adj.* Showing no sense of responsibility or concern for consequences; not dependable, reliable, or trustworthy: *He is too irresponsible to be trusted with the job.* [Latin *in-*, not + *responsible*, from Latin *respondēre*, to respond.]

ir·ri·gate |ĭr´ĭ gāt´| *v.* **ir·ri·gat·ed, ir·ri·gat·ing.** To supply (farmland, crops, etc.) with water by means of streams, ditches, pipes, canals, etc.: *irrigate a field.* [Latin *irrigāre*, to lead water: *in-*, in + *rigāre*, to wet, water.]

ir·ri·tate |ĭr´ĭ tāt´| *v.* **ir·ri·tat·ed, ir·ri·tat·ing. 1.** To make angry or impatient; annoy, bother, or exasperate: *His endless questions irritated me.* **2.** To cause to become sore or inflamed: *The heavy smoke irritated her eyes.* [Latin *irritāre*, to excite, provoke.]

-ise. Variant of the suffix **-ize.**

i·so·met·ric |ī´sə mĕt´rĭk| *adj.* Of or involving muscle contractions in which the ends of the muscle are held in place so that there is an increase in tension rather than a shortening of the muscle: *isometric exercises.* [From Greek *isometros*, of equal measure: *iso-*, equal + *metron*, measure.]

is·sue |ĭsh´ōō| *n.* A single edition of a newspaper or magazine: *the June issue.*

i·tin·er·ar·y |ī tĭn´ə rĕr´ē| *n., pl.* **i·tin·er·ar·ies.** A schedule of places to be visited in the course of a journey: *Their itinerary includes stops in Denver and Salt Lake City.*

-ize. A suffix that forms verbs and means: **1.** To become, cause to become, or form into: **materialize. 2.** To treat or affect with: **pasteurize.** [Late Latin, *-izāre*.]

J

jai a·lai |hī´lī´| *or* |hī´ə lī´| *or* |hī´ə lī´| *n.* A game similar to handball, played on a walled court, in which the participants use a long basket strapped to the wrist to catch and throw the ball.

jew·el·ry |jōō´əl rē| *n.* Ornaments to be worn, made of precious metals set with gems or from inexpensive or imitation materials.

jour·nal |jûr´nəl| *n.* A periodical containing news and articles in a particular field: *medical journal.*

jour·nal·ism |jûr´nə lĭz´əm| *n.* The gathering and presentation of news, especially by newspapers and magazines.

judg·ment, also **judge·ment** |jŭj´mənt| *n.* **1.** The ability to choose wisely; good sense: *trust his judgment.* **2.** The act or an instance of judging; the forming of a decision or opinion after due consideration: *make a judgment.*

ju·ris·dic·tion |jŏŏr´ĭs dĭk´shən| *n.* The authority to interpret and apply the law: *Federal courts have jurisdiction when a foreigner sues an American.* [Latin *jūrisdictiō: juris*, form of *jūs*, law + *dictiō*, declaration: from *dictus*, past participle of *dīcere*, to say.]

ju·ror |jŏŏr´ər| *n.* A member of a jury: *The juror listened carefully.*

K

ka·lei·do·scope |kə lī´də skōp´| *n.* A tube-shaped toy in which bits of colored glass contained at one end reflect light from a hole at the other end. [From Greek *kalos*, beautiful + *eidos*, form + *skopein*, to see.]

kay·ak |kī´ăk´| *n.* A watertight Eskimo canoe made of skins stretched over a light wooden frame and having a deck covering that closes around the waist of the paddler. [Eskimo *qajaq.*]

ker·nel |kûr´nəl| *n.* **1.** A grain or seed, especially of corn, wheat, or a similar cereal plant. **2.** The often edible part inside the shell of a nut or the pit of a peach, plum, etc.

kil·o·gram |kĭl´ə grăm´| *n.* A force equal to the weight of one kilogram mass, equal to 2.2046 pounds. [*kilo*, from Greek *khilioi*, a thousand + *gram*, from Latin *gramma*, a small unit, from Greek, letter.]

king·dom |kĭng´dəm| *n.* A country that is ruled or headed by a king or queen.

knowl·edge·a·ble |nŏl´ĭ jə bəl| *adj.* Well-informed: *knowledgeable about music.*

L

lab·y·rinth |lăb´ə rĭnth´| *n.* A network of winding, connected passages through which it is difficult to find one's way without help; a maze. [Greek *laburinthos*, probably akin to Greek *labrus*, double ax.]

land·scape |lănd´skāp´| *n.* A stretch of land or countryside forming a single scene or having its own special appearance or characteristics. [Dutch *landschap*, landscape, region.]

la·va |lä´və| *or* |lăv´ə| *n.* Molten rock that flows from a volcano or from a crack in the earth: *The lava flowed to the sea.*

lay·out |lā´out´| *n.* A planned arrangement of parts or items, especially on a flat surface: *a page layout of printing and illustrations.*

le·gal |lē´gəl| *adj.* **1.** Authorized or set down by law: *the legal heir.* **2.** Permitted by law: *legal activities.* [Old French, from Latin *lēgālis*, from *lēx*, law.]

le·gal·ize |lē´gə līz´| *v.* **le·gal·ized, le·gal·iz·ing.** To make legal.

leg·en·dar·y |lĕj´ən dĕr´ē| *adj.* Talked about frequently; famous: *His wit is legendary.*

leg·is·la·ture |lĕj´ĭs lā´chər| *n.* A body of persons empowered to make and change the laws of a nation or state.

length |lĕngkth| *or* |lĕngth| *n.* The measured distance from one end of a thing to the other along its greatest dimension. *Idiom.* **at length. 1.** After some time; eventually. **2.** Without being restricted in time: *spoke at length.*

length·en |lĕngk´thən| *or* |lĕng´-| *v.* To make or become longer.

le·o·tard |lē´ə tärd´| *n.* Often **leotards.** A tight-fitting garment, originally worn by dancers and acrobats. [Popularized by Jules Léotard, 19th-Century French aerialist.]

Pronunciation Key

ă	pat	ŏ	pot	û	fur
ā	pay	ō	go	*th*	**the**
â	care	ô	paw, for	th	**thin**
ä	father	oi	**oil**	hw	**which**
ĕ	pet	ŏŏ	book	zh	usual
ē	be	ōō	boot	ə	**ago**, item
ĭ	pit	yōō	cute		pencil, atom
ī	ice	ou	**out**		circus
î	near	ŭ	cut	ər	butter

li·bel |lī′bəl| *n.* **1.** A written or printed statement that unjustly damages a person's reputation or exposes him to ridicule. **2.** The act or crime of making such a statement: *The politician sued the writer for libel.*
Usage: **libel, slander.** *Libel* is a written or printed statement that unjustly damages a person's reputation. *Slander* is also a statement that damages a person's reputation through false accusation, but it is spoken, not written.

li·brar·i·an |lī brâr′ē ən| *n.* A person who works in or is in charge of a library.

li·chen |lī′kən| *n.* A plant consisting of a fungus and an alga growing in close combination and forming a crustlike, scaly, or branching growth on rocks and tree trunks.

lic·o·rice |lĭk′ə rĭs| *or* |-ər ĭsh| *n.* A chewy, often black candy flavored with an extract from the root of the licorice plant.

light·ning |līt′nĭng| *n.* **1.** A large, high-voltage electrical discharge that occurs in the atmosphere from natural causes. **2.** The flash of light that accompanies such a discharge.

light-year |līt′yîr′| *n.* Also **light year.** A measure of distance equal to the distance light travels through empty space in a year; about 5.878 trillion (5.878 x 10^{12}) miles: *Stars are more than four light-years away from our sun.*

lim·er·ick |lĭm′ər ĭk| *n.* A humorous five-line poem in which the first, second, and last lines rhyme with each other and the third line rhymes with the fourth. [From the line (of a verse) "Will you come up to Limerick?" after *Limerick*, Ireland.]

lit·er·ar·y |lĭt′ə rĕr′ē| *adj.* Of literature or authors: *a literary critic.*

lit·er·a·ture |lĭt′ər ə chər| *n.* **1.** A body of writing in prose or verse. **2.** Imaginative or creative writing, especially having recognized artistic value.

live·li·hood |līv′lē hŏod′| *n.* A person's means of support; a living: *He obtained his livelihood from carpentry.*

log·i·cal |lŏj′ĭ kəl| *adj.* **1.** Of, using, or agreeing with the principles of logic. **2.** Reasonable: *a logical choice.* **3.** Able to reason clearly. [From Late Latin *logica*, from Greek *logikē (tekhnē)*, "(art) of reasoning," from *logos*, speech, reason.]

lor·ry |lôr′ē| *or* |lŏr′ē| *n., pl.* **lor·ries.** *British.* A truck.

lu·bri·cate |lōo′brĭ kāt′| *v.* **lu·bri·cat·ed, lu·bri·cat·ing.** To apply or use a slippery substance, such as oil or grease: *lubricate the engine.*

lyr·ics |lĭr′ĭks| *pl. n.* The words of a song: *I am trying to learn the lyrics of the song.*

M

ma·chin·er·y |mə shē′nə rē| *n., pl.* **ma·chin·er·ies.** **1.** Machines or machine parts as a group. **2.** The working parts of a particular machine: *the machinery of a clock.*

mack·in·tosh |măk′ĭn tŏsh′| *n. British.* A raincoat. [Invented by Charles *Mackintosh* (1766–1843), Scottish chemist.]

mag·ma |măg′mə| *n.* The hot molten material under the earth's crust that often cools and hardens to form igneous rock.

mag·net |**măg´**nĭt| *n.* Something, such as a piece of metal or an ore, that attracts iron and other substances. [Greek *magnēs*, short for *Magnēs lithos*, "the Magnesian stone," from *Magnēs*, pertaining to *Magnēsia*.]

mag·nif·i·cent |măg **nĭf´**ĭ sənt| *adj.* Splendid in appearance; grand; remarkable. —**mag·nif´i·cence** *n.: the magnificence of the palace.*

mag·no·lia |măg **nōl´**yə| *or* |-**nō´**lē ə| *n.* **1.** A tree or shrub with large, showy, usually white or pink flowers. **2.** The flower of such a tree or shrub. [After Pierre *Magnol* (1638–1715), French botanist.]

mall |môl| *or* |măl| *n.* **1.** A street lined with shops and closed to vehicles. **2.** A shopping center. [From The Mall, an avenue in London; formerly an alley used in *pall-mall*, a game in which a ball was hit with a mallet through a ring at the end of an alley.]

mam·moth |**măm´**əth| —*adj.* Huge; gigantic: *a feeble fire in a mammoth fireplace.* [Obsolete Russian *mammot'*, used to describe an extinct elephant.]

man·tle |**măn´**tl| *n.* The layer of the earth between the crust and the core.

man·u·script |**măn´**yə skrĭpt´| *n.* A handwritten or typewritten book, paper, or article, as distinguished from a printed copy: *submit a manuscript to a publisher.* [Medieval Latin *manūscrīptus*, handwritten: Latin *manū*, by hand, from *manus*, hand + *scrīptus*, written, from *scrībere*, to write.]

Pronunciation Key

ă	pat	ŏ	pot	û	fur
ā	pay	ō	go	*th*	the
â	care	ô	paw, for	th	thin
ä	father	oi	oil	hw	which
ě	pet	ŏŏ	book	zh	usual
ē	be	ōō	boot	ə	ago, item
ĭ	pit	yōō	cute		pencil, atom
ī	ice	ou	out		circus
î	near	ŭ	cut	ər	butter

mas·sage |mə **säzh´**| *or* |-**säj´**| *n.* A body rub given to improve circulation and relax muscles. [French, probably from Arabic *mass*, to touch, handle.]

mast·head |**măst´**hěd´| *or* |**mäst´**-| *n.* The listing in a newspaper, magazine, or other publication of its owners and chief editors and information about its operation.

mav·er·ick |**măv´**ər ĭk| *or* |**măv´**rĭk| *n.* **1.** An unbranded calf or colt, traditionally belonging to the first person to brand it. **2.** A person who refuses to go along with the policies or views of his or her group. [After Samuel A. *Maverick* (1803–1870), Texas cattleman who did not brand his calves.]

max·i·mize |**măk´**sə mīz´| *v.* **max·i·mized, max·i·miz·ing.** To make as great or large as possible; increase to a maximum.

Ma·yan |**mä´**yən| *or* |**mī´**ən| *adj.* **1.** Of the Mayas, people of Central America and Southern Mexico whose civilization reached its height around A.D. 1000. **2.** Of the language and culture of the Mayas.

may·on·naise |mā´ə **nāz´**| *or* |mā´ə nāz´| *n.* A dressing made of beaten raw egg yolk, oil, lemon juice or vinegar, and seasonings. [French, possibly named in commemoration of the capture in 1756 of the city of *Mahon*, capital of the Spanish island of Minorca, by the Duke of Richelieu.]

mean |mēn| *n.* **arithmetic mean.** An average of a set of quantities or numbers obtained by adding all the members of the set and dividing the result by the number of members in the set.

me·an·der |mē ăn´dər| *v.* **1.** To follow a winding and turning course: *The river meanders through the town.* **2.** To wander aimlessly and idly. [From Greek *maiandros*, from *Maiandros*, a river in Phrygia noted for its windings.]

me·chan·ic |mə kăn´ĭk| *n.* A worker skilled in making, using, or repairing machines or tools.

me·dal·lion |mə dăl´yən| *n.* A round or oval ornament or design resembling a large medal.

me·di·an |mē´dē ən| *n.* In a set of numbers, a number that is greater than one half of the numbers and less than the other half. —*adj.* Located in the middle.

med·i·ca·tion |mĕd´ĭ kā´shən| *n.* A substance that helps to cure a disease or heal an injury; medicine: *an effective medication.*

me·di·um |mē´dē əm| *n., pl.* **me·di·a** or **me·di·ums.** A particular material used by a graphic artist: *the medium of oil paint.*

mel·o·dy |mĕl´ə dē| *n., pl.* **mel·o·dies.** The main voice or part in a musical composition; tune; air.

mem·brane |mĕm´brān´| *n.* A thin, flexible layer of tissue that covers surfaces or acts as the boundary between adjoining regions, structures, or organs in the body of an animal or plant.

mem·oir |mĕm´wär´| *or* |-wôr´| *n.* **1.** An account of experiences the author has lived through. **2. memoirs.** An autobiography, especially one written by a famous person at the end of his or her career: *I read her memoirs.* [Latin *memoria*, from *memor*, mindful.]

mem·o·ra·bil·i·a |mĕm´ər ə bĭl´ē ə| *or* |-bĭl´yə| *pl. n.* Facts or things from the past that are worth remembering or keeping: *a drawer full of souvenirs and other memorabilia.* [Latin *memorabilis*, from *memor*, mindful.]

mem·o·ra·ble |mĕm´ər ə bəl| *adj.* Remarkable; unforgettable: *a memorable event.*

mem·o·ran·dum |mĕm´ə răn´dəm| *n., pl.* **mem·o·ran·dums** or **mem·o·ran·da** |mĕm´ə răn´də|. A short note written as a reminder: *He sent a memorandum to his staff.* [Latin, from *memor*, mindful.]

me·mo·ri·al |mə môr´ē əl| *or* |-mōr´-| *n.* **1.** A monument, shrine, or institution established to preserve the memory of a person or an event. **2.** Anything kept or done in honor of a memory: *She lit a candle every Sunday as a memorial to her father.* [Latin *memorialis*, belonging to memory, from *memoria*, memory.]

mem·o·rize |mĕm´ə rīz´| *v.* **mem·o·rized, mem·o·riz·ing.** To commit to memory; learn by heart.

mem·o·ry |mĕm´ə rē| *n., pl.* **mem·o·ries. 1.** The capability of storing past experiences in the mind and recalling them at will; the ability to remember. **2.** Something remembered; a thought of someone or something out of the past: *She had happy memories of childhood.* [Latin *memoria*, from *memor*, mindful.]

-ment. A suffix that forms nouns and means: **1.** An action or process: **attachment. 2.** A condition: **amazement. 3.** The product, means, or result of an action: **entanglement.**

mer·chan·dise |mûr´chən dīz´| *or* |-dīs´| *n.* Things that may be bought or sold; commercial goods. —*v.* To promote the sale of.

me·ringue |mə răng´| *n.* A mixture of stiffly beaten egg whites and sugar, often used as a topping for cakes and pies.

mes·mer·ize |mĕz´mə rīz´| *or* |mĕs´-| *v.* **mes·mer·ized, mes·mer·iz·ing.** To hypnotize. [After Anton *Mesmer* (1734–1815), Austrian physician.]

me·te·or |mē´tē ər| *or* |-ôr´| *n.* The bright trail or streak seen in the sky when a fragment of solid material from space falls into the Earth's atmosphere and burns: *A meteor is sometimes called a falling star.*

me·te·or·ol·o·gy |mē´tē ə **rŏl´**ə jē| *n.* The scientific study of the atmosphere and its effects, especially those that influence weather and weather conditions.

me·ter |mē´tər| *n.* The basic unit of length in the metric system, equal to 39.37 inches. [Middle English from Old French *metrum*, from Greek *metron*, measure.]

-meter. A word part meaning "measuring device": **speedometer.**

met·ric |mĕt´rĭk| *adj.* Of, involving, or using the metric system. [French *métrique*, from *mètre*, from Latin *metrum*, from Greek *metron*, measure.]

met·ro·nome |mĕt´rə nōm´| *n.* A device that makes a series of clicks separated by precise, adjustable intervals of time. It is used to provide a steady beat for practicing music. [Greek *metron*, measure + *nomos*, rule, law.]

mi·cro·phone |mī´krə fōn´| *n.* A device that converts sound waves into electric signals, as in recording and radio broadcasting. [From Latin *micro*, from Greek *mikros*, small + Greek *phōnē*, sound, voice.]

mi·cro·scope |mī´krə skōp´| *n.* An instrument in which the light reflected from or projected through a tiny object is passed through a combination of lenses so as to produce a magnified image of the object that is large enough to be seen and studied. [New Latin *microscopium*: *micro-*, from Latin *mīcro-*, from Greek *mikros*, small + *-scope*, from Greek *skopein*, to see.]

mi·cro·scop·ic |mī´krə **skŏp´**ĭk| *adj.* **1.** Too small to be seen by the eye alone but large enough to be seen through a microscope. **2.** Very small; minute.

mile·age |mī´lĭj| *n.* **1.** Length or distance as measured or expressed in miles: *the mileage between two cities.* **2.** The

Pronunciation Key

ă	pat	ŏ	pot	û	fur
ā	pay	ō	go	*th*	the
â	care	ô	paw, for	th	thin
ä	father	oi	oil	hw	which
ĕ	pet	ŏŏ	book	zh	usual
ē	be	ōō	boot	ə	ago, item
ĭ	pit	yōō	cute		pencil, atom
ī	ice	ou	out		circus
î	near	ŭ	cut	ər	butter

distance a motor vehicle travels per unit of fuel: *What kind of mileage does your car get?*

Milky Way. The galaxy in which the solar system is located, visible as a bright band across the night sky.

min·er·al |mĭn´ər əl| *n.* **1.** Any natural substance that has a definite chemical composition and characteristic physical structure. **2.** Any substance, such as granite or other rock, composed of a mixture of minerals.

min·i·a·ture |mĭn´ē ə chər| *or* |mĭn´ə-| *adj.* On a greatly reduced scale from the usual: *a miniature computer.*

min·i·mize |mĭn´ə mīz´| *v.* **min·i·mized, min·i·miz·ing.** To reduce to the smallest possible amount, extent, size, or degree: *Heavy curtains minimized the noise from the street.*

min·i·se·ries |mĭn´ē sîr´ēz| *n.* A sequence of episodes that make up a televised dramatic production. [*mini-*, probably from both *miniature* and *minimum* + *series*, Latin *seriēs*, from *serere*, to join.]

mi·rage |mĭ **räzh´**| *n.* An optical illusion in which nonexistent bodies of water and upside-down reflections of distant objects are seen. It is caused by distortions that occur as light passes between layers of air that are at different temperatures: *The desert traveler saw a mirage that looked like a lake.*

mis·cel·la·ne·ous |mĭs´ə lā´nē əs| *adj.* Made up of a variety of different elements or ingredients: *a miscellaneous assortment of chocolates.*

mis·er·a·ble |mĭz´ər ə bəl| *or* |mĭz´rə-| *adj.* Very unhappy; wretched: *The living conditions are miserable.*

mis·spell |mĭs spĕl´| *v.* To spell incorrectly.

mo·bile |mō´bəl| *or* |-bēl´| *or* |-bīl´| *adj.* Capable of moving or being moved from place to place: *a mobile hospital.* —*n.* |mō´bēl´|. A sculpture (usually hanging) consisting of parts that move, especially in a breeze. —**mo·bil´i·ty** |mō bĭl´ĭ tē| *n.*: *She regained mobility in her leg.*

moc·ca·sin |mŏk´ə sĭn| *n.* **1.** A soft, heelless leather slipper, shoe, or boot, originally worn by North American Indians. **2.** A shoe resembling an Indian moccasin. [Proto-Algonquian *maxkeseni*.]

mode |mōd| *n.* The value that occurs most frequently in a set of data. For example, if the weights of six persons are, in pounds, 125, 140, 172, 164, 140, and 110, 140 is the mode for that set of data.

mo·del |mŏd´l| *v.* **mod·eled** or **mod·elled, mod·el·ing** or **mod·el·ling. 1.** To make or construct something out of clay, wax, or other material: *He was modeling animals in clay.* **2.** To pattern after or in imitation of something: *Our local library is modeled after the Library of Congress.*

mod·ern·ize |mŏd´ər nīz´| *v.* **mod·ern·ized, mod·ern·iz·ing.** To make modern; alter or bring up-to-date so as to meet current needs: *We modernized the kitchen with new cabinets and appliances.*

mol·e·cule |mŏl´ə kyōōl´| *n.* The smallest and most basic particle into which a substance can be divided and still be the same substance.

mon·soon |mŏn sōōn´| *n.* A system of winds that influences the climate of a large area and that changes direction with the seasons, especially the wind system that produces the wet and dry seasons in southern Asia. [Obsolete Dutch *monssoen*, from Portuguese *monção*, from Arabic *mausim*, monsoon season.]

Mos·cow |mŏs´kou| *or* |-kō|. The capital and largest city of Russia.

mo·tel |mō tĕl´| *n.* A hotel for motorists, usually opening directly onto a parking area. [mo(tor) + (ho)tel.]

mo·tor·cy·cle |mō´tər sī´kəl| *n.* A vehicle with two wheels, similar to a bicycle but larger and heavier, propelled by an internal-combustion engine. [From Latin *mōtor*, to move + Latin *cyclus*, from Greek *kuklos*, circle.]

mu·ral |myŏŏr´əl| *n.* A large picture or decoration applied directly to a wall or ceiling.

mus·cle |mŭs´əl| *n.* **1.** A type of body tissue composed of fibers that contract and relax to cause movement or exert force. **2.** Strength; brawn: *He has plenty of muscle.*

mus·cu·lar |mŭs´kyə lər| *adj.* Having strong, well-developed muscles: *a muscular fellow.*

mu·si·cian |myōō zĭsh´ən| *n.* Someone who performs or composes music, especially as a profession.

mu·ta·tion |myōō tā´shən| *n.* Any change in the genes or chromosomes of a living thing that can be inherited by its offspring.

mys·te·ry |mĭsʹtə rē| *n., pl.* **mys·te·ries.**
1. Anything that arouses curiosity because it is difficult to explain or is a secret: *Her whereabouts remain a mystery.* **2.** A piece of fiction dealing with a puzzling matter, often a crime.

N

Nai·ro·bi |nī rōʹbē|. The capital of Kenya.

na·ive, or **na·ïve** |nä ēvʹ| *adj.*
Showing a lack of experience or judgment; unsophisticated: *naive remarks.* [French, natural, from Latin *nātīvus*, native, from *nāscī*, to be born.]

nar·rate |nărʹāt´| or |nă rātʹ| *v.*
nar·rat·ed, nar·rat·ing. To supply the running commentary for a motion picture or other performance: *He narrated the story.* [Latin *narrāre*, from *gnārus*, knowing.] — **narʹra´tor** *n.*

nar·ra·tive |nărʹə tĭv| *n.* A story or description; a narrated account: *The children listened to the old man's narrative.*

nau·se·a |nôʹzē ə| or |-zhə| or |sē ə| or |-shə| *n.* A stomach disturbance that causes a feeling of the need to vomit: *Nausea was one symptom of the illness.*

nec·es·sa·ry |nĕsʹĭ sĕr´ē| *adj.* Needed to achieve a certain result or effect; essential.

ne·go·tia·ble |nĭ gōʹshə bəl| or |-shē ə-| *adj.* Capable of being negotiated, or discussed in order to come to an agreement: *a negotiable contract.*

-ness. A suffix that forms nouns and means "a state, condition, or quality": **rudeness.**

neu·ron |noŏrʹŏn´| or |nyŏŏrʹ-| *n.* Any of the cells that make up the tissue of nerves and of the nervous system, consisting typically of a main portion that contains the nucleus and threadlike stuctures that extend from this portion, carrying impulses to and away from the cell; a nerve cell: *Motor neurons carry instructions from the brain to muscles.*

Pronunciation Key

ă	pat	ŏ	pot	û	fur
ā	pay	ō	go	*th*	**the**
â	care	ô	paw, for	th	**thin**
ä	father	oi	**oil**	hw	**which**
ĕ	pet	ŏŏ	**book**	zh	usual
ē	be	ōō	**boot**	ə	**ago, item**
ĭ	pit	yōō	**cute**		pencil, atom
ī	ice	ou	**out**		circus
î	near	ŭ	cut	ər	butter

no·mad |nōʹmăd´| *n.* A member of a group of people who have no permanent home, live mainly by keeping livestock, and move about from place to place seeking food, water, and grazing land.

non·de·script |nŏnʹdĭ skrĭptʹ| *adj.*
Lacking in distinctive qualities and thus difficult to describe: *a nondescript rock.*
[*non-*, not + Latin *dēscriptus*, from *dēscrībere*, to copy, write down: *dē*, down + *scrībere*, to write.]

non·prof·it |nŏn prŏfʹĭt| *adj.* Not set up or managed for the purpose of making a profit: *a nonprofit organization.*

no·ta·tion |nō tāʹshən| *n.* A system of symbols or figures used to represent quantities, tones, or other values: *musical notation.*

noz·zle |nŏzʹəl| *n.* A projecting opening, as at the end of a hose or the rear of a rocket, through which a hot liquid or gas is discharged under pressure.

nu·cle·us |noōʹklē əs| or |nyoōʹ-| *n., pl.*
nu·cle·i |noōʹklē ī´| or |nyoōʹ-|. **1.** A central or essential part around which other parts are grouped; a core: *the nucleus of a city.* **2.** A complex, usually round structure contained within a living cell, controlling the metabolism, growth, reproduction, and heredity of the cell.

nui·sance |noōʹsəns| or |nyoōʹ-| *n.* A source of inconvenience; a bother.

nurs·er·y |nûr´sə rē| *or* |nûrs´rē| *n., pl.*
nurs·er·ies. A room set apart for the use of
babies or children.
nu·tri·tion |nōō trĭsh´ən| *or* |nyōō-| *n.*
Nourishment; diet: *good nutrition.*

O

o·a·sis |ō ā´sĭs| *n., pl.* **o·a·ses** |ō ā´sēz´|.
A fertile spot or area in a desert, watered by a
spring, stream, or well.
ob-. Also **oc-** (before *c*) or **of-** (before *f*) or
op- (before *p*) or **o-** (before *m*). A prefix
meaning "to, toward, in front of, against":
obstacle. [Latin *ob-*, from the preposition *ob*,
to, toward, in front of, on account of,
against.]
ob·jec·tive |əb jĕk´tĭv| *adj.* Not
influenced by emotion or prejudice; impartial:
an objective decision. —*n.* Something worked
toward; a goal; a purpose: *Our objective is to
plant more trees in town.* [Latin *objectus*, an
object.]
ob·ser·va·to·ry |əb zûr´və tôr´ē| *or*
|-tōr´ē| *n., pl.* **ob·ser·va·to·ries.** A place
designed and equipped for making
observations, as in astronomy or meteorology:
weather observatory.

ob·serve |əb zûrv´| *v.* **ob·served,**
ob·serv·ing. To perceive, notice, or watch
attentively.
ob·sta·cle |ŏb´stə kəl| *n.* Something that
stands in the way of progress toward a goal; a
hindrance. [From Latin *obstāre*, to hinder:
ob, against + *stāre*, to stand.]

ob·vi·ous |ŏb´vē əs| *adj.* Easily perceived
or understood; evident: *an obvious advantage.*
oc·tave |ŏk´tĭv| *or* |-tāv| *n.* The interval
between one musical tone and the eighth tone
above or below it: *From middle C to the C
above it is an octave.*
op·er·ate |ŏp´ə rāt´| *v.* **op·er·at·ed,**
op·er·at·ing. To function in an effective
way; work: *a machine that operates well.*
[Latin *operari*, to work, labor, from *opus*, a
work.]
op·er·a·tion |ŏp´ə rā´shən| *n.* **1.** The
condition of being capable of operating or
functioning: *a machine no longer in operation.*
2. A surgical procedure for curing a disease,
disorder, or injury in a living body.
op·po·nent |ə pō´nənt| *n.* A person or
group that opposes another in a battle,
contest, controversy, or debate. [Latin *ob-*,
against + *pōnere*, to put.]
op·por·tu·ni·ty |ŏp´ər tōō´nĭ tē| *or*
|-tyōō´-| *n., pl.* **op·por·tu·ni·ties.** A time
or occasion that is suitable for a particular
purpose; a favorable combination of
circumstances: *opportunity for advancement.*
[From Latin *ob-*, to + *portus*, harbor.]
or·ches·tra |ôr´kĭ strə| *n.* A large group
of musicians who play together on various
instruments, generally including string,
woodwind, brass, and percussion instruments.
or·di·nar·y |ôr´dn ĕr´ē| *adj.* Commonly
encountered; usual; normal.
or·gan·ize |ôr´gə nīz´| *v.* **or·gan·ized,**
or·gan·iz·ing. 1. To put together or arrange
in an orderly way: *organize one's thoughts.*
2. To form a group in order to work together
for a particular purpose: *organize a club.*
or·i·gin |ôr´ə jĭn| *or* |ŏr´-| *n.* The
beginning or coming into being of something:
the origin of life; the origin of a word.
o·rig·i·nate |ə rĭj´ə nāt´| *v.*
o·rig·i·nat·ed, o·rig·i·nat·ing. To bring or
come into being: *The cymbal originated in
Greece.*

or·na·ment |ôr´nə mənt| *n.* Something that adorns or makes more attractive or beautiful; a decoration. —*v.* |ôr´nə mənt´|. To supply or furnish with ornaments; decorate.

-ory. A suffix that forms nouns and means "a place of or for": **reformatory.**

Ot·ta·wa |ŏt´ə wə| *or* |-wä´| *or* |-wô´|. The capital of Canada.

P

pan·ic |păn´ĭk| *v.* **pan·icked, pan·ick·ing, pan·ics.** To be stricken with panic—a sudden, overwhelming terror: *Stay calm; don't panic.* [From Greek *panikos*, of Pan (in Greek mythology, a god who would arouse terror in lonely places).]

Pan·the·on |păn´thē ŏn´| *or* |-ən| *n.* A circular temple in Rome, completed in 27 B.C., and dedicated to all the gods.

pa·py·rus |pə pī´rəs| *n.* **1.** A tall, reedlike water plant of northern Africa and nearby regions. **2.** A kind of paper made from the stems and pith of this plant by the ancient Egyptians.

par·a·graph |păr´ə grăf´| *or* |-gräf´| *n.* A division of a piece of writing that begins on a new, usually indented line and that consists of one or more sentences on a single idea or aspect of the subject. [Medieval Latin *paragraphus*, sign marking a new section of writing, from Greek *paragraphos*, from *para*, beside + *graphein*, to write.]

par·al·lel·o·gram |păr´ə lĕl´ə grăm´| *n.* A plane, four-sided geometric figure in which each pair of opposite sides is parallel. [From Greek *parallēlos*, (*para-*, beside + *allēlōn*, of one another) + *grammē*, line.]

par·a·lyze |păr´ə līz´| *v.* **par·a·lyzed, par·a·lyz·ing. 1.** To affect with paralysis; make unable to feel or move. **2.** To make helpless or motionless: *paralyzed by fear.* **3.** To block the normal functioning of; bring to a standstill: *The blizzard paralyzed large sections of the city.*

Pronunciation Key

ă	pat	ŏ	pot	û	fur
ā	pay	ō	go	*th*	**the**
â	care	ô	paw, for	th	thin
ä	father	oi	oil	hw	which
ĕ	pet	o͞o	book	zh	usual
ē	be	o͞o	boot	ə	ago, item
ĭ	pit	yo͞o	cute		pencil, atom
ī	ice	ou	out		circus
î	near	ŭ	cut	ər	butter

---

par·a·med·ic |păr´ə mĕd´ĭk| *n.* A person who assists a highly trained medical professional, as a laboratory technician or a nurse. [Latin *para-*, beside + *medic* from *medicus*, physician.]

par·a·site |păr´ə sīt´| *n.* An organism that lives in or on a different kind of organism from which it gets its nourishment and to which it is sometimes harmful: *A parasite needs a host.*

par·ka |pär´kə| *n.* A warm fur or cloth jacket with a hood. [Eskimo from Aleutian, skin, from Russian, reindeer pelt, from Samoyed.]

Par·me·san |pär´mĭ zän´| *or* |-zän´| *or* |-zən| *n.* A hard, dry Italian cheese, usually served grated. [From *Parma*, Italy.]

Par·the·non |pär´thə nŏn´| The temple of the goddess Athena built on the Acropolis in Athens in the fifth century B.C.

par·tic·i·pate |pär tĭs´ə pāt´| *v.* **par·tic·i·pat·ed, par·tic·i·pat·ing.** To join with others in being active; take part: *participate in a discussion.* —**par·ti´ci·pa´tion** *n.*: *We need the participation of all members.* [From Latin *particeps*, a partaker: *pars*, to grant + *cepo*, taking.]

par·tic·u·lar·ly |pər tĭk´yə lər lē| *adv.* To a great degree; especially: *These strawberries are particularly sweet.*

pas de deux |pä də dœ´| *n., pl.* **pas de deux.** A ballet figure or dance for two persons: *perform a pas de deux.*

329

pa·tience |pā´shəns| *n.* Calm endurance of a trying, tedious, or annoying situation.

pa·tient |pā´shənt| *adj.* Enduring trouble, hardship, annoyance, delay, etc., without complaint or anger: *Please be patient.*

pat·i·o |păt´ē ō´| *n., pl.* **pat·i·os.** A space for dining or recreating, next to a house or apartment. [Spanish, untilled land, courtyard.]

pa·vil·ion |pə vĭl´yən| *n.* An ornate tent.

pe·nal·ize |pē´nə līz´| *v.* **pe·nal·ized, pe·nal·iz·ing.** To subject to a penalty, as for an offense or an infringement of a rule.

pen·dant |pĕn´dənt| *n.* A hanging ornament, as one worn dangling from a necklace or from the ear. [From Latin *pendēre*, to hang.]

pen·du·lum |pĕn´jə ləm| *or* |-dyə-| *n.* **1.** A mass hung by a relatively light cord so that it is able to swing freely. **2.** An apparatus of this kind used to regulate the action of some device, especially a clock. [Latin, neuter of *pendulus*, hanging down, from *pendēre*, to hang.]

pen·i·cil·lin |pĕn´ĭ sĭl´ən| *n.* Any of a group of related antibiotic compounds obtained from molds and used to treat various diseases and infections.

pen·in·su·la |pə nĭn´sə lə| *or* |-nĭns´yə-| *n.* A portion of land nearly surrounded by water and connected with a larger land mass.

pen·sion |pĕn´shən| *n.* A sum of money paid regularly as a retirement benefit. [Latin *pendere*, to weigh, pay.]

pen·sive |pĕn´sĭv| *adj.* Showing or engaged in deep, often melancholy, thought: *a pensive mood.* [From Latin *pendere*, to weigh.]

pent·house |pĕnt´hous´| *n.* An apartment or dwelling, usually with a terrace, located on the roof of a building. [Medieval Latin *appenticium*, to attach: *ad*, on + *pendēre*, to hang.]

per·for·mance |pər fôr´məns| *n.* **1.** The act, process, or manner of performing. **2.** A public presentation of something, such as a musical or dramatic work.

pe·rim·e·ter |pə rĭm´ĭ tər| *n.* **1.** The sum of the lengths of the sides of a polygon. **2.** The total length of or distance around any closed curve, such as a circle or ellipse. [From Greek *peri-*, around + *-meter*, from *metron*, measure.]

per·i·scope |pĕr´ĭ skōp´| *n.* Any of several instruments in which mirrors or prisms allow observation of objects that are not in a direct line of sight. [Greek *peri*, about, near + *skopein*, to see.]

per·ish·a·ble |pĕr´ĭ shə bəl| *adj.* Liable to decay or spoil easily: *perishable fruits.*

per·ju·ry |pûr´jə rē| *n., pl.* **per·ju·ries.** In law, the deliberate giving of false or misleading testimony while under oath: *guilty of perjury.*

per·ma·frost |pûr´mə frôst´| *or* |-frŏst´| *n.* Permanently frozen soil or subsoil occurring in arctic or subarctic regions.

per·ma·nent |pûr´mə nənt| *adj.* Lasting or meant to last indefinitely; enduring.

per·mis·si·ble |pər mĭs´ə bəl| *adj.* Such as can be permitted; admissible, allowable.

per·mit |pər mĭt´| *v.* **per·mit·ted, per·mit·ting. 1.** To give consent or permission to; allow; authorize: *permit them to enter.* **2.** To afford opportunity to; make possible: *The assembly line permitted mass production.* —*n.* |pûr´mĭt| *or* |pər mĭt´| A document or certificate giving permission to do something; a license.

per·pen·dic·u·lar |pûr´pən dĭk´yə lər| *adj.* Intersecting at or forming a right angle or right angles: *perpendicular lines.*

per·pet·u·al |pər **pĕch´**ōō əl| *adj.*
1. Lasting forever or for an indefinitely long time: *perpetual friendship.* **2.** Ceaselessly repeated or continuing without interruption: *perpetual nagging.* [Latin *perpetuus*, continuous, permanent, from *perpes*, throughout, uninterrupted: *per-*, thoroughly + *petere*, to go toward.]

per·sim·mon |pər **sĭm´**ən| *n.* **1.** An orange-red fruit with a pulp that is sweet and edible only when fully ripe. **2.** A tree that bears such a fruit. [Of Algonquian origin; akin to Cree *pasiminan*, dried fruit.]

per·sist·ent |pər **sĭs´**tənt| *adj.* Refusing to give up or let go; undaunted: *a persistent salesperson.* [Latin *persistere*: *per-* + *sistere*, to stand firm, + *-ent.*]

pe·tite |pə **tēt´**| *adj.* Small and slender; dainty. [From French *petit*, small.]

pe·ti·tion |pə **tĭsh´**ən| *n.* An entreaty, especially to a person or group in authority: *a petition sent to the governor.* —*v.* To make a formal request: *His lawyer petitioned for a retrial.* [Latin *petītiō*, attack, solicitation, from *petītus*, to seek, demand.]

phar·ma·cy |**fär´**mə sē| *n., pl.*
phar·ma·cies. A place where medicines are sold; a drugstore.

pheas·ant |**fĕz´**ənt| *n.* Any of several long-tailed, often brightly colored birds, frequently hunted as game. [Greek *phasianos*, "the Phasian (bird)," of the Phasis River in the Caucasus, from Phāsis, the Phasis River.]

Pronunciation Key					
ă	pat	ŏ	pot	û	fur
ā	pay	ō	go	*th*	**the**
â	care	ô	paw, for	th	**thin**
ä	father	oi	**oil**	hw	**wh**ich
ĕ	pet	ōō	book	zh	usual
ē	be	ōō	boot	ə	ago, item
ĭ	pit	yōō	cute		pencil, atom
ī	ice	ou	**out**		circus
î	near	ŭ	cut	ər	butter

phe·nom·e·na |fĭ **nŏm´**ə nə| *n.* A plural of **phenomenon.**

phe·nom·e·non |fĭ **nŏm´**ə nŏn´| *n., pl.*
phe·nom·e·na |fĭ **nŏm´**ə nə| *or*
phe·nom·e·nons. **1.** Any occurrence or fact that can be perceived by the senses: *Floods are natural phenomena.* **2.** Someone or something that is unusual or noteworthy: *Ball lightning is an unexplained phenomenon.*

-phone. A word part that forms nouns and means "sound, voice": **earphone.** [From Greek *phōnē*, sound, voice.]

pho·net·ic |fə **nĕt´**ĭk| *adj.* Representing the sounds of speech with a set of symbols, each denoting a single sound: *phonetic spelling.* [Greek *phōnētikos*, from *phōnein*, to sound, speak, from *phōnē*, sound, voice.]

phono-. A word part meaning "sound, voice, or speech": **phonograph.** [Greek *phōnē*, sound, voice.]

pho·no·graph |**fō´**nə grăf´| *or* |-gräf´| *n.* A device that reproduces sound from a groove cut into a disk. [From Greek *phōnē*, sound + *graphein*, to write.]

pho·to·graph |**fō´**tə grăf´| *or* |-gräf´| *n.* An image formed on a light-sensitive surface by a camera and developed by chemical means to produce a positive print. [From Greek *phōs*, light + *graphein*, to write.]

phys·i·cal |fĭz´ĭ kəl| *adj.* **1.** Of the body rather than the mind or emotions: *physical fitness.* **2.** Solid; material: *a physical object.*

phy·si·cian |fĭ zĭsh´ən| *n.* A person licensed to practice medicine; a doctor. [From Latin *physica*, natural medicine or science, from Greek *phusis*, nature, from *phuein*, to make grow.]

phy·sics |fĭz´ĭks| *n. (used with a singular verb).* The science of matter and energy and the relations between them. [From Latin *physica*, natural medicine or science, from Greek *phusis*, nature, from *phuein*, to make grow.]

phys·i·ol·o·gy |fĭz´ē ŏl´ə jē| *n.* A scientific study of the processes, activities, and functions essential to and characteristic of life. [From Latin *physicus*, natural, from Greek *phusis*, nature, from *phuein*, to make grow.]

phy·sique |fĭ zēk´| *n.* The body, considered in terms of its proportions, muscle development, and appearance: *the physique of an athlete.*

pi·an·o |pē ăn´ō| *n., pl.* **pi·an·os.** A keyboard musical instrument in which the movement of a key by the player's finger activates a felt-covered hammer that strikes a metal string and produces a tone.

pic·to·graph |pĭk´tə grăf´| *or* |-grăf´| *n.* A picture that represents a word or an idea: *That pictograph represents rain.*

pi·ña·ta |pēn yä´tə| *n.* A decorated container filled with candy and toys and suspended from the ceiling. During celebrations in certain Latin American countries, blindfolded children try to break the piñata with a stick.

pir·ou·ette |pĭr´ōō ĕt´| *n.* In dancing, a full turn of the body on the tip of the toe or the ball of the foot: *performed a pirouette.*

pis·ton |pĭs´tən| *n.* A cylinder or disk that fits snugly into a hollow cylinder and moves back and forth under the pressure of a fluid, as in many engines, or moves or compresses a fluid, as in a pump or compressor.

plaque |plăk| *n.* An ornamented or engraved plate, slab, or disk, used for decoration or to carry an inscription on a monument. [From Old French, metal plate, coin, from Middle Dutch *placken*, to patch, paste.]

pla·teau |plă tō´| *n.* A relatively level area that is at a higher elevation than the land around it. [French, from Old French *platel*, a flat piece, from Greek *platus*, broad, flat.]

plat·i·num |plăt´n əm| *n.* One of the elements, a silver-white metal. [From Spanish *platina*, diminutive of *plata*, silver, plate.]

plau·si·ble |plô´zə bəl| *adj.* Appearing true or reasonable: *a plausible excuse.*

pla·za |plăz´ə| *or* |plä´zə| *n.* A public square or similar open area in a town or city. [Spanish, from Vulgar Latin *plattea*, broad street, courtyard, from Greek *plateia*, broad, flat.]

plea |plē| *n.* In law, the answer of the accused to the charges against him: *a plea of "guilty."*

poin·set·ti·a |poin sĕt´ē ə| *or* |poin sĕt´ə| *n.* A tropical plant with small, yellowish flowers surrounded by showy, usually bright-red petal-like leaves. [Discovered by J.R. *Poinsett* (1799–1851), U.S. minister to Mexico.]

pol·len |pŏl´ən| *n.* Powderlike grains that contain the male reproductive cells of flowering plants and that unite with female reproductive cells, or egg cells, in the process of fertilization.

pol·y·gon |pŏl´ē gŏn´| *n.* A flat, closed geometric figure with three or more sides: *A triangle is a polygon.*

pon·cho |pŏn´chō| *n., pl.* **pon·chos.** A blanket-like cloak with a hole in the center for the head, worn in South America. [American Spanish, from Araucanian *pontho*, woolen fabric.]

por·ce·lain |pôr′sə lĭn| *or* |pōr′-| *n.* A hard, white, translucent material made by baking a fine clay at a high temperature and glazing it with one of several variously colored materials. [French *porcelaine*, from Italian *porcellana*, cowry shell. (Chinaware made of porcelain was thought to resemble the surface of the shells.)]

port·a·ble |pôr′tə bəl| *or* |pōr′-| *adj.* Easily or conveniently carried: *a portable radio.* [From Latin *portabilis*, from *portare*, to carry.]

por·ter |pôr′tər| *or* |pōr′-| *n.* A person hired to carry baggage at a station, airport, or hotel. [From Latin *portare*, to carry.]

port·fo·li·o |pôrt fō′lē ō′| *or* |pōrt-| *n.,* *pl.* **port·fo·li·os.** A portable case for holding loose papers, documents, etc. [Latin *port-*, to carry + *foglio*, leaf, sheet.]

por·tion |pôr′shən| *or* |pōr′-| *n.* A part of a whole; a section or quantity of a larger thing.

por·trait |pôr′trĭt′| *or* |-trāt′| *or* |pōr′-| *n.* A painting, photograph, or other likeness of a person, especially one showing the face. [From Old French *portraire*, from Latin *prōtrahere*, to reveal: *pro-*, forth + *trahere*, to draw.]

pos·si·bil·i·ty |pŏs′ə bĭl′ĭ tē| *n., pl.* **pos·si·bil·i·ties.** The fact or condition of being possible.

post-. A prefix that means: **1.** After in time; later: **postoperative. 2.** After in position; behind: **postscript.** [Latin, from *post*, behind, after.]

post·date |pōst dāt′| *v.* **post·dat·ed, post·dat·ing.** To put a date on (a check, letter, or document) that is later than the actual date. [Latin *post-*, after + *datus*, to give.]

post·grad·u·ate |pōst grăj′ōō ĭt| *or* |-āt′| *adj.* Of or taking courses beyond the level of a bachelor's degree: *postgraduate courses.* [Latin *post-*, after + *gradus*, degree, step, grade.]

Pronunciation Key					
ă	pat	ŏ	pot	û	fur
ā	pay	ō	go	*th*	the
â	care	ô	paw, for	th	thin
ä	father	oi	oil	hw	which
ĕ	pet	ŏŏ	book	zh	usual
ē	be	ōō	boot	ə	ago, item
ĭ	pit	yōō	cute		pencil, atom
ī	ice	ou	out		circus
î	near	ŭ	cut	ər	butter

post·pone |pōst pōn′| *v.* **post·poned, post·pon·ing.** To put off until a later time: *postpone a trip.* [Latin *post-*, after + *pōnere*, to put.]

post·script |pōst′skrĭpt′| *n.* **1.** A message added at the end of a letter, after the writer's signature. **2.** Something added to a book, article, etc. [Latin *post-*, after + *scribere*, to write.]

po·ta·to |pə tā′tō| *n., pl.* **po·ta·toes.** The starchy tuber, or enlarged underground stem, of a widely grown plant, eaten as a vegetable. [Spanish *patata*, from Taino *batata*.]

pre·cip·i·ta·tion |prĭ sĭp′ĭ tā′shən| *n.* Any form of water that condenses from the atmosphere and passes to the surface of the earth; rain, snow, sleet, etc.: *four inches of precipitation for the month.*

pre·cise |prĭ sīs′| *adj.* **1.** Distinct from others; particular: *on this precise spot.* **2.** Done, made, or capable of operating within very small limits of error or variation: *a precise measurement.* [From Latin *praecīdere*, to cut off in front, shorten: *prae*, in front + *caedere*, to cut.]

pre·cis·ion |prĭ sĭzh′ən| *n.* The condition, property, or quality of being precise, or exact: *the precision of a chemist's scales.* [French, from Latin *praecīsio*, act of cutting, from *praecīdere*, to cut off in front, shorten.]

pre·dic·a·ment |prĭ **dĭk´**ə mənt| *n.* A difficult or embarrassing situation. [Late Latin *praedicāmentum,* something predicted, condition (especially an unpleasant one), from *praedicāre,* to proclaim.]

pre·dic·tion |prĭ **dĭk´**shən| *n.* **1.** The act of foretelling, or telling in advance. **2.** Something that is predicted: *The prediction came true.* [Latin *prae,* before + *dīcere,* to tell, say.]

pre·lim·i·nar·y |prĭ **lĭm´**ə nĕr´ē| *adj.* Leading to or preparing for the main event, action, or business: *preliminary sketches for a statue.*

pre·mière |prĭ **mîr´**| *or* |-**myâr´**| *n.* The first public performance of a play, motion picture, or other theatrical work: *the première of the play.*

prep·a·ra·tion |prĕp´ə **rā´**shən| *n.* **1.** The action of preparing. **2.** The condition of being prepared; readiness: *a ship in good preparation for a voyage.*

pre·scribe |prĭ **skrīb´**| *v.* **pre·scribed, pre·scrib·ing.** To order or recommend the use of (a drug, diet, remedy, etc.).

pre·scrip·tion |prĭ **skrĭp´**shən| *n.* A written instruction from a physician indicating what treatment or medication a patient is to receive.

pres·sure |**prĕsh´**ər| *n.* The application of a continuous force on one body by another with which it is in contact.

pre·ven·tion |prĭ **vĕn´**shən| *n.* **1.** The act or an example of preventing: *the prevention of illness.* **2.** Something that prevents; a hindrance: *a prevention against colds.*

pri·ma·ry |**prī´**mĕr´ē| *or* |-mə rē| *adj.* **1.** First in time or sequence; original: *the primary stages of the project.* **2.** First in importance, degree, or quality; chief: *The primary function of furniture is comfort.* —*n.,* *pl.* **pri·ma·ries.** **1.** Something that is primary. **2. A primary election.** A preliminary election in which registered voters, usually the voters of each party, nominate candidates for office. [Latin *prīmārius,* of the first rank, chief, basic, from *prīmus,* first.]

prime time. In radio or television, the hours, usually during the evening, when the largest audience is available.

prin·ci·pal |**prĭn´**sə pəl| *adj.* First and foremost in rank, degree, or importance; chief: *the principal character in the story.*

prin·ci·ple |**prĭn´**sə pəl| *n.* A rule or standard of behavior: *a woman of dedicated political principles.*

pri·or |**prī´**ər| *adj.* Preceding in time or order: *his prior employment.* **Idiom. prior to.** Before: *Prior to that time, no inspection was made.*

prob·a·ble |**prŏb´**ə bəl| *adj.* Likely to happen or to be true: *the probable cost of the expedition.*

pro·ce·dure |prə **sē´**jər| *n.* A manner of proceeding; a way of doing something or going about getting something done.

prod·uct |**prŏd´**əkt| *n.* **1.** Something produced, as by nature, manufacturing, etc.: *industrial products.* **2.** A direct result: *The vaccine was the product of many years of research.*

pro·fes·sor |prə **fĕs´**ər| *n.* A teacher of the highest rank in a college or university.

pro·gram |**prō´**grăm´| *or* |-grəm| *n.* Also *chiefly British* **pro·gramme.** A listing of the order of events and other pertinent information for some public presentation.

pro·jec·tor |prə **jĕk´**tər| *n.* A machine that uses lenses and a source of light to project images, as of motion pictures, onto a surface. [Latin *prōjectum,* a projecting, projection, from *prō(j)icere,* to throw forth: *pro-,* forth + *jacere,* to throw.]

prompt |prŏmpt| *adj.* On time; punctual: *prompt to arrive.*

pro·scribe |prō skrīb´| *v.* **pro·scribed, pro·scrib·ing.** To make unlawful; prohibit.

pros·e·cute |prŏs´ĭ kyōōt´| *v.* **pros·e·cut·ed, pros·e·cut·ing.** To initiate or conduct a legal action against (someone): *prosecute for grand theft.* [From Latin *prosequi,* to follow up or forward: *pro,* forward + *sequi,* to follow.]

pros·e·cu·tion |prŏs´ĭ kyōō´shən| *n.* **1.** The act of prosecuting a person or case in a court of law. **2.** The condition of being thus prosecuted: *risked prosecution by breaking the law.*

pros·pect |prŏs´pĕkt´| *n.* Something expected or foreseen; an expectation: *hurried home with the prospect of a good dinner.*

pro·tein |prō´tēn´| *n.* A substance that contains nitrogen, occurs in and forms the basis of all living plant and animal tissue, and is necessary to life. Milk, eggs, cheese, meat, fish, and nuts are sources of protein.

pub·li·ca·tion |pŭb´lĭ kā´shən| *n.* **1.** The act of publishing printed matter. **2.** Printed matter, such as a magazine or newspaper, offered for sale or distribution.

pulse |pŭls| *n.* The rhythmical expansion and contraction of the arteries as blood is pushed through them by the beating of the heart.

pum·ice |pŭm´ĭs| *n.* A lightweight rock of volcanic origin.

punc·tu·ate |pŭngk´chōō āt´| *v.* **punc·tu·at·ed, punc·tu·at·ing.** To provide (written or printed material) with punctuation: *punctuate the sentence.* [Medieval Latin *punctuare,* to mark with a point, *punctuate,* from Latin *punctum,* point, from *pungere,* to pierce.]

punc·tu·a·tion |pŭngk´chōō ā´shən| *n.* **1.** The use of standard marks in writing and printing to separate sentences and parts of sentences in order to make the meaning clear. **2.** A mark or the marks so used.

Pronunciation Key					
ă	pat	ŏ	pot	û	fur
ā	pay	ō	go	*th*	the
â	care	ô	paw, for	th	thin
ä	father	oi	oil	hw	which
ĕ	pet	ōō	book	zh	usual
ē	be	ōō	boot	ə	ago, item
ĭ	pit	yōō	cute		pencil, atom
ī	ice	ou	out		circus
î	near	ŭ	cut	ər	butter

pyr·a·mid |pîr´ə mĭd| *n.* A massive monument having a rectangular base and four triangular faces with a single apex, or peak, and serving as a tomb or temple.

Q

qua·drille |kwŏ drĭl´| *or* |kwə-| *n.* A square dance of French origin, performed by four couples.

qual·i·fy |kwŏl´ə fī´| *v.* **qual·i·fied, qual·i·fy·ing, qual·i·fies.** To make, be, or become eligible or qualified, as for a position, task, etc.: *Her grades qualify her for the Honor Society.*

quan·da·ry |kwŏn´drē| *or* |-də rē| *n., pl.* **quan·da·ries.** A condition of uncertainty or doubt; a dilemma: *in a quandary over what to do next.*

quan·ti·ty |kwŏn´tĭ tē | *n., pl.* **quan·ti·ties.** An amount or number of a thing or things: *a large quantity of fruit.*

quin·tu·plet |kwĭn tŭp´lĭt| *or* |-tōō´plĭt| *or* |-tyōō´-| *or* |kwĭn´tōō plĭt| *n.* One of five children born in a single birth.

R

rac·coon |ră kōōn´| *n.* A North American animal with grayish-brown fur, black, masklike face markings, and a bushy, black-ringed tail. [Algonquian *aroughcoune, arathkone.*]

rac·quet·ball |răk´ĭt bôl´| *n.* A court game that is identical to handball but utilizes a short racquet and a larger, softer ball. [Old French *rachette*, *raquette*, from Arabic *rāhet*, palm of the hand + Middle English *bal*.]

ra·di·a·tor |rā´dē ā´tər| *n.* A cooling device, as in automotive engines.

ra·di·us |rā´dē əs| *n., pl.* **ra·di·i** |rā´dē ī´|. The length of a line segment that joins the center of a circle with any point on its circumference: *The radius of a circle is equal to 1/2 of the diameter.*

range |rānj| *n.* An extent or region within which something can vary: *a range of prices.*

rank |răngk| *n.* A relative position on a scale of performance, production, value, quality, etc.: *in the middle rank of his class.* —*v.* **1.** To hold a certain rank: *ranked eighth in a class of 160.* **2.** To assign a rank to; evaluate in a certain way: *Sports writers rank the team second in the nation.*

rap·port |ră pôr´| *or* |-pōr´| *n.* A relationship of mutual trust and understanding. [Latin *apportāre*: *ad-*, to + *portāre*, to carry.]

rasp·ber·ry |răz´běr´ē| *or* |räz´-| *n., pl.* **-ber·ries.** A sweet, many-seeded berry that grows on a prickly plant with long, woody stems.

rat·ing |rā´tĭng| *n., pl.* **rat·ings.** An estimate of the popularity of a television or radio program, made by polling the audience.

re-. A prefix meaning: **1.** Again, anew: **reassemble. 2.** Back; backward: **recall.**

[From Latin *re-*, back, backward, away, again, behind, contrary, against, in response to.]

re·al·i·ty |rē ăl´ĭ tē| *n., pl.* **re·al·i·ties.**
1. The condition or quality of being real; actual existence: *the reality of the situation.*
2. The sum total of things that actually exist; *the real world.*

re·al·ty |rē´əl tē| *n., pl.* **re·al·ties.** Land and the property on it; real estate.

re·ceipt |rĭ sēt´| *n.* A written acknowledgment that a sum of money has been paid or received or that a certain article or delivery of merchandise has been received.

rec·og·nize |rĕk´əg nīz´| *v.* **rec·og·nized, rec·og·niz·ing.** To know or identify from past experience or knowledge: *recognized his voice.*

rec·om·men·da·tion |rĕk´ə měn dā´shən| *n.* Something that recommends, as a letter or a favorable statement about someone's qualifications or character.

rec·tan·gle |rĕk´tăng´gəl| *n.* A parallelogram that contains an angle of 90 degrees.

ref·er·ence |rĕf´ər əns| *or* |rĕf´rəns| *n.* A note in a book or other publication that directs the reader to another part of the book or to another source of information.

re·fract |rĭ frăkt´| *v.* To cause the path of (light or other radiation) to bend or turn aside. [Latin *refringere*, to break off: *re-*, away + *frangere*, to break.]

re·frain |rĭ frān´| *n.* A phrase or verse repeated several times throughout the course of a song or poem, especially at the end of each stanza: *We sang the refrain over and over again.*

re·ha·bil·i·tate |rē´hə bĭl´ĭ tāt| *v.* **re·ha·bil·i·ta·ted, re·ha·bil·i·ta·ting.** To restore to useful life, as through training, therapy, etc.: *a program to rehabilitate blinded veterans.*

reign |rān| *v.* To exercise the real or symbolic power of a monarch: *Queen Victoria reigned.*

re·ject |rĭ **jĕkt´**| *v.* To refuse to accept, use, grant, consider, etc.: *He rejected the offer.* [Middle English *rejecten* from Latin *rejectus*, to throw back: *re-*, back + *jacere*, to throw.]

rel·e·vant |**rĕl´**ə vənt| *adj.* Related to the matter at hand; pertinent: *a relevant question.* —**rel·e·vance** *n.*: *a matter of great relevance.*

re·li·a·ble |rĭ **lī´**ə bəl| *adj.* Capable of being relied upon; dependable.

re·mem·ber |rĭ **mĕm´**bər| *v.* To recall to the mind; think of again. [Latin *rememorārī*, to remember again: *re-*, again + *memorārī*, to remind, from *memor,* mindful.]

re·mit·tance |rĭ **mĭt´**ns| *n.* Money or credit sent to someone.

remote control *n.* **1.** The control of an activity, a process, or a machine from a distance, especially by radio or coded signals. **2.** A device used to control a device or machine from a distance.

rep·e·ti·tion |rĕp´ə **tĭsh´**ən| *n.* **1.** The act or process of repeating: *the repetition of a sound.* **2.** Something repeated or produced by repeating: *an exact repetition of a design.* [Latin *repetītiō*, from *repetere*, repeat: *re-*, again + *petere*, to go toward.]

re·place·ment |rĭ **plās´**mənt| *n.* The act or process of replacing.

re·port·er |rĭ **pôr´**tər| *or* |-**pōr´**-| *n.* A person who gathers information for news stories that are written or broadcast. [Middle English from Old French *reporter*, to carry back, from Latin *reportare*: *re-*, back + *portare*, to carry.]

re·quire·ment |rĭ **kwīr´**mənt| *n.* Something that is needed: *daily food requirements.*

res·cue |**rĕs´**kyōō| *v.* **res·cued, res·cu·ing.** To save from danger, harm, capture, evil, etc.: *rescue a drowning person.* —*n.* An act of rescuing or saving: *A passerby came to our rescue.*

res·er·voir |**rĕz´**ər vwär´| *n.* A natural or artificial lake used as a storage place for water. [From French *réserver*, to reserve,

Pronunciation Key

ă	pat	ŏ	pot	û	fur
ā	pay	ō	go	*th*	**the**
â	care	ô	paw, for	th	**thin**
ä	father	oi	**oil**	hw	**which**
ĕ	pet	ōō	book	zh	usual
ē	be	ōō	boot	ə	**a**go, it**e**m
ĭ	pit	yōō	cute		penc**i**l, at**o**m
ī	ice	ou	**out**		circ**u**s
î	near	ŭ	cut	ər	butt**er**

from Latin *reservāre*, to keep back: *re-*, back + *servāre*, to save, keep.]

re·sign |rĭ **zīn´**| *v.* To give up or quit (a position.) [Middle English from Old French from Latin *resignāre*, to unseal: *re-*, back + *signāre*, to seal, sign, from *signum,* a mark, sign.]

res·ig·na·tion |rĕz´ĭg **nā´**shən| *n.* The act of giving up, leaving, or retiring from a position: *The president announced his resignation.*

re·sis·tance |rĭ **zĭs´**təns| *n.* The act, process, or capability of resisting: *The enemy offered little resistance.* [Latin *resistere*, to stand back, resist: *re-*, back, against + *sistere*, to set, place.]

res·o·lu·tion |rĕz´ə **lōō´**shən| *n.* **1.** Firmness; determination: *Face this with courage and resolution.* **2.** A vow or pledge to do something or refrain from doing something: *She made a New Year's resolution to keep her room neat and clean.* [Latin *resolūtionem*, from *resolvere*, to loosen, resolve.]

re·solve |rĭ **zŏlv´**| *v.* **re·solved, re·solv·ing. 1.** To make a firm decision: *He resolved to work harder.* **2.** To find a solution to; solve: *resolve a problem.* [Latin *resolvere*: *re-*, again + *solvere*, to loosen, release.]

re·spect |rĭ **spĕkt´**| *n.* **1.** A feeling of honor or esteem: *I have respect for my music teacher.* **2.** Regard or consideration: *respect for the law.* —*v.* To have or show respect for: *I respect your opinion.* [From Latin *respicere*, to regard, to look back: *re-*, back + *specere*, to look at.]

res·pi·ra·tion |rĕs´pə **rā´shən**| *n.* The act or process of inhaling or exhaling; breathing: *The patient's respiration was labored.*

re·spon·si·bil·i·ty |rĭ spŏn´sə **bĭl´ĭ tē**| *n., pl.* **re·spon·si·bil·i·ties.** **1.** The quality or fact of being responsible: *a sense of responsibility.* **2.** Something that one is responsible for; a duty or obligation.

res·tau·rant |rĕs´tər ənt| *or* |-tə ränt´| *n.* A place where meals are served to the public.

rés·u·mé |rĕz´o͝o mā´| *or* |rĕz´o͝o **mā´**| *n.* An outline of one's personal history and experience, submitted when applying for a job.

re·sus·ci·tate |rĭ sŭs´ĭ tāt´| *v.* **re·sus·ci·tat·ed, re·sus·ci·tat·ing.** To return to life or consciousness; revive: *The medic resuscitated the victim.*

ret·ro·spect |rĕt´rə spĕkt´| *n.* A review, survey, or contemplation of the past: *In retrospect, he could see where he had made his mistake.* [From Latin *retrōspicere*, to look back at: *retrō*, backward, behind + *specere*, to look at.]

re·vise |rĭ **vīz´**| *v.* **re·vised, re·vis·ing.** **1.** To edit in order to improve or bring up to date: *revise a paragraph.* **2.** To change or modify. [Latin *revīsere*, to look back: *re-*, again, back + *vīsere*, look at, from *vidēre*, to see.]

re·vi·sion |rĭ **vĭzh´ən**| *n.* The act or process of revising.

rhythm |**rĭth´əm**| *n.* **1.** A movement, action, or condition that recurs alternately or in regular sequence: *the rhythm of the tides.* **2.** A musical pattern formed by a series of notes or beats that are of different lengths and have different stresses.

ros·in |rŏz´ĭn| *n.* A translucent yellowish or brownish substance obtained from the sap of pine trees. It is used to prevent slipping on the bows of violins and other stringed instruments and on dancers' shoes; it is also used as an ingredient in varnish and other products.

rou·tine |ro͞o **tēn´**| *n.* A series of activities performed regularly; standard or usual procedure. [French, from *route*, beaten path.]

ru·in |**ro͞o´ĭn**| *n.* **1.** Severe damage, making something useless or worthless. **2.** Often **ruins.** The remains of a structure or group of structures that have been destroyed or have fallen into pieces from age: *Aztec ruins.* —*v.* To harm irreparably; make useless or worthless.

rup·ture |**rŭp´chər**| *n.* The act or process of breaking open or bursting: *The rupture began at a weak seam.* —*v.* **rup·tured, rup·tur·ing.** To break; burst: *The old tank ruptured.* [From Latin *rumpere*, to break.]

ru·ral |ro͝or´əl| *adj.* Of or in the country: *rural areas.*

S

sa·ble |**sā´bəl**| *n.* An animal of northern Europe and Asia that is related to the mink and weasel and has soft, dark fur.

salve |săv| *or* |säv| *n.* A soothing ointment applied to wounds, burns, or sores to heal them or relieve pain.

sand·stone |**sănd´stōn**| *n.* A type of sedimentary rock that occurs in a variety of colors, formed of sandlike grains of quartz held together by lime or other materials.

sar·dine |sär **dēn´**| *n.* A small herring or similar small fish, often canned for use as food. [From Greek *sardīnos*, possibly from *Sardō*, Sardinia.]

sat·el·lite |săt´l īt´| *n.* Any of various man-made objects launched so as to orbit a celestial body.

sat·is·fac·to·ry |săt´ĭs făk´tə rē| *adj.* Sufficient to meet a demand or requirement; adequate: *a satisfactory grade.*

sax·o·phone |săk´sə fōn´| *n.* A wind instrument having a single-reed mouthpiece, a curved conical body made of metal, and keys operated by the player's fingers. [Invented (1846) by Adolphe *Sax.*]

scal·lion |skăl´yən| *n.* A young onion with a small, narrow white bulb and long, narrow green leaves, both of which are eaten raw as a relish or used in cooking. [From Latin *Ascalōnia,* "Ascalonian (onion)," from Ascalon, a port in southern Palestine.]

scene |sēn| *n.* A section of a play, usually one of the divisions of an act, or a short section of a motion picture. [From Old French *scène,* stage, stage performance.]

schol·ar |skŏl´ər| *n.* A person of great learning.

scis·sors |sĭz´ərz| *n. (used with a plural verb).* A cutting tool consisting of two blades, each with a ring-shaped handle, joined on a pivot that allows the cutting edges to close against each other. [From Late Latin *cisorium,* cutting instrument, from Latin *caedere,* to cut.]

scribe |skrīb| *n.* **1.** An official copyist of manuscripts and documents. **2.** A public clerk or secretary. **3.** A writer.

Pronunciation Key

ă	pat	ŏ	pot	û	fur
ā	pay	ō	go	*th*	the
â	care	ô	paw, for	th	thin
ä	father	oi	oil	hw	which
ĕ	pet	ŏŏ	book	zh	usual
ē	be	ōō	boot	ə	ago, item
ĭ	pit	yōō	cute		pencil, atom
ī	ice	ou	out		circus
î	near	ŭ	cut	ər	butter

scroll |skrōl| *n.* A roll of parchment, papyrus, etc., used especially for writing a document.

sculp·ture |skŭlp´chər| *n.* **1.** The art of making figures or designs that have depth, as by carving wood, chiseling stone, or casting metal. **2.** A work of art created in this way.

sec·re·tar·y |sĕk´rĭ tĕr´ē| *n., pl.* **sec·re·tar·ies. 1.** A person employed to do clerical work, such as typing and filing. **2.** An officer of an organization in charge of the minutes of meetings, correspondence, etc. **3.** The head of a government department. **4.** A desk with a small bookcase on top.

seg·ment |sĕg´mənt| *n.* A part of a line that is included between any pair of its points; a line segment: *a segment of the curve.*

seis·mo·graph |sīz´mə grăf´| *or* |-gräf´| *n.* An instrument that detects and records motions of the ground. [From Greek *seismos,* from *seiein,* to shake + *graphein,* to write.]

selt·zer |sĕlt´sər| *n.* **1.** A bubbly mineral water. **2.** Artificially carbonated water. [From German *Selterser (Wasser),* "(water) of Nieder Selters," a district near Wiesbaden, Germany, locality of the springs.]

semi-. A prefix meaning: **1.** Part or partly: **semiprofessional. 2.** Half of: **semicircle.** [Latin *sēmi-,* half.]

339

sem·i·cir·cle |sĕm´ē sûr´kəl| *n.* An arc of 180 degrees; a half of a *circle.* [Latin *sēmi-,* half + *circle,* from Middle English *cercle,* from Latin *circulus,* diminutive of *circus,* ring.]

sem·i·co·lon |sĕm´ĭ kō´lən| *n.* A punctuation mark (;) indicating a greater degree of separation between elements in a sentence than a comma. [Latin *sēmi-,* half + *colon,* from Latin *cōlon,* from Greek *kōlon,* limb.]

sem·i·fi·nal |sĕm´ē fī´nəl| *n.* Often **semifinals.** A game or match that precedes the final, as in a tournament. [Latin *sēmi,* half + *finals,* from Latin *fīnālis,* from *finis,* end.]

sem·i·pre·cious |sĕm´ē prĕsh´əs| *adj.* Designating a gem, such as topaz, amethyst, or jade, that is less valuable than a precious stone. [Latin *sēmi-,* half + *precious,* from Old French *precieus,* from Latin *pretium,* price.]

sep·a·rate |sĕp´ə rāt´| *v.* **sep·a·rat·ed, sep·a·rat·ing.** To divide into parts. —*adj.* |sĕp´ə rĭt| *or* |sĕp´rĭt|. Set apart from the rest: *Libraries have a separate section for reference books.*

sep·tet |sĕp tĕt´| *n.* A group of seven people.

se·quoi·a |sĭ kwoi´ə| *n.* Either of two very large cone-bearing evergreen trees, the giant sequoia of the mountains of southern California or the redwood of northern California. [After *Sequoya,* known as George Guess, American Indian leader and scholar.]

se·ri·al |sîr´ē əl| *adj.* Presented in installments: *a serial television drama.* —*n.* A story or play presented in installments.

shelf |shĕlf| *n., pl.* **shelves** |shĕlvz|. A flat, usually rectangular piece of wood, metal, or glass, fastened at right angles to a wall and used to hold or store things.

sher·bet |shûr´bĭt| *n.* A sweet, frozen, often fruit-flavored dessert.

Si·be·ri·a |sī bîr´ē ə| A large region in the Asian part of Russia, extending from the Ural Mountains to the Pacific Ocean.

side·burns |sīd´bûrnz´| *pl. n.* Growths of hair down the sides of a man's face in front of the ears, especially when worn with the rest of the beard shaved off. [After Ambrose *Burnside* (1824–1881), Union general in the American Civil War.]

side effect. *n.* A secondary, often undesirable effect, especially from a drug: *a side effect of the medicine.*

si·es·ta |sē ĕs´tə| *n.* A rest or nap, usually taken after the midday meal. [Spanish, from Latin *sexta (hora),* sixth (hour after sunrise, noon).]

sig·nal |sĭg´nəl| *n.* A sign, gesture, or device that conveys information: *a traffic signal.* [French from Latin *signalis,* of a sign, from *signum,* distinctive mark or figure, seal, signal.]

sig·net |sĭg´nĭt| *n.* A seal, as one used to stamp documents. [From Latin *signum,* distinctive mark or figure, seal, signal.]

sig·nif·i·cance |sĭg nĭf´ĭ kəns| *n.* The state or quality of being significant; importance: *the significance of the event.*

sig·ni·fi·cant |sĭg nĭf´ĭ kənt| *adj.* Important; notable: *a significant event.*

sig·ni·fy |sĭg´nə fī| *v.* **sig·ni·fied, sig·ni·fy·ing.** To serve as a sign of: *What does this moment signify?* [From Latin *significāre: signum,* distinctive mark or figure, seal, signal + *facere,* to make.]

sil·hou·ette |sĭl´ōō ĕt´| *n.* **1.** A drawing consisting of the outline of something, especially a human profile, filled in with a solid color. **2.** An outline of something that appears dark against a light background. [After Etienne de *Silhouette* (1709–1767), French minister of finance in 1759.]

sim·i·lar |sĭm´ə lər| *adj.* Related in appearance or nature; alike though not the same.

si·mul·cast |sī´məl kăst´| *or* |sĭm´əl-| *v.* To broadcast simultaneously by FM and AM radio or by radio and television. [simul(taneous) + (broad)cast.]

sit·com |sĭt´kŏm´| *n.* A humorous television series with continuing characters. [Sit(uation) + com(edy).]

skate·board |skāt´bôrd´| *n.* A short narrow board having a set of four wheels mounted under it and usually ridden in a standing or crouched position.

skel·e·tal |skĕl´ĭ təl| *adj.* Of a skeleton.

sketch |skĕch| *n.* A rough preliminary drawing or painting: *a sketch of the park.* [Dutch *schets,* from Italian *schizzare,* to sketch, from Latin *schedius,* hastily put together, from Greek *skhedios,* without preparation.]

skunk |skŭngk| *n.* **1.** An animal that has black and white fur and a bushy tail and can spray a bad-smelling liquid from glands near the base of the tail. **2.** *Slang.* A mean person. —*v. Slang.* To defeat overwhelmingly, especially by keeping from scoring. [From Proto-Algonquian *shekākwa: shek-,* to urinate + *-ākw-,* a small mammal.]

slan·der |slăn´dər| *n.* **1.** A false statement uttered maliciously to damage someone's reputation. **2.** The act or crime of uttering such false statements. —See Usage note at **libel.**

slang |slăng| *n.* A kind of language used most often in casual speech, made up of words and special senses of words that name things with added vividness, humor, or other connotation; for example, "rap" for "talk," and "cool" for "good" are slang terms.

sleigh |slā| *n.* A light vehicle on low runners for use on snow or ice, having one or more seats and usually drawn by a horse. [Dutch (colonial) *slee,* short for *slede.*]

sleuth |slo͞oth| *n.* A detective.

snoop |sno͞op| *v. Informal.* To look at, pry, or search in a sneaky manner.

snow·mo·bile |snō´mō bēl´| *n.* A vehicle that is essentially a motorized sled, used for travelling over ice and snow. [Blend of snow + mobile.]

soap opera. A daytime radio or television serial drama, marked by sentimentality.

Pronunciation Key

ă	pat	ŏ	pot	û	fur
ā	pay	ō	go	*th*	**the**
â	care	ô	paw, for	th	**thin**
ä	father	oi	**oil**	hw	**which**
ĕ	pet	o͞o	book	zh	usual
ē	be	o͞o	boot	ə	ago, item
ĭ	pit	yo͞o	cute		pencil, atom
ī	ice	ou	**out**		circus
î	near	ŭ	cut	ər	butter

---

sol·emn |sŏl´əm| *adj.* Impressive; serious; grave: *a solemn occasion; solemn tones.*

so·lem·ni·ty |sə lĕm´nĭ tē| *n., pl.* **so·lem·ni·ties.** The condition or quality of being solemn; seriousness.

so·lo |sō´lō| *n., pl.* **so·los. 1.** A musical composition or passage for a single voice or instrument, with or without accompaniment. **2.** A performance of one or more such passages or compositions by a singer or instrumentalist.

sol·u·ble |sŏl´yə bəl| *adj.* Capable of being dissolved: *soluble aspirin.* [Late Latin *solūbilis,* from *solvere,* to loosen.]

so·lu·tion |sə lo͞o´shən| *n.* **1.** A mixture of two or more substances that appears to be uniform throughout except at the molecular level, and that is capable of forming by itself when the substances are in contact: *a solution of salt and water.* **2.** An answer to a problem. [Latin *solūtus,* from *solvere,* to loosen.]

sol·vent |sŏl´vənt| *adj.* Capable of dissolving another substance: *a solvent that removes paint.* [Latin *solvēns,* from *solvere,* to loosen.]

som·bre·ro |sŏm brâr´ō| *n., pl.* **som·bre·ros.** A large straw or felt hat with a broad brim and tall crown, worn in Mexico and the southwestern United States. [Spanish, hat, from *sombra,* shade.]

source |sôrs| *or* |sōrs| *n.* A person, place, book, etc., that supplies information: *What was your source for those facts?*

spe·cial·ize |spĕsh´ə līz´| *v.* **spe·cial·ized, spe·cial·iz·ing.** To focus on a special study, activity, or product: *a shop that specializes in sports clothes.*

spe·cies |spē´shēz´| *or* |-sēz´| *n., pl.* **spe·cies.** A group of similar animals or plants that are regarded as of the same kind and that are able to breed with one another.

spec·i·men |spĕs´ə mən| *n.* A sample used for analysis: *a blood specimen.* [Latin *specimen*, mark, example, from *specere*, to look at.]

spec·ta·cle |spĕk´tə kəl| *n.* **1.** A public performance or display. **2.** A marvel or curiosity: *the spectacle of the ocean's tides.* [From Latin *spectāre*, from *specere*, to look at.]

spec·tac·u·lar |spĕk tăk´yə lər| *adj.* Of the nature of a spectacle; sensational: *a spectacular view.* [From Latin *specere*, to look at.]

spec·ta·tor |spĕk´tā´tər| *n.* Someone who views an event; an observer or onlooker. [From Latin *spectāre*, from *specere*, to look at.]

spec·trum |spĕk´trəm| *n., pl.* **spec·tra** |spĕk´trə| *or* **spec·trums. 1.** The bands of color seen when white light, especially light from the sun, is broken up by refraction, as in a rainbow or by a prism. **2.** A broad range of related qualities, ideas, or activities: *a wide spectrum of emotions.* [Latin, appearance, image, form, from *specere*, to look at.]

spec·u·late |spĕk´yə lāt´| *v.* **spec·u·lat·ed, spec·u·lat·ing.** To think deeply on a given subject; ponder: *speculated about the meaning of life.* [Latin *speculārī*, to watch, from *specula*, watchtower, from *specere*, to look at.]

sphere |sfîr| *n.* **1.** A round, three-dimensional geometric shape, in which all the points on its surface are the same distance from the point in its center. **2.** An object or figure having this shape: *A globe is a sphere.*

sphinx |sfĭngks| *n., pl.* **sphinx·es. 1.** An ancient Egyptian figure with the body of a lion and the head of a man, ram, or hawk. **2. Sphinx.** The monumental sphinx having the head of a man at Giza, Egypt.

spore |spôr| *or* |spōr| *n.* A tiny, usually one-celled reproductive part produced by nonflowering plants such as ferns, mosses, and fungi.

spruce |sprōōs| *n.* Any of several evergreen trees with short needles and soft wood often used for paper pulp. [Short for *Spruce fir*, "Prussian fir," from *Spruce*, Prussia, Middle English *Sprewse,* alteration of *Pruce,* from Prussia.]

squall |skwôl| *n.* A brief, sudden, and violent windstorm, often accompanied by rain or snow.

squash |skwŏsh| *or* |skwôsh| *n.* A fleshy fruit related to the pumpkins and the gourds, eaten as a vegetable. [Short for *isquoutersquash,* from Massachuset *askōōtasquash: askāt-* + Proto-Algonquian *askw-,* plant + *ash.*]

stand |stănd| *v.* **stood** |stŏod|, **stand·ing. 1.** To take or stay in an upright position on the feet. **2.** *Chiefly British.* To be a candidate for public office; run: *stand for Parliament.*

stan·dard |stăn´dərd| *n.* **1.** A widely known and accepted measure used as a basis for a system of measures. **2.** A physical object from which such a measure can be determined under a given set of conditions. **3.** A rule or model used to judge the quality, value, or rightness of something. —*adj.* Serving as a standard of measurement, value, or quality: *a standard unit of volume.*

stan·za |stăn´zə| *n.* One of the divisions of a poem or song, composed of two or more lines. [From Latin *statuere*, to set up, stand.]

stat·ue |stăch´o͞o| *n.* A form representing a person or thing, made by an artist out of stone, metal, or another solid substance. [From Latin *statuere*, to set up, stand.]

stat·ute |stăch´o͞ot| *n.* A law enacted by a legislative body.

steppe |stĕp| *n.* A vast, somewhat arid plain, covered with grass and having few trees, as found in southeastern Europe and Siberia. [Russian *step'*, lowland.]

ste·re·o |stĕr´ē ō´| *or* |stîr-| *n., pl.* **ste·re·os. 1.** A sound-reproduction system that uses two separate channels to get more natural sound. **2.** Stereophonic sound.

ster·il·ize |stĕr´ə līz| *v.* **ster·il·ized, ster·il·iz·ing.** To make free from bacteria or germs.

steth·o·scope |stĕth´ə skōp´| *n.* An instrument used to listen to the sounds made within the body. [From Greek *stēthos*, chest + *skopein*, to see.]

Stock·holm |stŏk´hōm´| *or* |-hōlm´|. The capital of Sweden.

sto·ic |stō´ĭk| *adj.* Seemingly indifferent to pain, grief, etc. [From Greek *stōïkos*, from *stoa*, portico, the porch where Zeno taught.]

Stone·henge |stōn´hĕnj´| *n.* A prehistoric ceremonial ruin on the Salisbury Plain in Wiltshire, England, consisting of a circle of huge upright stone slabs and lintels, or horizontal beams, connecting some of the uprights.

Pronunciation Key

ă	pat	ŏ	pot	û	fur
ā	pay	ō	go	*th*	**the**
â	care	ô	paw, for	th	**th**in
ä	father	oi	**oi**l	hw	**wh**ich
ĕ	pet	o͝o	b**oo**k	zh	usual
ē	be	o͞o	b**oo**t	ə	**a**go, it**e**m
ĭ	pit	yo͞o	cute		penc**i**l, at**o**m
ī	ice	ou	**ou**t		circus
î	near	ŭ	cut	ər	butt**er**

---

stor·age |stôr´ĭj| *or* |stōr´-| *n.* **1.** The act of storing. **2.** A space for storing: *We have storage in the attic.*

stress |strĕs| *n.* The emphasis placed on the sound or syllable to be pronounced loudest in a word or phrase.

stuc·co |stŭk´ō| *n., pl.* **stuc·coes** or **stuc·cos.** A finish, usually of plaster and cement, used to cover walls: *walls of white stucco.*

stu·di·o |sto͞o´dē ō´| *or* |styo͞o´-| *n., pl.* **stu·di·os.** An artist's workroom.

sty·lus |stī´ləs| *n., pl.* **sty·lus·es** or **sty·li** |stī´lī´|. A sharp, pointed instrument used for writing: *Ancient peoples used a stylus to write by carving tablets of wax or clay.*

sub-. A prefix meaning: **1.** Under or beneath: **submarine. 2.** A subordinate or secondary part: **subdivision. 3.** Somewhat short of or less than: **subtropical.** [From Latin *sub*, under, from below.]

sub·jec·tive |səb jĕk´tĭv| *adj.* Existing within the mind or perception of an individual and not capable of being observed or experienced by anyone else. [From Old French *su(b)get*, from Latin *subicere*, to bring under: *sub-*, under + *jacere*, to throw.]

sub·poe·na |sə pē´nə| *n.* A court order requiring a person to appear in court and give testimony: *Issue a subpoena to the witness.*

sub·scribe |səb **skrīb´**| v. **sub·scribed, sub·scrib·ing.** To contract to receive and pay for a certain number of issues of a periodical: *subscribe to a magazine.* [From Latin *subscrībere*: *sub-*, under + *scrībere*, to write.]

sub·sist |səb **sĭst´**| v. To get nourishment and maintain life: *Horses can subsist entirely on grass.* [Latin *subsistere*, to stand still, stand up: *sub-*, from below, up + *sistere*, to cause to stand.]

suf·fice |sə **fīs´**| v. **suf·ficed, suf·fic·ing. 1.** To meet present needs; be sufficient: *The food will suffice until next week.* **2.** To be sufficient or adequate for: *enough water to suffice for three days.* [Middle English from Old French from Latin *sufficere*, to put under, substitute: *sub-*, under + *facere*, to do, make.]

suf·fi·cient |sə **fĭsh´**ənt| adj. As much as is needed; enough; adequate: *sufficient effort.*

sug·gest |səg **jĕst´**| or |sə-| v. To offer for consideration or action: *suggest that the books be stored.* [Latin *suggerere*, past participle of *suggestus*: sub, underneath + *gerere*, to carry.]

sug·ges·tion |səg **jĕs´**chən| or |sə-| n. The act of suggesting.

suite |swēt| n. An instrumental musical composition consisting of a set of pieces in the same or closely related keys: *The Nutcracker Suite is a well-known musical composition.*

sum·ma·rize |**sŭm´**ə rīz´| v. **sum·ma·rized, sum·ma·riz·ing.** To make a summary of; restate briefly.

su·per·no·va |soo͞ ´pər **nō´**və| n., pl. **su·per·no·vae** |soo͞ ´pər **nō´**vē´| or **su·per·no·vas.** A rare happening in which a star undergoes an extremely large explosion and becomes for a short time a very bright object radiating vast amounts of energy: *Scientists the world over studied the supernova.*

su·per·sti·tion |soo͞ ´pər **stĭsh´**ən| n. Any belief, practice, or rite unreasonably dependent on magic, chance, or dogma: *That's a silly superstition.* [Latin *superstitiō*, probably "a standing (in amazement and awe)," excessive fear, from *superstāre*, to stand over: *super*, over + *stāre*, to stand.]

sup·ple·ment |**sŭp´**lə mənt| n. A section added to a newspaper, book, document, etc., to give further information.

sur·mise |sər **mīz´**| v. **sur·mised, sur·mis·ing.** To conclude on slight evidence; suppose; guess: *I surmise that this will be a dry summer.*

sur·prise |sər **prīz´**| v. **sur·prised, sur·pris·ing.** To come upon suddenly and without warning. —n. The act of coming upon someone suddenly and without warning.

sur·veil·lance |sər **vā´**ləns| n. **1.** The action of observing or following closely: *The planes are used for surveillance.* **2.** The condition of being closely observed or followed, especially by the police or other authorities: *The house is under surveillance.* [French, from *surveiller*, to watch over: *sur-*, over + *veiller*, to watch.]

sus·pect |sə **spĕkt´**| v. To believe without being sure; imagine: *I suspect he got lost.* [From Latin *suspicere*, to look up at, watch: *sub-*, up from under + *specere*, to look at.]

sus·pend |sə **spĕnd´**| v. To cause to hang down from a place of attachment: *suspend a bell from a cow's neck.* [Latin *suspendere*, to hang up: *sub-*, up from under + *pendere*, to hang.]

sus·pense |sə **spĕns´**| n. Anxious uncertainty about what will happen: *I can't stand the suspense!* [Latin *suspendere*, to hang up: *sub-*, up from under + *pendere*, to hang.]

sus·pi·cious |sə **spĭsh´**əs| adj. Tending to suspect; distrustful: *Mary soon grew suspicious.*

syl·la·ble |**sĭl´**ə bəl| n. A single uninterrupted sound forming part of a word or in some cases an entire word: *an accented syllable.*

sym·bol·ize |sĭm´bə līz´| *v.* **sym·bol·ized, sym·bol·iz·ing.** To be or serve as a symbol of or for: *The poet uses rain to symbolize grief.*

sym·pho·ny |sĭm´fə nē| *n., pl.* **sym·pho·nies.** **1.** A usually long and elaborate sonata for orchestra, usually consisting of four movements. **2.** A symphony orchestra. [From Latin *symphonia* from Greek *sumphonia:* *sun-,* together + *phōnē,* voice, sound.]

syn·o·nym |sĭn´ə nĭm| *n.* A word having a meaning similar to that of another. For example, the words *wide* and *broad* are synonyms.

T

tab·u·late |tăb´yə lāt´| *v.* **tab·u·lat·ed, tab·u·lat·ing.** To condense and list, as in a table: *tabulate results.*

tack·y |tăk´ē| *adj.* **tack·i·er, tack·i·est.** *Informal.* Not stylish; dowdy: *tacky clothes.*

Taj Ma·hal |täzh´mə häl´| *or* |täj´|. A white marble mausoleum, or tomb, in Agra, India, built in the 17th century by Shah Jahan for his wife.

ta·ma·le |tə mä´lē| *n.* A highly seasoned Mexican dish made of fried chopped meat and crushed peppers or other foods rolled in cornmeal dough, wrapped in corn husks, and steamed.

tan·ger·ine |tăn´jə rēn´| *n.* A fruit related to the orange but somewhat smaller, having deep-orange skin that peels easily. [Short for *tangerine orange,* "orange of Tangier" (from which such oranges were first imported).]

tan·gi·ble |tăn´jə bəl| *adj.* **1.** Capable of being touched: *a tangible product, such as steel.* **2.** Concrete; real: *tangible evidence.*

ta·ran·tu·la |tə răn´chə lə| *n.* Any of several large, hairy, mostly tropical spiders that can give a painful but not seriously poisonous bite. [Italian *tarantola,* from Taranto, where it is common.]

tech·nique |tĕk nēk´| *n.* A systematic procedure or method by which a complicated task is accomplished, as in science or art.

tel·e·cast |tĕl´ĭ kăst´| *or* |-käst´| *v.* To broadcast (a program or programs) by television. —*n.* A television broadcast. [tele(vision) + (broad)cast.]

tel·e·gram |tĕl´ĭ grăm´| *n.* A message or communication sent by telegraph. [From Greek *tēle,* at a distance, far off + *gramma,* letter.]

tel·e·graph |tĕl´ĭ grăf´| *or* |-gräf´| *n.* A communications system in which a message is sent, either by wire or radio, to a receiving station. [From Greek *tēle-,* at a distance, far off + *-graph,* from *graphein,* to write.]

tel·e·phone |tĕl´ə fōn´| *n.* An instrument that reproduces or receives sound, especially speech, at a distance. [From Greek *tēle-,* at a distance, far off + *phōnē,* sound, voice.]

Pronunciation Key

ă	pat	ŏ	pot	û	fur
ā	pay	ō	go	*th*	the
â	care	ô	paw, for	th	thin
ä	father	oi	oil	hw	which
ĕ	pet	ŏŏ	book	zh	usual
ē	be	ōō	boot	ə	ago, item
ĭ	pit	yōō	cute		pencil, atom
ī	ice	ou	out		circus
î	near	ŭ	cut	ər	butter

Spelling Dictionary

tel·e·scope |tĕl´ĭ skōp´| *n.* A device that uses an arrangement of lenses, mirrors, or both to collect visible light, allowing observation or photographic recording of distant objects. [From Greek *tēle-*, at a distance, far off + *skopos*, watcher, from *skopein*, to see.]

tel·e·thon |tĕl´ə thŏn´| *n.* A long, continuous television program, usually to raise funds for charity. [From Greek *tēle-*, at a distance + (mara)thon.]

tem·per·a·ture |tĕm´pər ə chər| *or* |-prə chər| *n.* **1.** The relative hotness or coldness of a body or environment. **2.** A numerical measure of hotness or coldness referred to a standard scale.

tem·po |tĕm´pō| *n., pl.* **tem·pos** or **tem·pi** |tĕm´pē|. The speed at which a musical composition is played: *The song has a lively tempo.*

tem·po·rar·y |tĕm´pə rĕr´ē| *adj.* Lasting or used for a limited time only; not permanent.

ten·nis |tĕn´ĭs| *n.* A sport played between two persons (singles) or two pairs of persons (doubles) on a court divided in two by a net. A player strikes a ball with a racket, the object being to make the ball bounce in the opposing half of the court in such a way that the opposition cannot return it.

tes·ti·fy |tĕs´tə fī´| *v.* **tes·ti·fied, tes·ti·fy·ing, tes·ti·fies.** To make a declaration under oath: *Two witnesses testified against him.*

tes·ti·mo·ny |tĕs´tə mō´nē| *n., pl.* **tes·ti·mo·nies.** A declaration or affirmation made under oath: *the testimony of a handwriting expert.*

tex·ture |tĕks´chər| *n.* The composition or structure of a substance: *smooth texture.*

the·o·ry |thē´ə rē´| *or* |thîr´ē| *n., pl.* **the·o·ries.** An assumption or guess based on limited information or knowledge.

ther·a·peu·tic |thĕr´ə pyoo´tĭk| *adj.* Having the capability of healing or curing: *a therapeutic bath.*

ther·mal |thûr´məl| *adj.* Of, using, producing, or caused by heat. [From Greek *thermē*, heat, from *thermos*, hot.]

ther·mom·e·ter |thər mŏm´ĭ tər| *n.* An instrument that measures and indicates temperature, especially one that consists of a glass tube in which a liquid expands or contracts to reach a level that depends on the temperature. [From Greek *thermē*, heat, from *thermos*, hot + *metron*, measure.]

ther·mos |thûr´məs| *n., pl.* **ther·mos·es.** A container having double walls, a reflective coating, and a vacuum-insulated space between the walls, used to keep its contents from gaining or losing heat. [From Greek *thermos*, hot.]

ther·mo·stat |thûr´mə stăt´| *n.* A device that automatically controls a piece of heating or cooling equipment in such a way as to keep the temperature nearly constant: *I set the thermostat at 68 degrees.* [From Greek *thermos*, hot + *statēs*, one that causes to stand.]

the·sis |thē´sĭs| *n., pl.* **the·ses** |thē´sēz´|. Something stated or put forth for consideration, especially by a person who plans to maintain it by argument: *Her thesis is that people living in warm climates are generally happier.*

threat |thrĕt| *n.* **1.** An expression of an intention to inflict pain, injury, evil, etc.: *Kim's threat frightened Molly.* **2.** An indication of impending danger or harm: *The night air held a threat of frost.*

threat·en |thrĕt´n| *v.* To utter a threat against.

tight |tīt| *adj. Jargon.* Well-rehearsed: *The group will perform when it sounds tight.*

tis·sue |tĭsh´oo| *n.* **1.** A group or type of animal or plant cells that are similar in form and function, and often make up a particular organ or part: *lung tissue; leaf tissue.* **2.** Any cellular material of an organism: *muscle tissue.*

To·ky·o |tō´kē ō|. The capital and largest city of Japan, in the eastern part of the island of Honshu.

to·ma·to |tə mā´tō| *or* |-mä´-| *n., pl.*
to·ma·toes. The fleshy, usually reddish fruit of a widely cultivated plant that is eaten raw or cooked as a vegetable. [From Spanish, from Nahuatl *tomatl.*]

tongue |tŭng| *n.* A fleshy, muscular organ, attached in most vertebrates to the bottom of the mouth, that is the main organ of taste, moves to aid in chewing and swallowing, and in human beings, acts in speech. *Idiom.* **on the tip of (one's) tongue.** On the verge of being remembered or said.

to·pog·ra·phy |tə pŏg´rə fē| *n., pl.*
to·pog·ra·phies. 1. The technique or method of representing the exact physical features of a place or region on a map.
2. The physical features of a place or region. [From Greek *topographein,* to describe a place: *topos,* a place + *graphein,* to write.]

tor·til·la |tôr tē´yə| *n.* A round, flat Mexican bread made from cornmeal and water and baked on a grill. [American Spanish, diminutive of Spanish *torta,* a round cake.]

tor·toise |tôr´təs| *n.* A turtle, especially one that lives on land.

tour·na·ment |tŏŏr´nə mənt| *or* |tûr´-| *n.* A contest composed of a series of elimination games or trials: *a tennis tournament.*

tour·ni·quet |tŏŏr´nĭ kĭt| *or* |tûr´-| *n.* Any device, such as a tight band with a pad under it to concentrate the pressure, used to stop temporarily the flow of blood in a large artery in one of the limbs: *A tourniquet stopped the bleeding.*

trag·ic |trăj´ĭk| *adj.* **1.** Of dramatic tragedy. **2.** Bringing or involving great misfortune, suffering, or sadness. [From French *tragique,* from Greek *tragikos,* from *tragos,* goat.]

tran·scribe |trăn skrīb´| *v.* **tran·scribed, tran·scrib·ing.** To write or type a copy of; write out fully, as from shorthand notes. [Latin *transcrībere,* to copy, "write over": *trans-,* from one place to another, across + *scrībere,* to write.]

trans·mis·sion |trăns mĭsh´ən| *or* |trănz-| *n.* An assembly of gears and associated parts by which power is carried from an engine or motor to a load, as in an automobile.

trans·port |trăns pôrt´| *or* |-pōrt´| *v.* To carry from one place to another: *transport cargo.* [Latin *trānsportāre: trāns,* from one place to another + *portāre,* to carry.]

trau·ma |trou´mə| *or* |trô´-| *n.* A wound or injury, usually inflicted suddenly by some physical means.

treach·e·ry |trĕch´ə rē| *n., pl.*
treach·er·ies. Willful betrayal of trust; treason.

tri-. A prefix meaning "three": **triangle.** [From Latin *tres,* three.]

Pronunciation Key

ă	pat	ŏ	pot	û	fur
ā	pay	ō	go	*th*	**the**
â	care	ô	paw, for	th	thin
ä	father	oi	oil	hw	which
ĕ	pet	ŏŏ	book	zh	usual
ē	be	ōō	boot	ə	ago, item
ĭ	pit	yōō	cute		pencil, atom
ī	ice	ou	out		circus
î	near	ŭ	cut	ər	butter

tri·an·gle |trī´ăng´gəl| *n.* A closed plane geometric figure formed by three points not in a straight line connected by three line segments. [From Latin *triangulus*, three-angled: *tri-*, three + *angulus*, angle.]

tri·ath·lon |trī ăth´lən| *or* |-lŏn´| *n.* A race consisting of three parts: cross-country running, long-distance swimming, and long-distance bicycling. [Latin *tri-*, three + Greek *athlon*, contest.]

trig·o·nom·e·try |trĭg´ə nŏm´ĭ trē| *n.* A branch of mathematics concerned with calculations relating to triangles. [New Latin *trigonometria*: Greek *trigōnon*, triangle (from *tri-*, three + *-gon*, from *gōnia*, angle) + *-metry*, from Greek *metron*, meter, measure.]

tri·o |trē´ō| *n., pl.* **tri·os.** A group of three. [Italian variant of Latin *tria*, three.]

trip·le |trĭp´əl| *adj.* **1.** Of or having three parts; threefold. **2.** Three times as much or as many; multiplied by three. [From Latin *triplus*: *tri-*, three + *-plus*, fold.]

trip·let |trĭp´lĭt| *n., pl.* **trip·lets.** One of three children born at one birth. [From Latin *triplus* (*tri-*, three + *-plus*, fold) + et.]

tri·pod |trī´pŏd´| *n.* An adjustable stand with three legs, used especially to support a camera. [Latin *tripūs*, from Greek *tripous*, three-footed: *tri-*, three + *-pous*, foot.]

tri·umph |trī´əmf| *v.* To be victorious; win; prevail: *triumph over prejudice.* —*n.* The instance or fact of being victorious; success. [From Latin *triumphus*, a triumph.]

tri·um·phant |trī ŭm´fənt| *adj.* Victorious; successful: *a triumphant political campaign.*

triv·et |trĭv´ĭt| *n.* **1.** A three-legged stand for holding a kettle or pot over or near an open fire. **2.** A metal stand, usually with short legs, placed under a hot dish or platter. [Latin *tripēs*, "three-footed": *tri-*, three + *pēs*, foot.]

T-square |tē´skwâr´| *n.* A ruler with a short crosspiece at one end, used for drawing parallel lines.

tun·dra |tŭn´drə| *n.* A cold, treeless area of arctic regions, having only low-growing mosses, lichens, and stunted shrubs as plant life. [Russian, from Lapp *tundar*, akin to Finnish *tunturi*, an arctic hill, a bare hill.]

type·face |tīp´fās´| *n.* In printing, the size and style of printed characters.

U

un·a·bridged |ŭn´ə brĭjd´| *adj.* Not condensed, or shortened: *an unabridged book.*

uni-. A prefix meaning "one, single": **unilateral.** [Latin, from *ūnus*, one.]

u·ni·fy |yōō´nə fī´| *v.* **u·ni·fied, u·ni·fy·ing, u·ni·fies.** To make into a unit; unite: *Pride in their school unified the students.* [Old French *unifier*, from Late Latin *ūnificāre*: *uni-*, from Latin *ūnus*, one + *ficāre*, to make.]

u·nique |yōō nēk´| *adj.* Having no equal or equivalent; being the only one in kind, excellence, etc.: *a unique design for a house.* [French, from Latin *ūnicus*, only, solo, from *ūnus*, one.]

u·ni·son |yōō´nĭ sən| *or* |-zən| *n.* In music, the combination of two or more tones of the same pitch sounding at the same time. [Medieval Latin *ūnisonus*, of the same sound: *uni-*, from Latin *ūnus*, one + *sonus*, sound.]

u·nite |yōō nīt´| *v.* **u·nit·ed, u·nit·ing.** To bring together or join so as to form a whole: *unite the pieces to make a set.*

u·ni·ty |yōō´nĭ tē| *n., pl.* **u·ni·ties.** The condition of being united into a single whole; oneness: *In unity there is strength.* [From Latin *ūnitās*, from *ūnus*, one.]

u·ni·verse |yōō´nə vûrs´| *n.* All the matter and space that exists, considered as a whole; the cosmos. [From Latin *ūniversum*, the whole world, neuter of *ūniversus*, whole, "turned into one": *uni-*, from *ūnus*, one + *versus*, past participle of *vertere*, to turn.]

u·ni·ver·si·ty |yo͞o'nə **vûr**'sĭ tē| *n., pl.* **u·ni·ver·si·ties.** A school of higher learning that offers degrees and includes programs of study in graduate school, professional schools, and regular college divisions. [From Medieval Latin *ūniversitās (magistrorum et scholarium)*, "society (of masters and students)," from Latin *ūniversus*, whole: *uni-*, one + *versus*, turned.]

-ure. A suffix that forms nouns and means: **1.** An action or process: **erasure. 2.** A function, office, or group: **legislature.**

us·age |yo͞o'sĭj| *or* |-zĭj| *n.* **1.** The act or manner of using something; use or employment: *a car ruined by rough usage.* **2.** The customary practice or usual way of doing something.

u·til·ize |yo͞ot'l īz'| *v.* **u·til·ized, u·til·iz·ing.** To use for a certain purpose: *utilizing the stream's water to run the mill.* —**u'til·i·za'tion** *n.*

V

vac·u·um |văk'yo͞o əm| *or* |-yo͞om| *v.* **1.** To clean with a vacuum cleaner. **2. a.** The absence of matter. **b.** A space that is empty of matter. **c.** A space containing a gas at very low pressure.

vague |vāg| *adj.* **vagu·er, vagu·est. 1.** Not clearly expressed; lacking clarity: *a vague statement.* **2.** Lacking definite shape, form, or character: *the vague outline of a sailing ship on the horizon.* [Old French from Latin *vagus*, wandering, undecided, vague.]

val·e·dic·to·ri·an |văl'ĭ dĭk tôr'ē ən| *or* |-tōr'-| *n.* In some schools and colleges, the student ranking highest in the graduating class, who delivers the farewell address at commencement. [From Latin *valedīcere*, to say farewell: *valē*, vale (farewell) + *dīcere*, to say.]

Pronunciation Key

ă	pat	ŏ	pot	û	fur
ā	pay	ō	go	*th*	the
â	care	ô	paw, for	th	thin
ä	father	oi	oil	hw	which
ĕ	pet	o͝o	book	zh	usual
ē	be	o͞o	boot	ə	ago, item
ĭ	pit	yo͞o	cute		pencil, atom
ī	ice	ou	out		circus
î	near	ŭ	cut	ər	butter

valve |vălv| *n.* Any of various mechanical devices that control the flow of liquids, gases, or loose materials through pipes, channels, etc., by blocking and uncovering openings.

va·nil·la |və nĭl'ə| *n.* **1.** A flavoring made from the seed pods of a tropical orchid. **2.** Also **vanilla bean.** The long, beanlike seed pod from which this flavoring is obtained. [Spanish *vainilla*, "little sheath" (from its elongated fruit).]

va·por |vā'pər| *n.* Any faintly visible suspension of fine particles of matter in the air, as mist, fumes, or smoke.

va·ri·e·ty |və rī'ĭ tē| *n., pl.* **va·ri·e·ties. 1.** A number of different kinds, usually within the same general grouping; an assortment: *a variety of outdoor activities.* **2.** A kind or form: *plants of every variety.* [Old French *variété*, from Latin *varietās*, from *varius*, various.]

var·i·ous |vâr´ē əs| *adj.* Of different kinds.

ve·hi·cle |vē´ĭ kəl| *n.* A device for transporting passengers, goods, equipment, etc. [French from Latin *vehiculum,* from *vehere,* to carry.]

ve·hic·u·lar |vē hĭk´yə lər| *adj.* Of or being a vehicle or vehicles: *vehicular traffic.*

Vel·cro |vĕl´krō´| *n.* A trademark for a fastening tape used for cloth products. [vel(our) + cro(chet).]

ven·ti·late |vĕn´tl āt´| *v.* **ven·ti·lat·ed, ven·ti·lat·ing.** To cause fresh air to circulate through (a chamber, enclosure, etc.).

ver·dict |vûr´dĭkt| *n.* The decision reached by a jury at the end of a trial. [From Latin *vērus* + *dit,* saying, from Latin *dīcere,* to speak, say.]

verse |vûrs| *n.* **1.** Writing that has a meter or rhyme; poetry. **2.** A stanza of a poem or song.

vet·er·i·nar·i·an |vĕt´ər ə nâr´ē ən| *or* |vĕt´rə-| *n.* A person specially trained and qualified to give medical treatment to animals.

vic·tim |vĭk´tĭm| *n.* Someone made to suffer or undergo difficulty, as by trickery, unfair practices, or misunderstanding: *the victim of a hoax.*

vid·e·o |vĭd´ē ō´| *n., pl.* **vid·e·os. 1.** The visual part of a television broadcast. **2.** Television: *a star of stage, screen, and video.* **3.** A videocassette or videotape. [vi(sual) + (au)dio.]

vil·lain |vĭl´ən| *n.* A main character who harms or threatens the good or heroic characters in a story, play, etc.

vi·o·late |vī´ə lāt´| *v.* **vi·o·lat·ed, vi·o·lat·ing.** To break; disregard: *violate a law; violate a promise.* [From Latin *violāre,* from *vīs,* force.]

vi·o·la·tion |vī´ə lā´shən| *n.* **1.** The act of violating or the condition of being violated: *the violation of a truce.* **2.** An example of this: *a traffic violation.*

vis·i·ble |vĭz´ə bəl| *adj.* **1.** Capable of being seen; perceptible to the eye: *Only one ninth of an iceberg is visible above the water.* **2.** Easily noticed; clear; apparent: *showing visible signs of impatience.*

vis·u·al·ize |vĭzh´ōō ə līz´| *v.* **vis·u·al·ized, vis·u·al·iz·ing.** To form a mental image or vision of: *It is difficult to visualize infinity.*

vi·ta·min |vī´tə mĭn| *n.* Any of various fairly complex organic compounds that occur in small amounts in animal and plant tissues and that are needed for the continuation of normal life functions: *vitamin C.*

vo·cab·u·lar·y |vō kăb´yə lĕr´ē| *n., pl.* **vo·cab·u·lar·ies.** The sum of words used by a particular person, profession, etc.: *the writer's rich vocabulary; the vocabulary of economics.*

vol·ca·no |vŏl kā´nō| *n., pl.* **vol·ca·noes** *or* **vol·ca·nos. 1.** Any opening in the crust of the earth through which molten rock, dust, ash, and hot gases are thrown forth. **2.** A mountain or other elevation formed by the material thrown forth in this way. [From Latin *Volcānus,* after *Vulcan,* the god of fire and metalworking in Roman mythology.]

volt |vōlt| *n.* A unit for measuring the force of an electric current. [After Count Alessandro *Volta* (1745–1827), Italian physicist.]

vul·ner·a·ble |vŭl´nər ə bəl| *adj.* **1.** Open to danger or attack; unprotected: *The small boat was vulnerable to the crashing waves.* **2.** Easily hurt: *vulnerable to insult.*

wack·y |wăk´ē| *adj.* **wack·i·er, wack·i·est.** *Slang.* Crazy or silly; nutty.

waf·fle |wŏf´əl| *n.* A light, crisp batter cake baked in a waffle iron, an appliance having hinged metal plates marked with an indented pattern, as of squares, that is pressed into the batter as it bakes. [Dutch *wafel.*]

wal·rus |wôl´rəs| *n., pl.* **wal·rus·es** or **wal·rus.** A large sea animal of Arctic regions, related to the seals and sea lions and having tough wrinkled skin and large tusks. [Dutch, akin to Danish *hvalros.*]

wea·pon |wĕp´ən| *n.* Any instrument or device used to attack another or to defend oneself from an attack.

who's |hōōz| Contraction of *who is* or *who has.*

whose |hōōz| *pron.* **1.** The possessive form of *who: Do you know whose book this is?* **2.** The possessive form of *which: an old oak in whose branches I sat.*

wol·ver·ine |wŏŏl´və rēn´| *n.* A flesh-eating animal of northern regions, having thick, dark fur and a bushy tail.

xy·lo·phone |zī´lə fōn´| *n.* A percussion instrument consisting of a series of wooden bars tuned to a chromatic scale and played by striking the bars with wooden mallets. [From Greek *xulon,* wood + *phōnē,* sound, voice.]

yacht |yät| *n.* A relatively small sailing or motor-operated vessel used for pleasure trips or racing. —*v.,* To sail, cruise, or race in a yacht. [Earlier *yaught,* from obsolete Dutch *jaghte,* short for *jacht (schip),* "chasing (ship)," from *jagen,* to chase, hunt.]

Pronunciation Key

ă	pat	ŏ	pot	û	fur
ā	pay	ō	go	*th*	the
â	care	ô	paw, for	th	thin
ä	father	oi	oil	hw	which
ĕ	pet	ŏŏ	book	zh	usual
ē	be	ōō	boot	ə	ago, item
ĭ	pit	yōō	cute		pencil, atom
ī	ice	ou	out		circus
î	near	ŭ	cut	ər	butter

Yu·ca·tán |yōō´kə tän´|. A peninsula in southeastern Mexico and northern Central America.

-yze. A suffix that forms verbs and means "to become, cause to become, or form into": **paralyze.** [Late Latin, *-izere.*]

zep·pe·lin |zĕp´ə lĭn| *n.* A rigid airship with a long, tapering body, supported by cells containing a gas that is lighter than air. [Invented by Count Ferdinand von *Zeppelin.*]

zin·ni·a |zĭn´ē ə| *n.* A garden plant with showy, variously colored flowers. [After Johann Gottfried *Zinn* (1727–1759), German botanist and physician.]

Content Index

Numbers in **boldface** indicate pages on which a skill is introduced as well as references to the Capitalization and Punctuation Guide.

Dictionary Skills

alphabetical order, **26**
dictionary, using a, 32, **281**
etymology, **158**
guide words, **26**
homographs, **74**
parts of an entry, **32**, 281
parts of speech, **92**
prefixes, **200**
pronunciation, **140**
spelling table, **56**, 279
stress, **128**
suffixes, **200**
usage notes, **110**
variations, spelling and punctuation, **176**
word forms, **206**

Language Arts Skills

abbreviations, **247–248**
  of state names, **248**
  of titles, **247**
  of words in addresses, **247**
  of words used in business, **247**
agreement, subject and verb, **51**
capitalization, **250–252**
  in addresses, **135, 252**
  in dates, **135**
  in greetings and closings in letters, **147, 251**
  of proper adjectives, **251**
  of proper nouns, **135, 251**
commas
  in addresses, **135, 253**
  with appositives, **39, 253**
  in compound sentences, **15, 253**
  in dates, **135, 253**
  with interrupters, **123, 253**
  in letters, **147, 254**

in a series, **123, 253**
comparing with adjectives, **63**
comparing with adverbs, **69**
fragments, **21**
negatives, **87**
parts of a business letter, **256**
parts of a friendly letter, **255**
pronouns, **183, 195, 213, 219**
  compound objects, **195**
  compound subjects, **195**
  indefinite pronouns, **213**
  object pronouns, **183**
  after prepositions, **219**
  subject pronouns, **183**
proper adjectives, **105**
proper nouns, **105**
punctuation, **252–254**
quotation marks, **165, 249–250**
run-on sentences, **21**
titles, 171, **249–251**
using adjective or adverb, **99**

Literature

46, 82, 118, 154, 190, 226

Proofreading

for adjectives and adverbs
  of comparison, **63, 69**
  using correctly, **99**
for agreement
  of indefinite pronouns, **213**
  subject-verb, **51,** 83
for capitalization
  of dates, addresses, **135**
  in letters, **147**
  of proper adjectives, **105,** 119
  of proper nouns, **105,** 119
  of titles, **171**

for commas
  with appositives, **39**
  in compound sentences, **15,** 47
  in dates and addresses, **135**
  with interrupters, **123**
  in letters, **147**
  in a series, **123,** 155
for direct quotations, **165**
for double negatives, **87**
for fragments or run-ons, **21**
for letter form, **147,** 191
for pronouns, **183,** 227
  in compound subjects and objects, **195**
  after prepositions, **219**
for spelling. *See* Table of Contents

Spelling

See Table of Contents.
alphabetical order, 50, 98, 146, 194
self-assessment, 14, 20, 38, 50, 62, 68, 86, 98, 104, 122, 134, 146, 164, 170, 182, 194, 212, 218
spelling strategies, 12, 18, 24, 30, 36, 42–45, 48, 54, 60, 66, 72, 78–81, 84, 90, 96, 102, 108, 114–117, 120, 126, 132, 138, 144, 150–153, 156, 162, 168, 174, 180, 186–189, 192, 198, 204, 210, 216, 222, 225, 229–246
See also Vocabulary.

Spelling Across the Curriculum

art, 131
careers, 53, 89, 203, 221

352

health, 137, 179
industrial arts, 149
language arts, 17, 101, 161, 167, 209
life skills, 197
math, 59, 173
performing arts, 23, 107, 125, 215
science, 29, 35, 95, 113, 185
social studies, 41, 65, 71, 77, 143

Spelling and Meaning

absorbed prefixes
  ad-, **156,** 186, 192, 222, 225, 241, 244
  con-, **156,** 186, 189, 192, 222, 225, 241, 244
  in-, **156,** 186, 189, 192, 222, 225, 241
  ob-, **192,** 222
consonant changes, **12,** 42, 45, **48,** 78, 81, 229, 232
Greek word parts
  auto, **18,** 42, 229
  cris/crit, **112**
  cycl, **54,** 78, 232
  gram, **54,** 78, 232
  graph, **18,** 42, 229
  meter/metry, **54,** 78, 232
  phon, **18,** 42, 229
  phys, **54,** 78, 232
  scope, **88**
  therm, **54,** 78, 232
index, 271–278
Latin roots
  cis, **117**
  cred, **184**
  dict/dic, **162,** 186, 241
  fract/frag, **64**
  gest, **81**
  ject, **126,** 150, 238
  mem, **189**
  pend/pens/pent, **162,** 186, 241

pet, **225**
port, **126,** 150, 238
rupt, **90,** 114, 235
scrib/scrip/script, **90,** 114, 235
sign, **45**
sist, **202**
solve, **153**
spect/spec, **90,** 114, 235
sta/sti/st, **126,** 150, 238
vowel changes, **84,** 114, 117, **120,** 150, 153, 235, 238

Test-Taking Tactics

analogies, 16, 52, 88, 130, 166, 208
sentence completion, 64, 184, 202
vocabulary in context, 34, 100, 124

Thinking Skills

analogies, **13,** 16, 44, 49, 52, 78, 79, 85, 88, 103, 116, 127, 130, 139, 150, 163, 166, 175, 181, 186, 205, 208, 222, 230, 231, 232, 233, 234, 235, 238, 241, 243, 245
analyzing, 45, 46, 81, 82, 117, 118, 153, 154, 189, 190, 225, 226
classifying, 19, 37, 43, 55, 103, 139, 145, 151, 175, 187, 211, 232, 238, 239, 240, 242, 246
creative thinking, 15, 27, 33, 51, 63, 69, 87, 99, 105, 111, 123, 141, 147, 159, 177, 183, 195, 207, 213, 219
critical thinking, 17, 23, 29, 35, 41, 53, 59, 65, 71, 77, 89, 95, 101, 113, 125, 131, 137, 143, 149, 161,

167, 173, 179, 185, 197, 203, 209, 215, 221
making inferences, 19, 20, 25, 31, 32, 37, 38, 42, 43, 44, 55, 61, 62, 67, 68, 73, 78, 79, 81, 86, 91, 104, 109, 114, 116, 118, 121, 127, 133, 134, 150–152, 157, 163, 164, 169, 175, 181, 186, 188, 199, 200, 205, 211, 212, 217, 218, 222–224, 229–230, 232, 233, 235, 239, 241, 244, 245
using graphic organizers, 32, 40, 47, 63, 69, 83, 119, 140, 155, 160, 191, 208, 227

Vocabulary

absorbed prefixes. *See* Spelling and Meaning.
antonyms, **76,** 130, 169, 193, 208, 235, 237, 244
blends, 210, **214**
British English, **220**
clipped forms, **214**
cloze activities, 13, 17, 19, 23, 29, 31, 35, 41, 42–44, 49, 53, 59, 61, 64, 65, 67, 70, 71, 77, 78–80, 85, 88, 89, 95, 97, 101, 107, 112, 113, 114–116, 121, 125, 131, 137, 143, 145, 149, 150–152, 161, 167, 173, 179, 181, 184, 185, 186, 188, 196, 197, 202, 203, 205, 209, 215, 221, 222, 224, 229–231, 233–234, 236–238, 240, 242, 244–246
compound words, **58,** 210
connotation, **160**

Content Index

content area vocabulary, 17, 23, 29, 35, 41, 53, 59, 65, 71, 77, 89, 95, 101, 107, 113, 125, 131, 137, 143, 149, 161, 167, 173, 179, 185, 197, 203, 209, 215, 221

definitions, 13, 28, 31, 37, 43–44, 49, 55, 61, 67, 73, 80, 85, 91, 97, 103, 109, 114, 116, 121, 127, 133, 139, 145, 150, 152, 157, 163, 169, 188, 193, 199, 217, 222, 224, 229–231, 232, 234, 236, 238, 241, 243, 246

exact words, **136**

figurative language, **94**

Greek word parts. *See* Spelling and Meaning.

homophones, **36,** 44, 231

idioms, **148**

informal words, **34**

jargon, **124**

Latin roots. *See* Spelling and Meaning.

multiple meanings, **100**

prefixes
  ab-, **132, 151,** 239
  ad-, **132,** 151, 156, 186, 239, 241, 244
  anti-, **132,** 151, 239
  bi-, **24,** 43, 230
  con-, **156,** 186, 241, 244
  hept-, **26**
  in-, **156,** 186, 241
  ob-, **192**
  oct-, **28**
  post-, **132,** 151, 239
  quad-, **28**
  quint-, **28**
  semi-, **24,** 43, 230
  sept-, **28**
  tri-, **24,** 43, 230
  uni-, **24,** 43, 230

regional differences, **178**

slang, **142**

suffixes
  -able, **168,** 170, 187, 242
  adjective, **168,** 187, 242
  -ance, **198,** 222, 244
  -ant, **198,** 222, 244
  -ary, **96,** 115, 236
  -ate, **52**
  -dom, **60,** 79, 233
  -en, **52**
  -ence, **198,** 222, 244
  -ent, **198,** 222, 244
  -ery, **96,** 115, 236
  -ible, **168,** 170, 187, 242
  -ise, **204,** 223, 245
  -ize, **204,** 223, 245
  -ment, **60,** 79, 233
  noun, **60,** 79, 233
  -ory, **96,** 115, 236
  -ure, **60,** 79, 233
  verb, **204,** 223, 245
  -yze, **204,** 223, 245

synonyms, **40,** 73, 91, 97, 106, 172, 187, 193, 199, 208, 217, 231, 233, 235, 237, 240, 242, 243

test-taking tactics
  analogies, 16, 52, 88, 130, 166, 208
  sentence completion, 64, 184, 202
  vocabulary-in-context, 34, 100, 124

thesaurus, using a, **16, 257–258**

word origins
  French, **102,** 115, 236
  names, **30,** 43, 230
  other languages, **138,** 151, **239**
  places, **174,** 187, 242
  Spanish, **66,** 79, 233

words new to English, **210,** 223, 245

Writing

types of writing
  advertisement, 33, 195
  announcement, 135
  article, 15
  brochure, 207
  cause and effect, 83
  comparison and contrast, 21
  creative writing, 15, 27, 33, 39, 51, 63, 69, 87, 99, 105, 111, 123, 141, 147, 159, 177, 183, 195, 207, 213, 219
  description, 57, 63, 99, 105, 155
  dictionary entry, 165
  directions, 129
  essay, 75
  flier, 111
  interview questions, 93
  letter, 39, 123, 147
  menu, 177
  movie review, 69
  paragraph, 219
  personal narrative, 47, 51, 183
  persuasion, 87, 191
  poster, 141
  proposal, 213
  report, 171, 227
  script, 27
  sentences, 38, 86, 122, 182, 218
  story, 119, 159
  summary, 201
writing process
  cause and effect, 83
  description, 155
  personal narrative, 47
  persuasive letter, 191
  research report, 227
  story, 119

Credits

Design and Electronic Production: Kirchoff/Wohlberg, Inc.

Illustration   **4** Tom Leonard   **20** Mike DiGiorgio   **29** Arvis Stewart   **38** Andrea Wallace   **56** Colin Hayes   **70** Tom Leonard   **76** Tom Leonard   **86** Mike DiGiorgio   **94** Tom Leonard   **95** Arvis Stewart   **106** Kristen Goeters   **112** Tom Leonard   **128** Tom Leonard   **136** Kristen Goeters   **142** Ted Williams   **148** Rob Schuster   **160** Arvis Stewart   **178** Sharron O'Neil   **182** Mike DiGiorgio   **200** Mike DiGiorgio   **212** Ted Williams   **214** Ted Williams   **220** Rob Schuster

Assignment Photography   Gist, Inc., **10, 11** (bottom), **15** (top), **21, 23** (top), **27** (top), **33** (top), **35** (top), **39** (right), **41** (top), **51, 53** (top), **57, 59** (top), **65** (top), **69, 71** (top), **75, 77** (top), **82, 87** (top), **89** (top), **93, 95** (top), **101** (top), **105, 107** (top), **111** (top), **113** (top), **118, 123, 125, 131** (top), **135, 137** (top), **141, 143** (top right), **147, 149** (top), **154, 159, 161** (top), **163, 165, 167** (top), **170, 171, 173** (top), **177, 179** (top), **185, 197** (top), **201** (top), **203** (top right), **207, 209** (top), **213** (top), **219, 221 (**top), **226**

Photography   **3** Michael T. Sedam/Corbis;   **4** Kevin Schafer/Corbis;   **5** Robbie Jack/Corbis;   **6** (top), George Lepp/Tony Stone Images;   **6** (bottom), Culver Pictures **7** (top), Image Copyright © 2000 PhotoDisc, Inc.;   **7** (bottom), © The Topps Company;   **8** Microfield/Photo Researchers;   **11** (top), Gianni Dagli Orti/Corbis;   **13** Image Copyright © 2000 PhotoDisc, Inc.;   **14** Charles Gupton/Stock Boston;   **15** (bottom), Image Copyright © 2000 PhotoDisc, Inc.;   **17** (top), Image Copyright © 2000 PhotoDisc, Inc.;   **17** (bottom), The Granger Collection, New York;   **19** Image Copyright © 2000 PhotoDisc, Inc.;   **23** (bottom), Lynn Goldsmith/Corbis;   **25** Roger Ball/The Stock Market;   **26** Image Copyright © 2000 PhotoDisc, Inc.;   **27** (bottom), Image Copyright © 2000 PhotoDisc, Inc.;   **28** Jeffrey L. Rotman/Corbis;   **29** (top), Image Copyright © 2000 PhotoDisc, Inc.;   **31** Mark Reinstein/FPG International;   **33** (bottom), Image Copyright © 2000 PhotoDisc, Inc.;   **35** (top inset), Bernd Kappelmeyer/FPG International;   **35** (bottom), Michael T. Sedam/Corbis;   **37** Joseph Sohm/Corbis;   **39** (left), Richard T. Nowitz/Corbis;   **41** (bottom), Dean Conger/Corbis;   **46** Image Copyright © 2000 PhotoDisc, Inc.;   **49** Image Copyright © 2000 PhotoDisc, Inc.;   **53** (bottom), Ron Chapple/FPG International;   **55** Travelpix/FPG International;   **59** (bottom), Lee Snider/Corbis;   **61** Image Copyright © 2000 PhotoDisc, Inc.;   **62** Image Copyright © 2000 PhotoDisc, Inc.;   **63** Michael Yamashita/Corbis;   **64** Tom Skrivan/The Stock Market;   **65** (bottom), Kevin Schafer/Corbis;   **67** Image Copyright © 2000 PhotoDisc, Inc.;   **68** Danny Lehman/Corbis;   **71** (bottom), Stanley Schoenberger/Grant Heilman Photography;   **73** Grant Heilman Photography;   **77** (bottom), Jonathan Blair/Corbis;   **85** Raymond Gehman/Corbis;   **87** Image Copyright © 2000 PhotoDisc, Inc.;   **89** (bottom), Richard T. Nowitz/Corbis;   **91** Richard A. Cooke/Corbis;   **97** The Everett Collection;   **98** Image Copyright © 2000 PhotoDisc, Inc.;   **99** Image Copyright © 2000 PhotoDisc, Inc.;   **101** (bottom), The National Archives/Corbis;

103 Robbie Jack/Corbis;   **104** UPI/Corbis/Bettmann;   **107** (bottom), Stan Godlewski/Gamma Liaison;   **109** Ted Spiegel/Corbis;   **111** (bottom), Image Copyright © 2000 PhotoDisc, Inc.;   **113** Dan McCoy/The Stock Market;   **121** The Granger Collection, New York;   **122** Image Copyright © 2000 PhotoDisc, Inc.;   **125** (bottom), Museum of the City of New York/Archive Photos;   **127** Stephen Frisch/Stock Boston;   **129** Image Copyright © 2000 PhotoDisc, Inc.;   **131** (bottom), Culver Pictures;   **133**, Image Copyright © 2000 PhotoDisc, Inc.;   **137** (bottom), B. Seitz/Photo Researchers;   **139**, Andre Gallant/The Image Bank;   **143** (top), Galen Rowell/Corbis;   **143** (bottom), George Lepp/Tony Stone Images;   **145** Aaron Haupt/Photo Researchers;   **146** Don Spiro/Tony Stone Images;   **149** (bottom), Mark Joseph/Tony Stone Images;   **157** The Granger Collection, New York;   **161** (bottom), FPG International;   **167** (bottom), National Portrait Gallery/Photo Researchers;   **169** © The Topps Company;   **173** (bottom), Rafael Macia/Photo Researchers;   **175** Image Copyright © 2000 PhotoDisc, Inc.;   **179** (bottom), David Joel/Tony Stone Images;   **181**, Telegraph Colour Library/FPG International;   **183** Image Copyright © 2000 PhotoDisc, Inc.;   **185** (bottom), Joe Devenney/The Image Bank;   **190** Image Copyright © 2000 PhotoDisc, Inc.;   **193** Bob Daemmrich/Stock Boston;   **194** Image Copyright © 2000 PhotoDisc, Inc.;   **197** (bottom), Jim Cummins/FPG International;   **199** Felicia Martinez/PhotoEdit;   **201** (bottom), Image Copyright © 2000 PhotoDisc, Inc.;   **203** (top), Image Copyright © 2000 PhotoDisc, Inc.;   **203** (bottom), J. Pickerell/FPG International;   **205** Tony Freeman/PhotoEdit;   **209** (bottom), Rhoda Sidney/Stock Boston;   **211** Image Copyright © 2000 PhotoDisc, Inc.;   **213** Image Copyright © 2000 PhotoDisc, Inc.;   **215** (top), Image Copyright © 2000 PhotoDisc, Inc.;   **215** Jon Levy/Gamma Liaison;   **217** Chip Henderson/Tony Stone Images;   **218** Image Copyright © 2000 PhotoDisc, Inc.;   **221**, Microfield/Photo Researchers;   **255** Images Copyright © 2000 PhotoDisc, Inc.;   **256** James L. Amos/Corbis;   **285** Marvin E. Newman/The Image Bank;   **286** Josef Beck/FPG International;   **290** Alvis Upitis/The Image Bank;   **294** Kim Heacox/Tony Stone Images;   **297** Dale O'Dell/The Stock Market;   **298** Chris Rogers/The Stock Market;   **301** David Pollack/The Stock Market;   **303** Kevin R. Morris/Corbis;   **307** Chris Rogers/The Stock Market;   **308** Roy Morsch/The Stock Market;   **310** Philip D. Derenzis/The Image Bank;   **314** Mike McQueen/Tony Stone Images;   **316** GK & Vikki Hart/The Image Bank;   **318** Richard T. Nowitz/Corbis;   **322** Robert Essel/The Stock Market;   **323** Anne Heimann/The Stock Market;   **326** Robert Shafer/Tony Stone Images;   **328** Firefly Productions/The Stock Market;   **331** Laurie Campbell/Tony Stone Images;   **334** T. Stewart & R. Baxter/Tony Stone Images;   **336** Bruce Coleman, Inc.;   **339** David Ducros/Science Photo Library/Photo Researchers;   **342** Charlie Ott/Photo Researchers;   **345** William A. Graham/Photo Researchers;   **347** Schafer & Hill/Tony Stone Images;   **349** George Lepp/Corbis;   **351** (top), Tom & Pat Leeson/Photo Researchers;   **351** (bottom), John Maher/The Stock Market

Handwriting Models

a b c d e f g h i
j k l m n o p q r
s t u v w x y z

A B C D E F G H I
J K L M N O P Q R
S T U V W X Y Z